COMMUNITY DEVELOPMENT
APPLICATIONS FOR
LEISURE, SPORT, AND TOURISM

COMMUNITY DEVELOPMENT
APPLICATIONS FOR LEISURE, SPORT, AND TOURISM

EDITED BY
ERIN SHARPE, HEATHER MAIR, AND FELICE YUEN

VENTURE PUBLISHING, INC.
STATE COLLEGE, PA

Venture Publishing, Inc.
1999 Cato Avenue
State College, PA 16801
Phone (814) 234-4561
Fax (814) 234-1651

Cover Design by StepUp Communications, Inc.

Library of Congress Catalogue Card Number: 2016943210
ISBN-10: 1-939476-10-0
ISBN-13: 978-1-939476-10-4

TO FERN,
A STEADY FORCE
FULL OF WIT AND KINDNESS.

TABLE OF CONTENTS

FOREWORD

By Karen Fox

This book sits within a North American tradition beginning in the 1800s that connected recreation with community development. With industrialization came individuals and groups, such as George Williams and the Young Men's Christian Association (1844), the Massachusetts Emergency and Hygiene Association (1885), Jane Addams and the Hull House (1894), and the Playground Association of America (1906). All of these "founders" were recreation practitioners. Scholars since then have understood the potential of recreation to contribute to individual and societal well-being while inculcating dominant societal norms including religious participation, protection and nourishment of children, health, nationalism, productive citizenship and labor, and responsible work practices.

While these aims and relationships are important, less space in traditional scholarship has been devoted to understanding how leisure may, in fact, undermine—even harm—community development. Peukert (1987) wrote about everyday life in Germany under Hitler. His social history suggested leisure was the focus of controlling Germans through outlawing "deviant leisures" and framing organizations such as the "Brown Shirts" (an organization similar to the Boy and Girl Scouts) to report on other citizens, especially Jews. Although an extreme example, leisure and recreation historically were used to support dominant and normative governmental practices and reify racial distinctions and fragment Indigenous cultures worldwide. Framing the social world as a binary of leisure and work closes the spatialization of leisure spaces to the range of contradictory, paradoxical, and harmful as well as beneficial ways recreation can be used in service of societal goals.

This collection takes up a range of factors affecting the relationship between community development and recreation: planning assumptions and structures, class and racial influences on engagement processes, grassroots approaches, critical consciousness through young adult literature, questions about the relationship between community and economic development, and issues of inclusion, social justice, and community empowerment. As such, they create assemblages of complicated processes that contribute to, shape, and affect the dynamics of community, recreation, and development (Turnbull, 2003).

In a world of diversity and fluidity, the challenge for leisure/recreation practitioners and scholars becomes more complex and potentially exciting if we can become comfortable with uncertainty and ambiguity. The term 'community development' in a globalized and diverse world is problematic and carries with it a history of colonialism, Western expansion and hegemony, and neoliberal agendas in addition to being situated in a changing contentious world with nation-states and minority groups struggling over control. This volume initiates a discussion about the ways leisure, sport, and tourism might conceptualize the relationship with community development. The volume builds upon existing research and programs, extends or reframes theoretical approaches, questions, and posits alternative frameworks for playing with the intersection of community development, leisure, sport, and tourism. Its strength and relevance comes from the authors' willingness to seriously and playfully explore the limits, implications, and variations of community development relevant for recreation and leisure studies as well as construct alternative spaces for leisure practices. Whether it is reconceiving planning as a 'human arena' potentially facilitating how an individual comes to understand the self and communities, an exploration of how whiteness and privilege color community development and recreation, conceiving of a compassionate pedagogy for community and recreation facilitation, or returning to young adult literature and storytelling for knowledge, this collection interweaves current theories, ethical frameworks, practices, and critiques relevant to recreation and leisure practitioners and scholars.

Such a collection helps orient leisure practice and scholarship within larger international and North American currents of diversity, struggles over Indigenous rights and standing, economic and global agendas, political agendas that use leisure as power over or exclusion of others, the value of leisure beyond social and economic benefits, and the hegemonic commitment to an autonomous, self-initiating individual self. As the voices herein unfold spaces within dominant and "status quo" approaches in governments and academia, there are some voices yet to be heard.

I invite readers to hear the shifting of leisure practice and scholarship related to community development **and** notice the work that has yet to be done. Edited volumes such as this allow readers to reflect upon where the field has been and the aims of current research while inviting contemplation about what is missing, what still needs to be changed, and how larger societal forces or groups might critique or find the field wanting. For instance, the underlying community development framework still aligns itself with existing, dominant views of nation-states, healthy communities, individual psychological and physical well-being, and economic structures. As Lewis, Mowatt and Yuen (Chapter 9) point out, the majority of recreation and academic programs are white, middle-class individuals and groups focused on helping or making changes in non-white, low-income individuals and groups.

Given recent international events such as recessions and economic struggles, contagious diseases, environmental changes, mobility of large numbers of people, violence as a method for addressing grievances or differences, and sovereignty movements, successful leisure practice and scholarship might want to consider our role and connection with any of these and become responsive to the implications of these ripples at local, national, and international levels. This sensitivity requires theories, models, and programs that embrace multiple theories, views and approaches *and* a critical lens about the limits and harms that dominant and accepted ways of leisure practice and scholarship are complicit in processes that have excluded or harmed other peoples.

This volume initiates a number of conversations that can lead into discussions about what is absent. Some areas to consider are: care and stewardship for non-human communities; praxis grounded in other ways of knowing and being such as Indigenous perspectives; support and acceptance of scholars and experts from other ethnicities, Indigenous groups, and nations; our unintentional contributions to climate change, and nurturing leisure that challenges, resists, or shifts dominant ways of doing and being at leisure. Finally, and critically, leisure research and practice must seek to understand how some processes of community development may be intimately linked with colonialism, imperialism, violence, and globalization to the detriment of groups and people who are resisting or devising alternative ways of being.

This volume contributes to an ongoing discussion around the relationship of community development, sport, tourism, and leisure. Clearly, the frameworks, ethics, and goals of community development are being contested and employed in multifaceted ways that open space for multiple and alternative ways of being and knowing. There is innovation, appropriation, and modification from other practices and disciplines outside of sport, tourism, and leisure, and a commitment to equality and equity. In such a world of difference, multiplicity, and change, the authors support a leisure research and practice as humble and humbling.

REFERENCES

Peukert, D. J. K. (1987). *Inside Nazi Germany: Conformity, opposition, and racism in everyday life.* New Haven, CT: Yale University Press.

Turnbull, D. (2003). *Masons, Tricksters, and Cartographers.* London, UK: Routledge.

PART A
GUIDING PRINCIPLES AND THEORETICAL FRAMEWORKS

1
COMMUNITY DEVELOPMENT IN LEISURE: LAYING THE FOUNDATIONS

Erin Sharpe, Felice Yuen, and Heather Mair

Putting together a book like this forces one to ask: *what is leisure and why do so many scholars and practitioners argue it has an important role to play in community development*? Hopefully, this book will give you the tools you need to respond to that question and to engage members of society in a broader dialogue about leisure and community development. We also, however, don't want to shy away from the issue that leisure and its fields of practice—sport, tourism, recreation—are not always benign. In fact, we can draw a link between leisure (particularly leisure behaviors such as consumption and travel), and what are becoming increasingly serious threats to the social, cultural, economic, and environmental well-being of our neighborhoods. Indeed, our seemingly disposable electronic gadgets clog landfills and their production processes are laden with social and environmental problems. Our endless 'screen time' keeps us and our children indoors and arguably disconnected from the realities of life in our local communities. Our holiday travel to sunny and interesting destinations in faraway places serves to reinforce social and economic inequalities and has clear environmental repercussions. And so, while the main point of this book is to encourage you to think about the potential of leisure, we want you to think critically about leisure and to challenge your own assumptions about what the link is (and could be) between leisure and community development. Further to this, we encouraged contributing authors to write chapters that moved beyond an uncritical acceptance of the relationship between leisure and community and to create space for mindful dialogue through which to examine this relationship, warts and all.

UNDERSTANDING COMMUNITY

COMMUNITY OF THE PAST

When you think of community, warm and cozy thoughts might come to mind. Characteristics such as *tightly knit*—where everyone knows everyone, and *stable*—where you are continually surrounded by family, or friends that feel like family, who are willing help with child care or offer you some sugar for your coffee because you have run out, can be used to describe community (Shaffer & Anundsen, 1993). Some of you might think about your grandparents who lament on how a sense of community has been lost in today's society. This sense of community is typically associated with classic historical conceptualizations of community, which can be referred to as *Gemeinschaft*—a term coined by sociologist Ferdinand Tönnies in 1887. The closeness of relationships and the closeness of physical proximity are what make Gemeinschaft possible (Tönnies, 1957). However, as argued by Shaffer and Anundsen, "as tightly knit and stable as most old-style communities were, they were also homogeneous, suspicious of outsiders, socially and economically stratified, emotionally stifling, and limited in opportunities for personal and professional development" (p. 6). Indeed, communities of the past were typically exclusive and considered in the realm of geographic space.

COMMUNITY OF THE FUTURE

While we aim to create community, we are not aiming to build the communities our grandparents once knew. Rather, we are striving for a community that is heterogeneous and dynamic, with members that are interdependent, committed to one another, participate in common practices, and identify themselves as a part of something bigger than the sum of their individual parts (Shaffer & Anundsen, 1993). Such a community requires a sense of solidarity. *Solidarity* encompasses, 1) *a shared identity*, which comes from shared place, interest, affiliation, and ideology and 2) *shared norms*, which involves a code of conduct or social norms (Bhattacharyya, 2004). While there is a sense of solidarity that unites members, the kind of community we are advocating for is also inclusive and heterogeneous.

SOLIDARITY

Solidarity is a key concept in community development; however, it is also a concept that is difficult to define. Most scholars think of solidarity as sense of community based on shared understandings, feelings of togetherness, and common interests or values (Borner, 2013). Zimiles (2009) uses the term solidarity interchangeably with cohesion. Bhattychara (2004), who views the promotion of solidarity as a key goal of community development, defines it in terms of shared identity and shared norms. However, perhaps solidarity also requires something *from* us rather simply giving something *to* us. Schweigert (2002), for example, defines solidarity as "shared membership characterized by mutual care and mutual respect, that is, a sense of belonging enriched by a commitment to human dignity—to love one's neighbour as oneself" (p. 33). For Schweigert, community exists when we engage with one another through *relations of care*; it is the *principle of action* that defines community.

There are numerous definitions of community, with some focusing on social interaction, while others relate to geographical space and the functionality of community (Allen, 1991). As previously mentioned, community as a geographical space is the way in which community is traditionally viewed. For example, community is the pre-industrial village, a small town, or the local neighbourhood. A functional community can be described as a community of purpose, where there is a shared activity or project that brings members together (Pedlar & Haworth, 2006). For example, a running group where members share an appreciation for physical activity, health, and well-being can be conceptualized as a functional community. In this textbook we encourage you to consider the social dimension of community. One way to understand community from a social perspective is to consider the community spectrum by Shaffer and Anundsen (1993) (see Figure 1.1). This spectrum can also be viewed as an evolution of community. As connections and bonds form within the functional community, a conscious community may eventually evolve. Members in a conscious community recognize their interdependence with each other and with others. This interdependence tends to foster a willingness to embrace new people and ideas, rather than exclusivity and homogeneity (Shaffer & Anundsen). Eventually attitudes and behaviors of the group become so internalized that they become a part of natural everyday behavior and solidarity is solidified. Shaffer and Anundsen identify this normalcy of a conscious community as deep community.

Application Question

Think of an example for each type of community on the spectrum. Would you consider these communities a positive or negative contribution to society? We often think of community as something that is good, but it is important to highlight that community does not necessarily lead to good things, rather it is the goal of the community (e.g., cure for cancer, white supremacy) that reflects the benevolence or malevolence of the community.

Functional	Conscious	Deep
Focuses on external task: supports physical, social well-being of members. Traditionally slow to change and structured according to a hierarchy of fixed roles. Pays little or no attention to group process.	Focuses on internal dynamics and external task. Attends to whole system: individual and group development, process as well as task, interaction with larger communities. Characterized by openness, fluidity, diversity, roles sharing, use of group skills, regular renewal.	Conscious group skills/processes and systems orientation are so ingrained they are part of natural everyday behavior.

FIGURE 1.1 COMMUNITY SPECTRUM (SHAFFER & ANUNDSEN, 1993, P. 17)

THE LOSS AND REVIVAL OF COMMUNITY

As we mentioned earlier, some of you might have heard your grandparents remarking on a loss of community. They certainly aren't alone. Numerous researchers have observed the breakdown of social networks in Western society (Shaffer & Anundsen, 1993; Bellah, Madsen, Sullivan, Swidler & Tipton, 1996; Oldenburg, 1998; Putnam, 2000). The weakening of community bonds (Putnam, 2000), the loss of public space (Oldenburg), along with the decline of civic consciousness and sense of obligation (Bellah, et al., 1996) are noted as major concerns in the erosion of communities. *Why is this happening?* Individualism, consumption, and privatization have become dominant pillars of Western society and we have come to adopt and accept these ideologies as measurements of success. In other words, independence, economic wealth, and individual choice are indicative of a high quality of life, but our focus on achieving this status has contributed to the loss of community. Globalization has also been identified as a culprit in the loss of community as it threatens individual rights and freedoms (Arai & Pedlar, 2003). Ife and Tesoriero (2006), argue that the neoliberalist approach, which was an attempt to solve social problems, has in fact made them worse. That is, the dismantling of government structures and services and replacing them with private-sector, market-driven approaches have contributed to the decline of community and the unravelling of our social fabric.

NEOLIBERALISM

A way of organizing our lives socially, politically, and economically, which has at its core the assumption that the market system is the best way to allocate our access to goods and resources efficiently and, some would say, fairly. The hallmarks of neoliberalism are individualism, reduced government involvement in the lives of everyday people, increased public and private partnerships, and the increasing marketisation of every aspect of life (e.g., water, clean air, heritage, health, public space).

Leisure has played its part in the shift within individualization towards consumption and privatization, and ultimately the loss of community. Specifically, the focus on individual choice and autonomy in leisure provision and research has constrained attempts to develop a framework that moves beyond individualism (Arai & Pedlar, 2003). This textbook is a response to a call for action (Arai & Pedlar, 2003; Hemingway, 1999; Hutchison & McGill, 1995; Coalter, 1998; Glover & Stewart, 2006; Mair, 2009).Our response is founded on a social and political philosophy called *communitarianism*. There are varying divisions within this philosophy, such as democratic communitarianism—which argues that we can only flourish through community, or radical communitarianism—which believes that minority rights can be compromised at the expense of community values and traditions (Pedlar & Haworth, 2006). Nonetheless, the heart of communitarianism is social relationships (Arai & Pedlar) and the belief that community is needed for personal development and fulfillment (Pedlar & Haworth). Mutual support, reciprocity, and solidarity are essential components as communitarianism attempts to balance individual rights with collective responsibility and duty (Arai & Pedlar). We encourage you to consider communitarianism as an alternative to individualism and join us and the other authors in this textbook as we discuss ways in which leisure and leisure-service providers can engage in community development.

WHAT DOES LEISURE HAVE TO DO WITH COMMUNITY?

Felice writes: When I tell people I teach and do research in the field of leisure studies, they generally laugh and say something like "So, you get to study how to have fun. Lucky you!" I laugh along and reply "Yeah, but it's more than that. I study how leisure can be used as a context to build communities." I tell them about how leisure can be used as a vehicle for youth to be engaged in their communities, how leisure can be used as a bridge for women re-entering society after incarceration, how leisure can bring newcomers and locals together, and the list goes on. Leisure is the carrot to community building (I tell my students it's the chocolate); it's what motivates people to participate in community. Below is a quote that explains leisure's connection to community. It's a quote that I keep around in my back pocket and use quite often (thanks to my Master's and Ph.D. advisor):

> *People are not interested in the project of community building. It is the thing, its charms and traditions, that have captivated their good will.*
>
> —Albert Borgmann, 1992, p. 136

Leisure is the thing! Leisure is the charm and the tradition!! Participating in community is way more exciting with leisure in it. Leisure is a powerful tool. It can contribute to environmental degradation, social isolation, marginalization, and reinforce stereotypes, but it can also be used to develop and maintain the kind of relationships, skills, and capacities required for strong inclusive and heterogeneous communities. And yes, lucky us, we have the honour and privilege of using it in our practice.

UNDERSTANDING DEVELOPMENT

Let's now consider the other aspect of our title. What is *development*? Chambers (2004, p. 3) argues that we generally think of development as *good change*. Encompassed in this definition is the notion that development is both a vision and a process. Thinking about development requires us to consider our vision of society—in other words, what we think of as good, as well as the process of change that moves communities and societies closer to that desirable vision. However, even this simple definition raises a number of important questions. For example, what sort of change matters? Is my vision of 'good' the same as yours? Whose values and interests underlie the process of change (Sumner & Tribe, 2008)? These questions become even more heightened when development unfolds as part of a process of planned change or community intervention. Among advocates and scholars of development there are strongly conflicting views regarding the vision, processes, or even the legitimacy of 'doing development'. Anyone involved in development practice must consider deeply the values and interests that underlie their work, as well as be able to consider these 'post-development' critiques. Let's now wade into the definitions and debates.

DEVELOPMENT AS A VISION

Thinking about development as a vision leads us to consider the intent of development. If development is about good change, what do we think of as good? Again, here there is not one consistent answer. Our vision of a desirable society or community has changed over time, and visions of development also differ when considered through different theoretical or philosophical perspectives.

There is certainly one dominant view that the development vision is about an improvement of social conditions. In the early decades of development (1950s and 1960s), notions of improvement of social conditions were closely tied to notions of *modernization*. At this time, development was primarily about introducing countries and communities to the technologies and processes they might need to better engage in the kinds of social, economic, and political systems that characterize the West (Thomas, 2004). We can imagine the kind of development work that might be undertaken under this vision of development; the focus would undoubtedly focus on so-called 'developing' countries and initiatives might focus on introducing Western techniques of production to industries such as healthcare, agriculture, or manufacturing (Thomas, 2004).

The development-as-modernization vision has been critiqued on a couple of fronts. One critique is that it is very Western-centric; this vision has been characterized as the 'following in the footsteps of the West' approach as it establishes the societal conditions of the West as the ideal that is to be emulated and ideally achieved (Thomas, 2004). The Western-centric critique is one that the development field continues to wrestle with, as it raises questions about the values and societal visions that are being idealized through development. As we noted at the beginning of the chapter, Western society is not necessarily a societal model worth emulating as it has a number of its own problems (perhaps caused by *over-development!*) including obesity, inequality, and environmental degradation.

DEVELOPMENT AS WESTERNIZATION

The idea of development as Westernization has been discussed in a famous speech by the well-known philosopher and social critic Ivan Illich. Illich was invited to give an address at a conference for U.S. students volunteering in Latin America. In the address, which has since been titled "To Hell with Good Intentions," Illich (1968) challenged the students to think deeply about what it is that their presence in Latin America might really be doing. In his biting and sarcastic style, Illich told the students that they were no more than "vacationing do-gooders" who were working not as developers but as "salesmen . . . for the middle-class 'American Way of Life'." In other words, their presence and position as 'developers' worked to position Western values and practices as those which should be desired and emulated. Illich's address, given in 1968, is certainly of its time; however its questions and concerns have kept their potency.

A second critique is that this vision views development too narrowly. The modernization vision conceptualizes development primarily in terms of improving the productive capacity of societies and communities. Over the years, people have argued that the development vision needs go beyond expanding economic potential to include other factors that shape the extent to which people are able to realize their potential (Thomas, 2004). A broader umbrella that envisions development as *realizing human potential* takes into consideration factors such as health, hygiene, safety, security, and community. It also considers access to important institutions such as the education and legal system. Promoting inclusion, belonging, and recognition of marginalized groups is also part of this broader vision of development.

The definition of community development as presented by the United Nations captures this idea. The United Nations defines community development as "a process designed to create conditions of economic and social progress for the whole community with its active participation and the fullest possible reliance on the community's initiative" (United Nations, 1955, p. 6). This vision of development is also closely aligned with a philosophy of *social justice* because it suggests that access to basic human rights must be in place in order for human potential to be fully realized (Ife & Tesoriero, 2006). Social justice refers to principles of equity and justice for all people, regardless of race, gender, ability, status, sexual orientation, physical makeup, or religion, with emphasis on those who are underrepresented or underserved (Fouad, Gerstein, & Toporek, 2006; Rawls, 1999). Young (1990) extends this definition and emphasizes that "justice should be concerned not only with fair distribution of resources and advantages, but should also strive toward "institutional conditions necessary for the development and exercise of individual capacities and collective communication and cooperation" (p. 39). In other words, it is not sufficient to redistribute wealth or resources and assume all is just, because the oppressive structures that contribute to inequality would remain intact.

HOW CAN WE ENGAGE IN SOCIAL JUSTICE?

Political theorist Iris Marion Young (1990) would tell us to adopt a *politics of difference*, which argues "that equality as the participation and inclusion of all groups sometimes require different treatment for oppressed or disadvantaged groups" (p. 158). To fully understand this statement let us examine the meaning of equality. *Does equality mean sameness or fairness?* Sameness indicates that every person is treated according to the same principles and standards. This idea of equality means that all participants of municipal recreation centers are charged the same user fees. Fairness acknowledges that we need to give special treatment towards disadvantaged groups. Equality in the realm of fairness means that municipal recreation centers in lower-income neighborhoods would charge lower user fees than other areas of the city. Sameness has dominated the quest for equality, causing much criticism when change is made based on fairness. A politics of difference recognizes the world is structured to privileges certain groups such as men, the economically wealthy, and people who are white. In acknowledging this discrepancy, we strive for change by providing extra support to those who are disadvantaged such as women, the economically poor, and visible minorities. Young suggests social policies and adopting "a principle of representation for oppressed groups in democratic decisionmaking bodies" (p. 158) as specific ways that we can move towards social justice.

Another strand of thinking about the development vision shifts away from a focus on improving economic and social conditions and towards a focus on expanding freedom, choice and agency. Nobel laureate Amartya Sen has been influential in promoting this vision. For Sen (1999), development is not something to be bestowed on people. Instead, development is about engaging in a process of expanding the freedoms that people value and enjoy. Bhattacharyya (2004) describes this development vision:

> The ultimate goal of development should be human autonomy or agency—the capacity of people to order their world, the capacity to create, reproduce, change, and live according to their own meaning systems, to have the powers to define themselves as opposed to being defined by others. (2004, p. 12)

A vision of development as the expansion of human freedom involves two kinds of work. It involves removing major sources of 'unfreedom', including poverty, tyranny, poor economic opportunities, social deprivation, neglect of public facilities, as well as intolerance (Sen, 1999). It also involves working with people and communities in the expansion of assets and strengthening of capabilities of people to participate in, negotiate with, influence and build accountable institutions that affect their lives. Capabilities that can be strengthened include human capabilities such as good health, education, production and other life-enhancing skills; social capabilities like leadership, trust, and the ability to organize, and political capabilities such as the capacity to represent oneself or others, access information, or participate in political life (Sen, 1999). For Sen, development is ultimately a process of empowerment.

AGENCY AND EMPOWERMENT

Agency and empowerment are terms that are at the heart of community development. They are sometimes used interchangeably, because they both relate to a process of *increasing power.* Agency is, as Bhattacharyya and Sen describe, about freedom: it is "what a person is free to do and achieve in pursuit of whatever goals or values he or she regards as important" (Sen, 1985, p. 203). Empowerment is a process of *expanding and realizing agency*. McArdle (1990), for example, describes empowerment as "a process whereby decisions are made by the people who have to wear the consequences of those decisions." Rappaport (1987) defines it as a process through which people gain greater control over their lives, such that they are more able to realize their life goals and dreams. Empowerment requires work at both the individual and institutional level, as it may be that our ability to exert agency is restricted by broader social or institutional constraints (Ibrahim & Alkire, 2007).

DEVELOPMENT AS A PROCESS

Thinking about development as a process leads us to consider how it is that societies and communities change. Thomas (2004) reminds us that societies and communities are dynamic; the conditions in which we live and the values by which we live are in a process of ongoing and imminent change. However, when we think about development, most often we associate it with a process of intentional social or community change. The work of 'development agencies' certainly fits this conceptualization. Development agencies, working globally and locally, embark on projects and programs that have intended change-oriented goals and objectives.

Processes of community change do not necessarily have to be restricted to the work of development agencies. Much community change can (and should!) be undertaken in less formally organized ways, directed by individuals or groups of volunteers who are simply passionate about a change and willing to work to make it happen. For example, examine Matarrita-Cascante and Brennan's (2012) definition of community development. They describe community development as "a process that entails organization, facilitation, and action, which allows people to establish ways to create the community they want to live in" (p. 297). Note how this definition captures the elements of community development while also keeping open the options for who can be the actors or agents in this change process.

Although self-organized community development continues to be fundamentally important, recent decades have been characterized by a proliferation of development agencies, to the point that we now refer to them collectively as the *development sector*. In fact, we imagine the main audience of this book as those who are working as 'developers' in agencies that are to some degree entrusted with the development of groups and communities. Working in this role, although exciting and rewarding, is also highly complex and can at times be ethically ambiguous. This is because development agencies are "entrusted with the responsibility of acting on behalf of another—in this case to try to ensure the 'development' of the other" (Thomas, 2004, p. 41). This is no small task. Indeed, the history of development is one of agencies abusing this trust—for example, falsely claiming to have the capacity or the legitimacy to act on behalf of a community. A fundamental question that needs to be answered is whether the interests of those being developed are represented through the actions of the agency acting on their behalf (Thomas, 2004). For any agency, the answer must be a clear *yes*.

There are also broader and more fundamental questions being asked of contemporary development work. For example, an important critique has been raised by 'post-development' scholars who argue that rather than 'good change', development may in fact do more harm than good. For example, Esteva (1985) and Escobar (1995) contend that development is a 'myth'—that rather than creating community change, development simply creates an opportunity for more powerful entities (nations, groups) to intervene in and control the community in the name of development. Development has also critiqued for how it may work to reproduce troubling narratives about communities and nations as the 'needy other' (Todd, 2011). Critics argue that narratives such as these actually *constitute* the problems that they claim to analyze and solve (Escobar, 1995).

THE TROUBLE WITH DEVELOPMENT?

Erin writes: I was confronted with the question of whether development work was doing more harm than good in my early years of teaching community development. In one class, I required students to work with a local community development agency that had received funding to run after-school programs in neighborhoods that had been identified by our region as 'high priority' based on a range of indicators related to family income, education, and health status. Most student groups planned a recreation program of some kind, such as a Halloween dance, a sports program, or a video-making project. In the last class of the term, students reported on their experience. One student talked with enthusiasm and pride about her group's program. She talked about what her group did and how much she enjoyed it. 'It felt so good to help those kids in need', she said.

Her comment has stayed with me for many years. It sparked my own thinking about what this course was actually accomplishing. For example, how was this course reasserting distinctions between the students (as heroic helpers) and the community members (as needy others)? Might the consequences of the Othering and hierarchy reinforced in this class outweigh the direct benefits of the programs? This is what Escobar (1995) means by development actually constituting the problem, in that the act of constituting a people as 'in need of development' gives legitimacy to actions (e.g., intervention, control, removal of rights) that are ultimately oppressive and disempowering.

Application Question

People are often drawn to work for development agencies out of a desire to 'help,' or 'make a difference.' However, Cook (2008) contends that this is a stance that also positions the host culture as 'in need of help'. Reflect on this idea in relation to your own motivations and experiences. What is driving your interest to learn more about community development?

So, what are we to make of the definition of development as good change? Although appealing for its simplicity, we can see that it is too limiting a definition. Development work is not inherently good, ethical, or heroic (Todd, 2011). Instead, it is complex, ethically ambiguous, and best viewed as a *cautious practice* (Todd, p. 118) that requires us to engage in ongoing and reflexive questioning regarding its 'goodness' and ultimately, who it is good for.

UNDERSTANDING COMMUNITY DEVELOPMENT AS A FIELD OF PRACTICE

COMMUNITY DEVELOPMENT IN THE 'DAY-TO-DAY'

Heather writes: When I was a university student, some of my best friends were activists! I always admired how engaged they were, how politically-savvy they seemed to be, and how they were so deeply committed to living their lives in-tune with a commitment to social justice. Then, one day, I found myself at a large, international protest. I was marching alongside my friends and feeling I was a part of a global movement to claim space to talk about the political, social, environmental, and economic implications of unjust international trade practices. Not long after that, I was in a store, staring hard at the various labels and packaging and working to make choices about what I was purchasing that adhered to my own social justice goals. I realized that these experiences, coupled with a growing involvement in the labor movement, meant I too was becoming an activist . . . or perhaps I was trying to live my life in a way that made the principles of social justice and community development come to life. I was trying to live, enact, and practice a set of ideals about the way I wanted the world and humans to be (socially-conscious, environmentally-aware, and civically-engaged).

Today, I can't say I'm in deep with the activist community but I do always feel a sense of connectedness with them—or what we might call solidarity—and I will always defend and support their right to claim space to talk about those issues that are essential to ensuring a just and meaningful life for all. I still try to think hard about my consumption and travel patterns (in leisure and in work) as well as to be aware of my very privileged place in society—or what we might call agency. I use my status as a teacher and a professor to point out the ways we all need to be working hard to redress gender, race, and class power imbalances in society. When I teach in this area, I am most heartened when I see my students becoming both more critical of the way the world is but also more hopeful about their role in shaping how the world should be. I want my students to see how community development is a life's project—a project that we continually undertake in every area of our life.

If the main elements of community development are that it promotes solidarity and agency, then the practice of community development means working to ensure that these elements are protected and fostered. This might seem a bit abstract and you might find yourself asking "well, how do I promote solidarity and agency for people in communities?" The answer is complicated, of course, but here are some things you might find yourself *doing* if you become a community development practitioner. Most simply put, you might be involved in one or more of a series of roles: process, technical, organizational, advisory or challenging, resource, or system, Following Cavaye (2006), they are listed below with a few examples to give you a better picture. Most of all of the chapters included in this book will also offer examples of these and others roles a community development practitioner may be involved in. As you read along, try to imagine yourself in one or more of these roles.

Of course, no one practitioner can do all of these things; and so quite possibly the single most important task of the community development practitioner is to identify her own skills and to recognize her weaknesses and to then build a team, which includes people who can add their own knowledge and skills into the process. In this way, skills such as group development, educating, facilitating, representing, establishing trust, forming partnerships, also become important (as if the first list

Roles	Examples of Duties and Responsibilities
Process	• Helping members of communities identify concerns, needs and priority issues • Suggesting and conducting techniques for community engagement, group formation and decision-making • Helping develop leadership skills among community members
Technical	• Informing members of communities about the technical issues involved in community economic analysis • Providing technical information about the feasibility of development options • Directing people to sources of information
Organizational	• Helping members of communities organize committees or working groups • Facilitating the formation and function of existing or new community groups
Advisory or Challenge	• Challenging existing views among members of the community • Suggesting alternative ways of addressing issues • Advising members of the community on process or action options • Awareness-raising and stimulation of critical thinking
Resource	• Providing information about funding options and requirements • Assist members of communities in recognizing and using existing resources
System	• Ensuring that networks function effectively • Seeing that members of communities and groups liaise with outside individuals, groups and other communities

FIGURE 1.2 ROLES AND RESPONSIBILITIES FOR THE COMMUNITY DEVELOPMENT PRACTITIONER (ADAPTED FROM CAVAYE, 2006)

wasn't long enough!). (Ife & Tesoreiro, 2006; Hutchison & Nogradi 1996). Indeed, community development is hard work and because it is so oriented towards process, there are no hard and fast rules about what will work in any given situation.That's why those who write and think about community development talk about *principles* and not *answers*. All you can do is work towards sticking with the principles of community development and be open to having to change direction if things aren't working.

Additionally, a good practitioner works themselves out of a job or at least a particular project! Writing about the work of community development after more than 30 years of experience, Langin and Ensign (1998) argue, the mindset of community development practice demands that the practitioner ". . . should always be thinking of his [sic] withdrawal, of his [sic] leaving. He is not meant to be a fixture there. He is to be there in such a way that his ultimate goal is the non-necessity of his continuing to be there." (p. 133)

When thinking about community development practice as a way of living, it is important to realize that just as the ability to embrace the various roles outlined above, practice is also about knowing yourself—what we call reflexivity—and being able to identify your own assumptions, values, and yes, even weaknesses as is noted above. There are many chances throughout the book to do some deep thinking about who you are and how that will shape your approach to community development and we encourage you to take advantage of the opportunities to engage this inner learning. As Langin and Ensign (1998) describe, the Community Developer is a 'lighthouse'—particularly important in times of turbulent and so along with skills, a number of general personal and interpersonal ways of being are also important. To this Langin and Ensign add, being nonjudgmental, impartial, and empathetic. Being a really good listener. Being who you say you are. Being reliable and available. Keeping your personal issues to yourself.

PRAXIS

Praxis is the ongoing ability to link practical action with theoretical assumptions and ideas about social change, which shape that action. Practitioners do not just follow a set of rules unthinkingly, they are in a constant dialogue with themselves, others, and with community development theory in order to continue to learn, reflect, and act in purposeful ways.

All of this introspection and action, shaped by critical self-awareness—or praxis as is described above—leads to, as Ledwith notes (2005, p. 3), a process that is:

"based on confidence, critical consciousness and collectivity, consciousness being the linchpin between the two. Confidence grows as people begin to question their reality, and act together for change. Collective action grows in strength as individuals form groups, groups identify issues and develop projects, and projects form alliances that have the potential to become social movements."

As you move through the book, we hope you can see how community development is not some set of prescribed outcomes but a life-long journey, which full of learning, changing, and acting to meet challenges. Importantly, is also incredibly rewarding.

WHERE THE BOOK GOES FROM HERE

The book is divided into three major sections and we encourage you to move in and between the sections as topics and ideas strike you. The first section, **Part A: Guiding Principles and Theoretical Frameworks**, is designed to help you develop a familiarity with major concepts, theories and principles that undergird community development thinking and practice. **Part B: Community Development Practice** includes very practical descriptions and reflections upon community development in action. The last section, **Part C: Contemporary Context and Future Directions**, includes chapters that take the principles and practice of community development more directly into our substantive field of leisure studies (as comprised of sport, tourism and recreation).

Even after reading this brief introductory chapter, we hope it is becoming clear there are likely as many theories and ideas about community development as there are scholars and practitioners! Nonetheless, each of the authors involved with this book adheres to a common set of principles—principles that demand a consistency with notions of praxis, critical reflexivity, and a sense of 'cautious optimism' that community development is a journey worth undertaking.

REFERENCES

Allen, L. (1991). Benefits of leisure services to community satisfaction. In B. L. Driver, P. J. Brown, & G. L. Peterson (Eds.), *Benefits of Leisure* (pp. 331–350). State College, PA: Venture Publishing, Inc.

Bellah, R. N., Madsen, R., Sullivan, W. M., Swidler, A., & Tipton, S. (1996). *Habits of the heart*. Los Angeles: University of California Press.

Bhattachrayya, J. (2004). Theorizing community development. *Community Development, 34*(2), 5–34.

Borgmann, A. (1992). *Crossing the post-modern divide.* Chicago, IL: Chicago University Press.

Borner, S. (2013). *Belonging, solidarity, and expansion in social policy.* London: Palgrave Macmillan.

Cavaye, J. (2006). Understanding community development. Retrieved from http://www.communitydevelopment.com.au/publications.htm

Chambers, R. (2004). *Ideas for Development.* IDS Working Paper 238. Sussex: IDS.

Coalter, F. (1998). Leisure studies. leisure policy and social citizenship: The failure of welfare or the limits of welfare? *Leisure Studies, 17*, 21–36.

Cook, N. (2008). Shifting the focus of development: Turning 'helping' into self-reflexive learning. *Critical Literacy: Theories and Practices, 2*(1), 16–26. Retrieved from http://criticalliteracy.freehostia.com/index.php?journal=criticalliteracy&page=issue&op=view&path%5B%5D=1&path%5B%5D=showToc

Escobar, A. (1995). *Encountering development: The making and unmaking of the Third World.* Princeton, NJ: Princeton University Press.

Esteva, G. (1985). Beware of participation, and Development: Metaphor, myth, threat. *Development: Seeds of change, 3*, 77–79.

Fouad, N., Gerstein, L., & Toporek, R. (2006). Social justice and counseling psychology in context. In N. Fouad, L. Gerstein, T. Israel, G. Roysircar, & R. Toporek (Eds.), *Handbook for social justice in counseling psychology: Vision, leadership, and action* (pp. 1–16). Thousand Oaks, CA: Sage.

Glover, T. D., & Stewart, W. (2006). Introduction to special issue: Rethinking leisure and community research: Critical reflections and future agendas. *Leisure/loisir, 30*(2), 315–327.

Hemingway, J. L. (1999). Leisure, social capital, and democratic citizenship. *Journal of Leisure Research, 31*(2), 150–165.

Hutchison, P., & Nogradi, G. (1996). The concept and nature of community development in recreation and leisure services. *Journal of Applied Recreation Research, 21*(2), 93–130.

Hutchison, P., & McGill, J. (1995). *Leisure, integration and community.* Concord, ON: Leisurability Publications.

Ibrahim, S., & Alkire, S. (2007). Agency & empowerment: A proposal for internationally comparable indicatoars. Paper prepared for the workshop 'Missing dimensions of poverty data', 29-30 May 2007, Oxford, UK. Retrieved from www.ophi.org.uk

Ife, J. W., &. Tesoriero, F. (2006). Community Development: Community-Based Alternatives in an Age of Globalisation. Frenchs Forest, NSW: Pearson Education Australia.

Illich, I. (1968). To hell with good intentions. Address delivered to the Conference on InterAmerican Student Projects, Cuernavaca, Mexico, April 20, 1968. Retrieved from http://www.swaraj.org/illich_hell.htm

Langin, F. R., & Ensign, G. (1998). Ways of working in a community: Reflections of a former community development worker. *Canadian Journal of Native Studies, 8*(1), 131–145.

Ledwith, M. (2005). *Community development: A critical approach.* Portland, OR: Policy Press.

Mair, H. (2009). Club life: Third place and shared leisure in rural Canada. *Leisure Sciences, 31*(5), 450–465.

Matarrita-Cascante, D., & Brennan, M. A. (2012). Conceptualizing community development in the twenty-first century. *Community Development, 43*(3), 293–305.

McArdle, J. (1990). Community development—Tools of the trade. *Community Quarterly, 16*, 47–54.

Oldernburg, R. (1998). *The great good place: Cafés, coffee shops, bookstores, bars, hair salons, and other hangouts at the heart of a community*. New York: Marlowe.

Pedlar, A., & Haworth, L. (2006). Community. In C. Rojek, S. M. Shaw, & A. J. Veal (Eds.), *A handbook of leisure studies* (pp. 518–532). New York: Palgrave Macmillan.

Putnam, R. (2000). *Bowling alone: The collapse and revival of American community.* New York: Simon & Schuster.

Rappaport, J. (1987). Terms of empowerment/exemplars of prevention: Toward a theory for community psychology. *American Journal of Community Psychology, 15*(2), 121–148.

Rawls, J. (1999). *A Theory of Justice* (Revised ed.). Cambridge, MA: Harvard University Press.

Schweigert, F. J. (2002). Solidarity and subsidiarity: Complementary principles of community development. *Journal of Social Philosophy, 33*(1), 33–44.

Sen, A. (1999). *Development as freedom.* New York: Anchor Books.

Sen, A. (1985). Well-being, agency and freedom: The Dewey lectures 1984. *The Journal of Philosophy, 82*(4), 169–221.

Shaffer, C., & Anundsen, K. (1993). *Creating community anywhere: Finding support and connection in a fragmented world.* New York: G. P. Putnam's Sons.

Sumner, A., & Tribe, M. A. (2008). *International development studies: Theories and methods in research and practice.* Thousand Oaks: Sage.

Thomas, A. (2004). Meanings and views of development. In T. Allan & A. Thomas (Eds.), *Poverty and Development into the 21st Century* (pp. 23–41). New York: Oxford University Press.

Todd, S. (2011). "That power and privilege thing": Securing whiteness in community work. *Journal of Progressive Human Services, 22,* 117–134.

Tönnies, F. (1957). Community and Society (S. P. Loomis, Trans.). East Lansing, Michigan: The University of Michigan Press

United Nations. (1955). *Social progress through community development.* New York Author.

Young, I. M. (1990). *Justice and the politics of difference.* Princeton, NJ: Princeton University Press.

Zimiles, E. (2009). Sites of solidarity: Ethnic belonging in Northern Ireland, the Netherlands, and a world of difference." *Macalester International*: Vol. 22, Article 16. Retrieved from http://digitalcommons.macalester.edu/macintl/vol22/iss1/16

2
COMMUNITY CAPACITY

David Matarrita-Cascante and Michael Edwards

INTRODUCTION

Starting off the review of key concepts in the community development field, this chapter focuses on the notion of *community capacity.* Community capacity is a construct, as it is comprised of multiple notions (discussed below) that altogether reflect the ability of a community to "get things done." By this we mean community capacity reflects a series of characteristics that a community possesses that provides its residents and organizations with the capability to fix problems and/or improve local living conditions. The foundation of community capacity is the idea of self-help (e.g., the ability of communities to solve their own local problems). This idea reflects current trends in the world that are promoting bottom-up approaches to development as opposed to top-down ones (Agrawal & Gibson, 1999; Chambers, 1983; Goldman, 2003). As a key concept for community development, community capacity takes an "asset" instead of a traditional "needs" approach (Beaulieu, n.d.; McKnight and Kretzmann, 1996). That is, community capacity as a local development process takes an optimistic spin by placing emphasis on what the community has instead of focusing on what the community does not have, which some believe is critical when engaging in successful community development initiatives (Beaulieu, n.d.).

Because of these qualities, community capacity has gained popularity in many disciplines including public health, sociology and social work, political science, natural resource management/conservation, tourism, and more recently, leisure. In this chapter we will touch on current definitions of community capacity, list its dimensions, and highlight ways in which community capacity is linked with leisure studies.

DEFINITIONS OF COMMUNITY CAPACITY

Scholars from multiple fields have attempted to define community capacity (e.g., Wendel et al., 2009; or Chaskin, 2001), yet there is no universal definition of this notion. We believe this is, to a large extent, the result of the multiple aspects of a community—including resources, capitals, skills, and systems—that have to be considered when trying to define community capacity. Due to its complexity, as well as the fact that community capacity is studied by scholars working from multiple disciplines, a diversity of definitions exist.

Differences in how community capacity has been defined likely stem from the different perspectives that scholars hold about what constitutes 'capacity.' Some scholars see community capacity from a *structural* perspective; in this perspective, the emphasis is placed on communities achieving a certain level of appropriation of assets, resources, or capital, for instance infrastructure, money, or even education. Mendis-Millard and Reed (2007) noted that this emphasis is concerned with an initial and critical step of "developing an inventory of key characteristics typically grouped into natural and social forms of capitals" (p. 544). Lyons and Reimer (2006) noted that, from this perspective, community capacity is a sought-after state that communities thrive to achieve. Marré and Weber (2010) added that such desired state is often thought of as a *static* condition, in the sense that capacity an asset that a community can use when it needs it. That is, some believe that community capacity needs to be defined and understood from the angle of achieving a particular set of assets that are sought after.

Many others, according to Lyons and Reimer (2006), define community capacity as a *dynamic* resource. More specifically, advocates of this approach believe that community capacity reflects a continual effort. This second perspective "emphasizes actions that mobilize [. . .] assets through social relationships" (Mendis-Millard and Reed, 2007; p. 544). In contrast to the previous approach, community capacity is not seen as a static goal, but it is understood as a process that is always in motion and that is highly dependent on the 'interactional' abilities of a community. While static resources like infrastructure are clearly important for the betterment of a community, in the dynamic perspective it is the constant ability of its residents to communicate and interact to reach desired goals that defines community capacity (Mendis-Millard and Reed, 2007). Thus, advocates of this perspective believe developing connections and communication between individuals is the most important factor towards increasing community capacity. Building on these ideas, we define community capacity as:

> A process in which residents, nonprofits, government institutions, and for-profits (interested in community development) work together to secure and mobilize local and extra-local resources destined to solve existing community problems. Such goals are highly dependent on the attitudes and actions that local stakeholders possess and develop with the major goal in mind of helping the community better itself.

As a process, community capacity should be thought of as what academics and practitioners have called *capacity building*. This means that the goal is to establish ways in which community capacity can be built or enhanced (Goodman et al., 1998). Capacity can be enhanced through educational mechanisms (formal and informal) that increases community members' awareness, knowledge, and skills/abilities that will help them improve or develop the different dimensions comprising community capacity. In the following section, we detail some of the most common dimensions noted in the literature.

DIMENSIONS OF COMMUNITY CAPACITY

Many dimensions of community capacity have been identified in the literature. Recent work has attempted to organize these dimensions into categories, but even such attempts still present some shortcomings. Part of our challenge in defining and categorizing the dimensions of community capacity is because many of these dimensions are highly intertwined. Additionally, some of these dimensions are tangible (e.g., observable items like infrastructure or numbers of involved residents) while others are less tangible (e.g., harder to see items like levels of trust and sense of community). Finally, such dimensions can be seen as static assets or as dynamic processes, as described earlier. However, we think that looking at community capacity through its dimensions is a helpful way to both understand the concept and think about the different ways in which capacity building occurs in communities. Building on the work that has been previously done, we have categorized these dimensions of community capacity in the following forms (see Table 2.1).

The first dimension, *physical and economic assets*, refers to the necessary financial and physical resources (either built or natural) that are important for any community to move efforts like projects or programs forward. Almost any development project or activity implemented within a community requires funds and physical capital like buildings, infrastructure, or natural assets to succeed. In this chapter, we have chosen to include economic and physical assets together, as there is a close interrelationship between the two. Community development scholars often speak about the need to secure economic growth in order to have the resources necessary to fulfill needs at the community level (see Chapter 15 and also Christenson and Robinson, 1989; Kretzmann and McKnight, 1993; Matarrita-Cascante & Brennan, 2012; Roseland, 2000; Wilkinson, 1991). The role that these resources can play can be many. For instance, rural communities in Third World countries require funding in order to build infrastructure like sewage, electric systems, and roads. Local institutions like hospitals and municipalities require buildings in which they can function and do their everyday operations. Residents even need what Wendel et al. (2012) called spaces for community dialogue and action (p. 289). Thus, in order for community capacity to be developed, communities need to have financial and infrastructural assets to support their goals and aspirations. The desired condition in regards to these assets is to have diverse and multiple physical and financial resources in order to increase a community's capacity.

While not a mandatory first step, resource acquisition provides communities with a better chance to achieve their goals. Yet, this does not necessarily translate into effective usage and/or management. Thus, communities also require knowing how to use and manage resources. Furthermore, communities also need to know how to manage and coordinate other non-economic and physical resources in order to put into action desired community goals. *Skills and knowledge* is the second dimension of community capacity, which refers to aptitudes or know-how possessed by community members. That is, in order to make improvements or address a particular problem afflicting a community, residents and organizations need to have a series of abilities and understandings that will allow efforts to be put into action. Some of the most commonly noted skills and knowledge include critical thinking, analysis and assessment, problem solving, planning, organizing, ability to secure funding, ability to communicate effectively and collaborate, conflict management skills, and specific knowledge related to particular projects (Goodman et al., 1998; Wendel et al., 2009; Wendel et al., 2012). Thus,

TABLE 2.1 DIMENSIONS OF COMMUNITY CAPACITY (ORGANIZED BY THE AUTHORS)

Dimension	Description	Desired Condition
Physical and Economic Assets	Financial and physical capitals available in the community necessary to establish and support projects	Numerous and diverse assets
Skills and Knowledge	Aptitudes or know-how possessed by community members and organizations necessary to put into action desired goals and visions	Diverse skills and knowledge casting a wide range of community-relevant aspects
Leadership	Individuals or organizations in the community that lead the way in working to solve community problems	Numerous, dedicated, and strong leaders
Civic Participation	Involvement of residents and organizations in the decision making, establishment, and management of projects and activities	Large and diverse participation from different sectors of the community
Networks	Web of relationships from which community members share resources, information, and communicate to solve local problems	Well-established and wide-ranging networks
Disposition	Attitudes that community members and organizations have regarding working as one to solve local problems	Positive and constant disposition

the desired condition in terms of this dimension is to have a diverse base of skills and knowledge that altogether can be used to develop a community's capacity.

The third dimension, *leadership* consists of the ability of certain community members to lead the way in the community; to organize others, mobilize and manage resources and skills, and move projects forward. These leaders can be individuals or organizations that are both formally designated and informally held, all of which can lead the way in working to solve local problems (Goodman et al., 1998). Individuals can promote leadership through many different roles but among the most important skills in this regard are the ability to organize, communicate effectively, delegate functions, find and mobilize resources, recruit and develop other leaders, and coordinate collaborative efforts among community residents and/or local organizations (Chávez, 1973; Burns, 1978; Kahn, 1991; Korsching et al., 2007; O'Brien et al., 1991; Wendel et al., 2009). Without leaders, many of the ideas put forth to solve community problems could not be put into action. That is, leaders through their work empower residents and community members to put into motion their efforts seeking the betterment of their community (Burns, 1978; Kahn, 1991). Given their important role in the community, the desired condition in this dimension is to have numerous, strong, and dedicated leaders in order to develop community capacity.

Civic participation is the fourth dimension of community capacity, a notion that is among the most discussed and desired aspects of community development. Without constituents, leaders cannot achieve the many goals that they wish to achieve (including defining the desired local goals). Civic participation entails the involvement and passion of community members. For both ethical and democratic reasons, civic participation is a highly desired condition in communities. Civic participation recognizes that community members have important local knowledge and attachments that are worth "tapping into" and further, participation results in a series of benefits including power reversal/empowerment, promotion of self-reliance, higher rates of program/project success, and heightened sense of ownership, responsibility, and learning by community members (see Chapter 3 as well as Arnstein, 1969; Guaraldo, 1996; Mansori & Rao, 2004; Chambers, 1983;

Craig, 2002, Laverack, 2005; Pigg and Bradshaw, 2003; Goldman, 2003; Richards and Dalbey, 2006; Tosun, 2000). It is important to note that civic participation does not limit itself to community leaders or representatives of different sectors in the community, but should also include as much as possible, every single resident of a community. That is, civic participation should be as inclusive as possible in order to be an important and effective aspect of community capacity. Thus, the desired condition in terms of civic engagement is for it to be broad and as numerous as possible to develop community capacity.

Networks is the fifth dimension of community capacity. Networks refers to the web of relationships from which community members sustain a purposive connection with each other (i.e., the desire to work in collaboration for the overall community good; see Chapter 5). These networks can be social or inter-organizational stemming from formal and informal associations (Goodman et al., 1998; Wendel et al., 2009). The literature touches on some of the functions of these networks including facilitating and sharing resources and information, serving as a structure in which residents provide each other with emotional and intellectual (i.e., skills and knowledge) support, and providing a mechanism for communication (Wendel et al., 2009). That is, networks serve as the social structure in which community residents move their knowledge, ideas, and resources around the community. The desired condition, in order to develop community capacity, is for networks to be well-established and wide-ranging.

Finally, the literature is full of documentation calling for the importance of emotional or social-psychological aspects of a community for community capacity. In here, we have chosen to group all of these together under the name of community *disposition*. This sixth dimension refers to the attitudes that community members and organizations have regarding working for the betterment of the overall community. Scholars have discussed disposition in many different ways, mentioning aspects or factors that promote such attitudes. Oftentimes scholars talk about levels of collaboration and togetherness, sense of community, levels of concern for the community, social cohesion/connectedness, and positive values including positive and trustworthy social relationships, equity, learning culture, inclusion and tolerance among others (Goodman et al., 1998; Matarrita-Cascante, 2010a; Matarrita-Cascante et al., 2010; Wendel et al., 2009). That is, communities that display higher levels of community disposition have higher odds of achieving locally defined goals and improving quality of life. Based on the importance of this dimension, the desired condition is to have a consistently positive disposition in order to develop community capacity.

Application Question

Although we present these dimensions separately, as we noted earlier, they are highly intertwined. Can you think of an example of how a change to one dimension might impact another?

COMMUNITY CAPACITY IN LA FORTUNA, COSTA RICA

La Fortuna is a small rural town in Costa Rica. Historically, members of this community lived off agricultural practices and cattle ranching. Following an aggressive government strategy to promote tourism in the country during the 1990s (see Matarrita-Cascante 2010b), La Fortuna, as many other communities in the country, experienced a large increase of visitors attracted by the natural beauty of this place (e.g., the Arenal Volcano, the Arenal Lake, waterfalls, forests, and hot water springs). The arrival of tourism in La Fortuna meant that its residents had to "reinvent" themselves. La Fortunans had to shift their normal practices (i.e., those associated with farming) to new ones (i.e., those associated with hospitality and tourism). Despite this daunting task, La Fortuna is a well-documented case of successful community development in Costa Rica (see Estado de la Nación 2007). Local residents succeeded in reinventing themselves due to their high levels of community capacity, which was possible due to their membership in their Community Development Association (ADIFORT). Through ADIFORT, residents had the financial means (funds came from charging entrance fees to a waterfall owned by the association) that were used to develop local plazas (see Figure 2.1) and to pay for the development of projects that responded to the needs that emerged in the community after the incursion of tourism (e.g., increased traffic, pollution, crime rates). Local banks also made credit easily available for locals to invest in tourism development. Additionally, as local residents learned about the ins and outs of tourism and hospitality, they shared those skills and knowledge with other residents through formal meetings and informal conversations possible through established local social networks. Local leaders, some of which were on the board of ADIFORT, helped residents establish their businesses and encourage ideas like the promotion of local business ownership, consumption of locally-produced products, and the incorporation of sustainable practices in their businesses and the community overall. Residents of La Fortuna became instrumental in designing, developing, and running organizations whose goals included the establishment of carbon neutral practices in town, building a water treatment plant, and establishing a large number of organizations focused on environmental and social goals. All of these efforts were made possible because residents of La Fortuna possessed a great desire to work together and develop sustainable tourism. This desire was pushed by the idea that their collaboration would not just benefit the individuals involved in tourism-related businesses, but that it would benefit the rest of the locals, protect the local environment, and ultimately provide visitors with great experiences.

> ***Application Question***
>
> *What dimensions of community capacity can you infer from the previous text that were instrumental in the success of La Fortuna? Which ones of these seem to be more important than others (if any)?*

FIGURE 2.1 MAIN CENTRAL PLAZA IN LA FORTUNA CONVERTED FROM AN OLD SOCCER FIELD (PHOTOGRAPH BY DAVID MATARRITA-CASCANTE, TAKEN IN DECEMBER 2007 DURING FIELDWORK FOR HIS PH.D. DISSERTATION).

ON THE RELATION BETWEEN COMMUNITY CAPACITY AND LEISURE

Leisure can be a critical dimension of the capacity building process. Examples of individuals who have used their leisure time to be catalysts for social change in their community are plentiful (Hemingway, 1999). Think about people in your community who attend community meetings, volunteer their time in schools, or go door-to-door collecting signatures for a petition. The process of developing resources, capitals, and social systems within communities to build capacity occurs most often in leisure time. As a field, leisure may have a critical role to play in facilitating social change. Indeed, leisure practitioners may be the central professionals responsible for developing many of the local mechanisms for capacity building (Labonte, 1996).

LEISURE AND THE DIMENSIONS OF CAPACITY BUILDING

Although the market model of leisure services continues to dominate research and practice in this field, leisure remains a promising context for community capacity building. Using the previously discussed dimensions of community capacity as a guide, we will examine the practice of leisure and recreation to understand leisure's efficacy in promoting capacity building. Table 2.1 presents an overview of the relationship between leisure and the dimensions of community capacity.

Communities need numerous and diverse *economic and physical assets* to support capacity building. In terms of accruing these resources, it is important to note that investment in leisure and recreational infrastructure has been a critical part of sustainable economic development strategies. Communities that invest in infrastructure to promote quality of life, particularly as it pertains to leisure opportunities, are likely to perform better economically (Halstead & Deller, 1997). For example, it is recognized that providing parks, cafés, and art galleries is an important factor in attracting and sustaining vibrant industries and an educated workforce in urban areas (Florida, 2002). Additionally, creating access to natural recreation amenities and development of tourist destinations, as well as local recreational resources, is associated with increased economic performance in rural communities (Deller et al., 2001). While highly important for economic reasons, these economic and physical resources can also play an important role in capacity building. For instance, these avenues are excellent spaces for social interaction (see Chapter 6). Access to resources like parks, community centers,

TABLE 2.2 EXAMPLES OF LEISURE'S ROLE IN CAPACITY BUILDING

Dimension	Example of Leisure as a Context for Building Capacity
Physical and Economic Assets	Leisure as a context for building physical and economic assets through: Facilitating economic development and providing recreation facilities (e.g., parks, community centers) for meeting space
Skills and Knowledge	Leisure as a context for building skills and knowledge through: Providing education programs (e.g., accounting, public speaking) through recreation programs and skills developed through volunteer experiences and training
Leadership	Leisure as a context for building leadership through: Leadership development of volunteers, providing opportunities for career volunteering, and the credibility of leisure-service professionals (e.g., coaches, pastors) as trusted community leaders
Civic Participation	Leisure as a context for building civic participation through: Ensuring residents have access to leisure to participate in community activities, involvement in staging community events creating a heightened sense of citizenship among volunteers and participants, and encouraging shared decision making within community programs and events
Networks	Leisure as a context for building networks through: Providing leisure programs and spaces to encourage interpersonal social interaction and developing inter-organizational community partnerships to plan and implement leisure programs and events
Disposition	Leisure as a context for building disposition through: Facilitating shared experiences where collective identity and community capital can develop among participants and volunteers

libraries, or social clubs are often critical to facilitating the development of capacity building efforts (Barnes et al., 1997; Yuen et al., 2005). Leisure spaces like these are important physical assets that are often used for the public to meet, engage, and plan community activities.

The effective implementation of capacity building efforts is also dependent on local individuals with specific *skills and knowledge.* While many individuals develop these skills in specific educational programs or occupational settings, opportunities for personal development through leisure-based programs can be critical to this process (Hemingway, 1999). For example, in his or her spare time, an individual may sign up for a class to improve public speaking skills at a local community center or a basic accounting course online. Volunteers in community leisure programs (e.g., a sport tournament or cultural festival) receive training and gain experience to develop essential skills (e.g., planning, administration, fundraising, and communication) (Arai & Pedlar, 1997; Shaw, 2009). It should be noted, however, that due to perceived lack of leisure time and changes in leisure behaviors, communities are facing increasing challenges to mobilize volunteers (Sharpe, 2006). Additionally, poorly designed training and ineffective management may inhibit the development of skills, recruitment, and retention among volunteers.

Capacity building requires local community *leaders,* both individuals and organizations, to champion community initiatives, communicate goals, motivate citizens, locate resources, and facilitate implementation of projects. The presence of this leadership is especially important during a period of strategic initiating, where the leader tries to sell a vision to stakeholders and develop agreement around strategies (Jones, 2002). These type of leaders often emerge from the staging of community events; where the communication of goals, coordination of community resources, and implementation of strategies often occurs under the direction of volunteer leaders (Moscardo, 2007). Many of the key community leaders are indeed *career volunteers*–individuals who invest significant leisure time in volunteer roles and often become more associated with their volunteer role than other aspects of life (Stebbins, 2000). It is important for the success of capacity building efforts that leaders have the trust and respect of community members (Pérez et al., 2009). Interestingly, leisure-service professionals (e.g., program leaders, coaches, pastors) often have high levels of credibility among community stakeholders (Burnett, 2006). These professionals also have access to both organizational and external resources (e.g., expertise, space, social contacts) that can also be leveraged for community efforts (Autry & Anderson, 2007; Frisby & Millar, 2002). There has also been evidence to show that the staging of community sporting events can lead to the development of leadership characteristics among volunteers (Moscardo, 2007; Parent, Olver, & Séguin, 2009) and partner organizations (Skinner, Zakus, & Cowell, 2008) that is transferrable to other community projects.

To promote capacity building, significant *citizen engagement* across broad segments of the community is necessary (Wendel et al., 2009). However, civic participation is believed to have declined in recent decades (Putnam, 2000), to the extent that some scholars have even suggested that motivating individuals into direct civic participation is no longer possible in Western societies (Harris, 1998). Leisure and leisure-based social structures can be critical to nurture civic participation (Wendel et al., 2009). As Hemingway (1999) noted, participatory citizenship is dependent on leisure as a resource. This is important to note because while much capacity building is often facilitated by the resources of organizations and professionals, community capacity can be developed, led, and sustained through the active participation of citizens. Indeed, community involvement requires a significant investment of leisure time. Thus, people with less time or resources for leisure are often less likely to be involved citizens as are people who engage primarily in private or consumptive leisure activities (e.g., watching television or shopping) (Hemingway, 1999; Putnam, 2000; Yuen, Pedlar, & Mannell, 2005).

To ensure higher levels of participatory citizenship, leisure education programs can provide individuals with information to make informed decisions about time use. Additionally, community resources need to be used to overcome structural barriers to leisure participation (e.g., costs, transportation, and child care). Volunteer participation in sport clubs and cultural events can also serve as a mechanism for civic participation (Sharpe, 2006; Tonts, 2005). These settings are important as they provide critical public structures for community members to interact during leisure (Tonts, 2005; Trussell, 2009). Additionally, these settings provide opportunities for participants and volunteers to connect across the community, contributing to their awareness of local issues (Arai & Pedlar, 1997). For example, Glover (2004) found that volunteers at a community center became acquainted with previously unknown problems through interactions with patrons and fellow volunteers.

Community events may be another way to facilitate civic involvement. The production of local community events, even small-scale events, usually requires significant citizen involvement (Gibson, Kyriaki, & Kang, 2012). Volunteering for a local event, such as a sport tournament or cultural festival, may lead to a heightened sense of citizenship and interest in participating in other community activities (Glover, Parry, & Shinew, 2005; Kay & Bradbury, 2009). Moscardo (2007) found that many volunteers at local festivals and events sought opportunities to volunteer in other areas of the community. It is important to note that civic participation is higher when citizens have a sense of empowerment (Hemingway, 1999). Citizens are also more distrustful of community development initiatives if they are treated as recipients of a project's benefits, rather than as engaged partners (Autry & Anderson, 2007). Thus, it is important to ensure community programs and events encourage shared decision making among stakeholders (e.g., staff, volunteers, and participants) (Autry & Anderson, 2007; Glover, 2004).

Application Questions

Think of your own experience volunteering at events or the events that are regularly held in your hometown. How effective are these events at fostering civic participation? How might they be made more effective?

As noted above, a key dimension of capacity building is the development of both *social and organizational networks* to facilitate the sharing of resources, information, and support. In terms of interpersonal social networks, community capacity relies on *weak ties*—that is, social connections that are outside of stronger, more cohesive social networks (e.g., family, close friends) or homogenous groups (Granovetter, 1973). Leisure settings that bring people together, either as volunteers or participants, often provide mechanisms to develop these interpersonal networks (Moscardo, 2007). For example, the construction of a new hike-bike trail in a small US town provided community members with new opportunities to meet and interact with each other and develop networks (Lawson, 2005). Another type of setting that has potential for developing interpersonal networks is a community garden. Glover et al. (2005) found community gardens provided space for previously unknown neighbors, from a variety of backgrounds, to interact. Beyond interpersonal networks, leisure activities, particularly on a community scale, often encourage multi-sectorial organizational partnerships to facilitate planning and implementation (Chalip, 2006; Schulenkorf, 2012). This partnership development is one way in which communities can maximize resources, access a diversity of skills, and sustain activities (Cousens, Barnes, Stevens, Mallen, & Bradish, 2006; Frisby & Millar, 2002; Hartmann, 2003). Leisure services organizations (e.g., parks departments and sport clubs) are often leaders of these inter-organizational networks, particularly those that focus on staging community sport and recreation events. Critical to the capacity building process is the active participation of these organizations in coalitions that focus on other community projects. Because leisure-service organizations often lack the capacity to effectively lead numerous partnerships, leveraging the strength of existing partnerships to address different community issues may be key (Frisby, Thibault, & Kikulis, 2004).

Finally, one the most important foundations of capacity building, from our perspective, is a positive community disposition—a strong "sense of community," shared values, and energy for addressing common issues (Goodman et al., 1998). Much has been written about leisure's role in creating place attachment, or the emotional and symbolic meanings associated with specific places (for example, see Kyle et al., 2003). However, most of this research has focused on tourists in natural leisure settings, rather than the role leisure plays in local residents' attachment to community. Wilkinson (1991) argues that a process of social interactions within a community that encourages feelings of trust and a merging of values and culture leads to individual interest becoming more aligned with collective interests and, in turn, leads to collective action. Volunteers and participants in community-level events are often focused on common objectives. This process can lead to a stronger collective identity and connection to community (Arai & Pedlar, 1997; Glover, 2006; Tonts, 2005). However, and contrary to Putnam's (2000) perspective of social capital, unequal power relations often inhibit this process from occurring naturally, with the possible exception of homogenous communities. Thus, leisure setting may become a critical mediating process for developing community across unequal groups and structures. Recreation programs may provide a context for shared experiences as people often feel more comfortable interacting with people different from them in those types of environments (Autry & Anderson, 2007). Sport in particular may have promise for reducing social distances and constructing community spaces to engage in dialogue, even on difficult societal topics (Burnett, 2001; Sugden, 1991). In diverse communities, sport may be the only shared experience that connects different social or ethnic groups (Stodolska & Alexandris, 2004; Tonts, 2005), and can break down long-standing social barriers (Burnett, 2001). However, collective identity and understanding can form through interactions within parks, community centers, community pot luck dinners, or staging a multiethnic cultural festival.

LEISURE AS THE CONTEXT FOR BUILDING COMMUNITY CAPACITY IN ASHE COUNTY, NORTH CAROLINA, USA

Ashe County is a rural community in the Appalachian region of North Carolina, comprising 427 square miles of mountainous land with a total population of 25,000. Like much of the Appalachian region, Ashe is economically depressed, with more than 25% of children living in poverty and high unemployment rates. Ashe also has comparatively high rates of adolescent pregnancies, childhood obesity, and suicide. Thus, while community leaders sought to improve health and well-being of youth; they faced significant resource barriers to implementing programs and activities. However, these barriers did not stop the community from implementing an after-school program for ¾ of the county's student population (see Edwards, Miller, & Blackburn, 2011). The program provided health-promoting activities, health clinics, tutoring, nutritious snacks, and transportation home (a particular challenge in rural communities).

How did Ashe County do it? While Ashe County may have been low on financial resources, it had strong networks, high civic participation, and citizens with leadership skills. For example, the county 4-H program director became a natural leader for capacity building to address youth issues in the area. She was embedded in the community, trusted as an expert on local child health and well-being, and had access to organizational resources through 4-H and already established relationships with other community-based groups (e.g., schools, parks and recreation, local governments, and churches) and was able to form an inter-organizational partnership among these groups, along with volunteer parents and teachers. Citizen engagement also played an important role; for example, of the overall operating costs of the program, 90% was covered through grants and fundraising. Much of the grant writing and fundraising activities (including an annual canoe race) was administered by volunteers who invested time in developing competencies in these areas. Through parent advisory boards, community presentations, newsletters, and weekly appearances on local radio programs, program staff were able to both educate and engage local residents about broader issues related to children's health and build community support for initiatives.

The capacity that was activated and built in the after-school initiative had its own legacy. For example, during fieldwork in Ashe County in spring 2010, it was noted that the county's only public pool had recently been closed by state safety inspectors. At a time where many communities were closing public pools due to insufficient resources, many community leaders in Ashe County saw the loss of the pool as a threat to children's health and safety because of the need to provide swimming lessons and water safety classes. Collaborations among the school system, county government, and residents that developed from other projects like the after-school program were activated to develop a plan to raise funds and reopen the pool. The pool was reopened in spring 2013.

Application Questions

From the example of Ashe County, how might building dimensions of capacity to address one community issue (in this case, child health) be helpful to addressing other community issues? How did leisure serve as the context for building and activating community capacity?

SUMMARY

Community capacity is a construct that is very useful to understand the ability that a community has to fix their existing problems or fulfill desired goals. As a construct, it is composed of multiple dimensions that range from aptitudes, to attitudes, and to resources. Altogether, these dimensions conform the community's abilities to "get things done."

Leisure can play a large role in promoting community capacity, or as we call it here, capacity building. Either via the establishment of physical spaces where residents can meet, or by developing leaders in the community, leisure-based activities need to be considered in the light of this important notion that secures a better future for the residents of a community.

REFERENCES

Agrawal A. and Gibson C. (1999). Enchantment and disenchantment: the role of community in natural resource conservation *World Development* 27(4) 629–649

Apostle, R., Kasdan, L., & Hanson, A. (1985). Work satisfaction and community attachment among fishermen in Southwest Nova Scotia. *Canadian Journal of Fisheries and Aquatic Sciences, 42*(2), 256–267.

Arai, S. M., & Pedlar, A. M. (1997). Building communities through leisure: Citizen participation in a healthy communities initiative. *Journal of Leisure Research, 29*(2), 167–182.

Arnstein, S. (1969). A Ladder of Citizen Participation. JAIP 35(4): 216–224.

Autry, C. E., & Anderson, S. C. (2007). Recreation and the Glenview Neighborhood: Implications for Youth and Community Development. *Leisure Sciences, 29*(3), 267—285.

Barnes, M., Rodger, R., & Whyte, C. (1997). Empowerment through community development in recreation and leisure. *Journal of Leisureability, 24*(1), 47–52.

Beaulieu, Lionel J. (nd.) *Mapping the Assets of Your Community: A Key Component for Building Local Capacity.* Southern Rural Development Center, Mississippi State University. Available online at http://srdc.msstate.edu/publications/227/227_asset_mapping.pdf.

Burnett, C. (2001). Social impact assessment and sport development: Social Spin-Offs of the Australia-South Africa Junior Sport Programme. *International Review for the Sociology of Sport, 36*(1), 41–57. doi: 10.1177/101269001036001005

Burns, J. M. (1978). The Power in Leadership. Pp. 9–28 in *Leadership.* New York: Harper & Row.

Chalip, L. (2006). Towards Social Leverage of Sport Events. *Journal of Sport & Tourism, 11*(2), 109–127.

Chambers, R. (1983). *Rural Development: Putting the Last First.* London: Longman.

Chaskin, R. (2001). Building Community Capacity: A Definitional Framework and Case Studies from a Comprehensive Community Initiative. *Urban Affairs Review* 36(3): 291–323.

Chávez, C. (1973). The Organizer's Tale. Pp. 545–552 in *Introduction to Chicano Studies,* Duran, L & Bernard, H. (eds.). New York: Macmillan Publishing.

Christenson, J. and Robinson, J. (1989). *Community Development in Perspective.* Iowa StatePress.

Clark, J., & Stein, T. (2003). Incorporating the natural landscape within the assessment of community attachment. *Forest Science, 49*(6), 867–876.

Cousens, L., Barnes, M., Stevens, J., Mallen, C., & Bradish, C. (2006). "Who's your partner? Who's your ally?" Exploring the characteristics of public, private, and voluntary recreation linkages. *Journal of Park & Recreation Administration, 24*(1), 32–55.

Cowell, D., & Green, G. (1994). Community attachment and spending location: the importance of place in household consumption. *Social Science Quarterly, 75*(3), 637–655.

Craig, G. (2002). Towards Measures of Empowerment: The Evaluation of Community Development. *Community Development,* 33(1): 124–146.

Deller, S. C., Tsai, T. H. S., Marcouiller, D. W., & English, D. B. (2001). The role of amenities and quality of life in rural economic growth. *American Journal of Agricultural Economics, 83*(2), 352–365.

Edwards, M. B., Miller, J. L., & Blackburn, L. (2011). After-school programs for health promotion in rural communities: Ashe County Middle School 4-H After-school program. *Journal of Public Health Management and Practice. 17*(3), 283–287.

Estado de la Nación. 2007. *Estado de la Nación en el Desarrollo Humano Sostenible.* Informe 13. San Jose, Costa Rica: Lil.

Florida, R. L. (2002). *The rise of the creative class: And how it's transforming work, leisure, community and everyday life.* Basic Books.

Frisby, W., Crawford, S., & Dorer, T. (1997). Reflections on participatory action research: The case of low-income women accessing local physical activity services. *Journal of Sport Management, 11,* 8–28.

Frisby, W., & Millar, S. (2002). The actualities of doing community development to promote the inclusion of low income populations in local sport and recreation. *European Sport Management Quarterly, 2,* 209–233.

Frisby, W., Reid, C. J., Millar, S., & Hoeber, L. (2005). Putting "participatory" into participatory forms of action research. *Journal of Sport Management, 19,* 367–386.

Frisby, W., Thibault, L., & Kikulis, L. (2004). The organizational dynamics of under-managed parterships in leisure services departments. *Leisure Studies, 23*(2), 109–126.

Gibson, H. J., Kyriaki, K., & Kang, S. J. (2012). Small-scale event tourism: A case study in sustainable tourism. *Sport Management Review, 15,* 160–170.

Glover, T. D. (2004). The 'community' center and the social construction of citizenship. *Leisure Sciences, 26*(1), 63–83.

Glover, T. D. (2006). Toward a critical examination of social capital within leisure contexts: From production and maintenance to distribution. *Leisure/Loisir, 30*(2), 357–367.

Glover, T. D., Parry, D. C., & Shinew, K. J. (2005). Building relationships, accessing resources: Mobilizing social capital in community garden contexts. *Journal of Leisure Research, 37*(4), 450–474.

Goldman, M. (2003). Partitioned Nature, Privileged Knowledge: Community-based Conservation in Tanzania. *Development and Change,* 34(5): 833–862.

Goodman, R., Speers, M., McLeroy, K., Fawcett, S., Parker, E., Smith, S., Sertling, T., & Wallerstein, N. (1998). Identifying and Defining Dimensions of Community Capacity to Provide a Basis for Measurement. *Health Education Behavior,* 25(3), 258–278

Granovetter, M. S. (1973). The Strength of Weak Ties. *American Journal of Sociology, 78*(6), 1360–1380. doi: 10.2307/2776392

Guaraldo Choguill, M. (1996). A Ladder of Community Participation for Underdeveloped Countries. *Habitat International,* 20(3): 431–444.

Halstead, J. M. & Deller, S. C. (1997). Public infrastructure in economic development and growth: Evidence from rural manufacturers. *Journal of the Community Development Society, 28*(2), 149–169.

Harris, J. C. (1998). Civil society, physical activity, and the involvement of sport sociologists in the preparation of physical activity professionals. *Sociology of Sport Journal, 15,* 138–153.

Hartmann, D. (2003). Theorizing sport as social intervention: a view from the grassroots. *Quest (00336297), 55*(2), 118–140.

Hemingway, J. L. (1999). Leisure, Social Capital, and Democratic Citizenship. *Journal of Leisure Research, 31*(2), 150–165.

Jones, R. (2002). Partnerships in action: strategies for the development of voluntary community groups in urban parks. *Leisure Studies, 21*(3–4), 305–325. doi: 10.1080/02614360220000030623

Kahn, S. (1991). Leaders. Pp. 21–49 in *Organizing: A Guide for Grass Roots Leaders.* Washington DC: NASW Press.

Kay, T., & Bradbury, S. (2009). Youth sport volunteering: developing social capital? *Sport, Education and Society, 14*(1), 121–140. doi: 10.1080/13573320802615288

Korsching, P., Allen, J., Vogt, R., & Sapp, S. (2007). Community Leaders, Business Ownership, and Support of Entrepreneurship Development: The Role of Macro entrepreneurs. *Community Development, The Journal of the Community Development Society,* 38(4): 28–45.

Kretzmann, J. and McKnight, J. (1993). *Building Communities from Inside Out.* Center for Urban Affairs Northwestern University. Evanston, Il.

Kyle, G., Graefe, A., Manning, R., & Bacon, J. (2003). An examination of the relationship between leisure activity involvement and place attachment among hikers along the Appalachian Trail. *Journal of Leisure Research, 35*(3), 249–273.

Labonte, R. (1996). Community empowerment and leisure. *Journal of Leisureability, 23*(1), 4–20.

Laverack, G. (2005). Using a Domains Approach to Build Community Empowerment. *Community Development Journal,* 41(1), 4–12.

Lawson, H. A. (2005). Empowering people, facilitating community development, and contributing to sustainable development: The social work of sport, exercise, and physical education programs. *Sport, Education and Society, 10*(1), 135–160.

Lyons, T. and Reimer, B. (2006). A Literature Review of Capacity Frameworks: Six Features of Comparison. *Paper Presented at the National Rural Research Network Conference.* Twilingate, Newfoundland, Canada. June 8, 2006.

Mansuri, G. & Rao, V. (2004). Community-Based and -Driven Development: A Critical Review. *World Bank Research Observer,* 19(1), 1–39.

Marré, A. and Weber, B. (2010). Assessing Community Capacity and Social Capital in Rural America: Lessons from two Rural Observatories. *Community Development* 41(1), 92–107.

Matarrita-Cascante, D. (2010a). Beyond Growth: Reaching Tourism-led Development. *Annals of Tourism Research* 37(4), 1141–1163.

Matarrita-Cascante, D.. (2010b). Tourism Development in Costa Rica: History and Trends. *e-Review of Tourism Research, 8*(6), 136–156.

Matarrita-Cascante, D. & Brennan, M.A. (2012). Conceptualizing Community Development in the 21st Century. *Community Development* 43(3), 293–305.

Matarrita-Cascante, D., Brennan, M., & Luloff, A. E. (2010). Community Agency and Sustainable Tourism Development: The Case of La Fortuna, Costa Rica. *Journal of Sustainable Tourism* 18(6), 735–756.

Mendis-Millard, S. and Reed, M. (2007). Understanding Community Capacity Using Adaptive and Reflexive Research Practices: Lessons from Two Canadian Biosphere Reserves. *Society and Natural Resources* 20(6), 543–559.

McKnight, J. and Kretzmann, J. (1996). Mapping Community Capacity. Institute for Policy Research, Northwestern University. Evanston, Il.

Moscardo, G. (2007). Analyzing the role of festivals and events in regional development. *Event Management, 11*(1/2), 23–32.

O'Brien, Hassinger, E., Brown, R., & Pinkerton, J. (1991). The social networks of leaders in more or less viable communities. *Rural Sociology,* 56(4), 699–716.

Parent, M. M., Olver, D., & Séguin, B. (2009). Understanding Leadership in Major Sporting Events: The Case of the 2005 World Aquatics Championships. *Sport Management Review, 12*(3), 167–184. doi: http://dx.doi.org/10.1016/j.smr.2009.01.004

Pedlar, A. M. (1996). Community development: What does it mean for recreation and leisure? *Journal of Applied Recreation Research, 21*(1), 5–23.

Pérez, D., Lefèvre, P., Romero, M. I., Sánchez, L., De Vos, P., & Van der Stuyft, P. (2009). Augmenting frameworks for appraising the practices of community-based health interventions. *Health Policy and Planning, 24*(5), 335–341. doi: 10.1093/heapol/czp028

Pigg, K. E. and T. Bradshaw. (2003). Catalytic Community Development. Pp. 385–396 in Challenges for Rural America in the Twenty-First Century, edited by D. Brown and L. Swanson. University Park, PA: Penn State University Press.

Putnam, R. D. (2000). *Bowling alone: The collapse and revival of American community.* New York: Simon & Schuster.

Richards, L. and M. Dalbey. (2006). The Critical Role of Citizen Participation. *The Journal of the Community Development Society* 37, 18–32.

Roseland, M. (2000). Sustainable Community Development: Integrating Environmental, Economic, and Social Objectives. *Progress in Planning* 54(2), 73–132.

Schulenkorf, N. (2012). Sustainable community development through sport and events: A conceptual framework for Sport-for-Development projects. *Sport Management Review, 15,* 1–12.

Sharpe, E. K. (2006). Resources at the Grassroots of Recreation: Organizational Capacity and Quality of Experience in a Community Sport Organization. *Leisure Sciences, 28*(4), 385–401.

Shaw, S. (2009). "It was all 'smile for Dunedin!'": Event Volunteer Experiences at the 2006 New Zealand Masters Games. *Sport Management Review, 12*(1), 26–33. doi: http://dx.doi.org/10.1016/j.smr.2008.09.004

Skinner, J., Zakus, D. H., & Cowell, J. (2008). Development through Sport: Building Social Capital in Disadvantaged Communities. *Sport Management Review, 11,* 253–275.

Stebbins, R. A. (2000). Leisure education, serious leisure, and community development. In A. Sivan & H. Ruskin (Eds.), *Leisure education, community development, and populations with special needs* (pp. 21–30). New York: CABI Publishing.

Stodolska, M., & Alexandris, K. (2004). The Role of Recreational Sport in the Adaptation of First Generation Immigrants in the United States. *Journal of Leisure Research, 36*(3), 379–413.

Sugden, J. P. (1991). Belfast United: Encouraging Cross-Community Relations through Sport in Northern Ireland. *Journal of Sport & Social Issues, 15*(1), 59–80. doi: 10.1177/019372359101500104

Tonts, M. (2005). Competitive sport and social capital in rural Australia. *Journal of Rural Studies, 21*(2), 137–149. doi: http://dx.doi.org/10.1016/j.jrurstud.2005.03.001

Tosun, C. (2000). Limits to Community Participation in the Tourism Development Process in Developing Countries. *Tourism Management, 21*, 613–633.

Trussell, D. E. (2009). *Organized youth sport, parenthood ideologies and gender relations: Parents' and children's experience and the construction of "Team family."* Doctoral Dissertation. University of Waterloo. Waterloo, ON.

Wendel, M. L., Alaniz, A., Kelly, B. N., Clark, H. R., Drake, K. N., Outley, C., Garney, W., Dean, K., Simpson, L., Allen, B., Finke, P., Harris, T., Jackson, V., Player, D., Ramirez, A., Sutherland, M., Viator, C., McKeyer, E. L. J., McLeroy, K. R., & Burdine, J. N. (2012). Capacity building in rural communities. In R. A. Crosby, M. L. Wendel, R. C. Vaderpool, & B. R. Casey, (Eds.), *Addressing rural health disparities.* San Francisco: Jossey-Bass.

Wendel, M., Burdine, J., McLeroy, K., Alaniz, A., Norton, B., and Felix, M. (2009). Community Capacity: Theory and Application. In R. DiClemente, R. Crosby, & M. Kegler (Eds.), *Emerging theories in health promotion practice and research* (pp. 277–301). New York: Wiley and Sons.

Wilkinson, K. (1991). *The Community in Rural America.* Middleton, WI: Social Ecology Press.

Yuen, F. C., Pedlar, A. M., & Mannell, R. C. (2005). Building community and social capital through children's leisure in the context of an international camp. *Journal of Leisure Research, 37*(4), 494–518.

3

FOSTERING INCLUSION AND BELONGING

Colleen Whyte and Erin Sharpe

KEY CONCEPTS: INCLUSION AND BELONGING

In this chapter, we focus on the two closely aligned concepts of inclusion and belonging. Although we present these themes as mutually exclusive for the purpose of discussion, pulling at the concept of belonging undoubtedly weaves inclusion into the conversation, and vice versa. Each concept is shaped by and shapes the other. Our job in this chapter is to tease out the nuances of the terms, explore their relationship and consider their practical and theoretical implications for practitioners within the field of community development. We have three overarching objectives for this chapter: to demonstrate the association between inclusion, belonging, and personal and societal well-being; to explore the characteristics of inclusion and belonging, highlighting individual and community qualities that contribute to or impede a person's sense of belonging; and to offer a framework that CD practitioners can apply to their own inclusion practices.

For practitioners in the community recreation and leisure field, inclusion and belonging are at the heart of practice. For CD practitioners, a philosophical commitment to inclusion is driven by and intricately connected to fostering belonging. In fact, belonging has been conceptualized as the 'feeling' or psychosocial dimension of an inclusive society (Ponic & Frisby, 2010; Schultz & Sankaran, 2006). We can even think of belonging as the *goal* of community building. Leisure also has a role to play in the process of fostering belonging; oftentimes it is through recreation and leisure that community members come together and learn about each other. Indeed, Glover and Stewart (2006) write that it is opportunities for leisure which "connect humans who are in need of being connected" (p. 325). Thus we ask: as students and future practitioners, what is our role in fostering deep relationships in order to create belonging among and between community members? How can we create spaces of community belonging where citizens within our communities feel empowered to contribute to the betterment of community and its members?

APPRECIATING INCLUSION AND BELONGING WITHIN COMMUNITY DEVELOPMENT

Our desire to develop and nurture social bonds is so powerful that psychologists consider the *need to belong* to be a fundamental human need (Baumeister & Leary, 1995). The significance of belonging has been theorized as far back as Abraham Maslow (1943), who contended that people yearn for relationships with others and are naturally inclined to seek out people with whom to establish these relationships. In Maslow's theory, fulfillment of the need to belong is an essential step in the path toward achieving self-esteem and self-actualization. Our sense of belonging is also intimately tied to our personal and social well-being. Consider the following research findings:

- *Strong connection to community contributes to good health.* When compared to people who reported a 'very' or 'somewhat' weak sense of belonging to their local community, those who reported a 'very strong' connection to their local community had nearly twice the odds of reporting excellent or very good health, even when controlling for socioeconomic status, the presence of chronic disease, health behaviors, stress, and other factors (Ross, 2002).
- *Sense of belonging protects us against distress.* Feelings of belonging act to "protect" us from external stressors experienced in everyday life (Gold, 2007). As a result, we feel happier, experience better social support and a greater sense of meaning in life when we perceive a sense of belonging within a particular group.
- *Feeling a part of something fosters self-determination.* Greater feelings of belonging and acceptance improve our ability to make decisions, and take responsibility for our actions (Blackhart, Nelson, Winter, & Rockney, 2011).

Alternately, research has also shown the negative impact of an absence of sense of belonging:

- *Superficial connections fail to defend us against daily pressures.* When our sense of social connectedness is threatened, our ability to cope with daily challenges suffers (Walton, Cohen, Cwir, & Spencer, 2012).
- *Weak connection to community leads to greater health risks.* Feelings of loneliness and social isolation have a detrimental effect on personal health comparable to major health risk behaviors like high blood pressure, obesity, or smoking (Cacioppo & Patrick, 2008).
- *Social exclusion may reduce people's cognitive functioning.* In an experiment in which people were 'diagnosed' to expect a future of either belongingness or social exclusion, the people who were diagnosed to expect a future of social exclusion performed more poorly on a number of intelligence and memory tests (Baumeister, Twenge & Nuss, 2002).

> ***Reflection: What is the significance of belonging to you?***
>
> *As you read your way through this chapter, ask yourself about the communities to which you belong. Where do you experience belonging? How does a sense of belonging contribute to your own personal and social well-being? How is your life enriched by these affiliations?*

BELONGING AND INCLUSION: AN ENDURING PARTNERSHIP

Chances are a sense of belonging is not something you have spent a lot of time thinking about as it relates to your life. In fact, we go about our everyday lives without paying it much attention. The times in which we do become aware of our sense of belonging are those moments when we sense its absence—when we feel ostracized, excluded, isolated, alienated, or pushed toward some form of 'outsiderness' (Elkman et al., 2001). When we experience these feelings of exclusion, it is from a lack of connection that a sense of unease, of 'not belonging' emerges. When we feel a sense of valued involvement, we have the feeling that we are an important member of the larger community because we have something to offer that helps make the community stronger. In this way, belonging is about more than just people 'being there;' it is about people engaging in community life, making valued contributions, and being able to say to themselves: "*I'm meant to be here.*"

SENSE OF BELONGING

Throughout this chapter, we use a definition of sense of belonging adopted by Mahar, Cobigo and Stuart (2013), who describe it as a "personal feeling or perception of an individual as they relate to or interact with others, a group, or a system that is separate from an individual's actions, behavior or social participation" (p. 1029). It is important to note that these feelings, and sense of belonging as a whole, are experienced *subjectively.* In other words, sense of belonging is something that is experienced based on a person's perception of it—and someone's perception of not belonging is just as significant as the reality of not belonging (Hagerty, Lynch-Sauer, Patusky, Bouwsema, & Collier, 1992; Mahar et al., 2013).

Scholars conceptualize belonging as an experience that has a number of important dimensions. The first dimension of sense of belonging is feelings of being *included and accepted* (Hagerty, et al., 1992; Mahar, et al., 2013). When people sense they belong, they feel as though they are needed by others and integral to what is happening, that people respect them, and that people accept them for who they are. Baumeister and Leary (1995) are credited with advancing the belongingness hypothesis, suggesting that "human beings have a pervasive drive to form and maintain at least a minimum quantity of lasting, positive, and significant interpersonal relationships" (p. 497).

The second dimension of sense of belonging is the feeling of being *a part of something.* Sense of belonging is a concept that implies a referent; people need to belong to some system or community that is larger than themselves (Block, 2009). This dimension has been characterized as a feeling of 'fit' between the person and their surroundings (May, 2011) or with others in a social group (Hagerty et al., 1992). This aspect of sense of belonging has close conceptual ties to other prominent social-psychological constructs, such as feeling of connectedness and perceived cohesion (Mahar, et al., 2013).

Thirdly, sense of belonging is *dynamic.* As May (2011) noted, during the course of our lives we come into contact with many different people, contexts, and places, and the communities to which we feel a sense of belonging can shift over time. In some cases, a person's sense of belonging may be transitory while another's may be long-lasting and extend beyond any active involvement with that community. Additionally, Mahar et al. (2013) note that sense of belonging is "built on a foundation of shared experiences" (p. 1026) and is enhanced by activities such as sharing and socializing. As a result, a sense of belonging develops only after dedicated effort on the part of the individual joining a community, as well as existing community members who create a welcoming environment. It is enhanced by reciprocal actions—actions in which a community member both gives to and receives from the community (Maher et al., 2013; Stewart et al., 2009). Thus, with more time in a community, a stronger sense of belonging is likely to develop.

Finally, a sense of belonging is characterized by *freedom of choice*. For belongingness to develop, people must feel in control of their decisions to join a community, rather than feel as though the decision was forced upon them (Mahar et al., 2013). Research has suggested that freedom of choice could help explain differences in belongingness at times when people transition to new communities. For example, in her study of individuals living in long-term care (LTC) settings, Cooney (2012) found individuals who reported they had a say in the decision to move and were actively involved in choosing where to move had a stronger sense of belonging within their new residence than those who felt little or no choice in the decision to move to the LTC setting.

COLLEEN'S STORY ABOUT HENRY

I first met Henry when he agreed to participate in research exploring notions of inclusion and community in Westhill, a LTC home. One particular exchange with him stands out for me and changed the way I think about the concept of belonging, not to mention the direction of my research. When asked about his community within Westhill, Henry shared with me that he had a great community—he participated in a handful of structured recreation programs offered by Westhill, people knew him and when they saw him walking down the hall, they called out to him by name and asked how he was doing. Just as I was about to ask my next question, he continued: "but I don't have a feeling of belonging here." Intrigued, I asked him to elaborate. He shared that for him, community was external to an individual: it was about one's connections to other people. But belonging? That was about his internal sense of feeling comfortable and his ability to be himself within his environment—feelings he did not experience at Westhill. When asked about the personal implications of not belonging within his residence (he asked me not to call it his "home"), he acknowledged that he lived with deep regret, and his future well-being weighed heavily on him every day.

INCLUSION

Belonging is in many ways the outcome of community, as a community simply does not exist unless people feel a sense of belonging to it. A sense of belonging is what keeps people in communities, and the hallmark of a strong community is when its members feel that they belong. We feel a sense of belonging when we feel both a sense of inclusion and acceptance in the broader community, as well as a sense of valued involvement (Hagerty et al., 1992; Mahar et al., 2013). This valued involvement is deeper than mere presence within a community. Fabricant and Fisher (2002) argue that belonging emerges when community members feel they have a genuine voice and are confident to disagree with other members and still be validated by their peers.

Whereas belonging is the outcome of community, inclusion is the process that builds it. In other words, working to foster belonging necessitates a commitment to *social inclusion*. Gold (2007) describes a socially inclusive society as one in which all citizens feel valued, individual differences are respected, and individuals are able to have their needs met through social engagement. As described by Lord and Hutchison (2007), the ideal of social inclusion is one in which "communities are welcoming, diversity is respected, full participation or engagement is all aspects of community life is encouraged, and conditions enable everyone to be valued, contributing members of society" (p. 12).

Inclusion describes a course of collective action toward an ideal characterized "by a society's widely shared social experience and active participation, by a broad equality of opportunities and life chances for individuals, and by the achievement of a basic level of well-being for all citizens" (Sen, 2001, p. 74). In community development, inclusion is both an attitude and philosophy; it is a way of engaging community citizens as well as a collective aspiration. Thus, a commitment to social inclusion involves engaging in work that moves us closer to Lord and Hutchison's vision. It involves engaging in an ongoing process by which we—as individuals and as members of groups and community institutions—collectively take steps to engage citizens to participate in community life. However, this work involves doing more than fostering a feeling of belonging; it also involves working to foster a reality of belonging by looking 'upstream' and attending to issues of exclusion that might exist within our organizations, services, and programs.

Working to build the reality of inclusion involves real participation rather than tokenistic or manipulative participation (Chapter 4 discusses these ideas more fully). If inclusion is an ongoing process by which individuals, groups, and community institutions collectively take steps that expand citizens' engagement and participation in community life, then social exclusion occurs when individuals are not given opportunities to contribute to the social, economic, and political systems that promote the integration of individuals within society (Gold, 2007). People have been marginalized for reasons of race, religion, political views, culture, age, sexual orientation, gender, or financial status. Rather than constructing exclusion as a deficiency of these marginalized groups, we need to consider exclusion "as a consequence of the complex interactions between a wide range of factors, including the actions of the privileged" (Taket et al., 2014, p. 5). Thus, while community development practitioners need to work to foster the *feeling* of belonging, they also need to foster the *reality* of belonging. The relationship between belonging as a feeling and as a reality is displayed in Table 3.1. This framework was developed in a research project that brought together 200 people from over 70 community organizations. The researchers, Schultz and Sankaran (2006), worked with the participants to develop a framework that linked belonging to social inclusion and exclusion. As the authors describe, inclusion is characterized by both the feeling of belonging as well as a reality in which belonging is fostered through structures and services that are equitable and accessible. The feeling of belonging comes through caring, cooperation, and trust. We build the feeling of belonging together. The reality of belonging comes through equity and fairness, social and economic justice, and cultural as well as spiritual respect. We make belonging real by ensuring that it is accepted and practiced by society.

> **Application Question**
>
> *Using these characteristics of inclusion, what could be done at an organizational level by staff members at Westhill to support Henry's inclusion and sense of belonging?*

CONTRIBUTING TO INCLUSION AND BELONGING: ELEMENTS OF INDIVIDUAL AND COMMUNITY FIT

Although inclusion and belonging are associated with many positive outcomes, research has found that not everyone experiences a sense of belonging. In Canada for example, approximately two thirds of Canadians report a strong or somewhat strong sense of belonging to community (Statistics Canada, 2013). This means that for approximately one third of Canadians, their sense of belonging to community is weak or somewhat weak. What can explain the variation? Why might one person

TABLE 3.1 CHARACTERISTICS OF BELONGING AND INCLUSION (FROM SCHULTZ & SANKARAN, 2006)

	INCLUSION is characterized by:	EXCLUSION is characterized by:
FEELING of BELONGING	• Being accepted for who one is without judgments, being able to ask for and give support, being given responsibility, being part of community • Feeling of mutual respect, belonging, self-esteem, trust, comfort, courage, connection with neighbors and community, empowerment, togetherness, as well as of being heard and listened to, and welcomed	• Being ignored, unable to participate • Feeling rejected, discouraged, judged, diminished, humiliated, invisible, isolated, little, sick, sad and depressed, frustrated, abandoned, panic-stricken
REALITY of BELONGING	• Structures that are anti-racist, demonstrate diversity, are connected, where everyone has a place and can play a role, where doors are open and no one is left behind • Services that provide opportunities, are equitable, provide education for all, are accessible, and encourage growth • Behavior such as body language like a smile or eye contact, kindness, communicating in any language and in any way, culturally sensitive, empathy, team work, tolerance, value each other's gifts	• Structures that isolate and create silos, that are unjust, that are hierarchical • Services that are inaccessible because there are language barriers, no transportation, under-funded • Behavior that is derogatory, emphasizes differences and inequality, hypocrisy

have a strong sense of belonging to community whereas another person doesn't? In this section, we report on some of the elements that influence one's feelings of inclusion and belonging. As we discuss, elements that influence inclusion and belonging can be tied to the characteristics of individuals, of communities, as well as the interaction between an individual and his or her community.

INDIVIDUAL CHARACTERISTICS: ECONOMIC AND HEALTH STATUS

Researchers have investigated whether differences in a person's feelings of inclusion and belonging are related to personal characteristics such as age, gender, marital status, racial/ethnic identity, education, or economic status. From among this list, only health and economic status have been found to have an impact on sense of belonging. Specifically, research has found that individuals living on a high income report a stronger sense of belonging than individuals living on a low income (Green & Rogers, 2001; Hagerty et al., 1996; Stewart et al., 2009). Researchers have also found a relationship between personal income and the number and type of communities to which a person feels a sense of belonging. Stewart et al. (2009) found that people living on a low income were connected to fewer communities than people of higher income, and the communities were primarily neighborhood-based, whereas people living on a high income were connected to both neighborhood-based and activity-based 'elective' communities such as sport clubs and social groups.

The influence of economic status on sense of belonging reminds us of an obvious but important point: there are costs associated with engaging in community life. Costs such as membership or registration fees, or more hidden expenses such as transportation and child care costs, or equipment and clothing costs may limit or prohibit a person's engagement in a particular community. Indeed, in their study of sense of belonging among people living on high and low incomes, Stewart et al. (2009) found that people living on low incomes were less likely to initiate engagement in particular social activities because of the associated costs, which in turn reduced their opportunities to build sense of belonging.

Along with the costs of joining, there are costs associated with maintaining a meaningful involvement in a particular community. As noted earlier in the chapter, belonging is fostered by reciprocity, or the ability to receive and give (Mahar et al., 2013). Oftentimes, the ways that we reciprocate, such as by returning an invitation for dinner or contributing to the collection plate at church, have financial costs. Stewart et al. (2009) found that when people felt unable to reciprocate due to financial limitations, they made the decision to restrict their participation in a community rather than stay active but feel as though they were unable to contribute.

Along with economic status, there is also a bit of research which suggests that a person's health status plays an influencing role on sense of belonging. Stewart et al.'s (2009) study also found that participants reported a relationship between personal health and community involvement; engagement was more limited for people who experienced health challenges, illness, and/or a disability. Personal health status is thought to impact sense of belonging in a manner similar to economic status: our health is a resource that facilitates engagement in the kinds of activities and groups that enhance a person's sense of belonging. Good health opens up opportunities to engage in community life, whereas poor health can restrict or limit opportunities. Thus, while we know that sense of belonging improves health, it also appears to be the case that good health helps foster a sense of belonging.

COMMUNITY CHARACTERISTICS: OPPORTUNITIES FOR SOCIALIZING AND PERSONALIZING

What characteristics of a community influence a person's feelings of inclusion and sense of belonging? For example, for communities that have a spatial dimension (e.g., neighborhoods, schools, long-term care homes), does physical layout make a difference? What community spaces or features are needed? Although community characteristics are perhaps as equally as important an influence on sense of belonging as individual characteristics, they are more difficult to research.

However, there is strong theoretical support for the idea that community characteristics influence sense of belonging. For example, one of the tenets of the 'new urbanist' community planning perspective is that the built environment of a community can influence residents' sense of belonging (Talen, 1999). In new urbanism, sense of belonging can be fostered by building in environmental features that increase the frequency and quality of social contact among residents. Design features such as houses built close to the street, individuality in housing design, walkable streets and local amenities, and meeting grounds such as parks and plazas are all thought to foster the informal sociability that increases sense of belonging (Talen, 1999).

The prevalence of community organizations, and the opportunities these organizations make available, are also thought to make a difference to belonging. The richer a community is with coffee shops and restaurants, religious organizations, sport and leisure clubs, community centers, and nonprofit agencies, the better the community is positioned to foster belonging (Oldenburg, 1989). These spaces help unify neighborhoods in which they are located and can serve as introduction centers for newcomers and visitors to a neighborhood. (see Chapter 6 for further discussion).

While the relationship between belonging and physical features of a large-scale community is difficult to discern, there has been some interesting research conducted on this relationship at the level of an institutionally based community (e.g., long-term care home, school). For example, Cooney (2012) reported that in long-term care homes, both ample communal space as well as a personalization of spaces facilitated a sense of belonging. Personalization has also been found to foster sense of belonging in schools; in a comparison study of two elementary schools, Killeen, Evans, and Danko (2003) found that sense of belonging was significantly higher in schools where students were allowed to personalize their school, such as by hanging artwork on the walls.

A PROJECT OF BELONGING

Personalization can even extend to the broader community level. For example, the Village of Delburne, Alberta embarked on an initiative aimed at fostering community belonging. They did this by personalizing their town by displaying photographic murals of local residents on exterior building surfaces throughout the village. The village used the 'Faces of Delburne' project as a starting point for community conversations on community-wide priorities including Main Street revitalization and health and wellness (see http://ncdd.org/15617y).

In an effort to share their learnings with other communities embarking on community belonging initiatives, the Village of Delburne offered some recommendations based on their own experiences:

- engage everyone in the process
- invite community citizens who are already invested in the community and build connections from there
- trust in the process of community engagement
- don't rush the process—strengthening community engagement takes dedicated time and effort

FIT BETWEEN COMMUNITY AND PERSONAL NORMS AND VALUES

Another characteristic that is thought to affect sense of belonging is the perceived 'fit' between a person's values and beliefs, and the norms and values that are dominant in their community. Whereas sense of belonging is strengthened when the fit is strong, it is weakened when there seems to be a mismatch. Oftentimes we hear about mismatches in communities in which people have no choice but to be members such as schools, neighborhoods, or workplaces. In these settings, it can be the mismatch between personal and social norms and values that can lead people to feel that they 'don't fit in' or are 'outcasts' in their community. A poor fit may be less likely to be experienced in 'elective' communities or communities we choose to join such as those that develop around shared leisure interests.

The importance of fit between individual and community norms and values has been investigated in school communities, where ostracism and exclusion remain a major concern. Here researchers looked at who among the student body felt as though they 'fit in' the school culture and who did not. Research found that in schools, climate-related factors (e.g., school disciplinary climate, school and peer group academic expectations) were stronger predictors of sense of belonging than school context factors (e.g., size, socioeconomic status) (Goodenow & Grady, 1993; Ma, 2004). However, one group of students who have reported lower ratings of sense of belonging is students who are lesbian, gay, or bisexual (LGB) (Galliher, Postoskey, & Hughes, 2004). These findings have been attributed to the tendency for schools to be 'heteronormative' environments, in which students who are LGB are encouraged to remain invisible in and distanced from school, versus connected.

To address this, community development initiatives have been designed with the intent of strengthening a feeling of identity fit among members of a community. For example, Lowe (2000) chronicled the activities of two community building projects in Denver, Colorado, which both used art as a tool for building a collective identity among residents. In one project, participants painted tiles and collectively constructed a mosaic that celebrated the diversity of community residents. In the second project, participants wrote and performed a play about the history of the community. Lowe found that while the project's products were important for expressing community identity, so were the processes that were followed in the implementation of the project. These included following collaborative decision-making processes, creating a wide range of ways for community members to engage, and addressing community members' constraints to participation. In reflecting on the process of coming together to create community, Lowe (2000) emphasized that what worked were meaningful interactions that were "collaborative, cooperative, and nonjudgmental" (p. 26).

ADOPTING A CRITICAL LENS: CRITIQUES OF BELONGING

Belonging is a fundamental principle of CD practice; however, the concept is not without trouble spots. Trouble spots include the tendency for community development to present an overly optimistic view of belonging, the risk that promoting belonging leads to a sacrificing of unique personal qualities in order to "fit in," and a focus on belonging leading to unintentional exclusion. In this section, we examine some of the critiques of belonging and ask you to consider their impact on practice.

First, some authors would argue that the concept of belonging is laden with overly positive connotations. May (2011), for instance, questions whether the state of belonging is an ideal and if a lack of belonging should necessarily be thought of as harmful. If belonging is understood as a sense of ease with one's surroundings, then arguably not belonging can be characterized as a sense of unease. While a sense of not belonging can be uncomfortable for us, it is not necessarily bad and in fact, it may be an important state of being for promoting community change. May (2011) noted that "a sense of not belonging can open up new possibilities of, for example, political action if we become conscious of the fact that the routine paths we have so far traversed are not the only possible ones" (p. 373). May writes that not belonging can be motivating if, in questioning who we are, we come to construct alternative identities and ways of constructing the world around us.

For example, we can see the value of 'not fitting in' when we think of the people who have been the biggest "game changers" over the past 20 years. Sometimes, the biggest changes in society were implemented by people or ideas that did not fit or belong according to conventional wisdom. Oftentimes, it takes people from outside mainstream society to ignite social change. Consider the grassroots momentum of the Occupy movement that originated in the U.S. and spread to over 80 countries, including Canada. As described by Pickerill and Krinsky (2012), the Occupy movement "is not a simple movement, not a single issue, but instead embodies the frustration and energy that many of us have with the way society is organized" (p. 286). The impetus of the Occupy movement was to challenge rampant social and economic inequality, yet at its core, the grassroots movement was about challenging the status quo.

Application Question

Think about some of the biggest "game changers" of the past 10 years (people or social movements). Consider their sense of belonging within mainstream society. In what ways did this distancing from mainstream society fuel their initiative?

There is also the question of whether intentional inclusion of certain members of society inevitably results in unintentional exclusion of others (May, 2011; Yuval-Davis, 2006). In many cases, those who are excluded may be viewed as different from others, and as a result, are marginalized because of their differences (Lord & Hutchison, 2007; Pedlar, 2007). Crowley (1999) aptly defined the politics underlying the concept of belonging as "the dirty work of boundary maintenance" (p. 30). In other words, creating a sense of belonging oftentimes involves constructing boundaries that separate people into 'us' (those who belong) and 'them' (those who don't belong). Questions then arise over how we decide whether an individual stands inside or outside the imaginary boundary line of a community. Who gets to belong, and why? Who has the power to maintain the boundaries? Often the boundaries that are set are contested and challenged from within and beyond the community (Yuval-Davis, 2006).

The following story, about a community controversy over the use of a public library by people who are homeless, gives us an example of the contesting and challenging of boundaries. Although public spaces are meant to be settings in which community citizens gather and engage, not everyone feels welcome in such spaces. Research has illuminated examples in which people who are homeless are refused entry into public libraries (e.g., Hodgetts, et al., 2012). In some communities, in response to the public perception of people who are homeless "loitering" in public libraries, some libraries have hired guards to patrol the space, removing people who are homeless (Hodgetts et al., 2012). Seen as representing a social "problem," the issue of homelessness has manifested the tension between "us" and "them" and has revealed an uncomfortable truth in how society perceives its most marginalized citizens. Yet, rather than perpetuating the segregation of people who are homeless to shelters and other social service settings, public institutions such as libraries could foster a space in which people come together to learn from and about each other. In fact, Hodgetts et al. (2012) call for opening a space for "critiquing exclusionary practices and building coalitions to support the inclusion of homeless citizens" (p. 951).

Application Questions

Can you think of any 'boundaries' that are maintained, contested, or challenged in your community? Who gets to belong? Who doesn't?

COMMUNITY CONVERSATIONS ON BELONGING

More and more community groups are actively considering ways to apply these concepts to their city in order to build a stronger sense of community belonging. For the New Story Group of Waterloo Ontario Region, belonging is at the heart of social inclusion. In 2013, this group of concerned citizens and service providers launched a series of conversations to explore what belonging means to residents in the region. While engaging members of the community in these conversations, the group sought stories of belonging from citizens. As a result of these conversations and stories, the group identified three fundamental elements that must exist before people can experience a sense of belonging within a community: presence, participation, and relationships. In other words, people must be actively invited to community happenings that lead to active involvement becoming spontaneous and natural, with deep social bonds developed from personal connections. The work of the New Story Group is primarily about envisioning an ideal community in which citizens' experience deep belonging and strategizing ways to collectively work toward enacting this vision. The group is now working on ways to foster presence, participation, and relationships through further community conversations and initiatives that foster community connections, especially for citizens who are lonely or isolated, and developing indicators, or markers of belonging.

NURTURING INCLUSION AND BELONGING THROUGH LEISURE: REFLECTIONS FOR CD PRACTITIONERS

Planning opportunities that bring together community citizens to develop and nurture belonging and inclusion takes dedicated time and effort by practitioners willing to consider ways to advance inclusive practices and policies among community members. However, there are also many ways that practitioners can work toward fostering inclusion and belonging. Inspired by their involvement with a community-based health promotion project aimed at enhancing recreation opportunities for women living in poverty, Ponic and Frisby (2010) caution against a superficial understanding of inclusion. According to Ponic and Frisby (2010), inclusion is a multidimensional process that involved psychosocial, relational, participatory, and organizational dimensions. Figure 3.1 illustrates their relationship.

PSYCHOSOCIAL DIMENSION OF INCLUSION

This first dimension of inclusion refers to participants' understandings about their relationships with other members within the group. As explained by Ponic and Frisby (2010), women in their study identified acceptance, safety and trust, and recognition as key to the psychosocial dimension of inclusion. Feeling accepted was the most prevalent aspect of inclusion for the participants, as it helped reduce women's fears and increased their sense of safety and recognition in the group.

RELATIONAL DIMENSION OF INCLUSION

The second dimension of inclusion describes how project participants engaged and interacted with each another across issues of power and other differences. This dimension includes the elements of being welcomed, openness, social support, and treating each other with respect. When women spoke of what it meant to respect each other, they talked about the importance of valuing each other's differences (e.g., race, family situation, and health status).

PARTICIPATORY DIMENSION OF INCLUSION

This third dimension of inclusion refers to the ways in which participants chose to take action in a group. For women in the study with Ponic and Frisby (2010), elements in this dimension included contributing to the work of the organization, engaging in recreational activities, and having a voice. These actions gave evidence to participants' agency in inclusion processes, an aspect that is often overlooked when assumptions are made about who is meant to do the including (Shakir, 2005).

ORGANIZATIONAL DIMENSION OF INCLUSION

The fourth and final dimension of inclusion outlined by Ponic and Frisby (2010) refers to community-based organizing structures, processes, and values. The specific elements that participants identified were having the barriers to their participation addressed, having access to resources through partnerships with service providers and researchers, and creating an organizational culture based on an ethic of care.

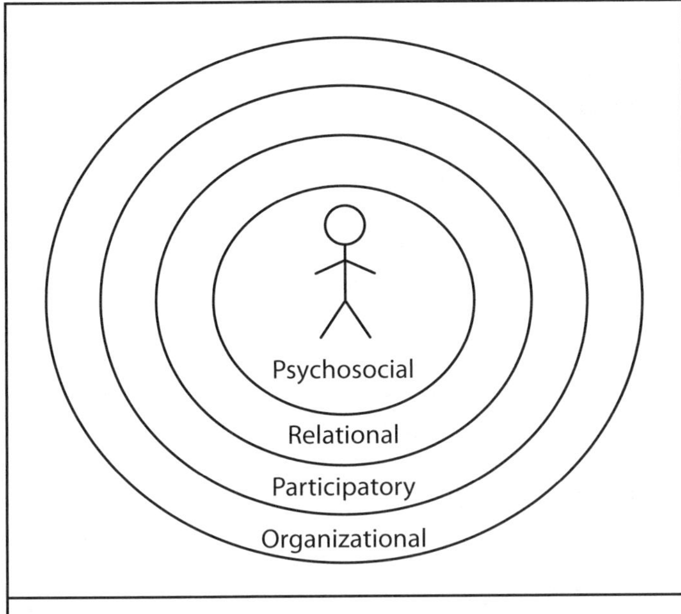

FIGURE 3.1 RELATIONSHIP BETWEEN DIMENSIONS OF INCLUSION

Rather than perpetuate the misperception that inclusionary practices are a one-size-fits-all community initiative by providing directives on ensuring inclusion, we offer in Table 3.2 the following reflection questions to act as discussion points—questions to ask yourself and your community groups—in order to ensure open and honest conversations among group members on the subject of belonging. It is our hope that these questions serve as a springboard for exploration into the aspirations of group members, the process, as well as any potential modifications to engagement. These questions are meant to be reflected on at regular intervals in the life history of a group, not merely at the onset of a group coming together.

As a key concept chapter, our prerogative was to delve into the concepts of belonging and inclusion, and apply the theoretical underpinnings of the terms to the field of community development. We had three overarching objectives for this chapter: to demonstrate the association between inclusion and belonging, and personal and societal well-being; to explore the characteristics of inclusion and belonging, highlighting individual and community qualities that contribute to or impede a person's sense of belonging; and to offer a framework that CD practitioners can apply to their own inclusion practices. At the conclusion of our chapter, we hope that we have answered some of your questions about the terms; however, we also hope that our chapter has spurned additional questions for you, based on your own experiences of belonging.

TABLE 3.2 REFLECTIVE QUESTIONS TO HELP BUILD INCLUSION AND BELONGING

Dimension	Questions
Psychosocial Dimension of Inclusion	• How are your safety and/or trust needs being met by group members? • How are members appreciated for their contributions within the group? • How can we create an environment in which new members feel accepted and welcomed into our group?
Relational Dimension of Inclusion	• How can we be welcoming and inclusive while still being open to dissent and conflict? • What do I need others to know about me? • How are group decisions made?
Participatory Dimension of Inclusion	• What are our individual strengths? • How can we engage our strengths toward our intent? • How are the qualities of our individual contributions valued?
Organizational Dimension of Inclusion	• How do we promote inclusion and sense of belonging for all? • How can individuals and organizations in our community contribute to a community of inclusion and belonging for all? • Who is involved in our group? Who is not? • What does it mean to be a "leader" in our project?

REFERENCES

Baumeister, R. F., & Leary, M. R. (1995). The need to belong: Desire for interpersonal attachments as a fundamental human motivation. *Psychological Bulletin, 117*, 497–529.

Baumeister, R. F., Twenge, J. M., & Nuss, C. (2002). Effects of social exclusion on cognitive processes: Anticipated aloneness reduces intelligent thought. *Journal of Personality and Social Psychology, 83*, 817–827.

Blackhart, G. C., Nelson, B. C., Winter, A., & Rockney, A. (2011). Self-control in Relation to feelings of belonging and acceptance. *Self and Identity, 10*, 152–165.

Block, P. (2009). *Community: The structure of belonging.* San Francisco: Berrett: Koehler Publishers.

Cacioppo, J. T. & Patrick, W. (2008). *Loneliness: Human nature and the need for social connection.* New York: W. W. Norton & Company.

Cooney, A. (2012). 'Finding home': a grounded theory on how older people 'find home' in long-term care settings. *International Journal of Older People Nursing, 7*, 188–199.

Crowley, J. (1999). The politics of belonging: Some theoretical considerations. In A. Geddes & A. Favell (Eds.), *The politics of belonging: Migrants and minorities in contemporary Europe* (pp. 15–41). Surrey, UK: Ashgate Publishers.

Ekman, I., Skott, C., & Norberg, A. (2001). A place of ones' one. The meaning of lived experience as narrated by an elderly woman with severe chronic heart failure. A case study. *Scandinavian Journal of Caring Sciences, 15*, 60–65.

Fabricant, M. B., & Fisher, R. (2002). *Settlement houses under siege: The struggle to sustain community organization in New York City*. New York, NY: Columbia University Press.

Galliher, R. V., Rostosky, S. S., & Hughes, H. K. (2004). School belonging, self-esteem, and depressive symptoms in adolescents: An examination of sex, sexual attraction status, and urbanicity. *Journal of Youth and Adolescence, 33*(3), 235–245.

Glover, T. D., & Stewart, W. (2006). Rethinking leisure and community research: Critical reflections and future agendas. *Leisure/Loisir, 30*, 315–327.

Gold, M. (2007). The gold standard: A sense of belonging. Retrieved from http://ontario.cmha.ca/network/the-gold-standard-a-sense-of-belonging/

Goodenow, C., & Grady, K. E. (1993). The relationship of school belonging and friends' values to academic motivation among urban adolescent students. *Journal of Experimental Education, 62*(1), 60–71.

Green, B. L., & Rodgers, A. (2001). Determinants of social support among low-income mothers: A longitudinal analysis. *American Journal of Community Psychology, 29*(3), 419–441.

Hagerty, B. M. K., Lynch-Sauer, J., Patusky, K., Bouwsema, M., & Collier, P. (1992). Sense of belonging: A vital mental health concept. *Archives of Psychiatric Nursing, 6*, 172–177.

Hagerty, B. M., Williams, R. A., Coyne, J. C., & Early, M. R. (1996). Sense of belonging and indicators of social and psychological functioning. *Archives of Psychiatric Nursing, 10*(4), 235–244.

Hodgetts, D., Stolte, O., Chamberlain, K., Radley, A., Nikora, L., Nabalarua E., & Schneider, S. (2012). A trip to the library: Homelessness and social inclusion. *Social & Cultural Geography, 9*, 933–953.

Killeen, J. P., Evans, G. W., & Danko, S. (2003). The role of permanent student artwork on students' sense of ownership in an elementary school. *Environment and Behavior, 35*, 250–263.

Lord, J., & Hutchison, P. (2007). *Pathways to inclusion: Building a new story with people and communities.* Concord, ON: Captus Press.

Lowe, S. (2000). Creating community: Art for community development. *Journal of Contemporary Ethnography, 29*(3), 357–386.

Ma, X. (2003). Sense of belonging to school: Can schools make a difference? *The Journal of Educational Research, 96*(6), 340–349.

Mahar, A. L., Cobigo. V., & Stuart, H. (2013). Conceptualizing belonging. *Disability & Rehabilitation, 35*(12), 1026–1032.

May, V. (2011). Self, belonging and social change. *Sociology, 45*, 363–378.

Maslow, A. H. (1943). A theory of human motivation. *Psychological Review, 50*, 370–396.

Oldenburg, R. (1989). *The great good place: Cafes, coffee shops, community centers, beauty parlors, general stores, bars, hangouts, and how they get you through the day.* New York: Paragon House.

Pickerill, J., & Krinsky, J. (2012). Why Does Occupy Matter? *Social Movement Studies, 11*(3–4), 279–287.

Pedlar, A. (2007). Community development. In R. McCarville & K. MacKay (Eds.), *Leisure for Canadians* (pp. 253–262). State College, PA: Venture Publishing, Inc.

Ponic, P., & Frisby, W. (2010). Unpacking assumptions about inclusion in community-based health promotion: Perspectives of women living in poverty. *Qualitative Health Research, 20*(11), 1519–1531.

Ross, N. (2002). Community belonging and health. *Health Reports. 13*, 3. Ottawa, ON: Statistics Canada.

Schultz, P., & Sankaran, S. (2006). *Inclusion: Societies that foster belonging improve health*. Toronto, ON: Ontario Prevention Clearinghouse.

Sen, A. (2001). *Development as Freedom*. Oxford, UK: Oxford University Press.

Shakir, U. (2005). Dangers of a new dogma: Social inclusion or else . . . ! In T. Richmond & A. Saloojee (Eds.), *Social inclusion: Canadian perspectives* (pp. 203-214). Halifax, NS, Canada: Fernwood.

Statistics Canada. (2013). Summary tables. Retrieved from http://www.statcan.gc.ca/tables-tableaux/sum-som/l01/cst01/health100b-eng.htm

Stewart, M. J., Makwarimba, E., Reutter, L. I., Veenstra, G., Raphael, D., & Love, R. (2009). Poverty, sense of belonging and experiences of social isolation. *Journal of Poverty, 13*(2), 173–195.

Taket, A., Crisp, B. R., Graham, M., Hanna, L., Goldingay, S., & Wilson, L. (2014). Scoping social inclusion practice. In A. Taket, B. R. Crip, M. Graham, L. Hanna, S. Goldingay, & L. Wilson (Eds.), *Practising social inclusion* (pp. 3–41). London: Routledge.

Talen, E. (1999). Sense of community and neighbourhood form: An assessment of the social doctrine of new urbanism. *Urban Studies, 36*(8), 1361–1379.

Walton, G. M., Cohen, G. L., Cwir, D., & Spencer, S. J. (2012). Mere belonging: The power of social connections. *Journal of Personality and Social Psychology, 102*, 513–532.

Yuval-Davis, N. (2006). Belonging and the politics of belonging. *Patterns of Prejudice, 40*, 197–214.

4

UNDERSTANDING AND ENHANCING CITIZEN POWER

Karen Gallant and Erin Sharpe

WHAT IS CITIZEN POWER?

At its most basic, power affords the ability to 'do' something. If we want to run our appliances, we need to power them somehow. When we get on our bicycle, we push on the pedals; this powers the bicycle and we can move. Citizen power follows this same idea. When a person or a group of people have power, it means that they have the ability to 'do' something; their efforts are consequential. When people are powerless, it means that no matter how hard they might try to make something happen, their efforts are ineffective; they are unable to influence the outcome of events.

The idea that citizens should have power is a foundational principle of community development practice. At its heart, citizen power is about a belief that rather than others having *power over* us, we should have control over the things that are important to us and affect our lives. In this sense, citizen power is comparable to the concept of *empowerment,* as empowerment relates to a process whereby "decisions are made by the people who have to wear the consequences of those decisions" (McArdle, 1990, p. 47). In contrast, *disempowerment* is a process whereby the control that people have over the important decisions of their lives is diminished.

The concept of citizen power is influenced by a *critical theoretical perspective.* One of the tenets of critical theory is the recognition that *power is not evenly distributed among people* (McLaren, 2003). Some groups and individuals have more power than others, meaning that they have a greater ability than others to do things that produce the outcomes they want. Another tenet is that *power is dynamic and relational, rather than absolute.* Although there are positions of power in different social, economic, and political realms, relations based on the power of these positions are not absolute. Power can be resisted, and power relations can be changed by the individuals and groups in those realms (VeneKlasen & Miller, 2007). A third tenet is that *power takes different forms*—it can be *visible, hidden,* and *invisible* (Gaventa, 1980). Visible power is the power embedded in our official and observable decision-making processes such as those found in the political or judiciary realms, or the power structures of institutions. Generally, a greater access to valuable resources (money, people) gives people greater access to visible power (Speer & Hughey, 1995). With resources (money, people, decision-making authority), people can more easily protect their own interests and control others who do not have resources. Hidden power is tied to the ability to set agendas and define issues. If a group can shape what people raise for public discussion, it can more easily protect its own interests. The third form, invisible power, is the power to influence shared consciousness through myths, ideology, and control of information. VeneKlasen and Miller (2007) consider invisible power to be the most insidious form of power because of the immense control that comes with the ability to shape what and how people think about their place in the world.

VISIBLE, HIDDEN, AND INVISIBLE POWER IN THE APPALACHIAN VALLEY

The conceptual framework of power as visible, hidden, and invisible has been best elaborated in the work of well-known development scholar John Gaventa. In the late 1970s, Gaventa undertook an ethnographic study of life in a rural coal mining town in the Appalachian region, one of the poorest parts of the United States. It was a region of glaring inequality of wealth; while the coal mining company was getting rich, the coal miners continued to live and work in appalling conditions. Gaventa asked: Why, in a social relationship involving the domination of a non-elite by an elite, does challenge to that domination not occur? (1980, p. 3). Gaventa found that all three forms of power—visible, hidden, and invisible—worked together to keep the coal miners powerless. First, the coal mining company's greater access to valuable resources was brought into the political decision-making arena, for example, to fund the campaigns of political candidates who were company loyalists (visible power). Further, the company was able to shape the issues that were raised for political discussion by influencing the people who were in positions of political power, most notably to keep economic and labor grievances off the political agenda (hidden power). Finally, the cumulative impact of miners' political defeat over time also increased the power of the elites because it internalized in the miners a sense of powerlessness, an attitude of submission and even an adoption of the values of the company (invisible power), which also strengthened the power of the company over the miners.While Gaventa's case study focuses on how powerlessness is upheld, he also maintains that power can be regained through efforts to increase access to any of the three forms of power.

Thus, enhancing citizen power in a community development context often translates into finding ways to shift the power balance toward those who are most impacted by the decision. Throughout the chapter, we will refer to the people who are most impacted as the 'citizens.' In the traditional sense of the word, citizens are the inhabitants of a particular defined community such as a city or country; further, if the community has a governing body, it is the citizenry that it is meant to respect and protect. Community development practice draws on this conceptualization of citizenship; however, it recognizes that the 'citizenry' can look different depending on the particular context, project, or issue at hand. For example, were a nursing home considering a policy or programming change, the people who would be most impacted by this change would be the residents (versus the paid staff, family members, or owner), and thus enhancing citizen power would involve an effort to foster the involvement of residents in determining the kinds of changes that will be made. There are a number of ways that this effort might be pursued. For example, staff might consult with residents through formal or informal meetings. Perhaps a resident advisory group is formed. Nursing home staff might distribute a survey to learn more about what residents think about the proposed changes. Or, the nursing home may even ask the residents to assess the problem and develop for themselves the policy or programming changes that are necessary. Now, contrast a resident home that attempts at least one of these approaches with a nursing home in which the staff do not consult, but instead 'decide and declare' to residents what the policy and programming changes are going to be. When held up against this scenario, we can see more clearly how all of the different approaches described above to some extent enhance citizen power, because they afford the residents more control over the decisions that will, ultimately, affect their lives the most.

A FRAMEWORK FOR UNDERSTANDING CITIZEN POWER IN DECISION-MAKING PROCESSES: THE LADDER OF CITIZEN PARTICIPATION

One of the most useful and influential tools for understanding citizen power has been Sherry Arnstein's (1969) *ladder of participation* (Figure 4.1). In developing the ladder, Arnstein drew on her experience as a community developer and chief presidential advisor on community participation in housing and development at the time of a large-scale federal housing initiative. One stipulation of the initiative was that the developers were required to consult with the residents of the community that had been selected to receive a new housing development, to ensure that the development that resulted was consistent with what the community needed and wanted. However, what Arnstein saw during this time was that while the community consultations were held, what she saw, more often than not, was not citizen power but instead, an "empty ritual of participation" (1969, p. 216). Her purpose in developing the ladder was to draw attention to this problem and provide a tool to help distinguish between participatory processes that involve *true* citizen power versus those that do not. Indeed, in her ladder of citizen participation, Arnstein considers only three of the eight levels to be exemplary of true citizen power as it is only in these levels where citizens have a meaningful role and actual influence in the decision-making process. She considers the other five levels as a form of either *nonparticipation* or *tokenism*.

Arnstein includes nonparticipation in her ladder as she notes that it is not uncommon for powerful groups to use the language and techniques of 'citizen participation' in manipulative ways. For example, if people are invited to participate in a decision-making process without being fully informed about the history of the project, who will benefit, or how their support will be used by those who are asking for it, this is a form of manipulation (Hart, 1992). These forms of nonparticipation are troublesome because they may in fact work to further silence and disempower the citizens that they are meant to empower. For Arnstein, tokenistic forms of citizen participation are those processes that are better than manipulative forms of nonparticipation because

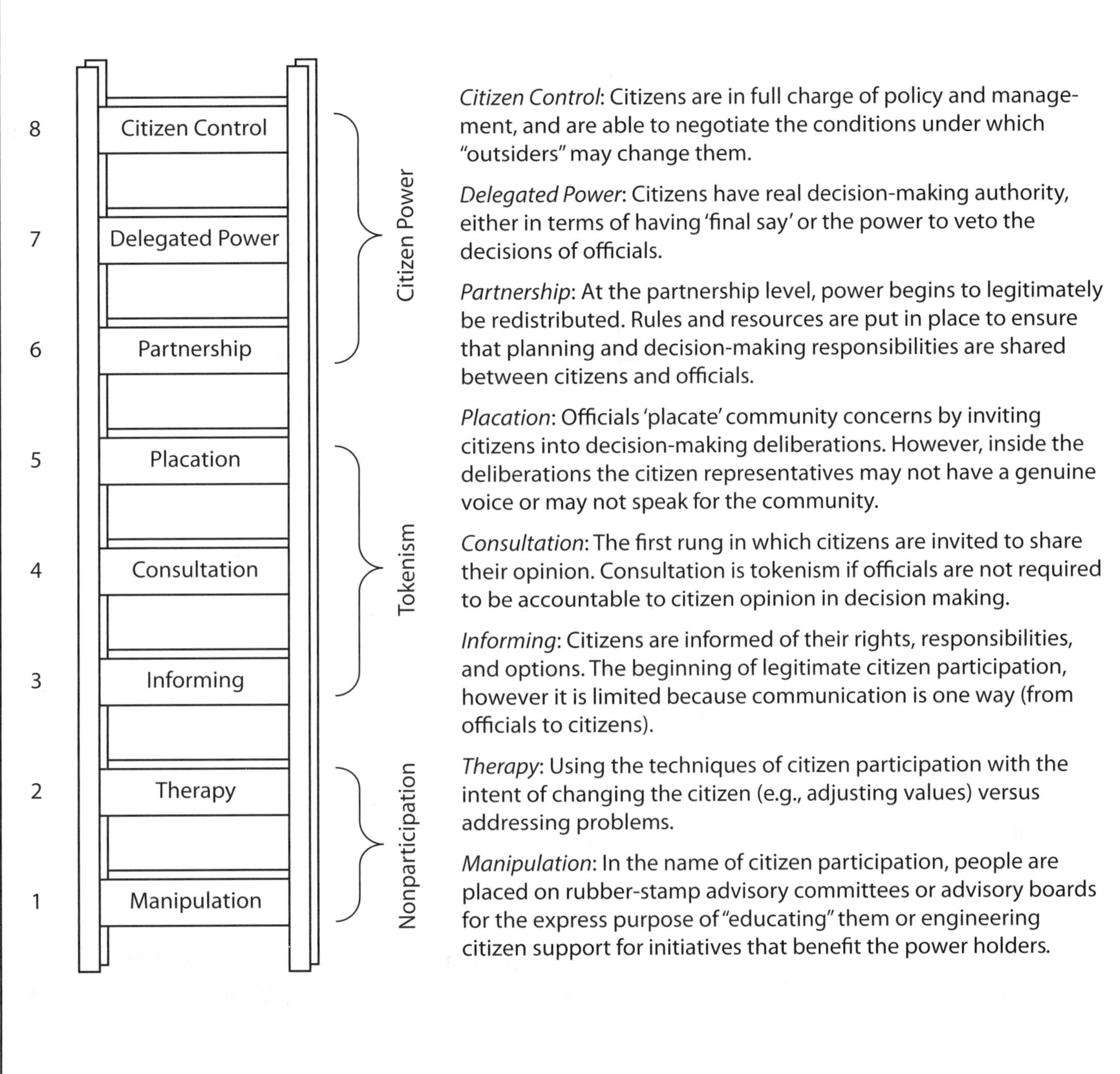

Adapted from: Arnstein, S. R. (1969). A Ladder of Citizen Participation. *Journal of the American Planning Association, 35*(4), 216–224.

FIGURE 4.1 ARNSTEIN'S LADDER OF CITIZEN PARTICIPATION

they are attempting to legitimately involve citizens in decision-making processes; however, they are limited because the actual influence of citizens over those decisions is minimal.

It is difficult to overestimate the influence of Arnstein's ladder on how citizen power and citizen participation have been conceptualized. It is a 'classic' piece of theorizing that has stood the test of time and influenced nearly every model that has emerged in the field since its publication. However, it has also been recognized that conceptualizing citizen power is more complex than what is captured in Arnstein's ladder and that more dimensions need to be considered. Fung (2006), for example, contends that to fully understand citizen power, we need to investigate three dimensions, one of which is the dimension in Arnstein's ladder: citizen influence over decisions. However, Fung notes that an analysis of citizen power needs to also consider the participants and the communicative processes that are used. In considering the participants, we need to ask: Who are the citizens who participate in the decision-making process? For Fung, in a process that truly expands citizen power, the people who participate in the decision-making processes must be representative of the citizenry at large, versus citizens who represent their own or special interests. In considering the communicative processes we need to ask: How deliberative are the processes being used in the decision making? Again, Fung contends that for a process to truly expand citizen power it must involve citizens engaged in a thoughtful discussion and debate of the issues at hand, versus simply listening to information.

Application Question

Where would you locate this scenario on Arnstein's ladder of citizen participation?

A 'youth action group' is established at a local nonprofit agency. The group wants to engage in a public campaign about homelessness but the agency says that homelessness is an issue beyond the scope of the agency. They want the group to organize a recreation activity like a dance or a field trip. If the youth do this, they will have the final say in all aspects, like the theme, location, decorations, food, and music.

WHY IS CITIZEN POWER IMPORTANT?

Citizen power is about people having some level of control over the decisions that shape their lives as well as an influence over how their community should grow and function. The ability to influence one's community, to have power over what happens there, is important for both *instrumental* and *intrinsic* reasons (Eversole, 2010). Instrumentally, community development advocates also argue that citizen power fosters a range of beneficial outcomes for communities and individuals. These instrumental benefits are summarized in Table 4.1. Intrinsically, citizen power is valued because the idea that citizens have a say over the decisions that affect their lives is fundamental to democracy and a cornerstone of social justice.

INSTRUMENTAL BENEFITS OF CITIZEN POWER: BENEFICIAL OUTCOMES FOR COMMUNITIES

Citizen power produces a host of beneficial outcomes for communities; indeed, the outcomes of citizen power are often very evident. Community features and facilities such as gardens, playgrounds, community centers, and churches are often the result of citizen power, as are countless programs, events, festivals, and educational campaigns. Citizens often come together to protect community structures they value such as local schools, churches, and meeting halls, particularly in rural areas. In addition, there is evidence that the outcomes of initiatives are strengthened through citizen power. When people have

TABLE 4.1 INSTRUMENTAL OUTCOMES OF CITIZEN POWER

Outcomes for Individuals	Outcomes for Communities
Development/strengthening of: **Social relationships**: development of new relationships, strengthening of existing relationships, and membership in groups and/or communication networks **Skills and knowledge**: usually related to the specific project or initiative, or about how to influence or work with government **Sense of community**: sense of belonging, influence, shared needs, and emotional connection with a group **Sense of personal empowerment**: sense of ability to control what happens in one's life	Development/strengthening of: **Social structures**: creation of new community groups and networks, or the strengthening of existing connections **Collective skills and knowledge**: development of assets that can be used in other community projects **Sense of collective empowerment**: sense of being able to work together to affect change

some power over changes in their communities, those changes are often better suited to the community and more sustainable. Community development theory suggests that the members of a community are uniquely suited to define and address the problems and issues that affect them, and that their local knowledge will lead to stronger outcomes that will be "owned" by the community (Matarrita-Cascante & Brennan, 2012; Tesoriero, 2010).

The story of the new library in Halifax, Canada (below) illustrates these points. In 2011, city officials invited citizens to participate in the planning of the design of a new public library. The story makes clear that citizen involvement helped produce a *better* library as the resulting design better suited the needs of its patrons. For example, a prime fifth-floor location offering expansive views of Citadel Hill and the harbour will be used as a public lounge and reading area rather than the offices that had been initially planned for that space.

Documenting the outcomes of citizen power can be challenging because these situations happen in real life, not in a laboratory. In the example about the development of the Halifax Public Library, it is not possible to directly compare the library designed as a result of citizen power with one where citizens were not involved in the design. At the same time, reflecting on the results of citizen power, it is possible to see that initiatives are positively altered through the meaningful involvement of citizens. For example, when citizens have some control over the outcome of an initiative, they are more likely to become and remain involved—and ongoing participation of community members is typically a hallmark of success of community programs and events (Chapter 7 expands on this topic).

LIBRARY CONSULTATIONS A LESSON IN COLLABORATION

The Halifax Chronicle-Herald
December 13, 2011
BY FRANCES WILLICK STAFF REPORTER

No one expected a blank piece of paper to cause such a commotion. But ever since the city showed up last year at the first public consultation meeting for the new central library with a blank sketchpad and an open mind, heads have been turning in our direction. And, for once, it's good news. Amid stories of municipal mismanagement and secret dealings at city hall, the story of Halifax's library consultations is an anomaly—a shining example for the world to follow.

Judith Hare has the passport to prove it. Since last year, the CEO of Halifax Public Libraries has traveled to Europe, New York and cities within Canada (on her own dime, she notes) to tell others about the open, collaborative process used here. She's also fielded phone calls from Helsinki, Finland and Bermuda asking about the project.

In October, the Ottawa Citizen heralded Halifax's consultation process as a model for that city's own central library development. "I think everyone is amazed by what we did," Hare said in an interview Tuesday. "Some people have said it was a very brave thing to do, to trust the design of your building to the public."

The consultations for the new central library branch, currently under construction at the corner of Spring Garden Road and Queen Street, were a clear departure from the usual type of public meeting, said George Cotaras, president of Fowler, Bauld & Mitchell, the architectural firm behind the $55-million project. Usually, what passes for consultation is really more of a presentation, Cotaras said, with an administrator or designer revealing an artist's sketch and then fielding questions from the community at a public meeting. "We went to our very first public consultation and we had nothing to show them. We said, 'We are here to get your ideas.' They were stunned," he said.

There were five public meetings from May to December 2010, each drawing up to about 250 people in person and up to 750 online, who watched a live stream of the session or joined an Internet chat. At the sessions, which used a "world café" style of collaboration, people sitting at tables of six or eight exchanged their opinions about the library project, then someone from each table presented their ideas to the entire room. So everyone had an opportunity to share their opinions with the architecture firm at the meeting.

At each successive meeting, Cotaras and his crew presented designs that incorporated those ideas. But the consultation went beyond those five sessions, said Tim Merry, the mastermind behind the process and the founder of Myrgan Inc., a leadership guidance company. "We went in with this really strong desire to set a new bar for how public consultation can happen in the city," Merry said. "How do we thin the gap between those who make decisions and those who are affected by them?"

In addition to social media staples such as Twitter, Facebook and YouTube, Merry and his team used chalk drawings on sidewalks, pumpkin people and yarn bombs—pieces of yarn stitched together to cover trees, buildings or signs in public places—to invite people to voice their opinions on the library project. The plan worked. Residents swayed the design of the building, nixing escalators in favor of stairs, lobbying for public space rather than offices in a prime fifth-floor area overlooking Citadel Hill and the harbour, and incorporating a teen hangout area and stroller parking into the plans. Merry hopes the consultation process used for the library, which was also used for the proposed stadium and the Cole Harbour Basin Open Spaces Plan, will serve as a template for more municipal projects in the future.

"I think there's an opportunity in Halifax to massively improve our democracy and the processes we use," he said. "I think often governments see public consultation as a burden, something they have to go to. So often we set ourselves in adversarial roles—the government against the people, the developers against the community. Maybe there's some way to move beyond that to improve this city together."

One study that has shed some light onto the relationship between involvement in decision making and ongoing participation has been Rimmer's (2012) study of community-based music programs for young people (see text box on p. 47). In the UK, a recent government-led initiative to promote 'youth engagement' through music led to the establishment of a number of music-focused youth programs in different community organizations. The intent of the initiative was to promote social inclusion and empower young people deemed to be 'at risk' by engaging them in weekly music-making workshops that focused on vocal or instrumental instruction, singing, songwriting, and related topics. All programs were developed with the intention of involving the youth participants in decision making about the goals and focus of the group; that is, the programs were intended to provide opportunities for citizen power. However, in practice, the level of involvement of young people in decision making varied across the programs that Rimmer observed. For example, in some programs, young people were not involved at all; the agendas for the weekly workshops were determined at meetings when the youth participants were not present, or young people's musical suggestions and preferences were not taken into account. Rimmer found that the programs that shared decision-making power with young people continued to retain and attract new members, whereas the programs that did not had difficulty retaining youth participants (more on community development in youth programming in Chapter 13).

INSTRUMENTAL BENEFITS OF CITIZEN POWER: BENEFICIAL OUTCOMES FOR INDIVIDUALS

Along with improved project outcomes, citizen involvement in decision making also offers benefits to the citizens themselves. Citizens exercising citizen power often gain a sense of empowerment, strengthen social relationships, develop a stronger sense of belonging to the community, and build new skills and knowledge (Arai & Pedlar, 1997; Glover, 2004; Matarrita-Cascante & Brennan, 2012; Ohmer, 2007). A sense of empowerment—the sense of power to control what happens in one's own life—is a key outcome of citizen power (Arai & Pedlar, 1997; Barnes, Rodger, & Whyte, 1997; Ohmer, 2007). A sense of personal empowerment encompasses several positive traits: self-confidence, developed as a result of increased problem-solving and decision-making abilities and opportunities, increased self-awareness, and openness and ability to change (Barnes, Rodger, & Whyte, 1997). Further, in exercising citizen power, individuals often develop new skills and knowledge, such as learning about local policies and how to work with local governments. Citizen power also typically involves citizens working together, resulting in the creation of new community groups and networks and/or the strengthening of existing connections. Working collectively with others in the community also nurtures citizens' sense of community—the sense of membership in a group dedicated to pursuing shared goals, which provides a shared emotional connection and the sense that one is able to influence others (McMillan & Chavis, 1986).

The benefits of citizen power for individuals and their communities are illustrated by the findings of a study that focused on citizens' leisure participation in social planning committees (Arai & Pedlar, 1997). Arai and Pedlar interviewed citizens who were involved in a 'Healthy Communities' planning group, which focused on discussing what was needed to make their communities healthier, and then developing strategies to address those needs. The groups pursued various activities to achieve their goals. For example, a group focused on stream rehabilitation first had to educate themselves about stream sustainability. After this, the group held a creek assessment day to evaluate the health of a local river, built a retaining wall for a local creek bank using discarded Christmas trees, and educated local farmers about what they could do to protect the creek. Through their involvement, citizens noted that they acquired individual skills and knowledge related to their particular area of focus as well as a sense of empowerment exemplified by the ability to be more vocal. Feelings of camaraderie within their groups, and a general sense of connectedness to the community, also developed. Further, participation in this group initiative provided benefits to the group, such as a joint sense of accomplishment, and an awareness of their ability to influence change.

The outcomes of involvement in citizen power are also thought to have a 'spin-off' or 'snowball' effect (Gaventa, 2006). One of the most important outcomes of citizen involvement is that it can result in a sense of community empowerment. Community empowerment refers to a collective sense of concern for and joint ability to impact the community (Barnes, Rodger, & Whyte, 1997). Further, citizen power is self-reinforcing: through the process of involvement in initiatives that offer opportunities for citizen power, individual and collective skills and attributes can be strengthened, such that the individual or group is able to take on even greater challenges. For example, in a citizen power initiative described by Glover (2003), a neighborhood group successfully advocated for new sidewalks, and this accomplishment spurred them to acquire a piece of untended land in their neighborhood that was being used for drug trafficking and prostitution, where they proceeded to establish a community garden. In addition, the new relationships, groups, or communication networks that formed through a particular initiative can facilitate communication and involvement for other purposes.

INTRINSIC VALUES OF CITIZEN POWER

In addition to the instrumental reasons for valuing citizen power, the intrinsic value of citizen power refers to the philosophical or abstract reasons that citizen power is important to us as a society. In particular, we view citizen power as critical to the way in which we act as members of a democratic society. Democracy at its root is defined as 'rule of the people,' although the extent to which citizens 'rule' varies in different societies, groups, communities, and levels of government. At the level of national governments, for example, it is unwieldy and impractical for all citizens to rule the country, and so we elect representatives who exercise power on our behalf. However, within smaller groups such as clubs, community groups, and neighborhoods, it is possible for citizens to have some direct control over issues and decisions that affect them. In other words, citizen power is foundational to the definition of a democracy, and the democratic nature of a community, large or small, is evidenced by opportunities for citizen power within it. Similarly, citizenship involves both rights and obligations associated with having status as a full member of a society (Glover, 2004). We are often aware of the rights that accompany citizenship, such as the right to vote or the right to free speech. Accompanying the rights of citizenship are obligations, most notably the obligation to take on active roles of citizenship necessary to ensure a democratic society—that is, a society ruled by the people.

We also value citizen power because it provides opportunities for individuals to be self-determined—to make choices about what happens in their own lives. The phrase 'nothing about me without me'—a phrase which has been important in the disability rights movement—captures the idea of self-determination. Self-determination is so important that we consider it to be both a human right and a foundational principle of social justice. Indeed, Glover (2004) writes of citizen power as a means of pursuing social justice, and thus making our values explicit. Overall, we value citizen power as a society because it reflects the value we place on citizen involvement in a democratic society and enables us to pursue our common values of social justice and democracy.

ENABLERS AND INHIBITORS OF CITIZEN POWER

The arguments in favor of enhancing citizen power are so extensive that decision makers no longer need to be convinced of its merits—the 'why' question has been well answered. The new question is: how? If the intent is to have citizens be the drivers of a decision-making process, how do we do this? Where do we start, and how do we get there?

Certainly, one starting point is for citizens to start the process themselves. This often happens; citizens organize themselves around an issue or an initiative and simply get to work, without any involvement of traditional decision-making authorities. Sometimes citizens band together to demand authorities listen to them and take their perspective into consideration when decisions are being made. However, citizen power also results from opportunities for citizen involvement created by someone else. For example, decision-making authorities take the initiative and reorient decision-making processes so that citizens are more involved and have more of a say. Municipal governments may conduct public consultations to gather input on new initiatives, seek citizen representatives to sit on committees or boards, or invite citizen volunteers to lead community events. These are all examples of *invited* participation (Cornwall, 2008). We can see the difference between invited participation and opportunities for participation that citizens create for themselves in an example of a community skating rink. For example, a municipality may want to see more citizen involvement in skating rinks, and offer funding to community groups that are willing to build and maintain a rink in a local park. In contrast, a group of community members may decide that they want to create a community skating rink and then take the steps to do so—thus creating a citizen power opportunity for themselves. These two community groups, while involved in similar ventures, may have different opportunities for citizen power because of the origin of their projects as invited or created.

Even with an invitation, however, initiatives do not always result in citizens being effectively engaged in decision making. Other factors come into play. Policy analysts Lowndes, Pratchett, and Stoker (2006) conducted a review of the different citizen participation initiatives—both the successes and failures—and identified the key factors that promoted successful citizen participation in decision making. They suggested that participation is most effective when citizen participation is CLEAR: when citizens Can do, Like to, are Enabled to, are Asked to, and are Responded to. Each of these factors are discussed below:

Can do. According to Lowndes et al. (2006), 'can do' refers to the resources and skill set that are required for a citizen to be effective within the political sphere. In their review, they found that when people had the appropriate skills and resources, they were more able to participate. Because two of the key resources for political participation are time and money, it may be no surprise that research has found positive associations between socioeconomic status indicators and the level of 'activeness in the community' of residents (e.g., Mattarita-Cascante et al., 2006; Vezina & Crompton, 2012). The implications of this research are that any effort to engage citizens must consider how to ensure the involvement of people who have limited financial means. Some agencies are proactive in this way, for example, by providing free child care or small honoraria to help citizens overcome financial barriers.

'Can do' also refers to the requisite skills that foster effective political participation. As the authors note, these skills are tied to communication, such as the ability and confidence to speak in public or write letters, to leadership, such as the capacity to organize events and inspire others to join in the case. Skills in acquiring resources, such as fundraising, collecting donations, or securing grants, are also valued for how they help sustain public involvement, particularly if the initiative is contentious, complex, and potentially long-lasting.

In some citizen-driven campaigns, a major focus can be in the area of skills training. For example, Arney and colleagues (2010) wrote about an initiative in which young people in a neighborhood in Tampa, Florida, organized in an effort to influence city council to roll back its recent increases in fees to participate in the city's after-school and summer recreational programming, as the young people found the fee increase to be prohibitively expensive. Working with university students, the young people learned research skills as well as the skills to communicate their research findings to their intended audience. After collecting data, the young people put the skills to use by writing a report and preparing a documentary film, which they presented at a city council meeting. Soon after, the city council retracted the fee hike.

Like to. As Lowndes et al. (2006) discuss, 'like to' rests on the idea that people's engagement is fostered and sustained when they feel a sense of affiliation with the issue or the community that is at the center of the decision-making process. For example, research has found that residents who are more involved had more interest in and attachment to their community (Mattarita-Cascante et al., 2006). Participation is also positively influenced by a sense of community, trust, and connection with the other people involved in the process. Lowndes et al. (2006) also found that the dynamics and processes that unfold in the decision-making processes (e.g., in the advisory group, planning meetings, etc.) are also important considerations for citizens. Participation is sustained when people feel welcomed into the decision-making process and comfortable in the environment. In contrast, when people feel excluded or devalued in the process, they are less likely to continue their involvement.

Enabled to. This factor is based on Lowndes et al.'s (2006) observation that most participation is facilitated through groups or organizations. Community groups and organizations provide opportunities for participation

YOUNG PEOPLE AND DECISION MAKING IN COMMUNITY MUSIC PROJECTS

In the three community-based music programs with young people introduced earlier in this chapter, Rimmer (2012) was able to capture the myriad ways that participation is nurtured or shut down in the 'micro-dynamics' of a community project. When Rimmer looked closely at what went on in the programs, he was able to identify how the program success was tied to leader-participant dynamics and group processes. Here is some of what he found:

Projects fail when project leaders force their own agenda or interests on project participants. In the case of the music project, the leaders that were hired were local musicians. The leaders had a lot of skill in music making but they also had musical interests that were different from the young people they were hired to work with. In the two projects that didn't work out, Rimmer found that the musicians developed the musical project around their own musical interests, rather than the musical tastes and interests of the young people. In the project that did work out, the musician set aside his own musical preferences and instead let the young people make the decisions around the kind of music they wanted to make.

Groups get into 'habits' of participation and nonparticipation. The music projects generally started out as participatory but over time, the leaders took more and more control over the direction of the project. When he watched group planning sessions, Rimmer found that in the programs that failed, the leaders gradually took over control of decision making. As this pattern continued, Rimmer noted that it became harder and harder to for young people to assert themselves in the decision-making process, as to do so required an effort of challenging the 'status quo' that created, for the young people, some potentially negative implications (e.g., being seen as a troublemaker, a poor relationship with leader).

Participation in decision making is an ongoing process. Participation in decision making is especially important in the early stages of a project, as this is when its course is being charted and many key decisions need to be made. However, Rimmer found that key decisions, which had an impact on the project's direction and that young people were invested in, were being made all the way through the program. In the program that was most successful, the leaders maintained a relationship with young people that was highly consultative throughout, meaning that whenever a decision was to be made, the leaders talked to the young people about it. Rimmer noted that consultation was particularly important any time a program experiences a significant change (e.g., a new leader joins, members leave).

on issues of common concern to members. For example, a parents' group associated with an elementary school could be asked to be provide feedback on a potential traffic calming intervention near the school. In this case, the parents' group provides a convenient means of inviting participation from individual parents, while participating as part of a collective can help participants to feel that their involvement will be consequential.

Asked to. As Lowndes et al. (2006) note, people are more likely to become engaged when they are asked to do so, preferably by those responsible for making a decision. For example, a local municipality may extend invitations to their citizens to provide feedback on issues of interest. It is important to provide several options for engagement, such as speaking up in a community meeting, tweeting questions to be answered in an online forum, or using post-it notes to leave comments on a poster located in a prominent community space. The use of incentives, such as honoraria or a chance to help make decisions (by casting a vote, for example) can be helpful making people feel that their participation is valued.

Responded to. 'Responded to' reflects the idea that people have to believe that their involvement is meaningful. Without this, people are unlikely to continue to participate. For example, leaders should communicate how decisions are made and the role of participant feedback within these decisions. While decisions may not always be in their favour, people can see their role within the bigger picture and feel "responded to" in the sense that their perspective was heard and taken into account.

WORKING TO BUILD CITIZEN POWER: CHALLENGES AND ISSUES

With the benefits and the ways of encouraging citizen power well-defined, what remains is to consider the challenges of facilitating citizen power. This section is focused on invited participation, which often poses challenges for citizen power because these opportunities for participation were inherently created by someone other than citizens themselves (Eversole, 2010). For example, a teen serving as a youth representative on the youth services committee of a municipality is able to exercise citizen power only because someone else created the committee and decided that there should be youth representation within it. The ability to create opportunities for citizen power, to *invite participation,* involves selecting the roles participants can play, the extent to which they do so, and how their contributions are used. Eversole writes of invited participation as a way of asking citizens to "participate on other people's institutional turf" (2010, p. 36). In other words, the very act of inviting participation reinforces a top-down rather than a citizen power approach. There is reason, then, to be thoughtful when inviting participation and particularly to consider the role for citizen power in these initiatives.

This chapter thus far has illustrated the many benefits of citizen power. We might draw the conclusion that more participation is always better, that it is always best to involve as many people as possible, as often as possible. However, is this the case? *Is more citizen power always better?* This idealized situation is not always realistic or advisable; having everyone affected by a decision involved in decision making at every stage of the decision-making process can be both cumbersome and impractical.

In fact, one critique of Arnstein's (1969) *Ladder of Citizen Participation* is that it implies that forms of participation higher up on the ladder are *always* preferable, that complete citizen power is always the ideal. The perspective that different degrees of participation might serve different purposes is not acknowledged (Cornwall, 2008). While the lower rungs of the ladder identified as non-participation (i.e., manipulation and therapy) are never appropriate or empowering forms of participation (and in fact are not forms of participation at all), different degrees of citizen power that may be appropriate for different community development projects. For example, Matarrita-Cascante and Brennan (2012) distinguished between imposed, self-help, and directed forms of community development. Imposed community development is led by professionals with technical expertise necessary for the provision of assets such as sidewalks and roads. In self-help forms of community development, citizens exercise complete control over changes to their communities. In between these two extremes is directed community development, where citizens are able to exercise limited power through invited participation such as providing feedback on the design of amenities such as playgrounds or bike paths. Their typology suggests that there are strengths and weaknesses associated with different degrees of citizen power. The high degree of citizen power evident in self-help forms of community development is more strongly associated with the benefits discussed in the previous section, such as sense of community, skills development, and more sustainable outcomes, while projects with little or no opportunity for citizen power (i.e., imposed community development) may sometimes be necessary where timelines are short or when projects are highly technical.

Another issue that community development advocates are beginning to consider is the potential burden that invited participation initiatives may place on citizens. Here the question is: *Does citizen power ask too much?* Although it takes time for practitioners to create opportunities for participation and to use citizens' contributions in thoughtful ways, they are compensated for doing so; however, citizens are rarely compensated for their contributions. Further, because citizen power initiatives are often aimed at increasing the power of those who have little, invited participation can rely heavily on the volunteerism of people with few resources. The demands of participation can be burdensome and, for some people, can compromise their ability to meet their own needs. For most people, citizen power is one commitment of many; citizens also have other responsibilities to their jobs, their families, their personal needs, and so on. Cornwall wrote of a community member who commented "You can't eat participation, can you?" (2008, p. 274), after being asked to recruit citizens to participate yet again in initiatives led by paid professionals.

Further, a small group of citizens tend to make the bulk of the contributions to citizen power. This trend is evident in research on volunteerism, where a comprehensive study of volunteering in Canada in 2010 revealed that 10% of volunteers contribute 53% of the volunteer hours (Vezina & Crompton, 2012). Citizens who become active can become known for their contributions, and can become the "go to" representatives of their communities (Reed & Selbee, 2001). This is troublesome for several reasons. First, the burden of citizen power lies disproportionately on a few citizens. In addition, having the same few people exercise citizen power can effectively disempower others, as power becomes vested in these few individuals rather than more broadly within a community. Finally, more broad representation also means that the benefits of citizen power are enjoyed more broadly.

Finally, an important question is: *How do we manage the process of relinquishing power?* Creating opportunities for citizen power requires those in power to relinquish some control; it is not possible to "keep" the power while "giving it away." This seems obvious, but can be difficult and uncomfortable in practice. For example, when citizens take part in decision making, they may make decisions that those traditionally in power, such as professionals or government leaders, would not have made. They may choose to do things differently. They may even decide to take a step back and focus on a different or broader issue than the one they were invited to be part of. For example, the text box below, *Considering Citizen Power,* presents an example of a group of older adults who came together to provide feedback to the seniors' community center to which they belonged. After a few months, however, they wanted to be able to access the center's financial records and to be briefed on the discussions held by the center's Board of Directors. Citizen power involves the redistribution of power and this can lead to conflict and discomfort as both citizens and professionals come to understand their role and decide how power should be shared. Frisby and Millar (2002) describe a citizen power initiative that brought low-income women together with public sector and recreation staff to work together to facilitate involvement of these women in sport and recreation. To ensure all members had power in making decisions, the group used a consensus-based approach where they discussed multiple perspectives when making a decision, and when reaching consensus, any member could "block" the group's decision by suggesting an alternative course of action, leading to further discussion. Both citizen participants and professionals reported finding this process frustrating and slow, but also said it allowed them to truly make decisions as a group.

CONSIDERING CITIZEN POWER

A community center for older adults has a members' council that was created to provide feedback and suggestion to the center's management, as well as to help plan and run events at the center. However, at recent meetings the group has become critical of the way the center is being managed, and they do not feel their feedback and suggestions are being considered. At the same time, the center's management staff have found the council uncooperative and unwilling to run events and meetings as they have in the past. Instead, the council has become focused on wanting to change some of the center's long-standing policies, so that, for example, members would have a vote on some of the decisions about how the center operates and would be able to access the center's financial records. The management team is considering shutting the members' council down as they are no longer fulfilling the role for which they were created.

What power does the community center's management hold? What power does the members' council hold? How does the "invited" nature of citizen power influence the power held by both groups?

MOVING FORWARD: RECONCILING THE CHALLENGES OF INVITED PARTICIPATION

Cornwall (2008) introduces the term *optimum* participation, which she defines as "getting the balance between depth and inclusion right for the purpose at hand" (p. 276). Achieving optimum participation means that practitioners should reflect on the form of invited participation that is appropriate and meaningful. *Who should be involved, and when? How can 'deeply' should citizens be asked to engage—that is, how much ownership should they be asked to take? How can opportunities for invited participation encourage citizen power despite their creation and existence within institutional settings?* These are not easy questions, but provide food for thought in the development of meaningful opportunities for citizen power.

REFERENCES

Arai, S. M., & Pedlar, A. M. (1997). Building communities through leisure: Citizen participation in a health communities initiative. *Journal of Leisure Research, 29*(2), 167–182.

Arney, L., Sabogal, M., & Moses House Youth (2010). Report from the field: The neoliberalization of community centers in Tampa, FL: Devastating effects temporarily reversed by local activism and community-based research. *North American Dialogue, 14*(1), 7–12.

Arnstein, S. R. (1969). A Ladder of Citizen Participation. *Journal of the American Planning Association, 35*(4), 216–224.

Barnes, M., Rodger, R., & Whyte, C. (1997). Empowerment through community development in recreation and leisure. *Journal of Leisurability, 24*(1), 47–52.

Cornwall, A. (2008). Unpacking 'participation': Models, meanings, and practices. *Community Development Journal, 43*(3), 269–283.

Eversole, R. (2010). Remaking participation: Challenges for community development practice. *Community Development Journal, 47*(1), 29–41.

Frisby, W., & Millar, S., (2002). The actualities of doing community development to promote the inclusion of low income populations in local sport and recreation. *European Sport Management Quarterly, 2*(3), 209–233.

Fung, A. (2006). Varieties of participation in complex governance. *Public Administration Review, 66,* 66–75.

Gaventa, J. (1980). *Power and Powerlessness: Quiescence and Rebellion in an Appalachian Valley.* Oxford: Clarendon Press.

Glover, T.D. (2003). The story of the Queen Anne Memorial Garden: Resisting a dominant cultural narrative. *Journal of Leisure Research, 35,* 190–212.

Glover, T. D. (2004). The 'community' center and the social construction of citizenship. *Leisure Sciences, 26,* 63–83.

Hart, R. A. (1992). *Children's Participation: From Tokenism to Citizenship.* Florence, Italy: UNICEF ICDC.

Hemingway, J. L. (1999). Leisure, social capital, and democratic citizenship. *Journal of Leisure Research, 31*(2), 150–165.

Lowndes, V., Pratchett, L., & Stoker, G. (2006). Diagnosing and remedying the failings of official participation schemes: The CLEAR framework. *Social Policy and Society, 5*(2), 281–291.

Matarrita-Cascante, D., Luloff, A. E., Krannich, R. S., & Field, D. R. (2006). Community Participation in Rapidly Growing Communities in Southern Utah. *Community Development, 37*(4), 71–87.

Matarrita-Cascante, D., & Brennan, M. A. (2012). Conceptualizing community development in the twenty-first century. *Community Development Journal, 43*(3), 293–305.

McArdle, J. (1990). Community development-Tools of the trade. *Community Quarterly, 16*, 47–54.

McLaren, P. (2003). Critical pedagogy: A look at the major concepts. In A. Darder, M. Baltodano & R. Torres (Eds.), *The Critical Pedagogy Reader* (pp. 69–96). New York: RoutledgeFarmer.

McMillan, D. W., & Chavis, D. W. (1986). Sense of community: A definition and theory. *Journal of Community Psychology, 14,* 6–23.

Ohmer, M. L. (2007). Citizen participation in neighborhood organizations and Its relationship to volunteers' self- and collective efficacy and sense of community. *Social Work Research, 31*(2), 109–120.

Reed, P. B., & Selbee, L. K. (2001). The civic core in Canada: Disproportionality in charitable giving, volunteering and civic participation. *Nonprofit and Voluntary Sector Quarterly, 30,* 761–780.

Rimmer, M. (2012). The participation and decision making of 'at risk' youth in community music projects: An exploration of three case studies. *Journal of Youth Studies, 15*(3), 329–350.

Speer, P., & Hughey, J. (1995). Community organizing: An ecological route to empowerment and power. *American Journal of Community Psychology, 23*(5), 729–748.

Tesoriero, F. (2010). *Community development: Community-based alternatives in an era of globalisation.* Frenchs Forest, NSW: Pearson.

Verba, S., Schlozman, K., and Brady, H. (1995), *Voice and Equality: Civic Voluntarism in American Politics,* Cambridge, MA: Harvard University Press.

VeneKlasen, L., & Miller, V. (2007). *A new weave of power, people, and politics.* Sterling, VA: Stylus Publishing.

Vezina, M., & Crompton, S. (2012). Volunteering in Canada. *Canadian Social Trends: Component of Statistics Canada Catologue no. 11-008-X.* Statistics Canada. Retrieved from http://www.statcan.gc.ca/pub/11-008-x/2012001/article/11638-eng.pdf

Willick, F. (2011, December 13). Public had major role in design of hew Halifax central library, Halifax Public Libraries. *The Chronicle-Herald,* p. xx. Retrieved from http://thechronicleherald.ca/metro/42423-library-consultations-lesson-collaboration

5
SOCIAL CAPITAL: THE VALUE OF SOCIAL NETWORKS IN COMMUNITY

Troy D. Glover

WHY SOCIAL NETWORKS MATTER

Communities function through webs of social relationships that form among their members. Those that thrive do so because they nurture and cultivate social networks that transcend self-interest; those that fail engender self-centeredness, apathy, and dysfunctional interactions. The quality and value of social networks matter insofar as they reflect a community's capacity to advance its members collective and individual interests. Social capital represents this value.

I like to think of social capital as ". . . the consequence of investment in and cultivation of social relationships allowing an individual access to resources that would otherwise be unavailable to him or her" (Glover et al., 2005, p. 87). Irrespective of how much human capital—skills, talents, abilities, and knowledge—we have at our disposal, we face scenarios in life that force us to rely on our social networks for assistance. In other words, we draw upon our social capital to act together (Graham & Glover, 2014), to get by, and get ahead (Glover & Parry, 2008). To develop social capital, we "invest" in relationships with others and build meaningful connections that lead to the establishment of norms of reciprocity and the creation of obligations to one another. These forms of social capital, among others (see below), can be drawn upon in times of need to access necessary resources and facilitate individual and collective actions. To extend the economic metaphor, then, our investment results in some sort of return. Thus, communities with a multitude of strong social networks provide greater access to resources than those without. For this reason, social capital merits serious attention from practitioners of community development.

> ***Application Questions:***
> ***Think of your 'social network.'***
>
> *1. To whom do you turn when you need support? What kinds of support do you look to your friends for? What about members of your family? Are there others in your life you feel comfortable reaching out to when you need resources?*
>
> *2. Do you think you form part of a social network for others? Who turns to you when they need help or support?*

Social capital, as a concept, captured the collective imagination of the world in the late 20th Century through the work of Robert Putnam, a Harvard political scientist and reportedly the most cited social scientist of the 1990s. His body of work sensitized us to the changing landscape of community relations and called for greater attention to address what he saw as a deepening deterioration in generalized trust and reciprocity, values he regarded as vital to the facilitation of social cooperation. You see, Putnam (1995, 2000) believed the dramatic erosion in social and civic engagement—operationalized as associational memberships in service clubs like the Rotary Club and leisure-based associations like bowling leagues—meant relative strangers were less likely to interact directly and routinely, thereby failing to forge meaningful relationships and create the social capital so necessary for a well-functioning civil society. Putnam's title of his work on this subject, *Bowling Alone,* neatly encapsulated these observations. His findings marked a disconcerting social trend with negative implications for community well-being. In many ways, Putnam simply refashioned an age-old idea in a new way. The decline of social capital, he observed, signaled a loss of community.

Social capital should not be confused with community, however. Recently, I described the two as "... different, albeit complementary. Community is a source of social capital, and social capital represents the value of community" (Glover, 2016, p. 3). That is, social capital represents a return on investments in community connections. Readers should note that social capital is a feature of all kinds of social structures (Coleman, 1990)—that is, the various patterns of social arrangements in society—not just community networks. Friendships, triads, dyads, and other forms of social networks all signify *sources* of social capital. With this in mind, the sources, and even outcomes, of social capital should not be conflated with social capital itself. Instead, social capital alerts us to the value embedded in our community relationships and memberships, albeit a value ultimately realized by individuals. In other words, the individual accesses and benefits from the social capital available to him or her. Because individuals, not communities, realize social capital, an understanding of social capital and its workings at the micro level help us appreciate the role leisure plays in its development.

UNDERSTANDING HOW SOCIAL CAPITAL WORKS: A MICRO LEVEL UNDERSTANDING

Together with my colleague Diana Parry, I modeled the process of social capital development (see Figure 5.1) in our research on friendships built subsequent to a stressful life event (see Glover & Parry, 2008). Though our model focused on friendships, the underlying process depicted in the model pertains to social capital built in other contexts, including social networks. Accordingly, I draw on the model as a useful heuristic to frame our discussion below. In so doing, I explain its workings, while paying deliberate attention to how it can be applied within the practice of community development.

HOW AND WHY PEOPLE COME TOGETHER

Our model begins with a premise consistent with something called the homophilous principle: that is, networks develop, first and foremost, among people who share a social identity (see McPherson et al., 2001). This principle makes intuitive sense. If we cannot connect with others on some level, we have no reason to connect with them at all. Accordingly, a social network

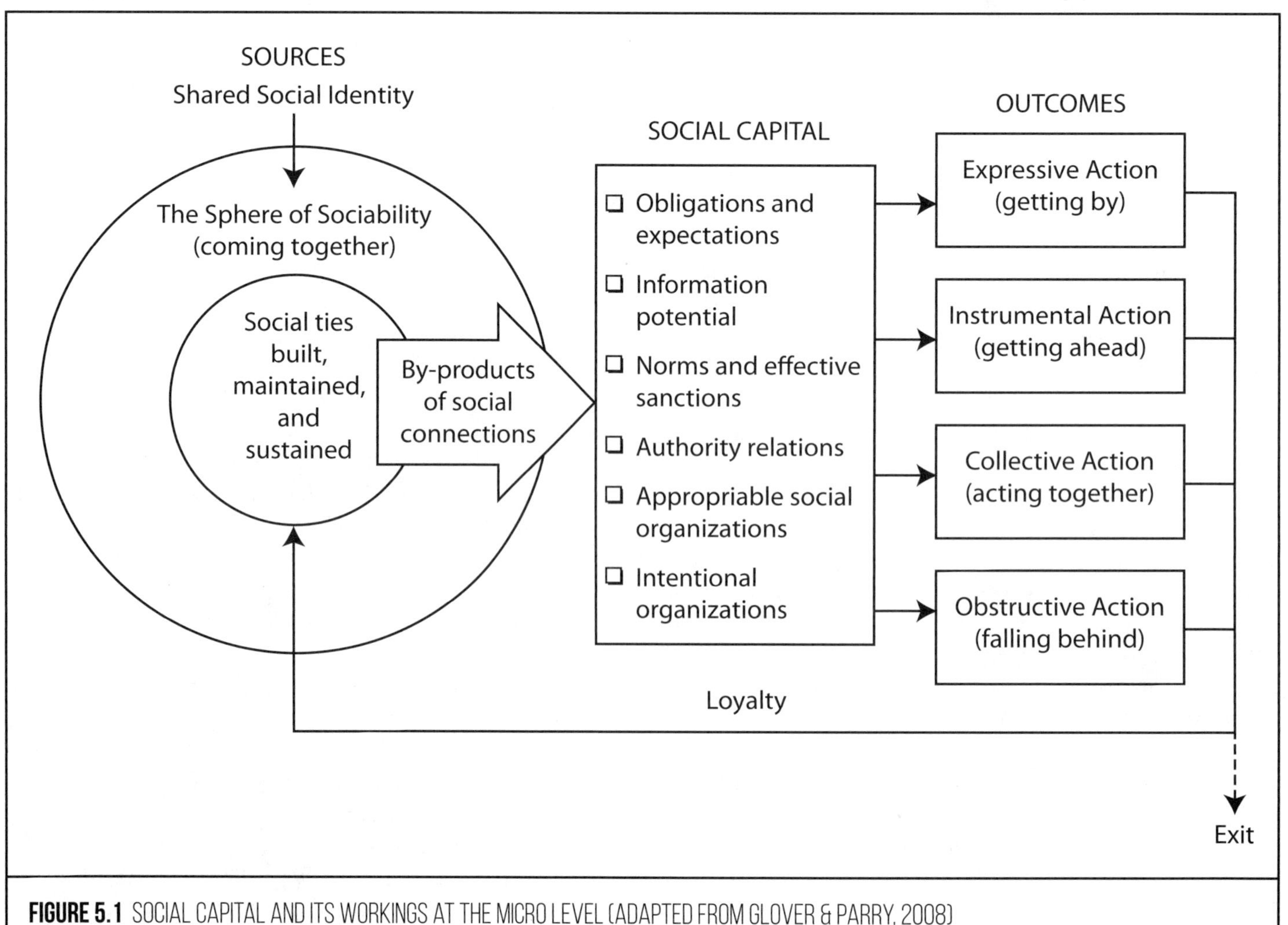

FIGURE 5.1 SOCIAL CAPITAL AND ITS WORKINGS AT THE MICRO LEVEL (ADAPTED FROM GLOVER & PARRY, 2008)

with members who feel no sense of shared identity is hard to imagine. Now, the complexity and multifaceted nature of our identities means there are always a variety of ways we can potentially see ourselves as similar to (or different from) our fellow community members. Perhaps we identify as neighbors, city dwellers, friends, coworkers, members of the same club, or fans of the same team. Maybe we belong to the same gender, race, ethnic group, social class, sexual orientation, or religion. What many scholars refer to as intersectionality (see McCall, 2005) or interconnectedness (see Parry & Fullagar, 2013) means there will always be some identity we share, just as there will always be identities that set us apart. Practitioners of community development who wish to build social capital must consider where identities intersect in a positive way, and bring people together under such a premise.

Along these lines, the social capital literature distinguishes between *bonding* and *bridging*, two types of relationships that provide individuals with access to resources. Bonding refers to connections among community members who see themselves as sharing a similar social identity, whereas bridging refers to connections among community members who believe themselves to be unalike in some socio-demographic (or social identity) sense (see Szreter & Woolcock, 2004). The distinction between the two complements the branch of social network theory in economic sociology on how information flows through a social network. Granovetter's (1973) "strength of weak ties" hypothesis asserts novel information flows to us through our weak ties (i.e., acquaintances), as opposed to our strong ties (i.e., family and close friends). Because our strong ties belong to the same, close-knit social circles, the information they have overlaps considerably with our own. Our weak ties, alternatively, know people unfamiliar to us, so they have better access to 'new' ideas and opportunities. In this sense, our weak ties fill 'structural holes' in our networks by functioning as 'brokers' between our circles of friends, thus extending our reach to more distant parts of our social system (Burt, 2009). We see this process unfold in our everyday interactions. For example, gossip often originates from a source outside of our social circle. It is shared with someone within our circle and passed along to other members of our network to strengthen our circle. Without the original source of information—the person who shared it—our social circle would remain in the dark about the content of the information he or she shared. In short, the bonding of strong ties and bridging of weak ties speak to the importance of diversifying our social connections for individual and collective gain.

Consistent with our discussion about intersectionality above, I noted elsewhere that "our multiple identities make it challenging to nail down definitively whether bonding or bridging took place" (Glover, 2016, p. 8). The strength of a social tie can be somewhat subjective. Correspondingly, Schuller (2007, pp. 15–16) argued the distinction between bonding and bridging is context dependent:

> It is only by understanding the particular context within which social capital is generated and applied, that we can identify what is bonding and what is bridging. Reaching out across a street in a given neighborhood may bridge ethnic, class or other lines; but seen in a broader context it may look like a community simply reinforcing its bonds against outsiders.

In an important conceptual development in the social capital literature, Schuller developed a useful matrix to better understand the interrelationships between bonding and bridging (see Figure 5.2). According to the matrix, a social network with high levels of bonding and bridging remains secure in its own identity and internally cohesive without having to close itself off to new ideas or differing values. By contrast, a social network with low levels of bonding and bridging works against itself from the outset. Its dysfunctional nature manifests itself in a lack of trust and tolerance, so it generates no resources from either internal or external connections. Its prejudice or apathy results in its inability to generate or sustain new capacities. A high bonding and low bridging social network functions in comfort, but lacks the ability to adapt to change. Thus, its self-isolation becomes its

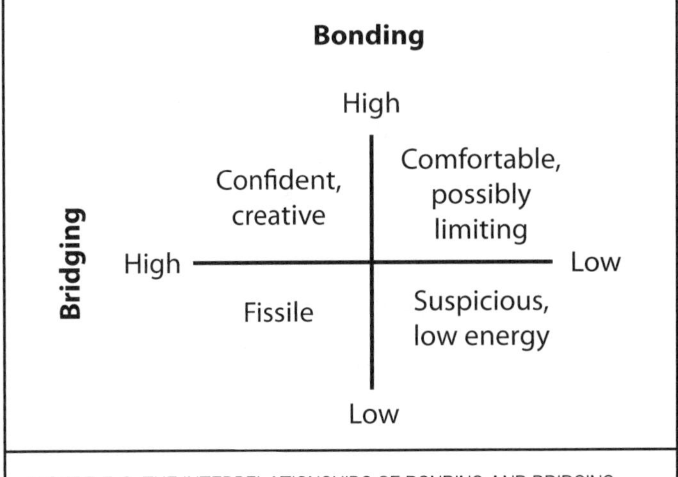

FIGURE 5.2 THE INTERRELATIONSHIPS OF BONDING AND BRIDGING (ADAPTED FROM SCHULLER, 2007)

own undoing, for high bonding can have culturally and economically constraining impacts that may lead to harmful forms of exclusion. Finally, a high bridging, low bonding scenario resembles a social network whose members fail to identify with the group as their primary reference point, but use it only instrumentally to advance their own interests. A social network under this context is highly combustible insofar as it is unlikely to remain intact and will likely dissolve. All told, Schuller insisted the relative importance of bonding and bridging social capital, for any social network, changes over time. As a result, his conceptualization forces practitioners of community development to consider when bonding needs to be complemented by bridging social capital or when the growth of bridging social capital leads to a transformation in the identity of the community.

Drawing People Together: The Role of Leisure

Shared identity may be important, but it only represents a starting point for coming together. Ultimately, people need a purpose to do so. For this reason, Diana Parry and I argued leisure plays a vital role in drawing people to socialize together and encouraging the development of durable social networks (Glover & Parry, 2008). Book clubs, sport teams, and local events, as well as neighborhood barbeques, happy hour at a local bar, and dinner parties, provide contexts in which members of a network engage in the ongoing social production of community. Even episodes of leisure that occur in work-like contexts (e.g., chatting around the water cooler, taking a coffee break) play a pivotal role in developing social capital by opening people up to the possibility of friendship and conviviality (Glover et al., 2005). Leisure, in each example, promotes sociability, thereby serving as an alluring draw for most individuals and the starting point for social capital production. Leisure opens up lines of communication among people and allows them to transcend the boundaries of their various social identities. In so doing, it serves as an indispensable vehicle for the development, maintenance, and sustainability of social networks (Glover, 2016) and the realization of community (Cook, 2003).

Social networks form and social capital develops within what Diana Parry and I called the "sphere of sociability" (Glover & Parry, 2008). To maintain their stocks of social capital, network members must routinely reinvest in their relationships by continuing to be social with each other, otherwise those relationships and the resources accessible through them are likely to wither (Putnam, 2000). Leisure provides a social context in which to build these relationships. After all, what troubled Putnam (1995) most about the decline of participation in organized bowling leagues in America was not the loss of revenue for bowling-lane proprietors, but rather "the social interaction and even occasionally civic conversations over beer and pizza that solo bowlers forgo" (p. 70). Far from trivial, then, leisure becomes a meaningful domain of everyday life in which we connect and renew our social bonds. For this reason, Kim Shinew, Diana Parry, and I described leisure as "the social lubricant" for social capital production (Glover et al., 2005).

The way community members experience leisure makes a difference in terms of the quality of social capital developed. Hemingway (1999) argued the more independence community members have in their leisure and the more leisure contributes to the development of their capacities, the more social capital will develop and transfer. He went on to venture that, to the extent individuals participate in creating their own leisure as opposed to simply consuming it passively, the more likely the resulting social capital will contribute to strong citizenship. Hemingway's propositions hold up well upon examination (see Doherty & Misener, 2008; Glover, 2002). Relatedly, Felice Yuen and I distinguished between leisure that encourages people to *socialize* (i.e., interact casually) and *mobilize* (i.e., act collectively to achieve a common goal), noting the former facilitates bonding, whereas the latter facilitates bridging (see Yuen & Glover, 2005). In both cases, social capital develops, so "the question is not if leisure is associated with civically relevant social capital, but what kinds of leisure in what kinds of settings" (Glover & Hemingway, 2005, p. 395).

Application Questions

Think about the benefits of social networks and social capital, as described above.

1. What role do you think recreation and leisure can play?

2. Are there certain kinds of leisure and recreation activities that are more conducive to building these relationships?

3. What initiatives could be put in place that can develop social capital in a neighborhood?

THE BENEFITS OF RECREATION TO BUILDING FAMILIES AND COMMUNITIES

Neighborhood Festivals: Can They Build Social Capital?

—Troy Glover & Felice Yuen

One of the long-standing lamentations of community life is how people no longer know their neighbors, that we now live in a world in which people are isolated, disconnected from their community, and disengaged from civic life.

The fragmenting of neighborhood and community networks is concerning for a few reasons. First, we feel more isolated and disconnected, which has an impact on personal well-being. Second, it decreases the productivity of a community as citizens have less "social capital" available to them.

With this in mind, in 2008 we investigated a program in Kitchener, Ontario called the *Festival of Neighbourhoods,* to see if it was effective in developing social capital. The Festival of Neighbourhoods program encourages local citizens to organize and enter neighborhood events (like picnics, street parties, or barbeques). Those neighborhoods that organize an event are then entered into a random draw for a $10,000 community improvement grant. The intent of the initiative is to encourage neighbors to build relationships that strengthen the social network of their area; however, the community improvement grant also becomes a resource that communities can use for further enhancement.

Two major themes emerged from our project. They were as follows:

The Role of Socializing: The Festival of Neighbourhoods program was set up deliberately to facilitate and strengthen informal connections among neighbors. The neighborhood events gave people a reason to come together that was informal, fun-focused, and celebrated what neighbors had in common rather than their differences. The events opened up the possibility for relationships to be developed or strengthened, and social networks to be enhanced. In this way, the event could be a starting point for other neighborhood initiatives or undertakings.

The Role of Mobilizing: Along with socializing, the festival events also encouraged neighbors to mobilize as a more cohesive group. Here, the community improvement grant played an important role, as the grant provided a reason for groups to talk about neighborhood needs and actively do something about it. Through this process, we found residents began to participate in community life and some took on leadership roles. The community improvement grant also created a process that engaged the municipality and residents together, which promoted mutual understanding.

The Importance of Facilitation: In the Festival of Neighbourhood project, the municipality stepped out of the role of direct-service provider in favor of a facilitative role in which it helped neighborhoods achieve the aims they had set for themselves. For the neighborhoods, the more participatory role has allowed them to develop projects that meet and characterize the uniqueness of their community.

Overall, we learned about the role that leisure can play in building social capital. The Festival of Neighbourhood project also emphasizes the role that informal leisure can play in this process. Participants also talked about *projects*—a short-term, one-time event—as particularly valuable for the first steps of community building, as it affords greater opportunity for success, and become a building block for further community development!

Source: Yuen, F., & Glover, T. (2005). Enabling social capital development: An examination of the Festival of Neighbourhoods in Kitchener, Ontario. *Journal of Park and Recreation Administration, 23*(4), 20–38

Even so, the liminal or short-lived, temporary nature of leisure and its implications for the durability of community relationships warrants attention from practitioners of community development. If social capital requires ongoing investments in social relationships, the liminality of leisure activities deserves monitoring to ensure the relationships that are built are meaningful. In my view, liminality and durability represent important matters that require the attention of leisure researchers (see Glover, 2016). Correspondingly, practitioners of community development ought to focus on how leisure can be mobilized to sustain relationships, not just build and maintain them.

SOCIAL CAPITAL: THE BY-PRODUCT OF COMMUNITY RELATIONSHIPS

The by-product of social networks built, maintained, and sustained through leisure is social capital, a sort of social credit amassed through social interactions upon which members of a social network can draw to access resources (Bourdieu, 1986). In other words, by investing in a relationship, we accrue the potential to draw on that relationship, when needed, to gain assistance or support. Social capital, as described above, speaks to the value of social networks and therefore the value of community to its members. If we invest in relationships with our neighbors, they are more likely to help us when we are in need of their assistance. Coleman (1990) distinguished among six forms of social capital that warrant description:

1. *Obligations and expectations* offer incentives to community members to invest in social networks and accumulate obligations, which are counted on to be reciprocated and repaid if and when needed. Stebbins (2000) argued agreeable obligation defines most group commitments in leisure contexts to ensure the group meets routinely and functions as intended.
2. *Information potential* involves the use of social ties to acquire specialized information without having to secure the information directly. In separate studies, Diana Parry, Catlin Mulcahy, and I found mothers who belonged to playgroups (Mulcahy et al., 2010) and social networking sites (Parry et al., 2013), respectively, accessed advice of other mothers through their social networks. Similarly, Taryn Graham and I found dog park visitors who connected on a regular basis commonly exchanged pet-related information concerning their dogs' daily care, grooming, and diet (Graham & Glover, 2014). In addition to pet-related information, some park visitors even used their connections to gain employment, find housing, or identify dating prospects.
3. *Norms and effective sanctions* convince network members to work for the collective interest of the social network. In research on the friendship networks of women experiencing infertility, research participants felt obliged to attend baby showers of their friends who conceived or adopted children, even though such support confronted them with their own infertility (Glover & Parry, 2008).
4. *Authority relations* occur when a social network transfers "rights of control" to one individual who then has access to an extensive network of social capital that can be targeted toward a specific goal. Johnson et al. (2009) revealed how community representatives worked with municipal officials to build trusting partnerships within their city. Their role enabled them to speak on behalf of the neighborhood and work toward desired improvements.
5. *An appropriable social organization* is an organization created for one purpose, but used for another. For example, in a 2003 study, I examined how a fractured neighborhood used a community garden as a symbol to elicit emotional affirmations of community identity (Glover, 2003).
6. *Intentional organizations* connect individuals together to benefit members, but also others. In previous work, I have (2004a) found volunteers described their community center as a "work in progress" that benefited volunteers and non-volunteer users alike.

All of these forms of social capital can be drawn upon by members of social networks to advance their individual, network, and/or community interests.

OUTCOMES OF SOCIAL CAPITAL: FACILITATING ACTION

The actions facilitated by social capital make the sustainability of positive social networks a vital part of the community development process. Diana Parry and I identified three types of action in our model (Glover & Parry, 2008). First, *expressive action* (or getting by) refers to emotional support. Social networks, in other words, assist community members in coping with their life situations through the receipt of empathetic support.

Second, *instrumental action* (or getting ahead), the material dimension of our social networks, gives members access to resources that help them advance their social position. Acquiring valuable information, as noted above, is a common example. Third, *obstructive action* (or falling behind) refers to actions taken by network members against their own interests. Diana Parry and I included this form of action to recognize the potential ill-effects of our social networks. Obstructive action represents a setback for people and often keeps them from getting ahead. As noted in the example above on sanctions, we can face peer pressures that result in unhealthy behaviors or actions.

The inclusion of obstructive action in our model alerts us to the darker side of social capital. Portes and Sensenbrenner (1993) recognized the very same social structures "that give rise to appropriate resources for individual use can also constrain action or even derail it from its original goals" (p. 1338). Like Schuller's point above, Portes and Landlot (1996) argued social capital can result in a high degree of conformity within a social network, thereby resulting in the rejection of difference. Any effort by a member to pursue advantage outside the network may be viewed as a danger to network solidarity and therefore discouraged. With this in mind, it is no surprise research participants in our study of women who experienced infertility (Glover & Parry, 2008) felt bound to support their friends by attending baby showers, even though doing so felt detrimental to their own well-being.

Though not included in the original model Diana Parry and I developed, practitioners of community development ought to naturally consider a fourth form of action, one that Graham and I (2014) recommended be added to the model: *collective action* (or acting together)—that is, the effort by more than one person to improve their shared conditions and achieve change through joint organization, mobilization, and negotiation. Community development in whatever shape or form advances the collective interests of its members, and so collective action represents a desirable aspect and outcome of the community development process.

EXIT AND LOYALTY: THE DURABILITY OF COMMUNITY RELATIONSHIPS

Community members can either choose to remain loyal members of their social networks or exit their networks altogether. The decision, either way, happens less deliberately and more likely because of a naturally occurring diminishment of investments in their networks (i.e., they just grow apart). Unlike financial capital wherein 'savings' can remain untouched and even grow without additional 'deposits,' social capital requires an ongoing investment, otherwise it withers and dies. As a result, we must continually reinvest in our network relationships if we want to benefit from them in the future. I am less likely to help someone with whom I have had little or no contact over the past 10 years, than I am someone with whom I connect on an everyday basis. At the social network level, a lack of investment by network members can result in the fragmentation or demise of the network itself.

In his definition of social capital, Bourdieu (1986, p. 248) emphasized the important of "a durable network of more or less institutionalized relationships of mutual acquaintance and recognition." By durability, he meant an enduring or lasting network upon which community members draw support or resources. The dynamic landscape of social networks within a community inevitably changes as networks grow and thrive, while others weaken and fade away. Practitioners of community development must aim to support the presence of durable networks so as to sustain or improve a community's resilience. They can do so by being sources of linking social capital.

Linking social capital refers to "norms of respect and networks of trusting relationships between people who are interacting across explicit, formal or institutionalized power or authority gradients in society" (Szreter & Woolcock, 2004, p. 655). That is, institutions provide a structural bridge to assist individuals in accessing needed resources, say for instance when a community organization connects a homeless person with supports within the community. Along these lines, community development agencies and community development practitioners play an active role in linking community groups to resources that strengthen and sustain the groups more effectively. In many ways, the development of linking social capital represents the enabling imperative of the community development profession. We see many examples of linking social capital in the literature. Arcodia and Whitford (2007), for example, revealed how event managers, by interacting directly with local businesses and the broader community in their event preparations, increased their knowledge of community resources, developed links among hitherto disparate networks, and largely inspired deeper interactions among existing community agencies. Similarly, Johnson et al. (2009) and Yuen et al. (2005) showed how municipal officials played an instrumental role in assisting neighborhood networks in accessing and acquiring resources to support their efforts at neighborhood improvements. Without the assistance of their municipal officials, the neighborhood would have been unlikely to make as much headway in their collective efforts. Connecting social networks to resources only strengthens the possibility of enabling positive outcomes for the community.

ISSUES OF ACCESS TO AND RETURNS OF SOCIAL CAPITAL

Member access to network resources signifies the presence of social capital in a social network. That is, if members cannot access resources from others in their network, social capital is not present. Where social capital exists, network resources tend to remain available to network members only (see intentional organizations above for a counter-example). Put differently, while community members draw on their social capital for assistance, the same resources can be inaccessible to outsiders. In DeFillippis's words (2001, p. 801), "People who realize capital through their networks of social capital do so precisely because others are excluded." The value of belonging to a community, in other words, stems from exclusive membership. Differences in the level of prosperity that exist among communities reflect differences in the pools of accessible resources available to its members. More prosperous communities, in other words, have more resources to share with their network members. However, not everyone prospers from their own network equally. Benefits distributed within a social network can differ significantly based upon the unique social positions its members occupy (Glover, 2006). All told, access to resources made available through social capital vary, both within and between social networks.

Effective practitioners of community development sensitize themselves to the actual distribution within and between social networks by understanding the degree to which community members actually secure social capital from their networks. As I outlined elsewhere (see Glover, 2006), access and return depend on at least three of factors. First, because of their position within the social hierarchy, certain community members enjoy differential rewards of network membership, even though they may contribute no more or perhaps even less than other network members. Lin (2001) referred to this inequality of outcome as a *return deficit*. For example, in my research on a neighborhood association's efforts to reclaim neighborhood space through the construction of a community garden, I found African American association members, in comparison to their Caucasian colleagues, had limited access to the community garden they helped build, even though they put equal energy into the project (see Glover, 2004b). Within group inequalities existed because of their return deficit.

Second, social class, gender, race, and ethnicity all shape the way certain social networks connect their members to resources (Foley & Edwards, 1999). While an individual may have open access to resources in his or her social network, the network all together may exist within a subjugated community. Lin (2001) referred to this inequality outcome as a capital deficit. Hunter (2010) revealed the importance of night clubs as spaces that assist poor urban African Americans negotiate their financial and social isolation. However, their club networks could get them ahead only so far because of the limited resources accessible within them.

Third, access to social capital depends on the quantity and quality of relationships. The more we bond with social actors who share a similar social identity and bridge with others to diversify our social identity, the more social capital we have at our disposal. By concentrating exclusively on quantity of social ties formed, however, we tend to ignore quality. The greater our social connections, the better. However, one tie may be sufficient to gain access to a crucial resource (Foley & Edwards, 1999). Moreover, the quality of the tie corresponds with its positive, as opposed to negative, influence. Here, peer pressure can serve as both a positive (see Rosenberg, 2013) and negative (see Portes, 1998) form of social capital, depending upon the actions it facilitates.

Practitioners of community development ought to do their best to advance principles of inclusion, shared benefit, and positive influence to address these issues. Doing so presents considerable challenges, however, given the unequal nature of the distribution of social capital. Perhaps the best approach is to resource networks more equitably to place them in a more prosperous position that enables the distribution of greater benefits for all members, irrespective of their structural position.

Application Questions

Imagine you are a municipal leader who is concerned about community development.

1. Are there specific actions you could take to help generate or facilitate the creation of the six forms of social capital that Coleman (1990) described?

2. What steps might you take to support initiatives in a neighborhood that is interested in working to change their community for the better?

Burt (2009) referred to this tactic as *structural autonomy,* a term he coined to conceptually merge the benefits of network closure (what I have referred to as bonding) and brokerage (what I have referred to as bridging). The best returns from social capital, he argued, come from social networks that nurture a cohesive group, yet connect its members to diverse external contacts.

WHY SOCIAL CAPITAL IS RELEVANT TO COMMUNITY DEVELOPMENT

For a variety of reasons, community development practitioners ought to take social capital and its creation, maintenance, and sustainability seriously. First and foremost, social capital strengthens a community's capacity to enact change, making it a necessary ingredient for the realization of a healthy community (Glover & Stewart, 2013). Its expansion in a community, moreover, bridges structural holes that exist, thereby enabling more efficient networking among its members (Burt, 2009), networking that can be mobilized to better the community as a whole. Finally, social capital facilitates collective action, something pivotal to the process of community development. As a result, Wilson (1997) argued social capital formation must be a central strategy for community development practitioners. Within the context of leisure, community development underscores the relevance of social and civic engagement as a means of nurturing social networks and building community capacity. Leisure represents a valuable tool in the community development process. Even so, while leisure may help facilitate social capital, the actual realization of social capital depends on those engaged in leisure themselves. As Field (2003) noted, we ". . . can bring people together, and ensure that the conditions exist for instrumental cooperation. We cannot force people to like each other, fall in love, or enjoy time in each other's company—and then go the extra mile in terms of trust and regard" (p. 133). With this in mind, he recommended, "probably the best role [for those interested in advancing social capita] is to serve as an enabler, and then stand back" (p. 134). Leisure, in our view, has genuine potential to enable social capital.

REFERENCES

Arcodia, C., & Whitford, M. (2007). Festival attendance and the development of social capital. *Journal of Convention & Event Tourism, 8*(2), 1–18.

Bourdieu, P. (1986). The forms of capital. In J. Richardson (Ed.), *Handbook of theory and research for the sociology of education* (pp. 241–258). New York: Greenwood.

Burt, R. S. (2009). *Structural holes: The social structure of competition.* Cambridge, MA: Harvard University Press.

Coleman, J. S. (1990). *Foundations of Social Theory.* Cambridge, MA: Belknap Press.

Cook, D. T. (2003). Recreation. In K. Christensen, & D. Levinson (eds.), *Encyclopedia of Community* (pp. 1146–1149). Thousand Oaks, CA: Sage.

DeFilippis, J. (2001). The myth of social capital in community development. *Housing Policy Debate, 12*(4), 781–806.

Doherty, A., & Misener, K. (2008). Community sport networks. In M. Nicholson, & R. Hoye (Eds.), *Sport and social capital* (pp. 113–142). New York: Butterworth-Heinemann.

Field, J. (2003). *Social capital.* New York: Routledge.

Foley, M. W., & Edwards, B. (1999). Is it time to divest in social capital? *Journal of Public Policy, 19*(2), 141–173.

Glover, T. D. (2002). Citizenship and the production of public recreation: Is there an empirical relationship? *Journal of Leisure Research, 34*(2), 204–231.

Glover, T. D. (2003). The story of the Queen Anne Memorial Garden: Resisting a dominant cultural narrative. *Journal of Leisure Research, 35*(2), 190–212.

Glover, T. D. (2004a). The 'community' center and the social construction of citizenship. *Leisure Sciences, 26*(1), 63–83.

Glover, T. D. (2004b). Social capital in the lived experiences of community gardeners, *Leisure Sciences, 26*(2), 143–162.

Glover, T. D. (2006). Toward a critical examination of social capital within leisure contexts: From production and maintenance to distribution. *Leisure/Loisir: Journal of the Canadian Association for Leisure Studies, 30* (2), 357–367.

Glover, T. D. (2016). Leveraging leisure-based community networks to access social capital. In G. Walker, D. Scott, and M. Stoldoska (Eds.), *Leisure matters: The state and future of leisure studies.* State College, PA: Venture Publishing, Inc.

Glover, T. D. & Hemingway, J. L (2005). Locating leisure in the social capital literature. *Journal of Leisure Research, 37*(4), 387–401.

Glover, T. D., & Parry, D. C. (2008). Friendships developed subsequent to a stressful life event: Links with leisure, social capital, and health. *Journal of Leisure Research, 40*(2), 208–230.

Glover, T. D., Parry, D. C., & Mulcahy, C. M. (2012). At once liberating and exclusionary? A Lefebvrean analysis of Gilda's Club of Toronto. *Leisure Studies.* DOI: 10.1080/02614367.2012.677057

Glover, T. D., Parry, D. C., & Shinew, K. J. (2005). Building relationships, accessing resources: Mobilizing social capital in community garden contexts. *Journal of Leisure Research, 37*(4), 450–474.

Glover, T. D., Shinew, K. J., & Parry, D. C. (2005). Association, sociability, and civic culture: The democratic effect of community gardening. *Leisure Sciences, 27*(1), 75–92.

Glover, T. D., & Stewart, W. P. (2013). Advancing healthy communities policy through tourism, leisure, and events research. *Journal of Policy Research in Tourism, Leisure and Events, 5*(2), 109–122.

Graham, T., & Glover, T. D. (2014). *On the fence: Dog parks and the (un)leashing of community and social capital. Leisure Sciences, 36*(3), 217–234.

Granovetter, M. (1973). The strength of weak ties. *American journal of sociology, 78*(6), l.

Hemingway, J. L. (1999). Leisure, social capital, and democratic citizenship. *Journal of Leisure Research, 31*(2), 150–165.

Hunter, M. A. (2010). The nightly round: Space, social capital, and urban black nightlife. *City & Community, 9*(2), 165–186.

Johnson, A. J., Glover, T. D., & Yuen, F. (2009). Supporting effective community representation: Lessons from the Festival of Neighbourhoods. *Managing Leisure, 14*(1), 1–16.

Lin, N. (2001). *Social capital: A theory of social structure and action.* New York: Cambridge University Press.

McCall, L. (2005). The complexity of intersectionality. *Signs, 30*(3), 1771–1800.

McPherson, M., Smith-Livin, L., & Cook, J. (2001). Birds of a feather: Homophily in social networks. *Annual Review of Sociology, 27,* 415–444.

Mulcahy, C. M., Parry, D. C., & Glover, T. D. (2010). Playgroup politics: A critical social capital exploration of exclusion and conformity in mummies groups. *Leisure Studies, 29*(1), 3–27.

Parry, D. C., & Fullagar, S. (2013). Feminist research in the contemporary era. *Journal of Leisure Research, 45*(5), 571–582.

Parry, D. C., Glover, T. D., & Mulcahy, C. M. (2013). From "stroller-stalker" to "momancer": Courting friends through a social networking site for mothers. *Journal of Leisure Research, 45*(1), 23–46.

Portes, A., & Landlot, P. (1996). The downside of social capital. *American Prospect, 26,* 18–21, 94.

Portes, A. & Sensenbrenner, J. (1993). Embeddedness and immigration: Notes on the social determinants of economic action. *American Journal of Sociology, 98*(6), 1320–1350.

Putnam, R. D. (1995). Bowling alone: America's declining social capital. *Journal of Democracy, 6*(1), 65–78.

Putnam, R. D. (2000). *Bowling alone: The collapse and revival of American community.* New York, NY: Simon & Schuster.

Rosenberg, T. (2013). Harnessing Positive Peer Pressure to Create Atruism. *Social Research: An International Quarterly, 80*(2), 491–510.

Schuller, T. (2007). Reflections on the use of social capital. Review of Social Economy, 65(1), 11–28.

Stebbins, R. A. (2000). Obligation as an aspect of leisure experience. *Journal of Leisure Research, 32*(1), 152–155.

Szreter, S., & Woolcock, M. (2004). Health by association? Social capital, social theory, and the political economy of public health. *International Journal of Epidemiology, 33*(4), 650–667.

Wilson, P. A. (1997). Building social capital: a learning agenda for the twenty-first century. *Urban studies, 34*(5–6), 745–760.

Yuen, F., & Glover, T. D. (2005). Enabling social capital development: An examination of the Festival of Neighbourhoods in Kitchener, Ontario. *Journal of Park and Recreation Administration, 23*(4), 20–38.

6
SPACE, PLACE, AND COMMUNITY DEVELOPMENT

Amanda Johnson and Felice Yuen

We live in spaces, we interact in spaces, and spaces are meaningful for individuals and communities. When you think about community spaces you may remember the park where you played as a child, the field where you participated in an active game of soccer, the school where you met your best friend, the trail you walked to work, or the shopping mall where you interacted with friends and strangers. These recollections and these spaces are meaningful because they provide a sense of self, a sense of place, a sense of community, and perhaps even a feeling of belonging. The meanings that specific spaces hold for people may not always be consistent—what that park means to you may not be what it means to me—but these meanings and connections remain important considerations for leisure professionals and community development practitioners.

In this chapter, we consider space and place and their contributions to community development. The idea that spaces and places play a central role in community development is founded on the understanding that they are important for creating opportunities for social interaction. As you know from Chapters 2 and 5, social interaction is necessary for civic engagement, community building, and active citizenship. The ideas we discuss can be applied to leisure because most of what we do in leisure and recreation occurs in a physical environment. As a result, leisure opportunities, leisure pursuits, and leisure activities incorporate a spatial component (Marans & Mohai, 1991; Smale, 1985, 1995, 2006). Thus, if we want to understand the relationship between leisure and community development, it is important that we consider the spaces where community is created and enacted.

AMANDA'S STORY: FARMERS' MARKETS AND COMMUNITY DEVELOPMENT

My doctoral research focused on a public space in my hometown, the Kitchener Farmers' Market (Johnson, 2013). Although farmers markets are primarily 'consumption spaces'—spaces meant for buying and selling—my experience of the Kitchener market was one of being a member of a diverse and well-established community that met and interacted every Saturday. This experience made me wonder if there was something about the space that fostered social interaction and the market community, or if it was fostered by the people and how they interacted. My study found that both the space and the people mattered. The people who attended the farmers' market on a regular basis shared a collective sense of connection to the farmers' market as a space, the individuals who formed the community, and the activities that occurred in the space. Relationships were formed through the space and the activities supported by the space. There was also a shared understanding between members of the community and feelings of commitment to these members. My research revealed that community members believed they knew other market participants (or community members) well enough to engage in informal conversation. Such conversations often revolved around market-related topics (e.g., how to pick a ripe melon) but also included conversation about everyday issues (e.g., the weather, politics). Furthermore, members expressed concern for specific vendors (e.g., the spice vendor closing her shop because of her ongoing battle with breast cancer) and other community members (e.g., people who may be unable to climb the stairs to the upper level). Overall, my research strengthened my conviction that the Kitchener Farmers' Market and other spaces we use on an everyday basis should not be considered "passive backdrops to human relations" (Mort, 1998, p. 891) where only individual needs are met. Instead, we should recognize them as important spaces in the building of community.

Understanding the spatial context of social life is important because individuals and communities "act and react to the different sociocultural settings in which they perceive themselves to be" (Mowl & Towner, 1995, p. 103). In other words, our social behavior is related to spaces and physical locations. To contribute to a broader understanding of the relevance and impact of community and leisure spaces, we must examine the natural and built environments where people are situated and where social interactions occur. When we do this, we quickly discover that some spaces are more conducive to community development. Similar to the farmers' market study, Glover's research (2004) on a community garden found that the space facilitated social interaction between local residents. It is important for us as leisure and community development practitioners to not only recognize but also enhance the relationship between space, place, and community development.

WHAT IS SPACE AND PLACE?

We use many different terms to describe or characterize spatial features. For example, location, node, spot, area, region, zone, territory, and site are all terms used to describe physical space. Other terms we use, such as neighborhood, city, community, place, park, home, or town, emphasize the nature or role of these physical locations in society. While the first list is technical terms used to denote space as it might be marked on a map, the second list is terms we use when talking about spaces that have a particular meaning to us. In some ways, this is what distinguishes a 'space' from a 'place' (e.g., Relph, 1981; Tuan, 1977). Well-known geographer Yi-Fu Tuan noted, "what begins as undifferentiated space becomes place as we get to know it better and endow it with value" (1977, p. 6). In other words, space is the *absolute dimension* of a geographic location; a space has physical and objective boundaries that can be systematically measured, it has specific limits, and can be identified as a physical property on a map or in person. Place, however, is considered to be a *relative dimension,* meaning that the dimensions of a place are subjective, perceived, and socially constructed (Mowl & Towner, 1995). In other words, places are experienced. Both the physical location and subjective experiences of spaces and places are important considerations in leisure and community development.We speak, write, and discuss these terms in ways that suggest there is an agreement on meanings. However, to better understand the role of place and space in community development we must acknowledge that oftentimes, spaces hold a multiplicity of meanings. For example, for some people a shopping mall is viewed as a place for meeting friends; however, for other people the same space is considered a place to purchase merchandise or commodities. Oncescu and Giles's work (2012) on a rural school closure highlights the multiple meanings we may attribute to everyday spaces. A major theme of Oncescu's research is that rural schools represent more than a space for learning and formal education. Instead, rural schools are also important spaces for community building and social interaction. As they noted, the "school related leisure activities cultivated informal social networks among community residents" (p. 120). Consequently, the closure of the school resulted in not only the loss of a space for learning, but also the loss of an important space for building community.

Spaces become meaningful—become places—through the experiences we have in them. They also become meaningful to us through the experiences that other people have in them, which we learn about through stories or collective memories. Because of our own unique histories, multiple meanings that spaces hold can at times be complex. For example, a 'baseball park' may invoke an image of a diamond shaped playing field, spectators in the stands, and perhaps a hot dog or a cold beverage in hand (i.e., absolute dimensions). For some of you, this image may conjure feelings of excitement and happiness as you recall memories of playing Little League baseball with your their friends. For others, such as the parents of African American baseball players identified in a study by Glover (2007), this leisure space may create feelings of anger and frustration as they reflect upon experiences of racism and marginalization in Little League (i.e., relative dimensions). As leisure practitioners working for community development, it is important to recognize the multiple meanings that exist for the leisure spaces in which we work. Leisure spaces are not benign and separate from prejudice and discrimination. Moreover, leisure spaces can be constructed to both reinforce and resist experiences of marginalization and oppression (see Glover & Bates, 2006; Shinew, Glover, & Parry, 2007). A deliberate and conscious effort is required to ensure that leisure spaces are inclusive and socially engaging, This process will be discussed in a later section.

PUBLIC SPACES IN COMMUNITY DEVELOPMENT

For community development to happen, we need spaces in which people can gather, build relationships, and act on collective concerns. As Lloyd and Auld (2003) noted, "without a space conducive to social life, community relations cannot prosper and grow" (p. 345). Or, as Carr, Francis, Rivlin, and Stone (1992) describe, communities need *public space,* which they define as "common ground where people carry out the functional and ritual activities that bind community" (p. xi). People interact and share experiences in public spaces and these spaces play an important role in the social prosperity of the local community. Public spaces, such as parks, farmers' markets, schools, and libraries, are characterized primarily by two features: a sense of collective ownership and ease of access (Johnson & Glover, 2013). Spaces for leisure and recreation are prominent on this list because they are a fundamental part of the informal organization, social activity, and cultural norms of diverse groups within communities.

Public spaces are important in the process of creating citizen involvement (Warpole, 1997), citizenship, and community. As spaces that can be accessed by the broader community, public spaces are often the site of efforts to draw attention to relevant social issues. In her examination of food activism, for example, Mair (2005) noted how activists used the downtown public square for the purposes of creating collaboration, sharing, education, and discussion between community members about food-related social issues. Similarly, parks and other public spaces, such as municipal libraries often function as forums for community involvement and community building (McInroy, 2000) because they are accessible spaces for all members of the community. By providing opportunities for social interaction, public spaces help create a sense of place, sense of belonging, and place attachment for community members (Low & Altman, 1992).

Leisure activities occurring in public spaces are also often cited for their function in community development in part for how they serve as a practical resource for social interaction and engagement, but also because they contribute to sense of place and belonging. For example, Amanda and her colleagues Troy Glover and Bill Stewart (2009) examined an urban brownfield redevelopment project, and their findings emphasized the importance of leisure in public spaces for sense of place, sense of community, and, ultimately, community development. Their research found that even an abandoned landfill site can be a meaningful space of interaction if local community members are able to interact within the space. We invite you to read the textbox below for more on the study and the specific elements of leisure in public spaces that contributed to community development (i.e., opportunity for social interaction, accessibility, sense of place).

FROM BROWNFIELD TO COMMUNITY SPACE: THE IMPORTANCE OF PUBLIC SPACE FOR COMMUNITY

The importance of public space for leisure was highlighted by my colleagues Troy Glover, Bill Stewart, and I (2009), in our study of a proposed redevelopment of an urban brownfield site, known locally as "Mt. Trashmore." Mt. Trashmore was a 39 hectare space in the middle of a growing community. The space was valued by the local community as an area for recreation and included walking/cycling trails, open field areas, a woodlot, and a prominent 35 metre hill used for tobogganing during the winter months. When the local government proposed a plan to redevelop Mt. Trashmore into a private snow tubing and mini-golf/driving range facility, local community members reacted negatively and rejected the proposal for private development. We examined the reactions of the residents to the planned redevelopment of the abandoned landfill site. We offered two reasons for the public outcry against the proposed redevelopment: sense of place and privatization of public space. Findings from our study indicated that local residents had an established community-based sense of place. In addition, Mt. Trashmore was utilized as a public space by local community members and although many people favored improvements to the area, most were against private development. The local community's sense of place relied largely on Mt. Trashmore remaining publicly accessible. We concluded that Mt. Trashmore was an accessible community asset that enhanced quality of daily life and social interaction. According to local residents, private redevelopment of the space would negatively impact the ability of community members to informally interact and connect in the space. In other words, the proposed private recreational facility would prevent social interaction and, ultimately, community development.

THIRD PLACES IN COMMUNITY DEVELOPMENT

The growing body of research on *third places* has also contributed to our understanding of the relationship between space, place, and community development. In his book, *The Great Good Place* (1999), Ray Oldenburg argued that third places are important sites of social interaction. Defined as places other than home or work, "the third place is a generic designation for a great variety of public places that host the regular, voluntary, informal, and happily anticipated gatherings of individuals beyond the realms of home and work" (Oldenburg, 1999, p. 16). For Oldenburg, third places are best described as welcoming, sociable, lighthearted, and fun places to be:

> The "fun" function of third places is better seen, perhaps, as the entertainment function. ... In third places, the entertainment is provided by the people themselves. The sustaining activity is conversation which is variously passionate and lighthearted, serious and witty, informative and silly. (Oldenburg, 1999, p. xxii)

Oldenburg's conceptualization of third places draws on Georg Simmel's (1950, 1972) idea of sociability. While sociability is found in virtually all types of interaction and spaces, Simmel (1950, 1972) argued that people require, and therefore seek out, *pure sociability*—a form of sociability where the individual's only motivation is to be in the company of others. Unlike work or home spaces, third places are especially conducive to pure sociability. For Simmel, "sociability in its pure form has no ulterior end, no content, and no result outside itself, it is oriented completely about personalities" (p. 255). In cases where pure sociability exists, individuals' interactions are not judged based on social qualifications (e.g., occupation or income). In other words, your profession or career (CEO vs. blue collar worker) or position of power (i.e., teacher vs. student) do not matter. Instead, individuals are acknowledged as different from one another and, regardless of social qualifications, all individuals are able to contribute to sociable values such as joy, relief, and vivacity (Simmel, 1950, 1972). Shields (1992) suggested that sociability "refers us back to the power of the collective, the sense of being together, the urge to 'get by' and the injunction 'to get along together'" (p. 106). In short, third places, which can exist in leisure spaces, provide avenues and possibilities for pure *sociable participation* and are thus conducive for community development.

Oldenburg's conceptualization of the third place examines the benefits that arise from being in places outside of the workplace and the home. According to Oldenburg, third places are meaningful because of the relative dimensions associated with the space—the memories, experiences, and emotions experienced within the space. Simply, he argued that participation in third places provides individuals with feelings of connectedness and community. Third places provide opportunities for members of the community to create and sustain relationships and experiences that may be unavailable to them in the realms of work, home, and other private spaces.

VIRTUAL WORLDS—A SPACE FOR COMMUNITY?

In this chapter we have conceptualized space and place primarily as concrete, physical locations. Given the prevalence of virtual spaces we encourage you to pause and consider the implication of such spaces on community development. Indeed, there are strong arguments for and against the use of the Internet and other technologically-based leisure pursuits in the realm of community development. Like any question in the realm of community development, there is no simple answer. Some researchers have argued that technology contributes to the weakening of community and facilitates socially isolating leisure experiences (Oldenberg 1999; Putnam, 2000). Delamere (2011), however, argued that virtual worlds can provide opportunities for meaningful social engagement and support, particularly for people with disabilities. She argued that multiplayer online virtual worlds, such as *Second Life,* can be what she refers to as *digitally mediated* third places. Information sharing, caregiver support, mentoring, and sociopolitical-oriented disability advocacy are a few examples of how social connections and support are fostered. Accordingly, Delamere stated (p. 245):

> As new technologies . . . shrink distance and erase limitation of geography, the creation of computer generated third places where empowered public emerge and communities of interest create social capital, results in intended or unintended social change.

> **Application Questions**
>
> *Think about the virtual worlds you know about or involved in. Do the same criteria of accessibility and sociability apply? Do you think that virtual space can be considered a third place? Could they play a particularly important role for people who are more likely to experience marginalization and oppression?*

ENHANCING LEISURE SPACES AND PLACES FOR COMMUNITY DEVELOPMENT

CHALLENGES AND ISSUES

As you have probably experienced firsthand, not all public spaces effectively build community. While a space may be designated as public, use of the space may be inhibited due to design or location. In some cases, groups with power effectively limit how public spaces are used and who is able to use them. Skateboarders, for example, are commonly and actively discouraged from using public spaces (as well as private spaces) for their recreation. Business owners, park management, and city planners overtly discourage and prevent use of public spaces by skateboarders with tactics such as "No Skateboarding" signs, bumps and spikes added to handrails and benches, or chains placed across ditches and steps (Borden, 1998). The deliberate determent of a recreation activity such as skateboarding reminds us public property is not necessarily accessible or open to everyone. In other words, the uses, control, access, and even the price of goods in public and community spaces can exclude individuals and groups based on race, physical ability, age, interest, and/or ability to pay.

Preventing or deterring use of public spaces by certain groups of people has negative consequences for community development. So-called 'community' spaces may in fact be subtly designed to encourage use by middle- and upper-middle-class consumers while simultaneously preventing low-income, minority, and generally marginalized populations (Byers, 1998). Pedestrian separated systems, such as city skyways and tunnels, are excellent examples of public spaces designed specifically for use by employed individuals traveling to or from their place of employment. Though considered to be public spaces, activities such as loitering or busking/performing are actively prevented in these spaces. In other words, some public spaces may encourage or create homogeneity and prevent access by certain demographics such as homeless populations, youth, and anyone who appears out of place. Thus, instead of promoting inclusion and interaction across social difference, this increasing specialization of public spaces potentially creates a "patchwork of specialised, monocultural enclaves defined by income bracket and identities of age, ethnicity and taste where people choose . . . to interact with 'people like themselves'" (Mean & Tims, 2005, p. 12). In his research on newcomer youth, recreation, and community, Glover (2013) similarly acknowledged that rather than enabling positive social interactions, recreation spaces may in fact create or contribute to an unwelcoming community. Discriminating factors, such as language barriers, may prevent full participation in leisure spaces.

According to Berman (1986), "implicit in our basic democratic rights... is the right to public space" (p. 477). Despite this conviction, public spaces are increasingly viewed as a commodity. Scholars have associated the loss of public space with globalization, neoliberalism, consumption, and capitalism (Mansvelt, 2005; Taylor, 2003). Further, access to these spaces is becoming more limited. The increase of public spaces constructed and controlled by private enterprises have become commonplace in North America. Friedmann (1987), for example, suggested streets must be recovered for use by people because "their place is being taken by private shopping malls" (p. 373). Some scholars have also argued citizens have been reduced to consumers and "public space has been privatized and evacuated" (Taylor, 2003, p. 7). These common spaces have been replaced with spaces designed for specific groups of people. In short, the loss of accessible public space has reduced sense of community and opportunities for leisure and community development.

While public spaces can facilitate interaction, they also have the potential to restrict interaction among friends, acquaintances, and strangers (Gehl, 1987). For example, among minority populations, experiences of perceived or actual discrimination in community parks and naturalized areas has been found to negatively influence leisure participation in community spaces (Floyd, 1998; Sharaievska et al., 2010). In their analysis of existing literature related to race, nature, and parks, Byrne and Wolch (2009) suggested the design of a park has the potential to impact how people perceive and use the space. Where parks may be perceived as welcoming, safe, and accessible for some user groups, the layout of the park space, signage, or even landscaping may prevent or discourage other user groups. Johnson and Glover (2013) acknowledged that it is important to consider "who is excluded from 'public' spaces, for no space is fully accessible to everyone at all times" (p. 195). In fact, it is not ownership of the place that makes a space public, but rather the accessibility and the presence of different individuals and groups (Mean & Tims, 2005; Oldenburg, 2009). In an examination of public spaces across the United Kingdom, Mean and Tims suggested ownership status, physical design, and aesthetic appearance had little to do with making spaces 'public.' Rather, the authors suggested a much better guide to whether a particular space is valued as a public space and conducive to community development is whether it is actively used and shared by different individuals and groups. Moreover, it is important to acknowledge that leisure spaces have the potential to create and recreate social practices and perceptions ultimately hindering or supporting community and community development.

Application Questions

Think about your own community in terms of where you live, work, and play. How do you interact socially in these spaces? Who has access to these spaces? Who is missing and why? How can these spaces be improved to allow more people to access them and create sociable participation?

STRATEGIES

Ideal public spaces rarely exist (Johnson & Glover, 2013); however, the possibilities to create leisure spaces that promote sociability and diversity, along with people's health, well-being, and happiness should be recognized. Converting a vacant neighborhood lot to a community garden (Shinew, Glover, & Parry, 2004), hosting a street party (Johnson, Glover, & Yuen, 2009), and participating in park(ing) day by transforming vehicle parking spaces into temporary public parks (parkingday.org) are all examples of how leisure spaces can be used towards community development.

It is important to build on local community assets to create accessible leisure spaces and places that promote social interactions. For example, local business ownership, a sense of pride among residents, and walkability are recognized as vital assets for community development. Here, we present two separate approaches that can be used to enhance leisure spaces for community development: 1) *The Rules of Engagement* (Mean & Tims, 2005) and 2) The *Place Diagram* (www.pps.org). These approaches help us understand the relationship between physical space and community development and additionally, offer strategies for how to strengthen this relationship.

The first approach, *The Rules of Engagement,* offers eight design principles for creating opportunities for social interaction and community in a public space (Mean & Tims, 2005). These principles have less to do with ownership of the space (i.e., commercial vs. non-commercial or public vs. private) and more to do with the conscious creation of community spaces to increase sociability, sociable participation, and ultimately opportunities for community development.

EIGHT DESIGN PRINCIPLES FOR CREATING COMMUNITY IN A PUBLIC SPACE: THE RULES OF ENGAGEMENT

(Mean & Tims, 2005)

1. **Access and availability:** Community development requires a range of publicly accessible and available spaces. Access and availability may be based on low/no cost to enter or hours of operation.
2. **Invitations from peers and others:** This principle suggests public spaces require people to become familiar with the space through word of mouth and "evangelisers" who promote the space.
3. **Exchange-based relationships:** People interact in spaces based on financial and non-financial exchange. Successful public spaces enable exchange and interaction between people.
4. **Visible and invisible choreography:** Community development in public spaces requires interaction and conviviality between users of the space. This principle recognizes the role of individuals in maintaining the spaces as public and accessible. These individuals may be official (e.g., an employee) or unofficial (e.g., a patron) representatives of the space.
5. **Diversity of activities and people:** Successful spaces encourage a mix of both activities and people. People feel uneasy or threatened when a space is dominated by a homogenous group of people who are engaged in one type of activity.
6. **Networked space:** To encourage movement and conviviality, accessible and available public spaces should be linked to other accessible and available public spaces.
7. **Props and permission:** While people often engage in private activities in public spaces, when users have the sense that other users

are in the space for a particular reason, there is greater tendency to share the space. "Props," such as dogs, babies, or shopping bags, are indications of reasons to be engaged in the space. Public spaces that provide a multitude of "props" or reasons to engage in the space such as trails, benches, or playgrounds, are more likely to be successful spaces of community development and social interaction.

8. **Safety:** Though a focus on safety is often blamed for the privatization of public space, the authors note that a sense of safety should be encouraged through developing social behavior (rather than focusing on regulating anti-social behavior or preventing specific activities within the space).

The second approach, *The Place Diagram* (Figure 6.1), was described and outlined by The Project for Public Spaces (www.pps.org). The Place Diagram illustrates the essential physical and social components of public spaces. According to this diagram, successful public spaces are those that include a mix of activities and are accessible, comfortable, and sociable. This approach helps to identify assets and evaluate elements of places conducive to community development. An underutilized park, for example, may be identified by the community as an asset. By considering absolute (dark gray) and relative (gray) qualities in relation to physical and social components (light gray), the Place Diagram helps community members, public officials, and community developers identify methods to improve the park's physical space to create a leisure space for community development.

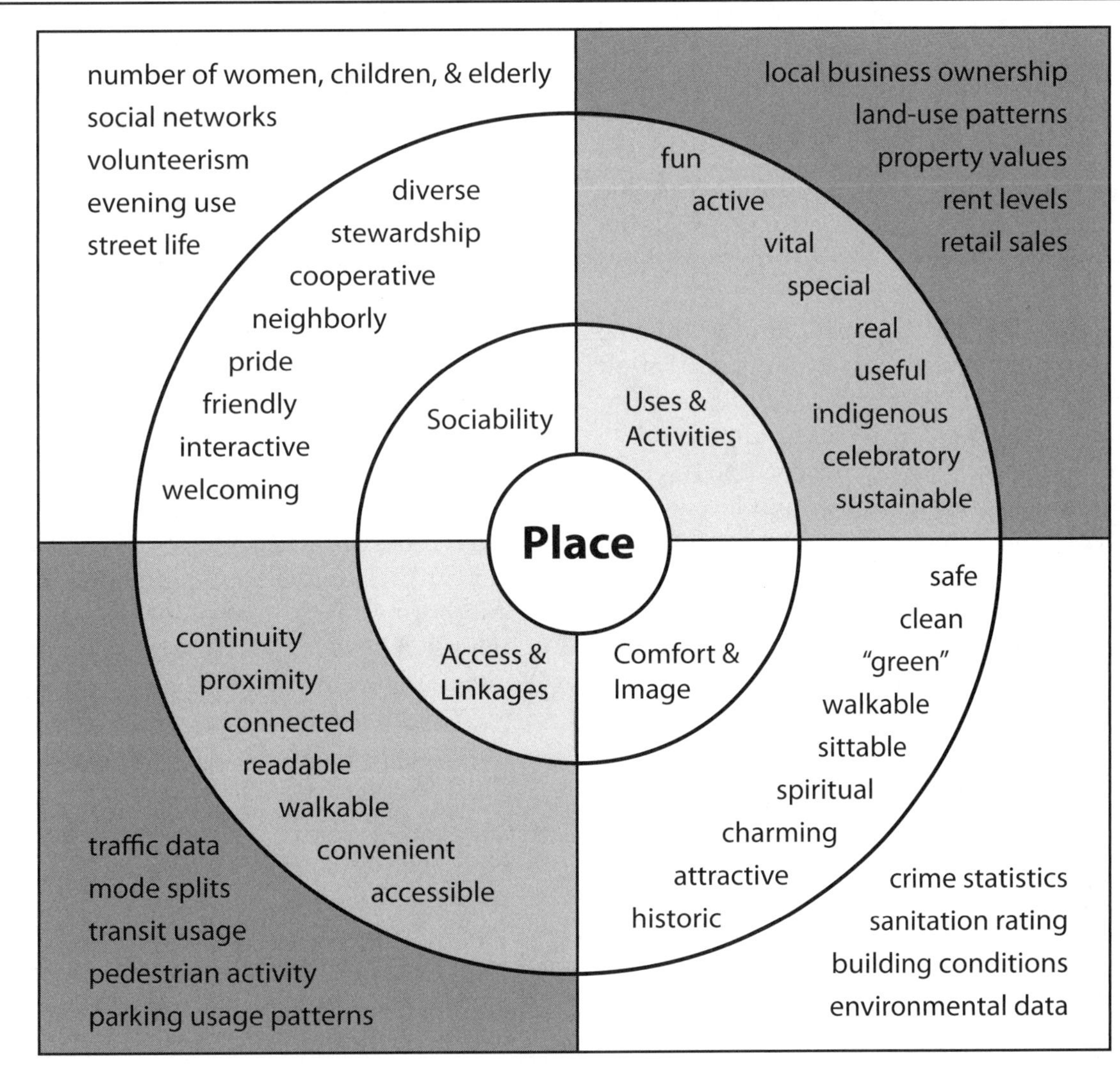

FIGURE 6.1 PLACE DIAGRAM (FROM WWW.PPS.ORG)

Application Questions: Creating community in leisure spaces

The existence of leisure space does not necessarily guarantee the existence of community. Think about a leisure space in your neighborhood or community. What characteristics of the space contribute to social interaction and a sense of belonging? Are there characteristics of the space that may make it inaccessible to the public? What about specific populations? What component(s) of the Place Diagram could you consider to improve this space and enable community development?

CONCLUSION

There is little doubt that spaces and places are important to the processes and outcomes of community development. From city parks to public squares, community activists and urban planners have pointed to the privatization and corporatization of public spaces as having a negative impact on community. However, there are individuals and groups of people committed to creating and maintaining meaningful and accessible spaces in both the public and private sphere, such the Kitchener farmer's market discussed at the beginning of the chapter.

Clearly, spaces and places play an important role in facilitating community development. For a recreation practitioner, using leisure spaces to create community generates many questions. What does an accessible public space look like? How can privatized spaces become community spaces? Who should have access to public space? How do we ensure accessibility and availability of public space? What dimension are contributing to or hindering sociable participation? And, how can we connect leisure in public space to community development processes and outcomes? These are important considerations as we endeavor to better understand and appreciate how our spatial environment shapes and creates both communities and individuals.

REFERENCES

Berman, M. (1986). Take it to the streets: Conflict and community in public space. *Dissent, 33*, 476–485.

Borden, (1998). *The gift of freedom? Skateboarding and socio-spatial censorship in the late twentieth century city.* Archis: Amsterdam.

Byers, J. (1998). The privatization of downtown public space: The emerging grade-separated city in North America. *Journal of Planning Education and Research, 17*, 189–205.

Byrne & Wolch (2009). Nature, race, and parks: Past research and future directions for geographic research. *Progress in Human Geography, 33*(6), 743–765.

Carr, S., Francis, M, Rivlin, L. G., & Stone, A. M. (1992). Public Space. Cambridge University Press: New York.

Delamere, F. M. (2011). Second Life as a digitally mediated third place: Social capital in virtual world communities. In G. Crawford, V. K. Gosling, & B. Light (Eds.), *Online gaming in context: The social and cultural significance of online games* (pp. 236–248). New York: Routledge.

Fletcher, J. (1997). *Fresh from the farmers market.* San Francisco: Chronicle Books.

Floyd, M. (1998). Getting beyond marginality and ethnicity: The challenge for race and ethnic studies in leisure research. *Journal of Leisure Research, 30*, 3–22.

Friedmann, J. (1987). *Planning in the public domain: From knowledge to action.* Princeton, NJ: Princeton University Press.

Gehl, J. (1987). *Life between buildings: Using public space.* New York: Van Nostrand.

Gieryn, T. F. (2000). A space for place in sociology. *Annual Review of Sociology, 26*, 463–496.

Glover, T. D. (2004). Social capital in the lived experiences of community gardeners. *Leisure Sciences, 26*(2), 143–162.

Glover, T. D. (2007). Ugly on the Diamonds: An Examination of White Privilege in Youth Baseball. *Leisure Studies, 29*(2), 195–208.

Glover, T. D. (2013). The role(s) of recreation in creating an (un)welcoming community. In J. Bocarro and J. Sibthorp (Eds.), *Abstracts from the 2013 Leisure Research Symposium.* Houston, TX.

Glover, T. D., & Bates, N. R. (2006). Recapturing a sense of neighbourhood since lost: Nostalgia and the formation of First String, a Community Team Inc. *Leisure Studies, 25*(3), 329—351.

Glover, T. D., Parry, D. C., & Mulcahy, C. M. (2012). At one liberating and exclusionary? A Lefebvrean analysis of Gilda's Club of Toronto. Leisure Studies, 1–20.

Johnson, A. J. (2013). "It's more than a shopping trip": Leisure and consumption in a farmers' market. *Annals of Leisure Research, 16*(4), 1–17.

Johnson, A. J., & Glover, T. D. (2013). Understanding urban public space in a leisure context. *Leisure*

Sciences: An Interdisciplinary Journal, 35(2), 190–197.

Johnson, A. J., Glover, T. D., & Stewart, W. (2009). One person's trash is another person's treasure: The public place-making of "Mount Trashmore." *Journal of Park and Recreation Administration, 27,* 85–103.

Johnson, A. J., Glover, T. D., & Yuen, F. C. (2009). Supporting effective community representation: Lessons from the Festival of Neighbourhoods. *Managing Leisure, 14,* 1–16.

Kretzman & McKnight (1993). *Building communities from the inside out: A path toward finding and mobilizing a community's assets.* Chicago: The Asset-Based Community Development Institute.

Lloyd, K. M., & Auld, C. J. (2003). Leisure, public space and quality of life in the urban environment. *Urban Policy and Research, 21*(4), 339–356.

Louv, R. (2005). *Last child in the woods: Saving our children from nature-deficit disorder.* New York: Workman Publishing.

Low, S. M., & Altman, I. (1992). Place attachment: A conceptual inquiry. In I. Altman & S. M. Low (Eds.), *Place attachment: Human behavior and environment* (Vol. 12, pp. 1–12). New York: Plenium Press.

Mair, H. (2005). A mouthful of change: Eating and acting for food democracy. In T. Delamere, C. Randall, and D. Robinson (Eds.). *Abstracts of papers presented at the 11th Canadian Congress of Leisure Research.* Nanaimo, BC.

Mansvelt, J. (2005). *Geographies of consumption.* London: Sage Publications

Marans, R. W., & Mohai, P. (1991). Leisure resources, recreation, activity, and the quality of life. In B. L. Driver, P. J. Brown, & G. L. Peterson (Eds.), *Benefits of leisure* (pp. 351–363). State College, PA: Venture Publishing, Inc.

McInroy, N. (2000). Urban regeneration and public space: The story of an urban park. *Space and Polity, 4,* 23–40.

Mean, M., & Tims, C. (2005). *People make places: Growing the public life of cities.* London: Demos.

Mitchell, D. (2003). *The right to the city: Social justice and the fight for public space.* New York: The Guilford Press.

Mort, F. (1998). Cityscapes: Consumption, masculinities and the mapping of London since 1950. *Urban Studies, 35,* 889–907.

Mowl, G., & Towner, J. (1995). Women, gender, leisure and place: Towards a more 'humanistic' geography of women's leisure. *Leisure Studies, 14*(2), 102–116.

Oldenburg, R. (1999). *The great good place: Cafés, coffee shops, bookstores, bars, hair salons and other hangouts at the heart of a community.* New York: Marlow & Company.

Oncescu, J., & Giles, A. R. (2012). Changing relationships: The impacts of a school's closure on rural families. *Leisure/loisir, 36*(2), 107–126.

Parking Day. (2014). www.parkingday.org.

Project for Public Spaces (2014). www.pps.org.

Relph, E. (1981). *Rational landscapes and humanistic geography.* London: Croom-Helm.

Roberts, J. (2013, June 12). How to grow a national park in your backyard. *Toronto Star,* p. A11

Schneekloth, L. H. & Shibley, R. G. (1995). *Placemaking: The art and practice of building communities.* New York: John Wiley & Sons, Inc.

Sharaievska, I., Stodolska, M, Shinew, K. J., Kim, J. (2010). Perceived discrimination in leisure settings in Latino urban communities. *Leisure/loisir, 34*(3), 295–326.

Shields, R. (1992). The individual, consumption cultures and the fate of community. In R. Shields (Ed.), *Lifestyle shopping: The subject of consumption* (pp. 99–113). London: Routledge.

Shinew, K. J., Glover, T. D., Parry, D. C. (2007). Leisure Spaces as Potential Sites for Interracial Interaction: Community Gardens in Urban Areas, *Journal of Leisure Research, 36*(3), 2004, 336–355.

Simmel, G. (1950). *The sociology of Georg Simmel,* translated by K. Wolf. New York: Tree Press.

Simmel, G. (1972). *On individuality and social forms.* D. Levine (Ed.). Chicago: University of Chicago Press.

Smale, B. (1985). A method for describing spatial variations in recreation participation. *Loisir et Société/ Society and Leisure, 8*(**2), 735–750.**

Smale, B. (1995). Spatially derived estimates of neighbourhood emissivity and park attractivity in explaining leisure behaviour in an urban context. Paper presented at *NRPA Leisure Research Symposium.* San Antonio, Texas.

Smale, B. (2006). Critical perspectives on place in leisure research. *Leisure/loisir, 30*(**2**), 369–382.

Smith, N., & Low, S. (2006). Introduction: The imperative of public space. In S. Low & N. Smith (Eds.), *The politics of public space* (pp. 1–16). New York: Routledge.

Soja, E. (1996). *Thirdspace: Journeys to Los Angeles and other real-and-imagined places.* Blackwell Publishers: Malden, MA.

Taylor, M. (2003). *Public policy in the community.* New York: Palgrave Macmillan.

Tuan, Y. F. (1977). *Space and place: The perspective of experience.* Minneapolis: University of Minnesota.

Warpole, K. (1997). *The richness of cities: Urban policy in a new landscape.* London: Comedia and Demos.

PART B
COMMUNITY DEVELOPMENT PRACTICE

7

COMMUNITY DEVELOPMENT PLANNING PROCESSES: FROM UNDERSTANDING TO MOBILIZING TO SUSTAINING

Heather Mair and Donald G. Reid

INTRODUCTION

Everyone plans. We all plan so we can make sure what we are undertaking is successful and satisfying. Not surprisingly, planning can—and should—play an important role in community development. The purpose of this chapter is to introduce you to the myriad ways those interested in community development engage in planning and to help you begin to think about how to approach planning from a community development perspective.

Simply put, planning is a process of thinking about a desired goal and then intervening in a social or physical environment to achieve that goal. Planners aim to work with others to set a course that will achieve clearly established goals and/or to reach a particular vision. As John Shaar so ably put it some time ago (1989: 321):

> The future is not a result of a predetermined path constructed by elites in society or conditions of the present, but a place created—created first in the mind and will, created next in discourse. The paths to it are not found but made, and the activity of making them changes both the maker and the destination.

In the context of community development, planning is not only concerned with developing some type of tangible product like a new park or built facility in the community, but it is also dedicated to listening, educating, mobilizing and even community transforming. Fundamentally, planning from a community development perspective is devoted to helping build community spirit and dialogue as much as it is oriented to a particular product development. It attempts to enhance community and environmental integrity while building social cohesion.

Planning is generally viewed as a product or outcome-oriented activity, but it should also be seen as a process of individual and community learning. Planning in the context of community development is dedicated to enhancing individual and community life. A good planner knows how to capture and work *with* the aspirations of community members, which are most often expressed as a set of values. Activities and strategies to achieve these values are then developed into a substantive plan of action, which includes an implementation strategy.

While the discussion above makes planning seems very straightforward, it is deeply complicated by the complexity of humanity, not to mention the natural world. Each of us has different aspirations in life, as well as unique ideas in terms of how the future should unfold. As such, planning to successfully reach a community's future aspirations depends on understanding individual's desires, as well as how they mix with the interests of others in the community. Often those aspirations and values are identified through a process of negotiation that is sometimes contentious. Then, these ideas and interests have to be understood within the context of broader societal values. Ideally, a planner working from a community development perspective provides the forum where the complexity is simplified and differences get resolved into some tangible and coherent plan of action, which community members can support. As you can imagine, the key is developing a process in which people can trust and with which they can become engaged.

Leisure, sport, and even tourism can be the arenas where an individual comes to understand him- or herself as well as their community. Planning can and should provide the structure where individuals can develop the skills to ask questions and learn about the leisure, sport, and tourism opportunities they want to see in their lives and in their communities. Moreover, good planning fosters a space, a forum, where discussions can revolve around how best to ensure those opportunities are provided. Ideally, being engaged in the community development and planning process is as much a leisure experience as it is devoted to producing a tangible resolution to a situation or problem or developing a strategy to meet an agreed upon goal. To prepare for writing this chapter, we have taken some time to reflect on our own ideas about what good planning for community development looks like. We both have been 'trained' to think about planning as a kind of top-down, expert-led endeavor where the planner takes charge and basically tells the community what should be done and why. However, life experience, shaped by learning and working with communities around the world, has taught us that community members are the best experts in determining their community needs and that makes them the most appropriate people to take charge of the planning process. A 'good' planner, then, in our view, is one who facilitates this process and steps in when the community agrees they are needed.

BASIC PRINCIPLES OF COMMUNITY DEVELOPMENT AND PLANNING

There are six basic elements of community development philosophy, which can and should guide the community planning process. Each is discussed in turn.

1. Community is the subject of the planning process

First, the community is *the subject* of the planning activity and not *the object*. Indeed, the community is not just something that planning *is done to* but is in fact the very substance of the planning endeavor. Put another way, sometimes we get so carried away with a focus on outcomes that we forget about the needs and desires of those most intimately involved in the process; we get lost in the technicalities of planning and providing a leisure, tourism, or sport service to the community. By thinking about the community as the object of community planning, planners risk becoming unchallenged experts and this can create an atmosphere where the planner's sense of what the community needs is the most prominent and yet it may not reflect what is actually desired or needed by community members themselves (Forrester, 1989). Related to this, and perhaps even more importantly, it can create a situation where community members do not feel they are being heard. When the community is the subject, then the focus is rightly put on the people who live there and planners become concerned with hearing their needs and building on their strengths.

2. Community members can discover and articulate their needs for themselves

Second, home-grown problem discovery and identification is fundamental to the planning process. This means that the community decides for itself what goals need to be set and they work to design the planning process to achieve those ends. With this principle in mind it is reasonable, perhaps even essential, for the planner to ask, 'what is the primary issue *the community* wishes to address?' In this sense, community development becomes as much or more of the focus of the planning process than the outcome.

3. Planners must understand and appreciate the uniqueness of each community

Third, the planner who works from a community development perspective must work to understand the special context and uniqueness of each community first and foremost. She or he cannot jump into solving problems, or designing facilities and programmes based on ideas gained through experience in other jurisdictions. As noted above, while the temptation for a planner might be to jump to a solution or an outcome that has worked in other places, each community needs to be understood on its own terms—as the subject of the planning exercise in its own right.

4. Community member participation in planning is essential, not an afterthought

A fourth key element of a community development approach to planning is the centrality of community member participation in the planning process. This approach to planning holds dear the idea that community members should be involved in the entire process and not just in limited ways or with only particular aspects of the planning process. Too often planners have the tendency to involve citizens at the plan approval stage and not at each of the many phases of the process. In this case, planning becomes a top-down process and not a community development exercise. More discussion on this important aspect is provided in the following sections.

5. **Community members can help themselves**

Fifth is the notion of 'self-help.' Community development planners assist communities as they work to meet their own needs instead of relying solely on government agencies and top-down programming. As is discussed in many parts of this text, members of communities have an abundance of resources and can generate appropriate responses to resolving their own issues. They can also develop the tools to tackle their own problems and planners can help with this process. Put another way, planners should work *with* members of communities in order to help them achieve their goals and not provide their 'expert,' ready-made solutions *for* communities.

6. **Community members must lead and control the planning process**

The last principle of community development that connects to planning is the notion that members of the community must not only lead but they must also control the process. Unfortunately, much of the education and training provided to planners in planning schools relies on the assumption that the planner needs to be in charge of the planning process. As a result, many planners often see themselves as experts rather than as facilitators who have expertise in helping to guide a community-led and controlled process. In the community development approach to planning, the role of the planner is often one of consultant, facilitator, or advisor (Healey, 1997; Forrester 1989). It is their role to shepherd members of a community through a course that the community controls.

Application Questions

Think about a recent leisure, tourism or sport-related development in your community. It might be something large like a new sporting facility or something small like improvements to the local park.

1. How aware are you of the processes that were used to plan for that development?

2. Do you remember seeing or hearing about meetings in the community to discuss the project?

Reflect on the six principles of community development and planning discussed above.

3. To your knowledge, were any of these principles reflected in the development in your community?

4. If some or all were absent, why do you think this was the case?

LEISURE, COMMUNITY DEVELOPMENT AND SOCIAL TRANSFORMATION: THE KAREN WALK NEIGHBOURHOOD

Back in 1996, Don and Elizabeth van Dreunen published a paper reporting on a study investigating the role of leisure in community development and transformation in a neighborhood in the City of Waterloo, Ontario. Using an Action Research approach (see Chapter 10 for a more thorough discussion of this approach to research with community members), Elizabeth worked closely with members of the Karen Walk Neighbourhood, which was also the community where she lived. She noticed that a plan to develop a subdivision in the community was being announced by the City and while that issue was of concern to her neighbors, Elizabeth also became aware of additional issues that were on the minds of community members. These included; children's safety, reckless driving through the area, growing levels of poverty, and issues of abuse. As the authors put it, "the resolution of these issues became the focus for action for the residents of Karen Walk" (p. 53). Residents created a neighborhood association and met to tackle issues that were important to them. They conducted their own traffic study of the area, undertook a door-to-door survey, and created a discussion workgroup that was open to all members in the community. The discussion workgroup undertook two visioning exercises.

Participants and residents were asked to reflect on four questions, which were developed by the Ontario Rural Learning Association:

1. What do I like most about my community?
2. What do I like least or feel I need to hide about my community?
3. What is sacred to me, what do I want to protect about my community?
4. What am I prepared to do to change my community?

These sessions and subsequent efforts to get broader community feedback through the use of a survey, which was built around these questions, resulted in a collective decision to create a locally run common house/community center that would serve the needs of the neighborhood. Faced with practical challenges to building the community center such as space and funding, the neighborhood association decided to focus on community building and worked with the local school and shopping mall to provide programming for youth and other ad hoc activities including a parent-and-tot group for young families. Other activities that sprang from this collective action included the restoration of part of the woodlot slated to be cut down to build the subdivision mentioned above and the development of an annual, community softball game. As Elizabeth reflected on her experience with the association and the community:

> The most actively involved residents of this community are those residents who have either attended neighborhood association meetings regularly and/or who were part of the discussion workgroup. The lives of these people have been transformed. Before their involvement in the community, many of them felt they had no control over their day-to-day existence. They had not dealt with issues that have been successfully resolved. (p. 59)

As the authors concluded their paper about the study, they made the point that leisure and recreation have the potential to provide a powerful context for generating opportunities for people to tackle issues that are important to their communities and to plan for a better future. Additionally, these opportunities lead to planning to achieve even more profound outcomes than just the programmatic or even structural changes to their communities, they can lead to social transformation.

Application Question

Which of the six principles outlined above were evident in this case?

There are many ways to think about the relationship between community development and planning. In fact, planners and those who write about planning and community development have long debated these issues. For instance, as far back as 1970, Sanders laid out the motivations of community development practice and connected them to the process of planning. He viewed these connections as a kind of continuum in terms of how much community involvement was needed (and when) in the planning process. Table 7.1 illustrates the connections Sanders made and more discussion of these points follows.

In the first point, using community development as a planning *method* focuses attention on the means for getting people involved (i.e., in terms of giving information about themselves and their views) in a project. Often the goal or intended outcome of the project is set from 'the top,' that is, by decision makers, before citizens are even engaged in the project. In this sense, the role of community members becomes one of encouraging community activity in order to accomplish the predetermined goal but not on bringing them into the process at the beginning or even at other stages of the process. In this approach it is quite possible that citizens will be involved only as respondents to surveys or for activities like fundraising but will not be involved in other stages in the planning process.

Next, using community development as a planning *program* moves closer to having the community members deeply involved in planning and implementing the project, but as the outcome or end goal is still determined by the 'top' or by those in power, the role of community remains somewhat circumscribed. Community members may feel they have had a meaningful say in the way a change is being brought to their community but not necessarily in regards to helping decide what that change may be.

Third, community development as a planning *process* links even more clearly to principles of community development discussed above. It is in this approach where community members have complete control of the steps of the process (discussed below) from creating the vision in the beginning, through setting and assessing objectives, to implementing and completing the process. The community is clearly in charge of the entire process in this form.

TABLE 7.1 BASIC FORMS OF CD THAT PROVIDE A MOTIVATION FOR THE PLANNING PROCESS

Form of Community Development	Approach to Planning
CD as a Method	Utilize a variety of methods to involve community members in some of the planning stages (outcome may be predetermined). [e.g., user surveys are filled out by community members to determine the need for building a pool in the community]
CD as a Program	Community members are involved in the stages of planning (the outcome is predetermined) [e.g., public are invited to give input at various stages of the process of building a pool—needs assessment, location decisions, etc.]
CD as a Process	Community members are in charge of all aspects of the planning process (outcome is not predetermined) [e.g., community members decide what is needed in the community and how that need will be met]
CD as a Movement	Community members are empowered and able to learn and develop the skills needed to transform their community

Finally, using community development as a *movement* encourages people to join in on a community-defined end goal of broader social change. Chapter 11 on grassroots organizing addresses some of these issues directly. Usually social movements are ideologically driven and most people who join in the process are in agreement with the stated goals and objectives of the movement as well as the means for achieving them.

It is important to note that these approaches have the most impact and value when they are used in the right context. Which method or framework used or set out in the plan is dependent upon the goals at hand. Importantly, of course, who decides what the goals are, as well as the nature of the situation being addressed, is the key to this process. Indeed, none of these approaches is more legitimate than any other; it is a matter of selecting the one that best fits the situation (as determined by members of the community) being addressed. However, community development, within the context of recreation and leisure, too frequently falls in the 'program' category as described above. Reid and van Dreunen (1996, p. 50) argued, "practitioners focus their effort on the activity, both its construction and delivery mechanism, rather than on what is happening to the actors as a result of the process." As noted above, we personally feel that there is much potential to move beyond a programmatic approach to planning and community development, and so we are focusing the bulk of the discussion in this chapter on alternative, less-traditional approaches. Nonetheless, it is important to understand the range of approaches that have shaped planning over time. The next section highlights important theories that underscore the various planning approaches.

THEORIES AND APPROACHES TO PLANNING

Although it is clear that we encourage approaches to community development planning, which center on the community members themselves, there really is no single approach that should be followed by everyone at all times. As noted above, how a planner decides which planning approach is the best fit depends on the issue at hand and the goals set out by members of the community. As is described below, in some planning activities the collection and analysis of data directs the planning process and the outcome. In other cases, as outlined in the Karen Walk Neighbourhood example, participants' reflections on their past, their present, and desired future are central to the process and the outcome. Further, planning from a community development perspective might even employ a mix of approaches. For this reason, it is important to understand the theoretical foundations of most modern planning approaches.

John Friedmann's (1987) classic treatise *Planning in the Public Domain* outlines a number of basic approaches to planning. Each approach—Social Reform, Policy Analysis, Social Learning, Social Mobilization, and

Radical Planning—is very different in both style and substance. While some of these approaches may not clearly align with what we have been describing as a CD approach, it is important to understand the variety of approaches that are available to all planners because they are options for the community development practitioner.

SOCIAL REFORM PLANNING

Social reform presupposes that community leaders and decision makers understand the issue facing a community completely and that they (including the planner) understand what is the best solution to that problem. As such, this approach is 'top down.' Not only is the planning process controlled by decision makers, the process of determining the outcome or the resolution of the issue is also controlled from the top. Most senior level members of government operate on this platform and within this mindset and while some seek public input in the planning process it is only at the level of consultation, what some might consider outright manipulation to achieve a predetermined goal. Indeed, if consultation occurs at all in this model, it may simply be a method of 'warming the public up' to accept what decision makers already know they want to provide.

POLICY ANALYSIS

Policy analysis is also seen as a top-down approach to planning. It differs from the social reform model in that expert-led research and data collection are the driving forces in terms of helping to solve the issue at hand. It is believed by those engaged in this approach that research, data collection and the analysis of these data will provide the answer to the problem in question. This approach does not put much emphasis on community involvement in the process other than to 'sell' the eventual product of the plan to the community. Not surprisingly, both the Social Reform and Policy Analysis approaches to planning are not models that generally fit the CD framework.

SOCIAL LEARNING

Social learning, on the other hand, repositions the process and the focus of the activity, involvement and control, from the 'top' to the 'bottom.' Those likely to be the most affected by the plan or the decisions taken are therefore in charge of the process. The social learning approach also changes the intention of the planning exercise from product generation or outcome orientation to community member learning and engagement. That is not to say that products and outcomes are not part of the Social Learning model but the emphasis is on the learning and empowerment that occurs when members of the community are intimately engaged in the process; indeed, learning is perhaps more important in this approach than product development or reaching a concrete outcome. This approach is more likely to be favored by planners who work from a community development perspective.

SOCIAL MOBILIZATION

Social Mobilization takes on many of the characteristics of the social learning model while adding the element of broader social change. And, while this may seem simple, social action or active engagement by members of the community to elicit change requires considerable effort to mobilize, educate and engage all participants in defining and addressing the issues at hand. This approach connects to the social movement idea noted above and draws on the work of Paulo Freire, the Brazilian educator and activist who argued that helping people to become aware of the power inequalities that shape their lives—a process he called *conscientization*—is key to building and mobilizing a social movement (Freire, 1970). Some scholars (e.g., Forrester, 1989) see a strong role for planners in this regard. This approach is closely linked to the next one.

RADICAL PLANNING

Like social mobilization, radical planning is an extension of the social learning approach but as the title would suggest, it radicalizes the activity and its participants. What this means is that the intention of this approach to planning is to change the foundation or the very roots of society (e.g., to address social inequality or long-standing issues of social marginalization). Radical planning takes social mobilization to its furthest point in that it works to build capacity in communities to generate deep social change and may be particularly appealing in situations where responses to social issues have been ineffective or unsatisfying. Most notably, radical planning was central to the civil rights movement in the 1960s and 70s in the United States, and it could be said that the Occupy movements of the early 21st century is a more recent examples of this approach. Often leisure activities provide a space where education, empowerment, and capacity can be built to address an issue that might become the focus of a radical planning initiative. Protests, street theater and music are just three examples where leisure and recreation activities connect with radial planning in that leisure provides the context for thinking critically about what is going on in the world and working to address major social issues (Mair, 2002, 2006; Sharpe, 2008). As stated earlier, John Friedmann's writing on these theories is essential reading for any student interested in gaining an in-depth understanding of these approaches to planning.

It is important to note that none of the ideas presented so far in this chapter stand alone; indeed, they are inter-related and overlapping. For example, if social learning is selected as the overarching theory to guide the planning process then CD as a process is likely to fit best.

> **Applications question:**
>
> *1. Why it is important to match the planning issue to be addressed with a planning paradigm? Conversely, what might be the consequences of using a planning paradigm that does not match the situation on the ground?*
>
> *2. Why should the involvement of citizens in the planning process matter as long as an efficient outcome of the issue planned for is accomplished?*

COMMUNITY DEVELOPMENT PLANNING IN ACTION: STAGES IN THE PLANNING PROCESS

With all these various theories and approaches in mind, it is time to get practical. In this section, we set out a series of steps or stages of a CD-oriented planning implementation. Typically, there are five stages and they are outlined below.

STEP ONE: BEFORE 'REAL' PLANNING CAN BEGIN: THE PRE-PLANNING PROCESS

Before presenting a discussion about stages of the formal planning process, it is important to consider some aspects of pre-planning, which can help address commonly found community and organizational issues. All too often planners treat communities in a generic fashion and fail to appreciate unique, existing social conditions. As we noted above, all communities are unique. Moreover, they have a distinct history of decision-making processes as well as a track record in terms of how active community members have been when able to be involved in the decision-making and planning process. It is likely that the decision-making process has been uneven and conflicts and even factions within the community have been building over the years. Indeed, a planning process can fail quickly if historic conflicts are not accounted for and addressed early. Figure 7.1 outlines pre-planning necessities that need to, or should, be addressed before a planning process that follows a community development approach is undertaken.

The major issues to be addressed in the pre-planning phase are the history of transparency in decision making in the community, the level of trust between decision makers and citizens, and the capacity of the community to engage in or control planning and decision-making activity. Although our work (with co-authors) was specifically in the context of community-based tourism planning and development, we (Reid, Mair, George, & Taylor, 2001; see also Reid, Mair & George, 2004) developed a method for analyzing the readiness of the community to plan for tourism development. Also important here are considerations of leadership and facilitation styles and skills. Chapter 8 provides an in-depth discussion on this topic.

> A community-assessment tool for planning tourism. In 2001, Don, Heather, and two colleagues devised an easy-to-use manual to help members of small communities plan for tourism. In developing the manual, we realized that many communities were not ready to jump into a traditional planning process. To help community members determine whether they were ready to plan, we developed a 13-item questionnaire, which members of communities could fill out and assess their planning potential. Below are some sample questions we included. Respondents chose from a five point scale (1 = strongly disagree and 5 = strongly agree):
>
> *1. There is a need for the community to be better organized to meet any tourism development needs that may arise.*
>
> *2. We do not have a clear process for solving problems as they arise.*
>
> *3. Everyone in the community needs to be involved in tourism development; it should not just be left to the business community.*
>
> *4. If tourism proposals are developed by certain people in the community, they are automatically opposed by others.*
>
> We advised that community members meet and fill out the questionnaires together. Then, by adding up the total scores from particular items on the questionnaires, the group could see whether they were ready to plan for tourism (i.e. move to the actually planning part of the manual

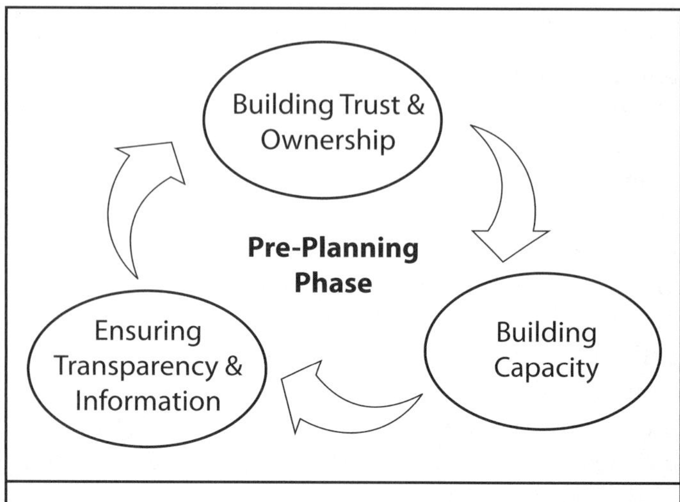

FIGURE 7.1 PRE-PLANNING NECESSITIES (SOURCE: REID, D. G., TAYLOR, J., & MAIR, H., 2000).

we had developed) or whether they needed to work on developing their readiness for planning (i.e., move to another part of the manual where they could undertake some additional preparation exercises). Importantly, at least in our view, we encouraged the community to use the questionnaire as a conversation-starter as much as a diagnostic tool. We felt the dialogue that the questions generated were likely more meaningful than the results of the scoring. (For more information, please see Reid, Mair, George, & Taylor, 2001; and Reid, Mair & George, 2004.)

STEP TWO: CHOOSING THE RIGHT APPROACH TO PLANNING

As noted above, choosing the appropriate planning approach (or mix of approaches) is critical. All of the pieces need to fit together in a coherent fashion. And, there is no off-the-shelf formula for making these choices. The critical action for making the right choices is to diagnose the situation and thoroughly understand what the desired outcome of the planning exercise is to be, from the perspectives of all the participants in the process. Some questions community development planners can ask to help in making the appropriate decisions are outlined in this section.

Perhaps the first question to be asked is: 'what is the issue to be addressed by the plan?' For example, is it purely a leisure issue (e.g., building a swimming pool in the community) or is it some larger social issue where leisure could potentially play a role (e.g., the need to provide a place for youth to become involved)? Various techniques for helping members of the community figure out the answer to this question can be employed and they include focus groups, facilitated brainstorming sessions, search conferences (Emery & Purser, 1996) and others. Once the issue at hand is identified, the second question a planner might ask is: 'what constitutes development or change in this case?' Not all individuals or groups in the planning process will initially agree on the answer to this question. Often the answer is a negotiated one, arrived at after considerable learning from one another about the issue by those engaged in the process. A plan is only as strong as the degree to which everyone agrees that the end goal (i.e., the purpose of the change or development) is actually achievable.

Next, the answer to the question: 'who is the community?' is also critical and yet deeply complicated. Certain groups will see themselves as the key players or those with the most at stake, while others may contest this notion. It is important for the planner to sort out the variety of interests and motivations at work among the various members of the community and to determine who is to benefit and who may be hurt by the plan. If there are potential negative outcomes for some members of the community, then mitigation strategies need to be part and parcel of the discussion throughout the process.

Finally, a community development planner must ask: 'who within the community needs to be in control or show leadership in the project?' The response to this question will depend on a number of variables, which are often not immediately obvious to the planner or to the members of the community. Further, the decision makers—usually politicians—often reserve the right to make the final decision on any issue that results from planning if the results of the plan require public expenditure. And so while we encourage a community-led process, the reality of the power structures of the community cannot be ignored and it would be a serious mistake for the planner to offer a level of control to a community if it is not truly there. To tell members of a community that they have sole authority for a plan, which has not been sanctioned by the final decision makers, will only result in calamity. So, the planning agent must be sure as to who will have ultimate authority and what type of authority that entails and they need to ensure that community leaders and power holders are part of the planning process too.

STEP THREE: DATA COLLECTION AND ANALYSIS TO SUPPORT THE PLANNING PROCESS

Data collection and analysis is generally a considerable part of the planning process. In order to do that effectively the planner normally constructs and implements a multi-method research program of data collection and analysis in aid of the decision-making process. There are a variety of data available to the planner (see Chapter 10 for more discussion on research with communities). While the type of data most familiar to community members including decision makers is likely quantitative or numerical, there are other ways of collecting information that can be relevant to planning and community development. Quantitative data are usually collected through surveys and are used to produce descriptive statistics such as demographic information about the community, as well as broad information about values, preferences, and frequencies of activities or behaviors. When the planner needs to know the preference among alternatives, rank ordering options using numbers is a likely method. Strength of preference can also be assessed in this way. Additionally, some attitudinal data can also be helpful and is quantitative in nature. Other methods that can be employed to collect quantitative data are secondary analysis of existing data. Often leisure planners will refer to national statistical data bases or census data. Communities may have undertaken numerical data collection for other projects and this information can also be useful for planning in the leisure domain. These types of documents can provide rich sources of information to the planner. For example, the quantitative analysis of registration and participation data collected by some recreation departments can also be rich sources of data that can provide useful information.

Qualitative data, on the other hand, lends itself to asking questions about meaning. When the planner is interested in the meaning of an activity to individual members of the community, then it is likely qualitative data that will be sought. Questions about values may also lend themselves to qualitative data collection and analysis. Regardless of which types of data are gathered and assessed by the planner, data collection can and should be undertaken in line with the values inherent in the CD approach. Indeed, what is important to keep in mind is that the CD approach does not specify specific types of data that are legitimate—what is important is how those data are used in the planning project.

There are a variety of methods for collecting qualitative data. Those most often used are notes and transcriptions from public meetings, visioning workshops, interviews, and focus group meetings. In addition to asking in-depth questions that usually require the participant to reflect on their experience and future aspirations, focus groups are excellent venues because participants can generate collective knowledge in a group setting. What is critical for implementing such data collection techniques is for the group facilitator to be highly skilled in group dynamics and experienced in such practices. These are not off-the-cuff conversations but complicated research methods and consequently, not for the uninitiated or those without adequate training.

STEP FOUR: BUILDING ENGAGEMENT AND CAPACITY FOR PARTICIPATION

An underlying assumption of this chapter is that participation from a broad array of community members is key to successfully developing a plan that keeps community needs in mind. However, as is discussed in many places in this book, building participation is complicated and requires thoughtful effort. John Forrester, a well-known planning analyst has provided a list of things a planner can do to encourage participation and meaningful involvement in the planning process (1989, pp. 155–156). We have summarized his main points in the text box below.

1. Cultivate community networks of liaisons and contacts.

2. Listen carefully to gauge the concerns and interests of all participants in the planning process to anticipate likely political obstacles, struggles, and opportunities.

3. Notify less-organized interests early in any planning process affecting them.

4. Educate citizens and community organizations about the planning process and both formal and informal "rules of the game."

5. Supply technical and political information to citizens to enable informed, effective, political participation and negotiation.

6. Work to see that community and neighborhood nonprofessional organizations have ready access to public planning information, local codes, plans, notices of relevant meetings, and consultations with agency contacts.

7. Encourage community-based groups to press for open, full information about proposed projects and design possibilities.

8. Develop skills to work with groups and conflict situations, rather than expecting progress to stem mainly from isolated technical work or elected officials.

9. Emphasize to community interests both the importance of the building their own power even before negotiations begin; take steps to make expertise available to professionally unsophisticated groups.

10. Encourage independent, community-based project reviews and investigations.

11. Anticipate political-economic pressures shaping design and project decisions and compensate for them.

STEP FIVE: KEEPING THE PLANNING PROCESS GOING

Unfortunately, planning is often seen as a one-time activity. It is a snapshot in time and while that has some use, it does not provide an ongoing picture of patterns and change. Today, planners working from a community development perspective recognize that ongoing data collection, analysis, and continuous efforts at planning are needed in order for the plan to remain current and relevant. This may involve efforts to meet regularly and even hiring someone who can pay attention to the details of the planning process as it goes along. Often one of the major shortcomings of community planning is that it is done as a 'one off' when there is a critical decision to be made in the community but suffers from the lack of a base line of data on which to measure change in the community.

THE POWER OF THE PLANNER

While we have tried to reinforce the notion that the planner who works from a community development perspective is ideally a facilitator, it is important to note that all planners carry a lot of power. As Healey, an expert in planning theory and approaches, has argued:

> Planning practice is thus not an innocent, value-neutral activity. It is deeply political. It carries value and expresses power. The power lies in the formal allocation of rights and responsibilities, in the politics of influence, the practices through which 'bias' is mobilized, and in the taken-for-granted assumptions embedded in cultural practices. (Healey 1997, p.: 84)

In our view, ensuring that everyone is aware of this power (i.e., the community members as well as the planner herself or himself) is an essential first step in opening the door to challenge that power and encouraging a collective, community-based planning endeavor.

FINAL THOUGHTS: PROCESS! PROCESS! PROCESS!

As authors and past-practitioners of community development planning, we have tried to present all of the major issues that face those who think about the role of planning in community development. We have taken you through the steps we think are central to the planning process as it relates to community development and have, we hope, reinforced the notion that it is the process that matters most. Community development is about participation and engagement and change. Planning is an important a tool for making that happen.

REFERENCES

Emery, M., & Purser, R. (1996). *The search conference: A comprehensive guide to theory and practice.* Jossey-Bass.

Friedmann, J. (1987). *Planning in the public domain: From knowledge to action.* Princeton: University Press.

Mair, H. (2006). Community development: Creating spaces for deep democracy, social action, and resistance. *Leisure/Loisir, 30*(2), 447–454.

Mair, H. (2002). Civil leisure? Exploring the relationship between leisure, activism and social change. *Leisure/Loisir, 27*(3–4), 213–237.

Forrester, J. (1989). *Planning in the face of power.* Berkeley, California: University of California Press.

Freire, P. (1970). Pedagogy of the Oppressed (trans. Myra Bergman Ramos). New York: Herder and Herder.

Healey, P. (1997). *Collaborative planning: Shaping places in fragmented societies,* Vancouver, British Columbia: University of British Columbia Press.

Reid, D. G., Mair H., & George, W. (2004). Community tourism planning: A self-assessment instrument. *Annals of Tourism Research, 31*(3), 623–639.

Reid, D. G., Mair, H., George, W., & Taylor, J. (2001). *Visiting your future: A community guide to planning rural tourism.* University of Guelph, Guelph, Ontario.

Reid, D. G., Taylor, J. & Mair, H. (2000). Rural Tourism Development: Research Report. Guelph: School of Rural Planning and Development, University of Guelph, p. 53.

Reid, D. G., & Dreunen, E. V. (1996). Leisure as a social transformation mechanism in community development practice. *Journal of Applied Recreation Research, 21*(1), 45–65.

Sanders, I. T. (1970). The concept of community development, In L. J. Cary (Ed.), *Community development as a process,* (pp. 9–31). Columbia, MO: University of Missouri.

Schaar, J. (1989). *Legitimacy in the modern state* (2nd Ed.). New Jersey: Transaction Publishers.

Sharpe, E. K. (2008). Festivals and social change: Intersections of pleasure and politics at a community music festival. *Leisure Sciences, 30*(3), 217–234.

8
LEADERSHIP ROLES AND GROUP FACILITATION SKILLS FOR COMMUNITY DEVELOPMENT

Alan Warner and John Colton

THE STORY OF STONE SOUP

A kindly old stranger was walking through the land when he came upon a village. As he entered, the villagers moved towards their homes, locking doors and windows. The stranger smiled and asked, "Why are you all so frightened? I am a simple traveler, looking for a soft place to stay for the night and a warm place for a meal."

"There's not a bite to eat in the whole region," he was told. "We are weak and our children are starving. Better keep moving on."

"Oh, I have everything I need," he said. "In fact, I was thinking of making some stone soup to share with all of you." He pulled an iron cauldron from his cloak, filled it with water, and began to build a fire under it. Then, with great ceremony, he drew an ordinary-looking stone from a silken bag and dropped it into the water.

By now, hearing the rumor of food, most of the villagers had come out of their homes or watched from their windows. As the stranger sniffed the "broth" and licked his lips in anticipation, hunger began to overcome their fear.

"Ahh," the stranger said to himself rather loudly, "I do like a tasty stone soup. Of course, stone soup with cabbage—that's hard to beat."

Soon a villager approached hesitantly, holding a small cabbage he'd retrieved from its hiding place, and added it to the pot.

"Wonderful!!" cried the stranger. "You know, I once had stone soup with cabbage and a bit of salt beef as well, and it was fit for a king."

The village butcher managed to find some salt beef . . . And so it went, through potatoes, onions, carrots, mushrooms, and so on, until there was indeed a delicious meal for everyone in the village to share.

Traditional story available from http://www.dltk-teach.com/fables/stonesoup/mtale.htm

In the Stone Soup story, the village contributed to and made the soup, but it was the caring stranger that brought people together, helped them to realize that they held the ingredients themselves, and facilitated a process through which they worked together. Communities in the 21st Century face a multitude of problems and just as in Stone Soup, too many face hunger, insecurity and fear. There is a need now, more than ever, for positive initiatives to address leisure, social, health, and sustainability issues at the community level, and increasingly there is a sense that a different sort of leader is required, not the 'hero,' but rather the 'host' and 'facilitator'

(Wheatley and Frieze, 2011). Communities have a multitude of gifts and assets amidst their citizens and organizations (McKnight & Block, 2012), but thoughtful, values-based leadership and facilitation from a range of citizens and professionals are desperately needed to find positive local solutions. This new leadership will not necessarily come from strangers to a local community, rather the leaders are likely to be engaged local citizens and/or professionals.

This chapter explores the characteristics of leadership necessary to community development in the 21st Century. It reviews key concepts and understandings about leadership and discusses facilitation skills for leaders to support community development. A key point is that every person has the potential to contribute to this community leadership process, and in fact everyone is called to serve given the multitude of problems to be addressed. The good news is that there is a wide array of examples across the world where these leadership and facilitation strategies have brought about dramatic change, and this chapter highlights just a few.

APPLICATIONS . . . PERSONAL DEFINITIONS OF LEADERSHIP

• On a piece of paper, list a few people in your life—people you admire, close relatives, teachers, coaches, or it could be someone famous—who have been positive role models for you. Think of examples of times when they supported you. Please address the following question: What are some of their positive qualities that make them special? Some examples: 'they were empathetic,' 'they listened to me without judging,' 'they challenged me,' 'they believed in me.'

• Take a whole sheet and fill it with the outline of a human being (great artistry is not required). Choose 3–4 people from the list above and write words or phrases inside the human being that stand out as representing positive qualities for these people. List as many qualities as possible.

• Reflect on these questions: Would you say these people are leaders in your life? Who are others that you respect and what are the qualities that they embody? What does leadership mean to you at this point in your life? What leadership qualities do you offer to others? For whom are you a role model?

• Finish by writing a definition of leadership and share your reflections with others as you see fit. Is your definition different than you might have expected? How is it similar or different to the leadership concepts in this chapter?

LEADER AS HOST RATHER THAN HERO

The traditional concept of the 'hero' is omnipresent in movies, books, history, and mainstream North American culture, hence the stereotypes are deeply engrained in our daily lives. This person (often characterized by the pronoun 'he') is bold, courageous, persistent, gifted, charismatic, and skillfully brings others to *his* cause. Captain James Kirk from the original *Star Trek* TV series is an example from Hollywood. George Mallory, the foremost English mountain climber of the early 20th century is an example from history. But Captain Kirk is a fictional stereotype and Mallory, despite his extraordinary climbing and 'leadership' skills, did not recognize his limits and died on the slopes of Mount Everest in his third attempt to be the first person to "conquer" the mountain (Davis, 2013). The 'hero' cannot single-handedly solve complex community problems, he or she cannot create affordable housing, eliminate teen pregnancy, or provide access to sustainable food for everyone. The 'hero' aims to 'save the world' and may have the best of intentions, but often ends up burnt-out and exhausted in the face of complex community problems involving conflicting perspectives and stakeholders (Wheatley & Frieze, 2011).

Traditional theories of leadership have also focused on what individuals should do to 'lead' others in various contexts, including what qualities they should possess and what strategies they should utilize to get the job done. Some theories emphasize the traits of the leader (e.g., charismatic, honest, extraverted; Zaccaro, Kemp, & Bader, 2004), or their behavioral characteristics (e.g., task- or people-oriented; Blake & Mouton, 1978), or particular leadership styles (e.g., autocratic, democratic or laissez-faire, Bass & Bass 2008)). Situational leadership theory emphasizes that leadership style should change depending on the context (Hersey, 1984). Regardless of the specific theory, implicit in this traditional thinking is the assumption that leadership is characterized by how an individual can best provide the right answers to address the issue and move followers in the appropriate direction (Luke, 1998).

Yet community problems are multifaceted and not solvable by one initiative, individual or organization. Take an increasing youth crime rate. The police need to be involved and reflect on how they work with young people, recreation organizations play a role through the services they offer, health providers must address addiction issues, and community centers can provide parents with skills and support. Moreover, members of one organization might believe that the best solution is to get the 'bad apples' off the street and lock young people in jail. Others believe that jail is a recipe for introducing new young offenders to a deeper criminal culture and set of values. In short, one person or one organization lacks the resources, multifaceted solutions, and ability to implement positive change.

Authority and responsibility for the issue are fragmented. Instead, more appropriate leadership involves bringing people and organizations together to reflect on the local circumstances and issues, and work collaboratively to find solutions (Hanleybrown, Kania & Kramer, 2012; Wheatley & Frieze, 2011). The leader needs to take on the role of a 'host' and help people with diverse perspectives have meaningful conversations. In the youth crime example, the question might be 'What contributes to youth delinquency and where are the leverage points to reduce it in a community?' The leader as host listens and facilitates instead of providing answers and dictating actions.

Communities have a wide array of resources and assets amidst their citizens, and given the right circumstances, citizens can work for positive change in areas they are passionate about and feel able to make a difference. Yet historically, traditional leaders and professional organizations have not listened to or supported citizen solutions, and instead have worked to rally them to their own causes (McKnight & Block, 2012). In contrast, the leader as host looks to the community and its organizations to address the key issues, much as the stranger finds the resources in the village to make the soup. Ultimately, leadership is about building engagement through facilitating relationships and networks rather than defining strategies and implementing solutions.

The work of Paulo Freire (1996), a renowned Brazilian educator and scholar, identifies the importance of the analysis of power and oppression to the process of hosting conversations among community members (Ledwith, 2011). For Freire, positive change toward social justice is only possible if and when community members have conversations that identify the power dynamics underlying the status quo. Freire began as an adult educator working to expand literacy in South America. Rather than using the literacy process as a means to transmit knowledge to students, he facilitated/hosted a process through which learners shared and analyzed the realities of their lives in poor communities so as to identify their passions, resources, and barriers to working for social justice and systemic change. His work was foundational to a global movement termed "popular education," which uses participatory educational practices to facilitate citizens to appreciate and reflect on their circumstances and mobilize to bring about positive change. The role of the leader in popular education is to be a host and facilitator seeking values-based change.

The leader as host concept is not restricted to social justice work. More recently it has been adopted as a prominent strategy by many local governments. In the United States there has been a movement to return power to citizens and neighborhoods so that they may define the nature of their communities and services. Seattle is a prime example of implementing an approach in which government established a Department of Neighborhoods that ceded power to neighborhood councils and supported citizens to actualize their powers (Diers, 2004). The result has been neighborhood developments with higher levels of citizen control while Department of Neighborhood organizers have served as hosts rather than decision makers.

CONCEPTS AND CHARACTERISTICS OF THE LEADER AS HOST

Core to the concept of the leader as host is the passion and values that enable one to serve others, rather than simply implementing one's own vision. Robert Greenleaf's concept of the 'servant leader' (see box) gets at the complexity of the hosting role and the notion that each person can both serve and lead simultaneously.

> *"The servant-leader is servant first. It begins with the natural feeling that one wants to serve. Then conscious choice brings one to aspire to lead. The best test is: do those served grow as persons: do they, while being served, become healthier, wiser, freer, more autonomous, more likely themselves to become servants? And, what is the effect on the least privileged in society; will they benefit, or, at least, not be further deprived?"*
>
> *Robert K. Greenleaf, 1970, p. 6*

Mahatma Gandhi was one of the most prominent servant leaders of modern times. Despite never having a formal political or governmental position and having no money and no military power at his command, Gandhi mobilized millions of people and was key to establishing India as the largest democracy in the world. Keshevan Nair (1997) identifies five key lessons from Gandhi's life

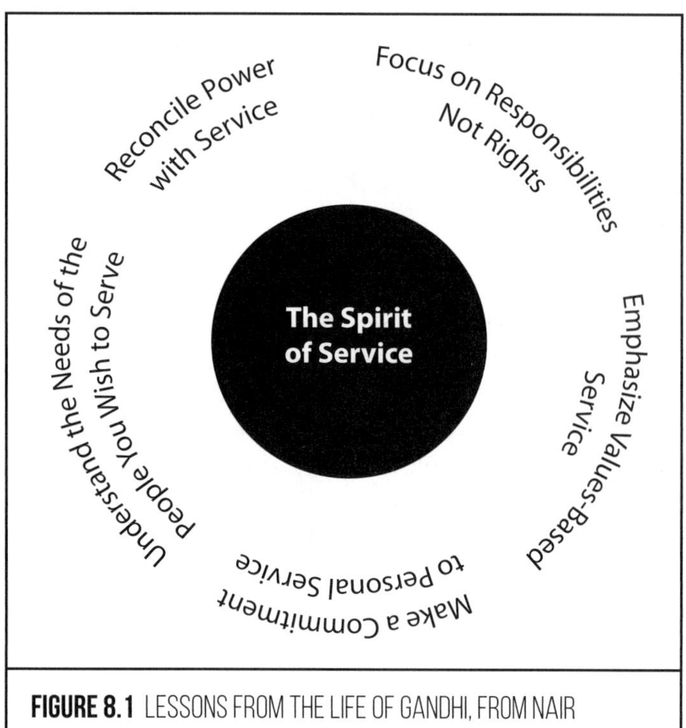

FIGURE 8.1 LESSONS FROM THE LIFE OF GANDHI, FROM NAIR (1997), P. 58

that define a high standard for leadership as service (see Figure 8.1).

Gandhi believed that service and leadership must be driven by clear and identifiable personal values. The essence of leadership is to treat others as one treats oneself—to be a role model, live modestly, and serve others in one's personal life. Gandhi, like Freire, emphasized that leadership involved the exercise of power, and this power has to be utilized in service to others. This requires deeply understanding the needs of others. The host in a community context brings people together to address community aspirations, issues and needs.

Ten characteristics of servant leadership have been defined based on the work of Greenleaf (see box on p. 90). These characteristics are not confined to great world leaders such as Gandhi or Nelson Mandela, rather they are present in each of us and can be nurtured for the benefit of others and our communities. Two young Canadians, Jessica Lax and Jocelyn Land-Murphy provide examples of the potential of each of us to be servant leaders and hosts that facilitate positive change in communities. They spent a semester as a part of their university degree studying in Kenya. Their experiences with the incredible warmth of the people, set within the broader context of inequity, injustice, and poverty there were transformational (Lax, 2006). They reflected on and critically analyzed their values and lifestyles, and recognized that excessive consumption in North America fueled inequity and poverty around the world. They returned to Canada and began shifting their own habits (role modeling change) and then worked with others to form the Otesha Project (which means "reason to dream" in Swahili). The Otesha Project (www.otesha.ca) educates young people through participatory education, theater, and long distance biking about how individuals can transform their lifestyles and simultaneously work for a more just and sustainable world. Otesha started in 2003 with 33 bicyclists traveling across Canada over 164 days while making more than 250 presentations to over 12,000 young people (Otesha Project, 2014). It has grown and evolved over the years but still uses bicycle tours and participatory education to role model and educate for a more sustainable and just world.

The ten characteristics of servant leadership are implicit in the work of Jessica Lax and Jocelyn Land-Murphy. They began in Kenya by *listening* with *empathy,* which led to *awareness* through reflection and then a commitment to *heal* themselves and *persuade* others to embark on a similar process. *Conceptualization* and *foresight* as to what a hopeful world could look like has been implicit in implementing the concept of 'reason to dream.' Finally, *stewardship, commitment to the growth of others* and *building community* are values inherent in the Otesha Project. Jessica and Jocelyn began their journey as university students seeking an adventure, like many other young people looking for a place in the world. They are realizing their potential as servant leaders and hosts, a path that is open to everyone, though each would actualize it in a different context.

STRATEGIES FOR FACILITATING LEARNING AND ACTION IN COMMUNITIES

At the core of community building is engaging and developing relationships among people who are willing to work for the common good. As discussed in Chapter 2, positive relationships and social networks represent the capacity of communities to get things accomplished for the benefit of all. This is frequently labeled as social capital in a community (Callaghan & Colton, 2008). A sense of camaraderie and trust is essential to overcoming the challenges of bringing diverse perspectives together to create a shared agenda. In fact, some argue that building relationships is the only important task of a community developer, and that if this is done well, the community will find ways to mobilize and take positive action (Rowson, Broome & Jones, 2010).

Bridgewater, Nova Scotia provides a small but powerful example of the value of developing relationships and using social networks. In the fall of 2009, Cate

APPLICATIONS . . . CHECKLIST FOR PERSONAL VALUES

Your personal values can drive your behavior and it is important to identify value when working as a leader and host. The following exercise adapted from *The Fifth Discipline Field Book* by Peter Senge (1994, pp. 209–211) can be helpful.

1. From this list of values, select the ten that are most important to you—as guides for how to behave, or as components of a valued way of life. Feel free to add any of your own to this list.

__ Achievement	__ Fitness	__ Physical challenge
__ Advancement & promotion	__ Freedom	__ Pleasure
__ Adventure	__ Friendships	__ Power & authority
__ Affection (love & caring)	__ Fun	__ Privacy
__ Arts	__ Growth	__ Public service
__ Challenging problems	__ Having a family	__ Purity
__ Change & variety	__ Health	__ Quality of what I take part in
__ Close relationships	__ Helping other people	__ Quality relationships
__ Community	__ Helping society	__ Recognition (respect from others)
__ Competence	__ Honesty	__ Religion
__ Competition	__ Independence	__ Reputation
__ Cooperation	__ Influencing others	__ Responsibility & accountability
__ Country	__ Inner harmony	__ Security
__ Creativity	__ Integrity	__ Self-respect
__ Decisiveness	__ Intellectual status	__ Serenity
__ Democracy	__ Involvement	__ Sophistication
__ Care for environment	__ Job tranquility	__ Stability
__ Economic security	__ Justice	__ Status
__ Effectiveness	__ Job tranquility	__ Supervising others
__ Efficiency	__ Knowledge	__ Time freedom
__ Equity	__ Leadership	__ Truth
__ Ethical practice	__ Loyalty	__ Wealth
__ Excellence	__ Market position	__ Wisdom
__ Excitement	__ Meaningful work	__ Work under pressure
__ Faith	__ Merit	__ Work with others
__ Fairness	__ Money	__ Working alone
__ Fame	__ Nature	__ Others . . .
__ Fast living	__ Openness & honesty	
__ Fast-paced work	__ Order	
__ Financial gain	__ Personal development	

2. Now that you have identified ten, imagine that you are only permitted to have five values. Which five would you give up? Cross them off.
3. Now reduce your list to your top three values. Then take a look at these and ask yourself . . .
   a) What do these values mean to me? To what extent are these values practiced in my life?
   b) How would my life be different if these values were prominent and practiced daily?

deVreede and Brian Briganza decided they would like to bring people together around a festive event that would build community in this town of 8000 residents (Bridgewater Community Christmas Society, 2010). They hit upon the idea of organizing a Christmas dinner that was free and open to everyone. Several friends were enthusiastic and they called a meeting to discuss the idea, and more than 30 people turned up. Although they started with no money and no resources, ultimately through lots of relationships, conversations, and meetings, nearly 200 volunteers served a free, delicious dinner on Christmas Day, including music and

TEN CHARACTERISTICS OF A SERVANT LEADER

These characteristics are abridged from the work of Larry Spears (2006, pp. 2–4) based on his study of Robert Greenleaf's writings on Servant Leadership.

1. Listening carefully, both to what is said and unsaid, working to understand and clarify the meaning and the intentions of others.

2. Empathy: Striving to understand and empathize with others. People need to be accepted and recognized for their special and unique spirits.

3. Healing: Working to heal relationships as a powerful force for transformation and integration of individuals, groups and communities.

4. Awareness helps one understand issues involving ethics, power and values. It allows one to view most situations from a more integrated, holistic position.

5. Persuasion: Using persuasion rather than one's positional authority in making decisions.

6. Conceptualization: Nurturing others abilities to dream great dreams. Conceptualizing an issue beyond day-to-day realities.

7. Foresight enables one to understand the lessons from the past, the realities of the present, and the likely consequence of a decision for the future.

8. Stewardship is holding something in trust for another, and is first and foremost a commitment to serving the needs of others.

9. Commitment to the growth of people, to the growth of each and every individual within an organization or community.

10. Building community is essential, both within teams and organizations and among them.

entertainment for more than 400 people. They served 190 kilograms of turkey, 32 liters of gravy and 20 liters of cranberry sauce. They ended up raising several thousand dollars that were contributed back to a community garden, and the dinner has been repeated with similar results over the last five years. Key ingredients for their success included setting positive core values, tapping into their friends and social networks, and perhaps most importantly, promoting inclusivity in participation. They actualized the old saying that 'it is not what you know, but who you know.'

Meaningful conversations, sometimes called "learning conversations" (Green, Moore and Obrien, 2006), are the fundamental act of community facilitation and organizing. Learning conversations are those in which a person is asked what they care about and in what areas they might be willing to take action. In short, "to mobilize a community, never do anything nobody wants" (Green, Moore, & Obrien, 2006, p. 60). In Bridgewater, a free community dinner was an idea that had traction and mobilized people to act. In some cases one might start a learning conversation with an open agenda. The question might simply be: what can be done in this community to improve things? More typically, conversations are convened with a broad issue in mind such as access to green space, recreational opportunities, youth issues, or sustainability initiatives.

In the spirit of the stranger in Stone Soup, Jeffrey Luke (1998, p. 33) defines the role of the leader to be that of a catalyst. This means "mobilizing or catalyzing a diverse set of individuals and agencies to address a public problem." There are four tasks of "catalytic leadership": (1) focusing attention on a public issue, (2) engaging diverse individuals and organizations to address it, (3) considering multiple strategies for action, and (4) sustaining action by sharing information and managing relationships.

First, it is important to focus attention on an issue. For Bridgewater, the purpose was to build a sense of community spirit and inclusion in a town that had been increasingly divided by income, social stigma, and stereotypes. A series of informal learning conversations ultimately resulted in the second step of convening a meeting that brought diverse people together to contemplate strategies for action. This generated the concept of a Community Christmas dinner, leading to the third step of carefully examining multiple options for how this might occur. As a part of looking at options, the group defined a clear set of core values that allowed for a broader and shared sense of purpose for the event. From there, individuals took on distinct and diverse roles that were needed to achieve success. Finally, based on the broader shared vision of building community capacity, the group used the relationships and increased sense of community to initiate other community projects such as a community garden and a community art space.

THE INGREDIENTS AND CHALLENGES OF EFFECTIVE GROUP PROCESSES

It all sounds so easy: call up your friends, hold a bunch of meaningful conversations and a group mobilizes and accomplishes great things. Indeed, very positive things are happening in lots of communities. But in many other locales there is anger, cynicism and despair, much as at the start of Stone Soup—the systems and structures of our societies do not necessarily work to empower citizens. Professionals and institutions with fragmented authority often accumulate resources and power in a manner that leaves citizens divided, isolated, and alienated from their communities (McKnight & Block, 2012). In fact, community initiatives only succeed with skillful hosting and facilitation of relationships, groups, and meetings. These are core processes of community development. It is easy to identify groups and meetings that fail due to poor facilitation, be they student project groups, neighborhood improvement groups, or municipal councils. In Bridgewater, despite lots of community support and eager volunteers, they are struggling to find facilitators who can continue the success as the current core group moves on to other activities.

There is a large body of knowledge that considers what makes group processes effective (see Johnson and Johnson, 2012). Two core factors are: (1) establishing a welcoming context with a climate of respect and trust among participants, and (2) enabling participatory processes where each person feels able to contribute while the group learns from its experience over time (Kaner et al, 2007; Yalom, 2005). First, people need to trust, value, and respect those they are working with if they are to persist with the many challenges of community work. This becomes particularly important if there is a need for adversaries to collaborate in solving a complex social problem. Thus both the police, and minority groups who have experienced abuse at the hands of the police, need to work together to address youth delinquency issues.

The second core factor is establishing positive participatory processes. Even if participants respect and trust each other, there is no guarantee that a group will not get mired in endless conversation with little resulting action. How many groups or meetings have you been at when you left feeling that it was unproductive, and yet did not have an opportunity or feel comfortable in sharing your perspective and trying to improve processes for the future? People need to feel they are making a contribution and the group needs to learn and make progress if it is to be an effective vehicle for positive change over time. Too often, groups falter because trust and/or positive participatory processes are lacking.

CORE FACILITATOR TASKS

Effectively hosting and facilitating group processes is both a science and an art. There are core principles, knowledge, and valuable tools that anyone can utilize with positive effect, yet expertise and skill also come through intuition, practice, and experience. This section introduces the core facilitator tasks.

The *Art of Hosting* (www.artofhosting.org) is the name both for an approach and an international network of practitioners who host conversations from a community development perspective. This is one valuable framework and set of tools, and there are many other individuals, organizations, and networks working to improve group processes in communities. This approach considers the whole group process, from the preparations through the conversations to the 'harvest,' where the results are collected and used to define subsequent actions (Art of Hosting, 2014).

The facilitator plays a crucial role in developing the group processes that are essential to effective groups. The facilitator's key tasks are: (1) to set norms and define a climate where a reasonable level of trust can be attained, (2) to establish and support processes where people feel empowered to engage in positive participatory decision making, and (3) to provide support and help the group address conflict (Yalom, 2005).

TASK #1: SETTING NORMS

Norms are the unwritten, implicit rules about how a group functions. Norms are the behavior group members actually demonstrate rather than what they say they do. They are quickly established and hard to change. For example, there are norms, or typical patterns of behavior in a group with regard to who starts conversations, who sets the agendas, who sits where, the tone and nature of the conversation, and the topics that are permissible and forbidden. A group that starts with a check-in during which each person shares how they are feeling that day operates from a different set of norms than a group that immediately dives into a packed agenda. A circle of chairs with snacks at the center establishes a different climate than a boardroom table with the chairperson at its head. A group may state that all participants treat each other with respect, but if some individuals dominate conversations and interrupt others, then there is not a norm of respect regardless of the stated intentions.

From the outset, meeting planners/facilitators need to consider how each decision that structures a meeting might influence and hopefully strengthen a climate of trust. They also make key decisions about norms. Setting positive norms for empowerment and participation begins with the group members playing an important role in defining a meeting agenda. For example, youth are often viewed as disinterested in community organizations and processes, yet the work of the Halifax Regional Adventure Earth Centre in Nova Scotia over many years contradicts the stereotype.

The Adventure Earth Centre (AEC), with only two full-time staff, provides environmental education and outdoor recreation programs for several thousand children each year, while supporting a youth leadership group with several hundred participants. Why do youth flock to this locale and lead its programs when many communities complain of youth alienation? Positive engagement norms are key. One AEC program is MindShift, a peer sustainability education program for high schools and communities that utilizes participatory theater (Halifax Regional Adventure Earth Centre, 2014). It has won a series of awards and has been a keynote presentation by youth at numbers of national, regional, and local conferences and gatherings. MindShift is designed, written, and delivered by youth. Thus the process of planning MindShift started with an invitation to a number of young people to be authors, followed by a brainstorming session in which the young people defined the characteristics of an excellent sustainability education program. The planning sessions started with fun activities and food. There were no formal agendas despite a clear understanding based on shared discussions about the purpose of a given session. If participants became tired during a session, there was frequently a break for an interactive game. The core youth design team became close friends, and encouraged and supported each other to come each week despite other stresses in their lives. At the core of the success was defining a set of norms and climate where young people felt included, trusted, and empowered. The facilitator does not to do the work but establishes a safe place where it can happen. Welcoming and empowering norms are particularly important for young people, but they are necessary with every group.

Power and privilege are key factors, often unstated, that enable or block the development of positive norms and trust. This is a particularly important issue for young people. Frequently adults indicate that young people's opinions are valued yet the experience of the young person is that adults seek input but then ignore it when it does not jive with their concerns or broader organizational needs. Similar dynamics can occur in communities when professionals consult but do not necessarily listen to community input. A privilege could be as simple as only some participants having vehicles

> ***Application Questions: Exploring Group Norms***
>
> *List as many norms as possible (at least twenty) for one group you are currently participating in: a class, workgroup, team, or an organization. Include, for instance, the physical nature of the meeting space, the patterns of interaction among group members, how newcomers are welcomed, the roles and style of the leaders, and the processes through which sessions begin and end. Given this list, consider...*
>
> *Which norms establish a positive climate and encourage group productivity and interaction?*
>
> *Which norms are counter-productive and block participation and/or progress on the group's tasks?*
>
> *How could you intervene to support positive norms or raise questions about counter-productive norms?*
>
> *What processes would you suggest to help establish group norms and positive methods of interaction?*

to get to meetings while most teenagers or people with low incomes have to arrange and depend on rides. If these barriers and others are not addressed when working on a community issue, then the process is not inclusive and perpetuates the existing power differences in the community.

The role, use, and perceptions of power in community processes are complex phenomena that connect to systemic practices, demographic, and socioeconomic characteristics, and personal attributes such as confidence and personality characteristics. Facilitators must attend to and use power to enable positive participation. Too frequently those with less power and privilege in society are left out of processes and decisions that affect their life circumstances. For example, young people (or people of color, new immigrants, those with lower incomes, those with less education, etc.) often do not have input into defining the programs and services developed for them. Their previous experiences in community processes and programs may make them appropriately suspicious and hesitant to accept the promises from professionals that this time 'it will be different.' The facilitator must authentically address these issues to establish basic trust.

One useful tool to help set norms with any group is to devote a significant session early on to working together to generate "community standards." These standards represent the group's expectations for participation that are agreed to at the outset as necessary to enable a safe, trusting and productive group. These are expectations, not norms (what participants do). However, by agreeing to clear expectations in a positive way at the outset, all of the group members can be more comfortable naming situations where participants are not living up to the expectations through their behavior.

TASK #2: ENABLING POSITIVE PARTICIPATION AND SHARED DECISION MAKING

Enabling positive participation and shared decision making is the second key to productive group processes. Kaner et al. (2007) have developed a valuable framework for facilitators to use to support participatory decision making. It begins with four core values: full participation, mutual understanding, inclusive solutions, and shared responsibility. Facilitators must clearly articulate these values and use them as a filter through which to analyze and enable positive group processes. Moreover, one needs to walk the talk with respect to values. If the value is full participation and yet some people are not contributing to group processes, one needs to look at the norms, structures, and processes shaping the participation experience. One must ask how things can be altered to actualize full participation, and this might include reflecting on issues of inclusion, power, and privilege (see Chapter 9).

The model for participatory decision making has five stages (see Figure 8.2). The first phase is *business as usual* in which the group is addressing routine issues with evident solutions. The facilitator's role is to ensure that norms conducive to trust and quality participation are occurring. Unfortunately, groups often rush to a decision using business as usual processes even when there are important issues under consideration where participants have divergent and conflicting perspectives. The rush to a decision can exclude alternative perspectives and prevent new ideas from being considered. Even though current strategies and solutions may not be working, they frequently continue to be recycled through business as usual processes. In this situation, the facilitator's task is to bring the group into the *divergent zone* whereby there is a pause in routines and everyone has an opportunity to examine the issue in depth and contribute their ideas and perspectives. This may require group brainstorming or sequential go-rounds with each person contributing. This puts a range of ideas on the table that are divergent and often conflicting.

The group then enters the *groan zone* where they must discuss and understand each other's perspectives. Struggle and conflict can ensue and the facilitator needs to support participants to positively work through this stage. Groups may try to avoid conflict and jump back to a comfortable place with an ineffective solution, or dissolve into chaos and indecision. This can leave the issue unsolved or leave someone else to make the decision for the group. Ideally, positive group dialogue leads the group into the *convergent zone* in which participants develop a shared framework for understanding and evaluating the divergent ideas.

Ultimately, in the *closure zone* a decision is made and the facilitator ensures it is broadly supported and transparent in its consequences. There are many choices

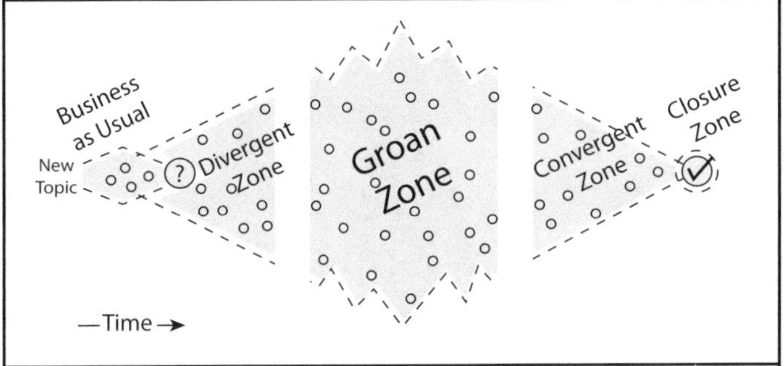

FIGURE 8.2 FRAMEWORK FOR PARTICIPATORY DECISION MAKING (FROM KANER, LIND, TOLDI, FISK, & BERGER (2007), P. 21)

for decision-making processes, which vary from decisions by consensus to majority vote to decisions by authority (Kaner et al, 2007). Each has pros and cons, but most importantly, whatever method is used needs to be clearly defined and undertaken in a transparent manner.

The participatory framework is relatively simple to grasp, but there are a multitude of pitfalls along the way such as refusing to change business as usual or failing to consider everyone's ideas. One example involves a large community garden that engages students, faculty, staff, and community members at our university. For several years, the level of student engagement in the garden had been low. The committee tried numerous ways to address the issue with limited success. Finally, at a regular meeting, the committee paused, reflected, and agreed that we needed to go back and revisit the mission statement and strategic aims of the garden, and bring in a facilitator to guide that process. The result was a deeper discussion and sharing retreat in which we discovered that some of our assumptions about each other's views were inaccurate. This helped us to converge on new and successful strategies to move forward.

Applications Questions: Reflecting on Group Processes

Analyze the process of a group you are a part of (possibly the one used in the previous exercise) and reflect on one recent meeting in relation to the Framework for Participatory Decision Making.

- *What zone do you feel your group was in with respect to particular priority issues?*
- *When has the group had conflicts? How have they been addressed? Has it been productive?*
- *What is your preferred style of addressing conflict: smoothing, confronting, collaborating, forcing, withdrawing, or compromising? Does this match the group's style?*
- *Does the group openly reflect on and discuss the process of its meetings, what things have gone well, and what things could be done better?*
- *What could you do to improve the process of the group to enable more effective performance?*

Why not try to take steps based on your analysis to improve the group's workings!

The framework for participatory decision making provides a guide for the facilitator. The facilitator must help the group move through the stages and encourage group members to reflect on how they are doing things, even though the group may be most interested in getting the job done. This reflection task is frequently ignored and groups may stumble on without asking deeper questions about their processes. How frequently have you been at a meeting when the chairperson openly and honestly invited participants to comment on what went well during the session and what was frustrating or could be improved? How frequently do groups finish by celebrating their successes and identifying ways to do better with the process next time? In our experience, this simple step is rarely undertaken. Often participants leave group processes frustrated and feeling unable to share their insights. "Done Wells" and "Do Betters" are one simple but powerful tool for a facilitator to utilize as part of the overall task of enabling shared decision making.

TASK 3: PROVIDING SUPPORT AND ADDRESSING CONFLICT

Two key aspects that enable groups to move through the stages in a productive manner are the ability to support each other and the need to productively address conflict. Conflict is an inevitable and important aspect of group process, be it a small work team or a larger community development process. The facilitator's key task is to make sure that conflict is addressed constructively rather than avoided. Once the conflict is in the open, the facilitator has to help ensure that it does not become personal and divisive to the extent that the group can never move on from the discussion of divergent ideas into the convergent zone. In fact, conflict comes with divergent interests and perspectives, and they are key to generating productive and innovative strategies that help the organization or community prosper. Unfortunately, particularly in North American mainstream culture, there are habits that block productive dialogue with respect to conflict (see box for examples). Moreover, each of us as individuals has a style and comfort level in addressing conflicts. Johnson and Johnson (2012) identify five styles through which people can approach conflict: teddy bears (smoothing); owls (confronting), turtles (withdrawing), sharks (forcing) and foxes (compromising). A facilitator must be aware of his or her own predispositions and be comfortable with raising and addressing conflict issues, otherwise the group may falter or possibly collapse.

Habits that Block Meaningful Conversations

• *The Culture of Advocacy: The purpose of a conversation is to push ones ideas and find supporters.*

• *Sending Not Receiving: The focus is on what one is going to say rather than listening and carefully considering the ideas of others.*

• *Possessing the Absolute Truth: There is one 'right' way and the person knows what it is.*

• *The Tyranny of the OR: Issues are often boiled down to limited choices or dichotomies. It is this way OR that, yet the best solutions may be emergent based on meaningful conversations and dialogue—it is possible to do this and...*

• *The Allure of Criticism: The easiest sort of comment is the negative one, rather than spending time understanding the ideas and then looking for positive ways to strengthen them.*

• *The Adversarial Mode: Views are often seen as mutually exclusive rather than interconnected and overlapping. People are too often judged in us-versus-them terms based on past experiences. Win-lose is often easier to achieve than win-win.*

from *The Art of Focused Conversation, 100 Ways to Access Group Wisdom in the Workplace*, edited by R. B. Stanfield, published by ICA Canada, Toronto, 1997.

The level of structure is key in determining how the host goes about the basic tasks of setting norms, facilitating positive participation, and addressing conflict. For example, some groups like city or town councils typically use Roberts Rules of Order with fixed agendas and clear rules governing all aspects of interaction, from who can speak when to proposing motions and voting procedures (Roberts, 2014). At the other extreme, important community development initiatives such as brainstorming how to improve a neighborhood may happen informally at the local coffee shop. Many groups fall in between in terms of their reliance on structure. Rigid structure is not friendly and welcoming, and fixed rules can inhibit participation from those unfamiliar with the process or those who feel like outsiders. Yet wide-open discussion may result in some voices dominating and the group spinning its wheels with little meaningful action to show for lengthy discussions.

There are a wide range of group facilitation techniques that define processes so that everyone can easily contribute without stifling positive, creative discussion with rigid rules. Valuable and popular techniques in community settings include: *circles* where people may check in, provide input and check out through a rotational process, *appreciative inquiry* in which people dream and design new approaches based on what is working, and *world café* which is a series of sequential small-group conversations amidst a large group on a broad and important issue (Art of Hosting, 2014).

BASIC FACILITATION SKILLS

Structured techniques may support positive participation but they cannot replace the expertise, experience, and skills of the facilitator. Ultimately, whether it is a town council, a community meeting, or an informal brainstorm, quality facilitation is essential to quality group performance. The facilitator has to exhibit three types of skills: to effectively *notice, reflect,* and *act* (HeartWood Centre for Community Youth Development, 2014). First, the facilitator must *notice* what is happening in all of its complex and subtle forms, from the sequence and frequency of who is talking and what they are saying to nonverbal body language and individual responsiveness and interest. The experienced facilitator is mentally recording everything that is happening in the room and can replay and examine the recording within the moment, or much later, to identify important issues, trends, and dynamics. Table 8.1 identifies some of the areas that require the facilitator's attention.

The second skill area for the facilitator is to *reflect* on the meaning of what he or she has noticed. Assume a recreation center is having a focus group to collect ideas for future programming from community members. What if the recreation director changes the topic in the middle of the session when one person suggests a weekly yoga program for seniors? It could mean any one of a number of things—maybe the recreation staff is not interested in yoga or is not listening. Possibly there are past conflicts between the two people, or maybe there is no budget for seniors programming and the staff member is embarrassed about this. The reflection step involves the facilitator exploring the meaning of observations in the context of other interactions within the group process and other sources of information from the broader context. Reflection can be instantaneous or

TABLE 8.1 POISE: ELEMENTS A FACILITATOR SHOULD CONSIDER WHEN **NOTICING** A GROUP PROGRESS (FROM HEARTWOOD CENTRE FOR COMMUNITY YOUTH DEVELOPMENT, 2014)

Participants	Ourselves	Interactions	Physical Space	Experiences
• Responsiveness • Interest • Capacity • Motivation • Relationships to participants & facilitators • Confidence • Energy • Food/water	• Health • Motivations • Co-facilitator • Skills • Values • Experiences • Knowledge • Energy • Instinct • Buttons	• Body language • Verbal comments • Cliques • Seating arrangements • Who speaks more • Who speaks less • Group dynamic • Outgoing • Withdrawn • Who takes initiative • Who doesn't • Relationships (existing or new) • Boundaries	• Room set up • Lighting & color • Breakout space • Outdoor space • Shared ownership • Accommodation • Creative options	• Meaningful • Authentic • Challenging • Fresh • Safety • Relevant • Community connections

occur over a longer period, possibly including discussion with a co-facilitator. Deliberate reflection helps the facilitator understand the situation so as to identify the most appropriate actions to take to facilitate the group process constructively.

The third skill area for the facilitator is to *act* based on what has been noticed, reflected upon, and understood. Knowing what should be done and doing it are two distinct steps. The facilitator may see the need to ask the recreation staff why he or she changed the subject, but may not have the confidence to do it because it puts the staff member on the spot. Acting in this sort of instance is often an interpersonal risk for the facilitator. Intervening in a clear but respectful manner takes confidence and skill, which often come with training and experience.

The stranger in Stone Soup was the perfect facilitator and knew just what to say to get all of the villagers to overcome their fears and volunteer to contribute. Yet there is no consideration of what was going on inside the stranger's head. What did he notice and how did he reflect on and understand the situation? We only know that he had the confidence and skill to take appropriate action. In fact, superb facilitators are often hard to find and the path to becoming one takes interpersonal sensitivity, training, and experience. They are absolutely essential to positive community development efforts. Facilitation skills are required for anyone aspiring to take a host role as a part of leadership in community development initiatives. Even with skilled facilitation, the challenges of community engagement are enormous, as the case study of the Wolfville Sustainability Initiative on the next page illustrates.

CONCLUSIONS

Communities face an enormous range of interconnected problems with regard to leisure, health, justice, planning, economy, and sustainability. They grapple with forces at global, national, and regional levels while trying to mobilize their internal assets to define a constructive future that builds on their strengths and addresses key community issues. There is little benefit in wishing away issues or in trying to return to an older, simpler time. A new approach is being utilized in numbers of locales whereby leadership involves taking on the role of host and facilitator rather than hero. The host brings people together through processes in which citizens work together to mobilize their resources and take initiative for the betterment of their lives and communities.

Key tasks of the host are to take steps to set positive group norms and to enable participatory processes and shared decision making as groups move forward. The host provides support and helps the group address conflict. This work requires effective facilitation skills, which take training, time, and experience to develop, yet are indispensable to successful community development processes. For those interested in a career in community development, training in facilitation is an invaluable investment.

The story of Stone Soup provides a simplistic, though captivating, depiction of an idealistic community

THE POTENTIAL AND CHALLENGES OF COMMUNITY DEVELOPMENT PROCESSES—THE WOLFVILLE SUSTAINABILITY INITIATIVE

In the mid-2000s, John Colton was involved in a community development project called the Wolfville Sustainability Initiative (WSI). WSI sought to move the Town of Wolfville, Nova Scotia toward becoming a sustainable community. It was managed through a partnership between the Town and the Centre for Rural Sustainability (CRS), a regional nonprofit organization. The purpose of the initiative was to:

- Enable the Town to effectively envision, plan, and maintain a sustainable future that considers such increasingly important variables as climate change, energy scarcity, water quality and quantity, food supply, job and skill base, and population demographics.
- Bring clarity to the community's sustainability needs by redefining progress as a function of genuine improvement in quality of life for the whole community.
- Create and maintain momentum for implementing sustainability initiatives based on the community's clearly articulated vision for sustainability. (CRS, 2004)

John's role in the project was to host and facilitate approximately 30 community circles (lengthy, semi-structured group discussions) with local residents and interest groups. The purpose of these community circles was to explore residents and other stakeholders' views on their community in the present and future. John and colleagues prepared a detailed report on the community circles process and outcomes, which was intended to inform a revised Municipal Planning Strategy.

The community circles generated considerable excitement and enthusiasm among participants who were encouraged by the town's leadership and its commitment to building a sustainable community. Friendships and networks were created among residents and stakeholder groups. A sense of momentum and urgency in moving toward a sustainable community developed among members of these stakeholder groups.

Not surprisingly, it became clear that there were conflicting paths envisioned to a sustainable community. While several local businesses were involved in the community circles, one umbrella organization representing local businesses was absent (the Wolfville Business Development Corporation (WBDC)). Our efforts to engage them directly had failed due to miscommunications, timing, and misperceptions. The WBDC had in fact, begun their own strategic planning around sustainability issues in a business context.

When John's final recommendations were made to the Municipal Planning Strategy, the draft plan was quickly tabled as a result of the growing unrest among numbers of community stakeholders. After significant collective effort and fundraising, the idea of working toward a sustainable community was finished; at least for the time being.

What went wrong and what lessons were learned? First, it quickly became obvious that community development can be a messy process despite the best intentions and involvement of local government, residents, local NGOs, and other stakeholders. When reflecting on the process it is easy to 'tick' many of the boxes in regards to community engagement. Yes, positive norms were established in how John and his colleagues interacted in the community circles and the overall project. Practices and principles were put in place to support positive participation. Lacking, however, were frameworks that supported broader shared decision making or methods for addressing conflict. Those with differing perspectives did not feel heard and instead began talking with others and ultimately organizing resistance outside of the planning processes.

development process. In fact, a more appropriate metaphor for an actual community process is a swamp rather than a kettle of soup. A swamp is teeming with life and includes many types of organisms, nutrients, waste products, complex interactions, and muck. A swamp can stagnate and decay for centuries when the interactions go badly or it can become a rich growing medium for an abundance of new life when the system processes are in balance. The leader as host plays an indispensable role in facilitating positive change and growth by helping to mobilize peoples' assets and willingness to act in the 'swamp' of a human community.

REFERENCES

Art of Hosting (2014). What is the art of hosting conversations that matter? Retrieved from http://www.artofhosting.org/what-is-aoh/

Bass, B. M., & Bass, R. (2008). *The Bass handbook of leadership: Theory, research, and managerial applications.* New York: Free Press.

Blake, R. R., & Mouton, J. S. (1978). *The New Managerial Grid.* Houston TX: Gulf.

Bridgewater Community Christmas Society. (2010). Who's it for? The key ingredients for the Bridgewater Community Christmas. Unpublished report.

Callaghan, E. G., & Colton, J. (2008). Building sustainable and resilient communities: A balancing of community capital. *Environment, Development and Sustainability 10,* 931–942.

Davis, W. (2012). *Into the silence: The great war, Mallory and the conquest of Everest.* Toronto, ON: Vintage Canada.

Diers, J. (2004). *Neighbour power: Building community the Seattle way.* Seattle WA: University of Washington Press.

Freire, P. (1996). *Pedagogy of the oppressed, revised edition.* Harmondsworth, UK: Penguin.

Green, M., Moore, H., & O'Brien, J. (2006). *When people care enough to act.* Toronto, ON: Inclusion Press.

Greenleaf, R. K. (1970). The servant as leader. Essay retrieved from https://www.leadershiparlington.org/pdf/TheServantasLeader.pdf

Halifax Regional Adventure Earth Centre (2014). MindShift. Retrieved from www.earthed.ns.ca/mind shift

Hanleybrown, F., Kania, J., & Kramer, M. (2012). Channeling change: Making collective impact work. Published by the *Stanford Social Innovation Review.* Retrieved from http://www.ssireview.org/articles/entry/collective_impact

Hersey, P. (1984). *The situational leader.* New York, NY: Warner.

HeartWood Centre for Community Youth Development (2014). HeartWood's facilitation approach. Unpublished report of the HeartWood Centre for Community Youth Development, Halifax, Nova Scotia, Canada.

Johnson, D., & Johnson, F. (2012). *Joining Together: Group Theory and Group Skills,* 11th Edition. Essex, UK: Pearson.

Kaner, S., Lind, L., Toldi, C., Fisk, S., & Berger, D. (2007). *Facilitator's Guide to Participatory Decision-Making,* 2nd Edition. San Francisco, CA: John Wiley & Sons.

Lax, J. (2006). Reasons to dream. In S. Cullis-Suzuki, K. Frederickson, & C. MacKenzie (Eds.), *Notes from Canada's young activists: A generation stands up for change.* Vancouver, BC: Greystone Books.

Ledwith, M. (2011). *Community development: A critical approach,* 2nd Edition. Bristol, UK: Policy Press.

Luke, J. S. (1998). *Catalytic Leadership: Strategies for an Interconnected World.* San Francisco, CA: Jossey-Bass Publishers.

McKnight, J., & Block, P. (2012). *The abundant community: Awakening the power of families and neighborhoods.* San Francisco, CA: Berrett-Koehler Publishers.

Nair, K. (1997). *A higher standard of leadership: Lessons from the life of Gandhi.* San Francisco, CA: Berrett-Koehler Publishers, Inc.

Otesha Project. (2014). Our History. Retrieved from http://www.otesha.ca/content/our-history

Roberts, H. (2014). Robert's Rules of Order, revised, 1915 version. Retrieved from http://www.constitution.org/rror/rror—00.htm

Rowson, J., Broome, S., & Jones, A. (2010). Connected communities: How social networks power and sustain the Big Society. Published by the RSA Action Research Centre. Retrieved from http://www.thersa.org/action-research-centre/reports/socialchange/how-social-networks-power-and-sustain-the-big-society

Senge, P. (1994). *The fifth discipline field book: Strategies and tools for building a learning organization.* Toronto, ON: Doubleday.

Spears, L. (2006). On character and servant-leadership: Ten characteristics of effective, caring leaders. Retrieved from http://www.regent.edu/acad/global/publications/jvl/vol1_iss1/Spears_Final.pdf

Stanfield, R. B. (1997). *The art of focused conversation: 100 ways to access group wisdom in the workplace.* Toronto, ON: ICA Canada.

Wheatley, M., & Frieze, D. (2011). *Walk out walk on: A living journey into communities daring to live the future now.* San Francisco, CA: Berrett-Koehler Publishers, Inc.

Yalom, I. (2005). *Theory and practice of group psychotherapy,* 5th edition. New York, NY: Basic Books.

Zaccaro, S. J., Kemp, C., & Bader, P. (2004). Leader traits and attributes. In J. Antonakis, A. Cianciolo and R. Steinberg (Eds.), *The nature of leadership*, (pp. 101–124). Thousand Oaks, CA: Sage Publications, Inc.

9

WORKING THROUGH DIFFERENCE: ACKNOWLEDGING POWER, PRIVILEGE, AND THE ROOTS OF OPPRESSION

Stephen Lewis, Rasul Mowatt, and Felice Yuen

Contemporary North American culture readily dismisses caste systems as 'medieval' and proclaims explicit practices of slavery and legislated racial, ethnic, and gender oppression as 'antiquated' and 'barbaric.' Yet, this same culture that espouses inherent qualities of justice and 'freedom for all' has made it difficult to recognize the roles we might play in perpetuating marginalization and powerlessness within our own communities. In this chapter we confront the roots of oppression, the meaning of privilege, and examine the role leisure plays in perpetuating and reinforcing these exploitive and exclusionary practices.

We wrote this chapter because we believe community developers in the field of leisure need to understand and have the ability to discuss issues of inequality such as gender oppression and equity, disability denial and access, and religious profiling and freedoms. These issues all stem from the same source, degrading superiority and privilege. Further, we believe that acknowledging one experience should not negate the experiences of others. As leisure facilitators engaging in community development practice, we must go through a "radical mutation of consciousness" to work through difference grounded in the roots of oppression (Gibson, 2003, p. 10). As we engage in critical action we need to, "feel in a fog on three counts: (1) what is the present situation? (2) what are the dangers? And most important of all, (3) what shall we do?" (Lewin, 1946, p. 34).

Engaging in a radical mutation of consciousness is not easy. In this process, we confront everyday interactions that we take for granted. Such an approach requires us to adopt a *reflexive practice*, which involves the conscious and deliberate inclusion of ourselves (i.e., our biases and our social positioning) in relation to others (Dupuis, 1999). Through this reflexive practice, we acknowledge our impact on the lives of others, and also recognize how our experiences impact our personal values, attitudes and behaviors. A reflexive practitioner is someone who frequently and thoughtfully reflects on how their personal biases may impact their world view, their expectations, the decisions they make, and the way they interact with other individuals and/or groups of people.

Throughout this chapter you will read a vignette from each author. Each vignette holds a personal story that has contributed to our own mutation of consciousness and depicts a reflexive practice. These vignettes were specifically chosen to be examples of the concepts we discuss and to provide a context through which you can pause to consider your own lives. The questions in this chapter were created to encourage you to apply the reading material to your lives and to facilitate a reflexive practice.

The chapter begins with discussions on oppression and privilege, what those terms mean, and how they manifest in our everyday lives. We then make the connection between oppression and privilege and broader systemic factors and cultural processes. The chapter also examines issues of Whiteness, and highlights the complexities of oppression when individuals experience discrimination on a variety of ways (i.e., discrimination for being lesbian, gay, bisexual, transgender, queer, *and* obese). We end the chapter on a hopeful note by offering three approaches you can use to work towards social change. The chapter concludes with an opportunity for you to explore and develop a personal manifesto that you can use to become an agent for justice. Without further delay, let us begin.

THE ROOTS OF OPPRESSION

We turn to Frantz Fanon to understand the depths of oppression. As a noted thinker of societal marginalization and social justice while also engaged in the actual struggle for liberation from France in Algeria, Fanon is often looked to for a description and analysis of oppression. In the years of practicing psychiatry in Algeria, he deduced that the reasons for the conditions, disorders, and other mental illnesses he was seeing in his patients were rooted in the oppressive system of colonialism, and more specifically, the French. He ultimately saw that the engagement in freedom by ending colonialism was the only way to would 'cure' their mental health and restore their human dignity. Oppression, according to Fanon (1963), was firmly grounded in violence. Fanon saw that all interactions of the authority were that of dominance over an oppressed populace, and this was ultimately violence in many forms.

At this point, you may be wondering how leisure fits into this violence. If oppression is systemic, or ingrained in the everyday functions of society, then it takes the actual violence from the justified power of the military (occupying army) or paramilitary (police). However, alongside these overt forms of violence, there is the everydayness of *peaceful violence,* which is enacted in the structures that produce and maintain social disparities, structured poverty, residential segregation, unequal opportunities, and discriminatory access. Though not on all accounts (see Mowatt's (2012) research on lynching as leisure), we can understand leisure's role in a structure of dominance and power as peaceful violence. That is, the majority of recreation programming is built upon Western White, upper and middle-class values. As explained by Fox and Lashua (2010), "dominant leisure practices and programs are imbricated in Euro-North American values related to capitalism, excellence, people as expendable resources, and profit lines that ignore the well-being and flourishing of human and non-human communities" (p. 238). Furthermore, the threat of violence fosters further dominance by way of a 'culture of silence' that defines oppressed people as Other by labeling and denigrating certain markers of identification (gay, woman, dark, savage, handicap) and controls their identities and roles through education and other institutions of socialization (Freire, 1970). This culture of silence has the power to render the oppressed concerns mute.

> *We may oppose cruel and oppressive labor conditions or child labour, but willingly buy the latest recreation equipment manufactured abroad at cheaper prices . . . No practice, including leisure, is free of power and its effects.*
>
> *—Fox (2000, p. 33)*

Race, ethnicity, gender, sexual orientation, disability, age, income, and religion are simply categories of difference and categories of people that this violence is applied to. In being applied to these categories, violence takes on an additional form, *internalized oppression.* As the oppressed populace fails to resist the system of oppression that they are experiencing, and as they experience the ongoing degradation and deprivation in their lives, they begin to violently turn inward on themselves as a matter of frustration and disorientation. Living under oppression results in the oppressed moving in and out of phases of capitulation (absorbed into dominant culture and rejecting original culture), revitalization (reject the dominant culture, yet becoming reactionary), or radicalization (committed to social change) (Bulhan, 1985). It is this inward turn that must be overcome for the oppressed to move towards empowerment (Hanna, Talley, & Guindon, 2000; Lea, 2012).

> **Reflection Questions**
>
> *Think of a story in the news related to a person or group who is marginalized. Which of the following best describes the behavior, attitudes, or actions of this person/group? Why?*
>
> *Capitulation*
>
> *Revitalization*
>
> *Radicalization*

The effects of oppression are psychological for Fanon (Hilton, 2011), as the oppressed learn at an early age that to grow and prosper under dominance means to "hate oneself" and to "invest in the hero, who is White" (Fanon, 1967, p. 114). This self-hatred leads one to aspire to be like the oppressor, and like the oppressor to violently victimize the inferior. As leisure practitioners we can help stop this cycle of violence by adopting a perspective that acknowledges oppression and the impact it has on the oppressed. The culture in our field needs to be changed to have the capacity to talk about the particular histories of the legacy of slavery and segregation, conquest and colonialism, and stolen lands and indigenous displacement as representations of the same oppressive power, and how acknowledging one moment should not erase the moments of other peoples. Such a capacity is realized by acknowledging and understanding the roots of oppression and the effects of privilege.

UNDERSTANDING PRIVILEGE

Privilege is unearned benefits based on real or perceived demographic attributes such as age, socioeconomic status, gender, and race. As previously mentioned, North American recreational and leisure practices are largely based upon White values. For this reason, to understand privilege, we believe it is imperative to understand *White privilege*. Peggy McIntosh (1988) described White privilege as, ". . . an invisible weightless knapsack of special provisions, assurances, tools, maps, guides, codebooks, passports, visas, clothes, compass, emergency gear, and blank checks . . ." (p. 95). McIntosh refers to Whiteness as a type of unearned currency. She also asserts that it is a cultural standard that is difficult for many people who possess such privilege to acknowledge and understand. In order to help illuminate how privilege might *look* in action, she created a series of more than 40 statements for readers to relate to, including the following:

- *I can, if I wish, arrange to be in the company of people of my race most of the time*
- *I can go shopping alone most of the time, fairly well assured that I will not be followed or harassed by store detectives*
- *I can turn on the television or open to the front page of the paper and see people of my race widely and positively represented*
- *When I am told about our national heritage or about "civilization," I am shown that people of my color made it what it is*
- *I can be fairly sure of having my voice heard in a group in which I am the only member of my race*
- *I did not have to educate our children to be aware of systemic racism for their own daily physical protection*
- *I can do well in a challenging situation without being called a credit to my race*
- *I am never asked to speak for all the people of my racial group*
- *I can criticize our government and talk about how much I fear its policies and behavior without being seen as a cultural outsider (pp. 97–98).*

Within the context of community development, those with such privilege may unintentionally contribute to the social marginalization of others through such mechanisms as socioeconomic exclusion (e.g., user fees), the absence of positive visual representations of non-White culture in the public arena (e.g., advertisements and other promotional material), and even disregard of the oppression faced by those identified within non-White ethnic and racial groups (Walter, 2010).

Well-intentioned community recreation initiatives often illustrate these issues, as they frequently target non-White and lower-income participants, but are usually designed and led by people idealizing activities and programs reflecting the interests of Western White, middle-class culture. In such cases, even thoughtful recreation programmers might overlook the complex needs of community members by basing their goals on personal experiences, expected skill sets, and cultural values. In the following vignette, Felice shares an example based on her experiences working with women in prison that helps to further unpack some of these ideas.

FELICE'S STORY

"Get real. They have no idea what you're even talking about"

I embarked on my Ph.D. eager to explore how leisure could contribute to the well-being of Indigenous women in prison. During my time as a graduate student, I also had the opportunity to be employed as a research assistant on a project that examined how women can be supported after incarceration so they may become valued and contributing members of society (Pedlar, Arai, Yuen, & Fortune, 2008). Recognizing that leisure is often limited for marginalized groups, I assumed: If the opportunity existed, whether it be in the prison or out in the community, participation (and all the good stuff that goes along with it) would prevail. For example, if costs were reduced, childcare provided, and transportation accessible, women would be more likely to participant in leisure activities. Looking back, I realize that I was naively optimistic. After four years of volunteering in the prison and doing research with both Indigenous and non-Indigenous women who are incarcerated, I came to realize that participation in leisure was far more complex than I initially thought.

Like many of us who pursue a degree in leisure studies, I had experienced the benefits of leisure in my childhood, youth, and young adulthood. I also grew up in a loving family; a big sister that I looked up to, a mother and father who encouraged and supported us in a variety of leisure pursuits, and yes, even a dog named Dexter to complete our family unit. One might say that I had a privileged upbringing. These experiences led me to develop a certain perspective of what leisure is supposed to be and the role it should play in our lives. For example, leisure was summer camp, the friends I made, and the fun we had. Thus, I developed the idea that leisure is conducive to positive emotions and contributes to the development of friendship. My assumptions of leisure and overall worldview came into question during the time that I spent with women in prison.

One pivotal moment was when one of the women asked me the difference between the yellow pages and white pages of a phonebook. This incident occurred when I began going to the prison in 2004, so looking for information in this manner wasn't totally unheard of. It was like asking what it means to 'Google' something. I came to realize people might have the desire to participate in a leisure activity or access certain services, but they might not know how to find it. Another turning point was when a woman told me how she wished she could volunteer upon her release from prison, but the criminal record checks would likely prevent her from doing so. Her awareness of this barrier, and the perceptions society has of incarcerated women as mad or bad, brought to life the stigma women have to endure and overcome (Pedlar, Arai & Yuen, 2007; Pedlar, Yuen, & Fortune, 2008).

A final point I wish to emphasize coincides with sociologist Hannah-Moffat's (2001) observation," [a] common false assumption is that women in prison often identify with middle-class reformers and are willing participants even though they are being involuntarily confined in prison" (p. 191). In other words, some women's understandings of leisure aren't necessarily the same as my privileged, middle-class perceptions of leisure (e.g., beneficial to one's life, opportunity for development). Numerous interviews suggest that some women viewed leisure as dangerous because it could lead to a return to old habits, including alcohol and drug use. For many women, leisure was something to avoid (Yuen, Arai, & Fortune, 2012). Further, common leisure activities such as crafts or sports where seen as foreign and meaningless. As one woman astutely remarked, *"you try to get these women to go into a craft workshop in the community. I mean, are you kidding? Get real. They have no idea what you're even talking about... You might as well be speaking Greek. It's just so far out of their realm."*

Personal experiences affect the way in which we see and understand the world, and the way in which we value and define leisure. My experiences with the women I met gave me a better understanding of women in prison and ultimately altered the lens I use to see the world. I am now a cautious optimist. There is still much to learn and my perspective will undoubtedly continue to change.

Reflection Questions

Before continuing, we want you to take a moment to consider your response to the following questions so that you may consciously position yourself in relation to the ideas that are presented later on.

What factors led to the development of your definition of leisure? As you move through this chapter, consider how your values and conceptualization of leisure, and your experiences of privilege might be a shaping force.

How might the prioritization of community resources be the same or differ for someone from a different socioeconomic background or cultural identity than yourself (especially if they have significantly fewer financial resources)?

How many citizens within your community experience stigma, prejudice and discrimination more intensely and frequently than you? Is there a difference? How do you think this impacts the way they conceptualize meaningful community and safe spaces in comparison to you?

ACKNOWLEDGING PRIVILEGE AND LOCATING YOUR PERSONAL SUBJECTIVE LENS

Privilege is something we often take for granted. Acknowledging privilege requires purposeful and mindful reflection of our everyday encounters. For example, those of us reading this textbook are privileged because we have the cognitive abilities needed to read and comprehend this material, literacy skills, opportunities for education, resources for access to this textbook, and time to read, process, and discuss the material. None of these are bad, but because privilege is often something we all take for granted it can lead us to unintentionally decide what is best for others without fully understanding the diverse contexts in which we all live.

The fact of the matter is that everyone reading this possesses some level of privilege. What's important is to acknowledge this privilege, and recognize how it affects the way we think and act in relation to others. In this chapter, you are invited to situate yourself in relation to the topics we discuss and to interrogate how your own experiences of privilege and oppression have created what you may consider to be "common sense" in community development work.

WHITENESS IN RECREATION, LEISURE, AND SPORT

While privilege clearly impacts the lens we use to view the world, many feel that racial discrimination is more of an historical *event* than a current practice. For example, based on frequent examples of athletes of color in some of the more visible sports, we may feel that segregation no longer exists (Edwards, 1979). However, many sports considered to be more 'elite,' such as golf and tennis, have only recently begun to offer strong examples of non-White representation (Harrison, 2013). Across all sports, there are culturally implied expectations of *racial spatiality,* or, what type of racialized body we automatically associate (or disassociate) with a particular sport (Carter, 2008; Harrison, 2013). David Sibley (1995) labeled these insidious expectations as *geographies of exclusion.* Such racialized expectations are examples of how leisure contributes to the peaceful violence of oppression.

The concept of *geographies of exclusion* can be readily seen within the context of snow skiing. Even with the efforts of Black ski clubs (Lee, 2006) and the economic need of ski resorts to expand beyond their clientele (Harrison, 2013), many people of color feel that recreational snow skiing is an exclusionary leisure space where they are not welcome. Others may want to attempt to fit in for both reasons of personal interest, and possibly also to try to reap the benefits of acceptance in such a privileged space; such attempts go beyond straightforward issues of privilege, into the more complex (and problematic) study of *Whiteness* in recreation and leisure studies (Harrison, 2013). White identity, in Western societies, is an identity that is desirable and sought after by all regardless of race, ethnicity, gender, sexual orientation, ability, religion, educational attainment, and economic status. Notably, we cannot assume that being White inherently induces privilege. For example, a person who is transgendered or disabled can be White, but experience marginalization and oppression. Despite McIntosh's (1988) explanation of White privilege and Whiteness as a type of unearned currency, we must go further and see both of them as a cultural ideal that all peoples (including people of color and people of difference) aspire to. This ideal establishes that White, upper and middle class, Western cultural values and norms are the standard for beliefs, thoughts, and actions. It is the way that Fanon's (1963) dominance conspicuously and inconspicuously exists in the lives of everyday people. White privilege and Whiteness tills the soil for discrimination and superiority to grow. Below, Rasul's story explores the process of Whiteness, and ultimately the process of oppression, in leisure.

RASUL'S STORY

Changing the Complexions of a Swimming Pool

Summer. As a youth, I can fondly remember the heat of the sun in June-August was unbearable at times. That heat was only curbed by our ability to find a store that had air conditioning, purchasing ice cream, or splashing in water. However, each required us, as children of color, to navigate an uneasy line of permission seeking that may not be favorable. Seeking this shelter and relief from the rays of the sun only placed us into confrontations of race, power, and space. The following is as much my story as it is their story; it is as much 1977 as it is 2009.

Nestled in the Somerton section of Northeast Philadelphia, the Valley Swim Club is located in Huntingdon Valley. Huntingdon Valley is an exceptionally White and somewhat wealthy suburb. The nearby Philmont Heights neighborhood houses the Russian and Jewish immigrants that had a history of restrictions of access to the

Valley Swim Club in the 1980s that sets the stage of what occurred over the summer of 2009.

The Creative Steps Daycare Camp, after the closure of the New Frankford Community YMCA, purchased membership via email to the Valley Swim Club for $1950 for the 65 Black, Brown, middle, and lower class children to continue swimming as an important activity in their day camp daily itinerary for 90 minutes for one day per week for the remainder of the summer. The camp swam indoors on Tuesdays and Thursdays at the Raymond and Miriam Klein Jewish Community Center in Northeast Philadelphia. The Valley Swim Club was an ideal outdoor replacement as it was only a 20-minute bus ride from the camp's location that was also in Northeast Philadelphia.

The Creative Steps Daycare Camp arrived to their new outdoor swim option on June 29, 2009 and the youth were excited and took a plunge into the sizable 110,000 gallon pool. Almost immediately, a member approached the Valley Swim Club President and was concerned that the pool was now overcrowded, a situation that is not expected to occur when members paid for privacy and exclusivity. Other members made overt comments that were heard by Creative Steps Campers, such as "What are all these Black kids doing here? They might do something to my child." The camp was approached by staff to leave. As they left, members shouted, "We're gonna see to it that they don't come back anymore." Two days later, the President of the Valley Swim Club called the Creative Steps Daycare Camp Executive Director and apologized and that the Swim Club membership overruled his decision by vote and the camp would not be able to come back without any other explanation. Creative Steps Camp was refunded their money. When media outlets caught wind of the occurrence, the Valley Swim Club President remarked that, "there was concern that a lot of kids would change the complexion... and the atmosphere of the club" (Lattanzio, 2009).

Although this incident caught the attention of the media and there was some form of restitution and support given to Creative Steps Campers, this is a far too common occurrence to simply be an incident. This is not one time. This is the norm, minus the attention and restitution. The experience of bodies of color being ostracized from movie theaters, game rooms, gyms, beaches, and swimming pools has gone on since the inception of those spaces. The history of segregated beaches and pools is as old as the end of slavery and colonialism. The attitudes that desire for segregated spaces still linger today in a younger generation of leisure-service professionals just as it did in previous generations. Laws of making discrimination illegal have only prevented the occurrences to be commonplace and confrontational. But I present this story less for the shock value but to encourage reflection:

- Has there been a value orientation to deny bodies of color these opportunities in your own life? Consider the movies you have seen and reactions of your friends and family. Consider your own reactions when you see people of color in a variety of leisure settings.

- Where does the resentment of a population begin and the passion to serve communities through recreation end? Can these two co-exist? Can leisure play a role in eliminating this resentment?

To understand the process of Whiteness, we offer four theoretical concentrations to consider: *Structural Privilege, Social Mechanisms, Discursive Meanings, Cultural Reproduction,* and *Institutional* (Mowatt, 2013). *Structural Privilege* focuses on the access to tangible goods and opportunities, as well as the freedom from social harm, such as persecution and incarceration. *Social Mechanisms* locates Whiteness in social interactions, social customs, social beliefs, and the social relationships, such as the stigmatizing and stereotyping of populations. *Discursive Meanings* analyzes the manner that White identity is upheld as the standard and norm in language, media, and other forms of discourse. While *Cultural Reproduction* concentrates on the process that Whiteness replicates itself even in the newest (social media) and most beneficent institutions (leisure-service agencies, social work, and public education). Lastly, *Institutional Theoretical Area* examines the formal, informal, and symbolic systems of Whiteness within societal institutions (political, educational, economic, health, and social) that are erected and maintained.

If we think of the Creative Steps Camp incident, the youth of color in the camp interfered with the standard or accepted *Social Mechanisms* of the Valley Swim Club of Pennsylvania. Even though there was no report indicating unruly or dangerous behavior, the youth's very presence either 1) presented a new set of behaviors that were generally not seen; and, 2) hindered the continued behaviors of those who frequented the Swim Club. The *Discursive Meanings* are evident in the staff of Valley Swim Club revoking the Creative Steps Camp temporary passes to the club based on stated and unstated rules and regulations. As they were questioned by news agencies, the leadership and staff of the Valley Swim Club re-affirmed their decision in revoking Creative Steps Camp, as if their rationale was just. This doubling down on their decision is an example of the *Cultural Reproduction Theoretical Area.* In following the incident further, it took legal action for the camp to be awarded some degree of restitution through the bankruptcy of the Swim Club. All parties involved agreed upon distributing the award to six youth serving bodies of Philadelphia with additional funds going to the children of Creative Steps Daycare Camp. But the sheer fact that it took the force of federal-level legal action (U.S. Bankruptcy Court) is indicative of the *Institutional Theoretical Area* and the Valley Swim Club power to block any lower court's decision or mediation.

> **_Reflection Questions_**
>
> *Rasul's story likely evoked strong emotions, but we ask you to go even deeper into the topic and answer the following questions as if you were an administrator working for the Valley Swim Club.*
>
> *What messages do you feel that the final decision sent out to the surrounding community/ communities?*
>
> *How would you simultaneously address the demands from private club members with fairness to the Creative Steps Camp?*
>
> *How could you facilitate a productive discussion between the administrators of the Creative Steps Camp and the private members of the swim club?*
>
> *How could you reach out to the Day Camp and members of the community to try to promote more justice and inclusion after the impact of this event?*

WHITENESS AS A CULTURAL PROCESS

We must understand Whiteness as a *cultural process* that is beyond White privilege. As Rasul has written before, White privilege discussions tend to:

> Reduce our conceptualization of "Whiteness" to isolated circumstances of benefits, opportunities, and advantages that White people have over populations of color rather than the process of dominance that determines and establishes these privileges based on a White identity" (Mowatt, 2013, p. 46).

By understanding this cultural process, we are better able to understand the process of oppression. Distancing ourselves in this discussion of Whiteness from White privilege allows us to understand the nuances that exist as it relates to 'rights, and the right of rule' (Mowatt, 2013). It is the ultimate cultural marker of prestige and achievement, and the more White sub-identities (Western, upper class, middle class, educated, male, able bodied, heterosexual) that you can aspire and attain, the greater your chance of having the ultimate quality of life.

However, even if you fall short of attaining all of the sub-identities there are rights, responsibilities, and privileges that can be earned in an honorary position. Creating such a 'rat race' is the by-product of a well-oiled machine that produces school systems that create aspirations of separation from one's cultural background; separates communities within a city so that one group is unseen or unheard unless linked to crime; and, discards and disposes of people if they do not have the requisite functional abilities, orientation, or income. The cultural process impacts our contemporary lived realities and is a creation of the greater structure of *White Supremacy* that spawns systems of powerlessness and power acquisition, nationalistic zeal, violence and social control, marginalization and accommodation, and lastly, exploitation and privileged benefits (Mowatt, 2013; Mowatt & Schmalz, 2014). As Ansley (1997) stated that White Supremacy refers instead to,

> "A political, economic and cultural system in which Whites overwhelmingly control power and material resources, conscious and unconscious ideas of White superiority and entitlement are widespread, and relations of White dominance and non-White subordination are daily reenacted across a broad array of institutions and social settings" (p. 592).

Leisure settings are significant social settings in society and are not exempt from the expanse of White Supremacy despite its beneficent and socially responsible origins. Philipp (2000) commented that,

It appears to be 'shocking' for many leisure researchers to even consider race in

> their understanding of leisure behavior. Yet, perhaps nowhere else does race matter as much as during leisure... [no] laws have been enacted to secure the racial integration of leisure spaces. (p. 121)

Due to the historic origin and the overt emphasis on service, most leisure scholars, students, and practitioners tend to avoid the possibility that community organizations and other leisure settings could be generators of the type of social order that is desirable under the conception of Whiteness, and the greater institution of White Supremacy. Allison (1999) remarked that,

> The historical grounding of the recreation profession in the early social reform movements (Sessoms, 1984), coupled with the professional credo (ideology) that recreation is a democratically based institution, may foster the belief that inclusionary practices are a "natural" component of the field and need not be addressed explicitly. (p. 80)

As a result, we do not fully understand how "leisure practices create, reinforce, and perpetuate racist practices in contemporary society" (Floyd, 2007, p. 249). For this reason, we urge community developers to continuously pause and reflect upon how their decisions and actions may impact the lives of marginalized groups.

INTERSECTIONALITY WITHIN OUR COMMUNITIES

The consideration of ethnic and/or racialized bodies and communities provides a strong foundation for exploring issues of privilege and oppression, but these dynamics are far from linear. Even when delving deeper into the process of Whiteness, we have to look beyond 'just' race to include cultural power play of gender, sexual identity, socioeconomics, ability, age, and other factors. Each of these demographic markers holds cultural significance by themselves, but it is examining the intersectionality of individuals, groups, and communities that allow us to more deeply understand the complexity and oppression of the lived experience within a community. *Intersectionality* considers the way different personal abilities, demographic characteristics, and attributes interact with one another to impact a person's level of privilege.

Crenshaw (1991) originally developed the concept of intersectionality to articulate the ways that Black feminist could address anti-discrimination laws that looked blindly onto their experiences as women being separate from their identity as being Black. The term has been repurposed to address the ways that multiple forms of power structures impede on the growth and development of people as their multiple identities. Crenshaw explored the simultaneously gendered and racialized experiences of women of color in incidences of sexual assault. Women of Color were often times overlooked in discussions of assault, in considerations when coming forward to legal entities, and disregarded and de-legitimized by Black men.

Intersectionality was an important step in engaging the experiences of Black women beyond their race but also their gender, sexual orientation, social class, etc. And now, intersectionality is an important step in understanding the multiple experiences of people with multiple identities. It is important to recognize that some identities are more culturally relevant and influential than others. For example, we often hear that men control a lot of resources, and possess significantly more privilege than women overall in our cultures. Embedded within this statement is the assumption that we are referencing *White, heterosexual, cis-gendered* men, as men of color, gay men, and trans-men (or any combination) are frequently marginalized by the patriarchal culture in North America within the context of their sexual and gendered identity. However, wealth and prestige may buffer some stigma if that person also possesses other characteristics that easily align with and support values of Whiteness. In this section, we provide specific examples of how intersectionality impacts oppression.

COMPLEXITIES OF INTERSECTIONALITY WITHIN THE LGBTQ+ COMMUNITY

Issues related to intersectionality are the foundation for much conflict within the lesbian, gay, bisexual, transgender, and queer (LGBTQ+; the "+" indicating a more inclusive spectrum with other implied identities including, but not limited to, questioning, intersex, and asexual) community. Media representations of PRIDE celebrations continued to gain traction in recent years, along with significant advances in civil rights for people within the non-heteronormative spectrum. However, even though social progress originated from a sense of a united front, the reality is that community includes much division, and all within the LGBTQ+ umbrella are not treated equally.

White men typically possess the potential for higher cultural privilege and power, but White men who fall outside of expected heterosexual norms frequently face prejudice and discrimination based on their queer identities (Connell, 1995; Sedwick, 1993). Due to such marginalization, White gay men may be unaware of the discrimination that they exert on people of color (Uwujaren, 2014) who are already at higher risk of discriminatory consequences based on intersections of sexual minority status and African American (e.g., Battle & Lemelle, 2002), Asian American (e.g., Chan, 1989), Latina/o American (e.g., Zea, Reisen, & Díaz, 2003), or indigenous American (e.g., Gilley & Co-Cké, 2005) heritage. In actuality, the same organized groups that worked tirelessly to gain 'gay acceptance' within North American culture, did so by promoting mainstream images reflecting Whiteness in order to make such acceptance more palatable (Bérubé, 2001).

For decades, gay bars have served as a safe haven for people with LGBTQ+ identities, but these supposedly inclusive social spaces also have a history of racial and gendered segregation. Practitioners need to be aware of the conflict and discrimination among various communities experiencing oppression. For example, gay institutions are notorious for excluding non-White representations from their marketing efforts (Han, 2007), and Black gays and lesbians generally do not experience any sense of community created from an entirely White perspective (Shuttlesworth, 2004). Even gay spaces that explicitly market some days and activities towards lesbians can be sites for hostility and misogyny by gay men (Johnson & Samdahl, 2005). Additionally, some gay men adopt and maintain a more virulent White identity of dominance as gay racialist skinheads (Waldner, Martin, & Capeder, 2006). This attitude and behavior serves as an example of how oppressed groups (i.e., gay men) can be oppressors of other groups.

Despite rights and respect for transgender and gender non-conforming people gaining significant ground in recent years, when trans-persons seek refuge from discrimination in gay leisure settings, they often find implicit and explicit prejudice, discrimination, and aggression from the gay men who usually dominate these spaces (Lewis & Johnson, 2011). As community developers, we need to be aware that activities created for the purpose of equality alone do not necessarily combat oppression.

Some intersections, such as body size and sexual identity may play out differently. Lesbians identified as overweight are stigmatized much less than gay men who do not fit the expected body standards, even though heterosexual men may not be stigmatized at all by excess weight (Fikkan & Rothblum, 2012). Body size and ability are frequently scrutinized within North American culture, regardless of sexual orientation or gender identity. Below, Stephen's story draws from his work on the stigmatization of obesity to further illustrate complexities of intersectionality and oppression in community recreation. Specifically, how an individual has overcome her struggles with being queer to her "super religious parents," yet continues to feel excluded because of body size.

STEPHEN'S STORY

My Big Fat Taxes

As someone who has struggled with issues of social exclusion on different levels based on weight and body image since early childhood, I became interested with the issue on an academic level while pursuing my Master's degree. However, I found that many of the faculty I described my interests to wanted me to focus on exercise and weight loss, even though I wanted to explore the stigmatizing effects of bigger bodies as a constraint to desired leisure of all kinds. At that time, I was able to find very little on this topic. About seven years later, I picked up where I left off and found a rapidly emerging body of literature on 'obesity-stigma.' Since that time, I have researched and written on its relevance to recreation and leisure studies. Participants in my studies seem eager to talk about this thing that they often haven't been able to name or discuss with anyone else.

The following narrative comes from a larger interview I conducted with a college professor (she chose the pseudonym of "Mary") who expanded on a previous comment regarding why she became a 'recluse' in her late twenties a decade later.

I survived coming out as a young queer woman to my super religious parents, taking a stand and claiming my identity in such a way that they could no longer think of it as just a phase I was going through, but I continued to allow my parents, my coworkers, and even my friends to put me down because I was a big girl without ever challenging it . . . I guess I was raised just like them, and even now I sometimes catch myself judging someone because they are fat . . . It's a cultural thing, but it is so dangerous and so toxic.

I tried to play the apologetic role of the fat girl who was doing everything she could to lose weight. I only ate salads without dressing in front of people if I ate anything at all, and I joined every kind of exercise class you can think of. I actually attended most of them for a while, even though it triggered every bit of anxiety within me to even show up to a gym. Here is what I found though. Exercise equipment—not made for someone with a body like mine. Exercise instructors—don't know what the hell to do with fat people. I even went to an "inclusive yoga" session, and the instructor told me afterwards that she didn't really know what to do with me unless I would participate like the people who used a wheelchair. Paying close attention to her tone and the way she looked me up and down with disgust prevented me from ever coming back . . .

*When I was around thirty, I decided to just say, "f*ck it." I was feeling more empowered, more subversive, and was tired of making excuses for not doing the things I really wanted to do. I stopped worrying about losing weight, but still found it really hard to get involved... I love going to parks for nature walks, but there aren't enough benches along the way to gracefully take a break when I start sweating profusely and scaring other hikers with my heavy breathing [laughs].... Everybody tells me that I need to get out more and be more active, and I do want to, but even when there are chairs, and kind people, and a friend to go with, I always worry that the chairs won't fit me, or will break, and the people are going to hurt me with good intentions! I may be a fat girl, but I pay my big fat taxes just like everybody else. When will the public park and recreation system actually start supporting big people? We are everywhere!*

This participant's narrative resonated strongly with me based on my own experiences of prejudice, discrimination, and internalized stigma based on intersections between my weight and other attributes. As a researcher, I can safely intellectualize these complexities of intersectionality and oppression, but then as I reflect on a more personal level, I often become frustrated that I haven't been able to free myself from weight-related stigma, even though I know it to be socially constructed. As a recreation professional, I internally evaluate how welcoming or constraining public recreation organizations and resources are, and ponder how others might feel more welcome and included than I do. It is my hope that frank examples such as these might open up important dialogue for recreation specialists and community planners so that they might tackle these challenging dilemmas and increase availability of leisure spaces and opportunities within the community that accommodate and truly support participation for all people.

CHALLENGING THE OBESITY PANIC

We are constantly bombarded with alarming statistics of an obesity crisis that threatens our modern existence. While statistics do indicate that the majority of North Americans can be classified as clinically overweight or obese (Rossner, 2002), much of the money allocated towards research and programs designed to address this issue is driven by cultural myths and presumptions that are not supported by research (Casazza, et al., 2014). Well-intentioned educational programs, public health campaigns, and recreational services have contributed to the discrimination and oppression of individuals who are overweight. Educational programs have been documented as explicitly privileging "fit" bodies and stigmatizing "overweight" bodies in extreme ways (Russell, Cameron, Socha, & Ninch, 2013). Public health campaigns often contribute to the stigmatization, depicting negative imagery and focusing blame on adults and children who are overweight (see Figure 9.1), rather than focusing on the more controllable aspects of physical activity, moderate dietary changes, or taking on big processed food corporations. Recreation providers, as evidenced in Mary's narrative, are not prepared to adapt their services to the needs of people who are obese.

Discriminatory attitudes and campaigns are problematic both for the marginalization that they create, as well as for foundations in ableism, or, privileging an embodied ideal of what it is to be fit, healthy, and beautiful—becoming instantly unobtainable for millions of people with diverse appearances and (dis)abilities. Unintentional, yet discriminatory tones from

FIGURE 9.1 NEGATIVE IMAGERY CONTRIBUTING TO OBESITY (SOURCE: DASGUPTA (2013)

well-meaning public health campaigns are problematic and counter-productive since stigma reduces the chances of people engaging in public recreation (West, 1984), and leads to personal, interpersonal, and structural constraints and barriers to community leisure participation (Lewis & Van Puymbroeck, 2008; Liechty, Freeman, & Zabriskie, 2006; Newhouse & Lewis, 2014). If increased health is the rationale and intended outcome for public scorn and scrutiny, these efforts are misdirected since overweight children and adults can reap several benefits from community participation in physical activity, even if no weight loss is ever achieved (Duncan, et al., 2003).

People who are stigmatized and marginalized by other demographic attributes or abilities may experience the stigmatization of obesity in different ways (e.g. Carr & Friedman, 2005; Latner, et al., 2005; Hebl & Turchin, 2005). Mary's experience is one experience of being a queer, overweight, white female. If she was a woman of color, her experiences of marginalization and oppression may have been exacerbated and compounded by racial prejudice and discrimination experiences of oppression are incredibly complex due to the intersectionality of personal abilities, demographic characteristics, and attributes. As leisure professionals engaging in community development, we must intentionally look for and mediate the variety of stigmas and oppressive factors that are keeping people from participating in your community building process.

Reflection Questions:

Stephen`s story highlights one person's narrative, but is congruent with emerging literature on recreation and leisure services inadequacy in addressing the needs of bigger participants. The good news is that those of us in the fields of recreation and community development can make a difference by acknowledging their own anti-fat biases and working to develop and promote more inclusive programming and recreational spaces. Please keep these ideas in mind when answering the following questions:

Considering the obstacles Mary faced in participating in community-based programs, what would you prioritize as the three top issues that need to be immediately addressed in order to promote inclusive, body-positive community-recreation programs?

What ties can you apply from this example to the way we design our urban landscapes in terms of recreational paths and spaces?

What specific recommendations can you make to academic programs in order to better empower emerging public recreation and community development professionals to promote non-stigmatizing health initiatives for all body types?

BECOMING AGENTS OF CHANGE

Consciously acknowledging issues of power, privilege, and oppression constitutes an important step towards becoming a more reflexive practitioner and an agent of change. However, in order to make real positive difference, this knowledge must be applied to a variety of approaches on a variety of levels as we strive to combat oppression. Collective action focuses on the programming process (micro level), policy change presents an institutional approach (meso level), and distributive justice offers a broader level of change (macro level). Confronting each level is important in resisting the peaceful violence of oppression. Notably, these approaches are not mutually exclusive. In others words changes on one level will influence the others. For example, an outcome of collective action may lead to a change in policy.

COLLECTIVE ACTION

Facilitating authentic relationships and recognizing humanity are key elements to collective action. Even when trying to enact justice by acting on behalf of a marginalized individual, group, or community, we must consider how much more powerful it would be to have authentic representation, and stand *by the side* of those who traditionally had less of a voice in such matters. For instance, when we act on behalf of others, we should do so as their ally, always considering oppressive forces that have created discrepancies in power. Acting *with* these communities provides more potential for bringing authentic information into the public arena (Lewis, Arnold, House, & Toporek, 2003).

AUTHENTIC RELATIONSHIPS

Mansuri and Rao (2004) identified the lack of outcomes associated with well-intended community development projects that aimed to be 'community-driven' with participation from targeted community groups. Typically, the power remained with the more privileged developers, creating barriers to authentic participation, particularly from those with less socioeconomic privilege. Within urban centers, it is not uncommon to find public arts programs directing inner-city youth to participate in collaborative efforts. However, it is difficult to find documented input from the families and communities of young people, and the young people themselves. In contrast, a program that effectively integrated the needs and voices of Indigenous Australians found that the collective voice created from such initiatives could serve as a bridge to authentic communication with non-indigenous community members (Sonn & Quayle, 2013).

As community developers and recreation professionals, we should always interrogate the role we play to facilitate the creation, implementation, and evaluation of programs; constantly balancing resources and the needs of the larger community with the buy-in and partnership with those representing different facets of the community which might otherwise be ignored. This can create a powerful platform for communication and self-advocacy. Indeed, opportunities for community leadership, organizing, and engagement are important to youth and adults, especially in communities struggling to achieve a level of social capital often needed to achieve community-level empowerment (Nissen, 2011). It is therefore urgent to enact reflexivity when partnering with community members to examine the best types of support to create pathways to these less tangible resources of power. Chapter 20 offers *compassionate pedagogy* as a specific approach towards reflexivity.

HUMANITY

We believe the cycle of oppression can be mediated by the recognition of humanity. Once we move away from overly simplistic, binary notions of community members as either 'insiders' or 'outsiders' and examine the complexity of all of the interacting forces (local government, community developers, recreation agencies, privileged and marginalized community members, activists, etc.), we can start building more authentic communication and partnerships (Sonn & Quayle, 2013). In other words, every person involved needs to be engaged in meaningful relationships and dialogue. While this is a lengthy process, it is crucial. Discovering the potential for change involves focusing on the assets and strengths of each person (see Chapter 8) and a desire to understand. As Yuen and Context(e (2013) state, "'we are not working with a building, we are not working with a job title, we are working with a person'... It is not enough to receive the empathetic response, '*I understand.*' True encouragement, support, and acceptance are communicated and felt by expressions of a desire to understand (p. 364).

ISSUES OF POLICY

Policies, whether within a specific a recreation center or at the federal level, inevitably influence the way in which leisure services are offered and have the potential to overcome, or exacerbate and legitimize, marginalization and oppression. In Canada, the Quebec provincial government proposed the Quebec Charter of Values in 2013. Under the premise of preserving the neutrality of the state and secularism, the Charter would ban 'overt and conspicuous' religious symbols by government sector employees (e.g., community recreation centers, teachers, judges). These symbols included large visible crucifixes, niqabs, turbans, hijabs, and kippas. The enactment of this Charter effectively targeted Orthodox Jewish men, Sikh men, and Muslim women. Such a policy privileged the dominant society and delivered a message of exclusion and intolerance. As noted by Glover's (2007) critique of color-blindness and exposure of White privilege in American Little League baseball practices and policies, the absence of representation of marginalized groups in the provision of leisure services can lead to a lack of role models, isolation of minority participants, and spectator behavior. The proposal of this Charter was labeled racist and discriminatory by politicians and citizens alike and never came to pass as a new government was elected into power the following year. Nonetheless, similar policies have been proposed and passed in France and other parts of the world.

From the example above, we can see how policies on the surface might seem benign, or possibly beneficial (in this case supposedly supporting "neutrality"), can actually result in divisiveness and oppression. Even though this example was at the provincial-level, the policies we create within workplaces and recreational centers may be embedded with discriminatory mechanisms less visible to those with multiple intersections of privilege. For example, consider how the creation of specific dress codes can marginalize people of not only different cultural backgrounds, but also diverse gender identities and expressions. The reflexive practitioner will frequently question existing policies that are unjust, and advocate for the creation of policies that help to promote inclusivity and honour the rich diversity within our communities.

DISTRIBUTIVE JUSTICE

Where a collective action approach emphasizes working with all stakeholders in the process of programming, and a policy approach emphasizes changing the institutionalized structure, the distributive justice approach encourages us to reconsider the values that guide our everyday actions. Discrepancies of power and privilege are often tied to unequal distribution of resources. This type of inequality is central to the need for distributive justice initiatives. The ways in which individuals and communities define and prioritize community resources varies significantly, but often factors such as financial resources, affordable housing, public safety, healthcare, transportation, employment opportunities, natural resources, and recreational spaces, are common discourse in this regard. The idea of *distributive justice* implies that citizens are entitled to the fair distribution of such resources. For example, over the past decades, we have witnessed huge developments in policy regarding access to resources by persons with disabilities. Something as simple (that many of us take for granted) as designated parking spaces and accessible toilets have provided increased empowerment to people with physical, cognitive, and other types of disabling conditions.

While the designated parking spaces and accessible toilets are simple steps towards distributive justice, the incorporation of this value, much less straightforward. The following example provides an idea of how distributive justice challenges our notions of entitlement and ownership. In the United States, the Lakota Sioux tribe is exerting a collective voice against the proposed strip-mining in the Black Hills. On one side, developers see this area as rich in natural resources that should be accessed and distributed, as well as create enormous profits for those in power. In contrast, The Lakota Sioux see clean water, air, and land as more valuable than the non-renewable resources that the developers are seeking. This battle is similar to that faced by many indigenous groups who place high value on their historical and spiritual ties to land that continues to vanish during continued post-colonial development (Moore, 2012). This example can serve as a metaphor to what some consider a type of urban colonization happening within our contemporary cultures. The likely outcome inevitably prioritizes the (profit-driven) values of the dominant White perspective.

Moving from the example of strip-mining to one that one that is more related to leisure are the decisions we make to significantly alter (improve) our communities. We take actions such as adding green spaces and parks and revitalizing districts in hopes of enhancing the aesthetics, and increasing safety, the economy, and social capital within that area. Paradoxically, some of the biggest 'success stories' raise property values so high that former residents are forced out. The same thing happens when areas of business and tourism become so popular that outside retailers and chains force local business out of business. There is no simple answer. Enacting distributive justice requires community developers to consciously consider the minority; the voices and the stories of people who are affected, but not yet been heard. It is our duty to ensure that they are heard, understood, and respected in the decision-making process.

Different neighborhoods and districts within each town and city have access to different types of resources. Such distribution is inequitable. As exemplified in Rasul's story, those with more privilege frequently feel a sense of entitlement to *all* areas, while questioning (and sometimes even opposing) the participation of people perceived to come from non-White racial and ethnic groups, and/or lower-income areas. The reflexive practitioner who embraces values of distributive justice, is charged with the difficult task of partnering with community members to advocate for and obtain needed resources that can remain within the grasp of community members. This will undoubtedly require creativity and innovation. When creating recreational programs and facilities, we strive for authentic input, engagement, and leadership from actual members of the community, and aim to embrace that community's culture without stereotyping or exotifying. A positive agent of change is an advocate who thinks beyond their own needs, values, and experiences to partner and facilitate enrichment within the communities they serve.

CONCLUSION: YOUR PERSONAL MANIFESTO

Throughout this chapter, you have been asked to consider oppression within our communities, originating from imbalances in power and privilege among citizens. You have also been charged with the task of actively processing how your own experiences shape your perceptions towards these discussions, as well as to explore some ways that you can help resist the perpetuation of an oppressive status quo and become an agent for justice and change. The idea of leisure as peaceful violence, and that it can and has contributed to the oppression of marginalized populations is unsettling. We urge you to become agents of change and develop the capacity to be in "sustained conversation[s] with those who are assaulted by oppression, resisting it and/or cleaning up the mess created by widespread social injustice" (Fine, 2006, p. 99). In working through differences, we can work with the oppressed to create human encounters that are reciprocally beneficial, non-oppressive, and most importantly capable of restoring human dignity.

We purposefully leave this chapter open-ended rather than trying to provide a distinct 'conclusion,' as communities are just as fluid and intersectional as those of individuals. There is unfortunately no handbook with all of the right answers, but we hope that this chapter has sparked meaningful thoughts, conversations, and goals for both current and future community development professionals specializing in the area of recreation and leisure. Rather than provide additional reflection questions, we leave you with an exercise that will help you to synthesize and further process the critical issues presented. We hope you will use this exercise to celebrate the professional you want to be, and the difference you can make.

Your Professional Manifesto

In order to process and apply this content to your intentions as a future or continuing practitioner in community development, please take a few moments to create a short "Professional Manifesto" consisting of at least ten statements of the type of professional you want to be. Each line should start with an "I statement" (e.g. I will; I believe; I respect; I value; etc.), and should be tied to your main "take-aways" from this chapter. You might want to look over your earlier reflections, as well as consider including statements related to the following:

How you will acknowledge and challenge your own privilege; especially in terms of the way it influences your worldview and practice in the field?

What positive ways do you see diversity/intersectionality creating richer, and more authentic communities?

What kind of reflexive practitioner you wish to be when serving as an ally to any of the frequently marginalized groups referenced within this chapter?

What are some opportunities we have to make recreation, leisure, and other community spaces safer, and more inclusive?

What are some intentional ways you plan to become more involved in policy creation and change, and justice initiatives?

After the completion of your professional manifesto, we encourage you to share the statements you have created that resonate most strongly with you. Also, as comfort allows, consider sharing some of the issues you continue to struggle with, and/or found the hardest to read and reflect upon with a friend or a colleague. Be supportive of one another and try to be open to differing points of view, especially considering how the different intersectionality within different group members creates different foundations from which to start.

REFERENCES

Allison, M. T. (1999). Organizational barriers to diversity in the workplace. *Journal of Leisure Research, 31*(1), 78–101.

Ansley, F. L. (1997). White Supremacy (and what we should do about it). In R. Delgado and J. Stefancic (Eds.), *Critical white studies: Looking behind the mirror,* (pp. 592–595). Philadelphia: Temple University Press.

Battle, J., & Lemelle, A. J. (2002). Gender differences in African American attitudes toward gay males. *Western Journal of Black Studies, 26*(3), 134–139.

Bérubé, A. (2001). How gay stays white and what kind of white it stays. In B. B. Rasmussen, E. Klineberg, I. J. Nexica, & M. Wray (Eds.), *The making and unmaking of whiteness.* Durham, NC: Duke University Press.

Bulhan, H. A. (1985). *Frantz Fanon and the psychology of oppression.* New York: Plenum Press.

Carr, D., & Friedman, M. A. (2005). Is obesity stigmatizing? Body weight, perceived discrimination, and psychological well-being in the United States. *Journal of Health and Social Behavior, 46*(3), 244–259.

Carter, P. L. (2008). Coloured places and pigmented holidays: Racialized leisure travel. *Tourism Geographies, 10,* 265–284.

Casazza, K., Brown, A., Astrup, A., Bertz, F., Baum, C., Bohan, B. M., . . . George, A. B. (2014). Weighing the evidence of common beliefs in obesity research. *Critical Reviews in Food Science and Nutrition,* (Epub ahead of print).

Chan, C. S. (1989). Issues of Identity Development among Asian-American Lesbians and Gay Men. *Journal of Counseling & Development, 68*(1), 16–20.

Connell, R. W. (1995). *Masculinities.* Cambridge, UK: Polity Press.

Crenshaw, K. (1999). Mapping the margins: Intersectionality, identity politics, and violence against women of color. *Stanford Law Review, 43*(6), 1241–1299.

DasGupta, S. (2013, April 13). Controlling portions, controlling pregnancies: Race and class panic in New York City public health campaigns [web log comment]. Retrieved from http://www.racialicious.com/2013/04/03/controlling-portions-controlling-pregnancies-race-and-class-panic-in-new-york-city-public-health-campaigns/

Duncan, G. E., Perri, M. G., Theriaque, D. W., Hutson, A. D., Eckel, R. H., & Stacpoole, P. W. (2003). Exercise training without weight loss, increases insulin sensitivity and postheparin plasma lipase activity in previously sedentary adults. *Diabetes Care, 26*(3), 557–562.

Dupuis, S. L. (1999). Naked truths: Towards a reflexive methodology in leisure research. *Leisure Science, 21,* 43–64.

Edwards, H. (1979). Sport within the veil: The triumphs, tragedies, and challenges of Afro-American involvement. *Annals of the American Academy of Political and Social Science, 445* (contemporary issues in sport), 116–127.

Fanon, F. (1963). *The wretched of the Earth.* (Constance Farrington, trans.). New York: Grove Press.

Fikkan, J. L, & Rothblum, E. D. (2012). Is fat a feminist issue? Exploring the gendered nature of weight bias. *Sex Roles, 66,* 575–592.

Fine, M. (2006). Bearing witness: Methods for researching oppression and resistance—A textbook for critical research. *Social Justice Research, 19*(1), 83–108.

Floyd, M. F. (2007). Research on race and ethnicity in leisure: Anticipating the fourth wave. *Leisure/Loisir, 31*(1), 245–254.

Fox, K. M. (2000). Echoes of leisure: Questions, challenges, and potentials. *Journal of Leisure Research, 32*(1), 32–36.

Fox, K. M. & Lashua, B. D. (2010). Hold gently people who create space on the margins: Urban Aboriginal-Canadian young people and hip-hop rhythms of "leisures." In D. Reid, H. Mair, & S. Arai (Eds.), *Decentring work: Critical perspectives on leisure, development and social change* (pp. 229–250). Calgary, AB: University of Calgary Press.

Freire, P. (1970). *Pedagogy of the oppressed.* New York: Continuum.

Gibson, N. C. (2003). *Fanon: The postcolonial imagination.* Cambridge: Polity Press.

Gilley, B. J., & Co-Cké, J. H. (2005). Cultural investment: Providing opportunities to reduce risky behavior among gay American Indian males. *Journal of Psychoactive Drugs, 37*(3), 293–298.

Glover, T. D. (2007). Ugly on the Diamonds: An Examination of White Privilege in Youth Baseball. *Leisure Studies, 29*(2), 195–208.

Han, C.-S. (2007). They don't want to cruise your type: Gay men of color and the racial politics of exclusion. *Social Identities, 13*(1), 51–67.

Hanna, F. J., Talley, W. B., & Guindon, M. H. (2000). The power of perception: Toward a model of cultural oppression and liberation. *Journal of Counseling & Development, 78,* 430–441.

Hannah-Moffat, K. (2001). *Punishment in disguise: Penal governance and federal imprisonment of women in Canada.* Toronto: University of Toronto Press Inc.

Harrison, A. K. (2013). Black skiing, everyday racism, and the racial spatiality of whiteness. *Journal of Sport and Social Issues, 37*(4), 315–339.

Hebl, M. R., & Turchin, J. M. (2005). The stigma of obesity: What about men? *Basic and Applied Social Psychology, 27*(3), 267–275.

Johnson, C. W., & Samdahl, D. M. (2005). The night they took over: Misogyny in a country-western gay bar. *Leisure Sciences, 27*(4), 331–348.

Lattinzio, V. (2009, July 10). Swim club members: "Nothing to with race." *NBC News10*. Retrieved from http://www.nbcphiladelphia.com/news/archive/Swim-Club-Members-Nothing-to-Do-With-Race.html

Lea, Y. S. (2012). From oppression to negotiation: Constructing a generative identity. International Proceedings of Economics Development & Research, 40, 71–76.

Lee, G. (2006, September 3). Black travelers join the club. *Washington Post*. Retrieved from http://www.washingtonpost.com/wpdyn/content/article/2006/09/01/AR2006090100506.html

Lewin, K. (1946). Action research and minority problems. *Journal of Social Issues, 2*, 34–46.

Lewis, J., Arnold, M. S., House, R., & Toporek, R. L. (2003). Advocacy competencies: American Counseling Association Task Force on Advocacy Competencies. Retrieved from http://www.counseling.org/Resources/Competencies/Advocacy_Competencies.pdf

Lewis, S. T., & Johnson, C. W. (2011). "But it's not *that* easy": Negotiating (trans)gender expressions in leisure spaces. *Leisure/Loisir, 35*(2), 115–132.

Lewis, S. T., & Van Puymbroeck, M. (2008). Obesity-stigma as a multifaceted constraint to leisure. *Journal of Leisure Research, 40*(4), 574–588.

Liechty, T., Freeman, P. A., & Zabriskie, R. B. (2006). Body image and beliefs about appearance: Constraints on the leisure of college-age and middle-age women. *Leisure Sciences, 28*(4), 311–330.

Mansuri, G., & Rao, V. (2004). Community-based and -driven development: A critical review. *The World Bank Research Observer, 19*(1), 1–39.

McIntosh, Peggy. (1988). White privilege and male privilege: A personal account of coming to see correspondences through work in women's studies. In M. Anderson and P. H. Collins (Eds.), *Race, class, and gender: An anthology*, (3rd ed), (pp. 94–105). NY: Wadsworth Publishing Company.

Moore, M. (2012). Resources, territorial right, and global distributive justice. *Political Theory, 40*(1), 84–107.

Mowatt, R. A. (2009). Notes from a leisure son: Expanding an understanding of Whiteness in leisure. *Journal of Leisure Research, 41*(4), 509–526.

Mowatt, R. A. (2012). Lynching as leisure: Broadening notions of a field. *American Behavioral Scientist, 56*(10), 1361–1387.

Mowatt, R. A. (2013). Constructing White Supremacy or privilege: Deconstructing "whiteness" in leisure studies. *Leisure Studies Association Newsletter, 94*, 45–50.

Mowatt, R. A. & Schmalz, D. L. (2014). The conspicuous nature of power. *Journal of Leisure Research, 46*(3), 353.

Newhouse, G., & Lewis, S. T., (in press). Obesity-stigma and the 'Why Try' model: Implications for outdoor recreation constraint negotiation. *Journal of Outdoor Recreation, Education and Leadership.*

Nissen, L. B. (2011). Community-directed engagement and positive youth development: Developing positive and progressive pathways between youth and their communities in Reclaiming Futures. *Children and youth services review, 33*, S23—S28.

Philipp, S. (2000). Race and the pursuit of happiness. *Journal of Leisure Research, 32*(1), 121–124.

Pedlar A., Arai, S., & Yuen, F. (2007). Media representation of federally sentenced women and leisure opportunities: Ramifications of social inclusion. *Leisure/Loisir, 31*(1), 255–276.

Pedlar, A., Arai, S., Yuen, F., & Fortune D. (2008). *Uncertain futures: Women leaving prison and re-entering community.* Retrieved from http://www.ahs.uwaterloo.ca/uncertainfutures/

Pedlar, A., Yuen, F., & Fortune, D. (2008). Incarcerated women and leisure: Making good girls out of bad? *Therapeutic Recreation Journal: Special Issue, Mental Health and transcending Life Challenges: The Role of Therapeutic Recreation Services, 42*(1), 24–36.

Rossner, S. (2002). Obesity: The disease of the twenty-first century. *International Journal of Obesity, 26*, S2–S4.

Russell, C., Cameron, E., Socha, T., & McNinch, H. (2013). "Fatties Cause Global Warming": Fat pedagogy and environmental education. *Canadian Journal of Environmental Education, 18*(1), 15–33.

Sedwick, E. K. (1993). Epistemology of the closet. In H. Abelove, M. A. Barale, & D. M. Halperin (Eds.), *The lesbian and gay studies reader* (pp. 45–61). New York: Routledge.

Shuttlesworth, F. (2004). Is gay rights a civil rights issue? *Ebony, 59*(9), 142–146.

Sibley, D. (1995). *Geographies of exclusion.* London, England: Routledge.

Sonn, C. C., & Quayle, A. F. (2013). Developing praxis: Mobilising critical race theory in community cultural development. *Journal of Community and Applied Social Psychology*. doi:10.1002/casp.2145

Uwujaren, J. (2014, April 24). The gay community tends to pride itself on being anti-discriminatory but is that true? *Media Diversified.* Retrieved from http://mediadiversified.org/2014/04/24/the-gay-community-tends-to-pride-itself-on-being-anti-discriminatory-but-is-that-true/

Waldner, L. K., Martin, H., & Capeder, L. (2006). Ideology of gay racialist skinheads and stigma management techniques. *Journal of Political and Military Sociology, 34*(1), 165–184.

Walter, M. (2010). Market forces and Indigenous resistance paradigms. *Social Movement Studies, 9*(2), 121–137.

West, P. C. (1984). Social stigma and community recreation participation by the mentally and physically handicapped. *Therapeutic Recreation Journal, 18*(1), 221–249.

Yuen, F., Arai, S., & Fortune, D. (2012). Women in prison, community dislocation and reconnection through leisure: A poetic representation of incarcerated women's experiences of leisure and connection to community. *Leisure Sciences, 34*(4), 1–17.

Yuen, F., & Context(e, G. (2013). A Bridge to Alien-Nation: Connecting through Humanity, Diversity and Relationship. *International Journal of Child, Youth and Family Studies, 4*(3), 357–370.

Zea, M. C., Reisen, C. A., & Díaz, R. M. (2003). Methodological issues in research issues on sexual behavior with Latino gay and bisexual men. *American Journal of Community Psychology, 31*(3/4), 281–291.

10
COMMUNITY-BASED RESEARCH: ENGAGING CITIZENS IN CREATING CHANGE

Peggy Hutchison, John Lord, and Theron Kramer

INTRODUCTION

Imagine you have a chance to do some research for a community organization or for your employer. You may be hesitant at first because you do not have much research experience. But hopefully you are also excited because you can see the possibility of research as a vehicle for change. Historically, research has been seen as one way to increase our understanding of the world around us by creating knowledge for innovation and community change (Patton, 2001).

You may not be the only one hesitant about research. It is not unusual for people and organizations in our communities to be cautious about getting involved in research. They may have heard about other research projects where the needs of the researcher rather than the community were paramount. They may have experienced research where the results were soon forgotten, without any meaningful change having taken place.

Based on a three-year collaboration between low-income women, community partners, and a research team using community-based research, Frisby and colleagues noted that community members may not always trust researchers or the research process, as one community partner in their project described:

> *Some of the older women were very suspicious of the research initially. In the past, researchers have come in and have taken what they need, and we never hear from them again. I told the women not to worry, that you were different, that you [the researchers] were a community development type of researcher who will listen to them and give something back.* (Frisby, Reid, Millar, & Hoeber, 2005, p. 374)

What if there is a research approach available to leisure, sport, or tourism professionals that could actually *address people's needs* by creating changes that could make a difference? What if there is a research approach that *fully engages stakeholders* and involved citizens in genuine and full participation with people at all stages of the research process (Ateljevic, Prichard, & Morgan, 2007; Veal, 2011)? What if there is research that is more *qualitative and inductive* with less concern about the research being objective and value-free as in quantitative research (Creswell, 2013; Dupuis, 1999; Henderson, 2006)? What if communities could do research that would allow them to address *issues of social justice?* Some of these issues are outlined in Table 10.1.

There is a particular way of approaching research that is uniquely designed for doing research in the community referred to as "community-based research" (Hutchison & Lord, 2012). This alternative approach to research is part of a new paradigm that is considered transformative. Its basic tenet is that the development of knowledge is not neutral and reflects the power and social relationships in society. Researchers committed to community-based research believe that people, particularly those who are marginalized due to age, disability, gender, sexual orientation, ethnicity, or poverty need to be engaged in creating knowledge that helps them to change society (Kirby, Greaves, & Reid, 2006; Mertens, 2009). As their issues are studied, community members and researchers work collaboratively to design and implement the research. This includes the provision of a research process, which not only includes the voices of study participants but also has the potential to raise people's awareness and change their lives (Cresswell, 2013; Dupuis et al., 2012).

Over the last 30 years, all three of us have been involved in a wide range of community-based research projects. We have played leadership roles in the Centre for Community-Based Research, which has completed over 300 research studies and evaluations using community-based research approaches (2014a). We have also

TABLE 10.1 POTENTIAL COMMUNITY DEVELOPMENT RESEARCH ISSUES

The following are potential research issues which could interest professionals working in the areas of leisure, recreation, sports, or tourism. Examples of a few of these subjects will be used throughout this chapter as we explore how community-based research can support you in your community development role.

As you explore the following issues that may be most pertinent to your field of interest, it may be useful to think about what you would be hoping to change as a result of your research, which would be affected by the results of your research (stakeholders), who would want to be involved in designing your research. This could include those who would be able to help determine the questions you want to ask, people you need to get data from, how and where you might reach the people who might want to talk to, who might be involved in giving feedback on your results, and who needs to see the final research report.

Target Groups	Health & Well-Being	Organizational Issues	Other
• Children involved in after-school programs • High risk, homeless, school drop-out youth • Seniors in need of day programs or other specialized services • Women or men in prison or other institutional care • Single parents • Persons with disabilities • People in group homes • First Nations, Indigenous, Aboriginal persons • Rural communities	• Active living strategies that work • Inclusion, social support, and sense of community • Building social capital • Family cohesion • Neighborhood safety and/or capacity • Isolated communities • Bullying • Loneliness • Obesity and fitness • Chronic illness and role of community support • Poverty and program/service access • Health and safety of tourism/recreation/sports/cultural workers	• Partnerships (e.g., between police and youth workers) • Volunteerism (e.g., effectiveness of current volunteer recruitment, training, retention) • Professionalism (e.g., advantages/disadvantages of professional associations) • Use of public spaces (e.g., use of schools after hours) • User fees (e.g., equitable access to subsidy programs) • Effectiveness of not-for-profit organizations (e.g., minor sports associations) • Training for sports/recreation/tourism/arts & culture workers (e.g., health & safety)	• Best practice in applying community development strategies to leisure and recreation program development • How community gardens contribute to health of participants • Role of municipalities in neighborhood development • Role of volunteers in park and trail maintenance • How current environmental concerns contribute to citizen willingness to support retention of urban natural areas • Citizen involvement in creation of municipal Leisure Master plans, Sports & Recreation Strategic Plans, etc.

been deeply committed to community development approaches in our own community as well as in several provincial and national initiatives.

Linking community development and community-based research in sport, tourism, and leisure studies. Research is often the first stage of the community development process as it helps the community determine its needs and concerns. However, long-standing community development initiatives may also benefit from research. For example, research that helps the community document what has been learned through the community development process and/or how that process may be improved as it progresses. Like community developers, community-based researchers pay attention to the context and the concerns reflected by local citizens.

Whether in the early stages of a community-based research project, or later, as part of an evaluation, it is important to choose a research process that is consistent with community development principles and practices as outlined in Part A of this book. Most importantly, the research process should be understandable to the citizens who are participating (Reid, 2006) and should involve them directly in its design. Including them fully also means paying attention to the power dynamics that are inherent in any inclusive community development process. Relative to research, that means paying attention to the perceived or actual power imbalance that may exist between the researcher (often seen as the expert) and the community participants.

One of the first sport and leisure researchers to realize that community development can be initiated and facilitated by community-based research was Wendy Frisby (2002). Frisby believes that community development research endeavors must utilize a new way of approaching the relationship between research, participants, and researcher. She suggests that it is vital for community researchers to be self-critical in order to ensure that researcher-participant relationships are based on mutual respect and equality.

> *If it is community development processes we want to understand as leisure researchers through theoretical critique and empirical analysis, we must turn the gaze on ourselves by critically*

> *reflecting on how our roles, responsibilities, and relationships with study participants may reinforce the very power imbalances that we are seeking to dismantle.* (Frisby, 2006, p. 438)

This chapter supports the premise that community-based research (CBR), because of its focus on citizen participation and action, is an excellent fit with community development.

WHAT IS COMMUNITY-BASED RESEARCH (CBR)?

The Centre for Community-Based Research (2014a), with a thirty-year history of doing CBR, has identified three essential components: community situated, collaborative, and action oriented.

Community situated means that research, and hence the learning and action that arises from the research, needs to be inclusive of the community that is being impacted. Researchers need to understand the nature of community and how it links with community development and citizen engagement.

Collaborative is about a working or cooperative relationship between researchers and individuals or members of community organizations. Collaborative research in CBR is concerned with addressing power imbalances between researchers and participants, particularly if the research is with underserved or marginalized citizens. This is essential in order that tokenism is avoided. Collaboration in this context may even mean using some research participants as co-researchers.

Action oriented in CBR means that any research endeavor must intentionally be concerned with the need for change. Furthermore, that change must be relevant to the lives of the participants. In other words, the process and results are useful to community members/organizations involved in making constructive social change.

The text box below provides a practical example of how the three components (community situated, collaborative, and action oriented) play out.

A STUDY TO ILLUSTRATE THE THREE ELEMENTS OF COMMUNITY-BASED RESEARCH

Support networks have long been considered an important part of people's quality of life. Community leaders, engaged citizens, and community-based researchers came together in one community to design a study that would enhance the support networks of citizens who were lonely and isolated. *Grounded in community,* this study began with a steering committee that was committed to using research as a way to build capacity in the community for strong, vibrant support networks with a number of local citizens. The goal was to implement several support networks, known as support clusters, study their process and outcomes, and learn from the experience.

This study was *collaborative.* The steering committee, comprised of two researchers, representatives from several local organizations, engaged citizens, and staff who were building the support networks, worked together on all aspects of the study. The researchers played the role of facilitators, as they created a process that enabled everyone to participate in designing the research and choosing appropriate research methods. Collaboration was also evident in the way the study was conducted. Researchers and volunteers participated in the network development, and jointly documented the progress and issues that networks faced as they evolved.

From the outset, the study had an *action component.* The steering committee saw the value in a design that would enable them to "learn as you go." Support network development was phased in, with surveys and interview questions being used at each three-month milestone period. Feedback from the research was then used to shape the next phase of the work. As a result of this focus on action, the study was able to disseminate an important document designed to assist facilitators and communities to be effective in nurturing support networks. (Ochocka & Lord, 1998)

These three components of community-based research are consistent with the underlying premises of community development. What links them together in practice are the principles that underlie their process. Community-based researchers use principles to guide their work and to assist community groups to stay on track in the research process. The Centre for Community-Based Research (2014b), for example, has ten principles that help ensure that community, collaboration, and action all remain central in any community-based research applied to community development. Four principles most relevant to our discussion are in Table 10.2.

TABLE 10.2 EXAMPLES OF PRINCIPLES THAT GUIDE COMMUNITY-BASED RESEARCH

Principle 1: Research should do no harm to participants, staff, users, and others.
Implications for Practice: If you are undertaking CBR, then you should have your research reviewed for ethical considerations. This ethics review will address issues such as free and informed consent, voluntary participation, and confidentiality.
Principle 2: Citizens who have a stake in the process and outcomes of the research should be actively involved in the research process.
Implications for Practice: For example, a study around the issue of poverty would include citizens who are living below the poverty line, anti-poverty activists, and employment services representatives in a steering group.
Principle 3: Listening to people affected by the issues is central to understanding.
Implications for Practice: Interviews, focus groups and other methods must include those who are affected by the issue. For example, in a study on issues related to aging, those who deliver service, so-called 'experts,' may be included but their voices will never dominate the research data.
Principle 4: Community development is best understood in context, including 'person in his or her environment.'
Implications for Practice: If the study relates to independent living for persons with disabilities, the study should interview people in their living situation, in order to get a sense of what it means to live independently. You would also want to interview people who support those individuals.

HOW DOES CBR SUPPORT COMMUNITY DEVELOPMENT?

There are several ways that community-based research supports community development: assessing needs for change, understanding process, considering impact and outcomes, and supporting developmental evaluation.

Assessing the need for change. Communities often find that community-based research is useful as they assess the need for change. In traditional research, the process often starts with the researchers' own interest in the issue, along with a literature search. However, within a community-based research framework, the researcher starts with the community and engages citizens in identifying what is important to them. In some cases, the community itself identifies a need and searches out a researcher.

Needs assessment has traditionally focused on a community's weaknesses or deficits. As community development practitioners have learned about the power of asset-based or strengths-based approaches (see Chapters 2, 7 and 8), they have been looking for complementary research approaches. CBR assists communities to identify assets and to consider how assets and capacities can be used to strengthen what needs to change in the community. For example, if we were looking at children's recreation programs, community members and the researcher might think together about the neighborhood and what needs to change in order to build on existing strengths related to diversity, location, skills, and experience of residents.

Understanding process. When you are committed to citizen involvement at all levels of the development and implementation of your research, then you understand that there will be dynamics in the CD process that heighten the need to pay attention to relationships and interactions among participants, including the dynamics between citizen participants and the researcher. For example, a researcher who is facilitating a steering group exploring the recreation needs in a neighborhood should pay attention to potential power dynamics between, for example, municipal recreation staff who have control and authority over how recreation facilities and programs are managed, and families who want to use these same facilities and programs but perhaps in a different way than how they are currently being provided.

By paying attention to context and process, not just outcomes, it is possible to gain insight into social change. Researchers do not need to wait until the end of a project for those insights. Instead, it is more useful to analyze the process along the way, including tracking and documenting lessons learned. This focus on context and process enables us to discover what works and what does not work. This idea of 'learning along the way' maximizes our insights into community development and social change.

Considering outcomes and impact. Although understanding process is vital in community development, people engaged in CD also strive to achieve positive outcomes that have community impact. Community-based research can be helpful for understanding both intended and unintended outcomes. For example, imagine that a community is considering hosting a large sporting event. While the hosting of sporting events typically receives support because of their economic benefits, they have also been criticized for how they can displace low-income residents—an unintended outcome (Olds, 1998). A community-based tourism research study could be designed to understand the commercial viability of a community development initiative that would attract tourists, without displacing low-income housing.

> **Application Question**
>
> *Can you think of any other community development initiatives that may produce unintended outcomes?*

As we design projects to measure the outcomes of community development, we come to understand that outcomes can be multilayered. Outcomes can be about individuals (personal), groups (organizational), or institutions (systems). Researchers that are considering outcomes pay attention to change that occurs as a result of community development activity. We must be aware that outcomes differ from outputs. While outputs are the things you do to achieve results, they may or may not result in positive outcomes. An example of an output might be the number of people attending a meeting. An outcome might be how the attitudes of people attending the meeting changed as a result of what they learned.

Community-based research is especially helpful for assessing outcomes as they emerge in community development. CBR researchers understand how to assess progress at various milestones in a project. Community members who are engaged in the community development process have a chance to mark their progress and make adjustments to their strategies and processes when needed. While a range of outcomes is important, community impact is the goal of community development. A range of outcomes taken collectively can give us a sense of community impact. Community-based research, because community members learn more about what really impacts community change, enhances the ability of community development to build the capacity of a community.

Supporting developmental evaluation. One theory that is beginning to influence the way community development is practiced is social innovation theory. Scholars who research social innovation understand that many problems are complex and require innovative solutions. Often with complex systems, "there are diverse elements whose interactions create unpredictable, emergent results" (Gamble, 2008, p. 14). In other words, ". . . developmental evaluators make expecting the unexpected fundamental to the work at hand" (Patton, 2011, p. 11). We may not always be able to know ahead of time what issues or outcomes may be most important. Developmental evaluation is about learning as the project unfolds and applying what is learned as the project continues to develop.

Community-based research is well suited to developmental evaluation. Researchers and innovators work together to conceptualize the issue during the early stage of such evaluations. Since innovators often test out quick solutions through feedback, researchers using a developmental evaluation approach may report early observations and suggest refinements.

Increasingly, community development practitioners are using developmental evaluation to make sure their interventions are tracked carefully and so that dissemination can provide insights into both process and outcomes. Patton's (2011) work on developmental evaluation is based on many of the same principles as community-based research.

RESEARCH DESIGN

There are three main research designs that are typically utilized when designing community-based research projects: Action Research (AR), Participatory Research (PR), and Participatory Action Research (PAR).

Action Research (AR). The earliest form of community-based research came in the form of 'action research.' The origin of "action research" came from Kurt Lewin (1946) to describe research that involves experiential learning leading to action or social change, which could improve organizations, programs/services and our communities. This research process has become synonymous with learning progressively from experience while working with the community to address issues that are pertinent to them. That learning process includes a spiral of problem-solving steps involving a recurring cycle of planning, acting, observing, reflecting, and re-planning. Sport, leisure, and tourism researchers who have analyzed and advocated for this approach are few and far between, but nevertheless important (e.g., Pedlar, 1995).

One example of a research study, which utilized action research because of its commitment to change, was a study on building community through leisure at the Woolwich Healthy Communities Initiative in Ontario, Canada. The researchers identified several important themes: citizens learned new skills; became more vocal; felt greater balance and renewal; experienced greater sense of group accomplishment and ability to influence change; and finally citizens developed a sense of community through opportunity for shared learning amongst a variety of people (Arai & Pedlar, 1997). Other examples of interesting action research can be found in a special issue on action research and social change in sport (Chalip, 1997). People interested in this approach will find there are several good resources to guide them through such a project (e.g., Reason & Bradbury, 2008; journals such as *Action Research* and *Canadian Journal of Action Research*).

Participatory Research (PR). Another early approach to community research came from Paulo Freire (1970), a Brazilian community development worker and adult educator. He stressed that empowerment is best facilitated through a self-reflective process of starting where people are at, and seeing learners as active participants in the learning process. Ordinary citizens generate knowledge by addressing their concerns as members of society through direct involvement as co-researchers. Unfortunately, it has been difficult to find a good example of a study in recreation, leisure, or tourism to illustrate how this approach to research can be implemented. This may be partially explained by the fact that participatory research requires a deep commitment to citizen engagement and control. Also, these types of methods are new to our field. In some cases, leisure and tourism researchers have found community-based research methods which are more powerful and an appropriate fit with their research question, such as Participatory Action Research (PAR) (see below). Two useful resources that are available for anyone pursuing this research approach are the books by Jason, Keys, Suarez-Balcazar, Taylor, and Davis (2004); and Minkler and Wallerstein (2011).

Participatory Action Research (PAR). PAR includes components of both action and participatory research. Proponents of this design believe that any community-based research should include both elements (participation and action) in this PAR approach. Historically, PAR was part of an activist approach, designed to empower individuals who were poor and exploited and to encourage social action. Once again, excellent resources are available to assist potential researchers (Kindon, Pain, & Kesby, 2007). There has been some interest by sport, leisure, and tourism researchers in PAR in general (Dupuis et al., 2012; Fortune, 2011) as well as in the context of community development (Ateljevic et al., 2007; Frisby, 2006; Frisby et al., 2005).

A recent study designed to create a culture of inclusion for people with disabilities on one university campus chose PAR as a research design, since those involved were interested in a method that included both participation and action (Gillies & Dupuis, 2013). A PAR team included researchers, staff, and students, four of whom were members with disabilities. All team members worked collaboratively to design the research study, provide insights throughout the study, and were involved in all decision making. The PAR team created an inclusion framework, based on the data that was collected. This framework was then shared with research participants and others to gain feedback, and to create practical strategies on how a culture of inclusion can be created and sustained. The final framework included a series of recommendations for action and implementation.

> ***Application Question***
>
> *Can you think of another research question that might lend itself to PAR?*

In conclusion, community researchers will be in the position of deciding which of these three approaches to choose. PAR, the last approach described above, is probably the best choice because community-based research within a community development context will be much stronger and more meaningful to those affected by the research if the design includes citizen participation (PR) and leads to action (AR).

IMPLEMENTING A CBR PROJECT—STEPS TO CONSIDER

Regardless of which approach or design researchers choose (e.g., action, participatory, or a combination), there are some steps in implementation that all approaches have in common.

Forming a steering committee. A steering committee is needed in most CBR projects. The role of a steering committee is to guide the research, not just to provide advice. Steering committees must have ownership over the need for change. Typically, steering committees will include people who care about an issue (whether identified by the community or researchers). This means including individuals or organizations that have a stake in the issue. The activities of the steering committee include developing principles of working together, understanding assumptions, setting parameters for the research, and designing research instruments. As well, steering committees assess changing contexts, emerging outcomes, the need for changes in the research; and draft reports.

Participants on a steering committee may be concerned citizens interested in or affected by the issues that have led to the research or they may represent stakeholder organizations. However, when a person is an organization's representative, he or she will have to get approval from the organization. Participants that form a steering committee should be there primarily to bring their knowledge and expertise, not just because their organization requires them to be in attendance. Sometimes a formal contractual approach between the researcher and the community participants may be useful during a complex project, but other times more informal arrangements will suffice.

Working with multiple stakeholders. In CBR, involving multiple stakeholders (e.g., citizens, professionals, and decisionmakers) ensures that the research addresses issues identified by the community. This may involve participation on the steering committee, funding the research, contributing input to the steering committee in defining the issues, or being participants in the study.

Involving multiple stakeholders means you might have multiple agendas and differing or competing interests. Many of these issues will need to be mediated, which requires good facilitation skills and the ability to work across differences by supporting a diversity of perspectives and experiences. This usually means finding common ground or negotiating with an individual or sometimes collective negotiation using a facilitated approach. The role of the facilitator is to mediate the power imbalances among stakeholders. The challenge for the researcher is to decide who is in the best position to be the facilitator. One of the key roles of the facilitator is to get everyone committed to the same vision of the research. For example, if a person does not keep coming to steering committee meetings, it may mean that he or she feels powerless and excluded, or it may mean that the person needs additional support, such as day care or bus tickets. The facilitator's primary role is to pay attention to process and the individual needs of participants. Because the primary role of the researcher is to guide the research itself, it is sometimes best to have someone else undertake the facilitator's role.

Understanding previous research. When a steering committee identifies a concern or issue, it is important to begin by examining other research that has been done. This is not dissimilar to other forms of research. Looking at other research (such as journals, books, and reports) will help you learn what knowledge already exists in the area under study. Previous research can also give insight into what methods other researchers have used in studying the issue.

Determining the role of citizens in carrying out the research. Any CBR project needs to determine specifically what role citizens will play as researchers. In keeping with the tradition of PAR research, citizens often help carry out the research, as interviewers or as analysts of research information. The degree to which citizens help with carrying out the research will be determined by people's experience, skills, and interest. Some community-based researchers have had significant success with engaging citizens in playing the role of citizen researcher (Reeve, Cornell, D'Costa, Janzen, & Ochocka, 2002). Traditional researchers may find it challenging to involve citizens as researchers. For this process to be successful, the researcher must have deep respect for the gifts of citizens and a belief in the potential of citizens to take on the researcher role. Having the time and resources to dedicate to training citizen researchers is crucial here (Stoecker, 2013; Van de Ven, 2007).

Asking good questions. Steering committees must spend time deciding on the purpose of the study. In CBR, this also involves creating research questions that the community wants addressed. This is very deliberate and challenging work, as citizens and researchers work together to synthesize a community's concerns into realistic research questions. An important part of this work in CBR is to share the questions with the key stakeholders to be sure that the research questions in fact reflect the concerns of the community. How one addresses this process depends on the purpose of the study. For example, a study that focuses mostly on the lived experience of members of one group (e.g. program participants) may give more weight to participant views of the emerging research questions, rather than to the perspective of the program designers/deliverers.

Choosing appropriate methods. Steering committees work closely with the researcher to select methods that are a good fit with the study purpose and objectives. For example, if a study would benefit from breadth of understanding, a survey of multiple stakeholders may be utilized. On the other hand, if the study demands an in-depth understanding of an issue or process, interviews with key stakeholders may be chosen. In more complex studies, steering committees may choose multiple methods that address both breadth and depth. In keeping with the tradition of PAR, methods are based on CBR principles, and, as much as possible, are able to be conducted by citizens who represent the major stakeholder group. In using a PAR approach, the role of the researcher then, in conducting a project with a low-income community, would be to design the draft of the survey, get input from the steering committee and train and provide support to members of the community, who would actually conduct the survey with neighbors.

Analyzing information. As information is being gathered, steering committees often assist the researcher to analyze the information. When the information is quantitative, it may involve a data analysis strategy such as charting. When the information is qualitative, citizens can learn how to make sense of interview data, through coding and pattern/theme development. In the tradition of CBR, information analysis is an ongoing process and may be linked to milestones which allow for revisions of goals and activities, based on the feedback from the data analysis.

TABLE 10.3 IMPLEMENTATION STEPS IN A CBR STUDY: JOHN'S EXPERIENCE

A few years ago, I was one of three researchers who were thinking about a study that would examine how one community supports its vulnerable citizens. When my research colleagues and I began talking with people in the community, we realized there were organizations and grassroots groups committed to change who were interested in enhancing the quality of life of vulnerable citizens. Other organizations and community leaders were also excited about the idea of a study that would explore how one community was working for change.

Following these exploratory conversations, a steering committee of engaged citizens, organization leaders, and representatives of vulnerable populations was formed. Three key organizations that represented diverse approaches agreed to be part of the study and the steering committee. The broad diversity on the steering committee was a challenge, but we had significant facilitation experience and played a strong role in enabling the steering committee to work across differences and to find common ground. Hospitality was also seen as a key ingredient that reduced power imbalances and lack of trust. Meetings included food, lots of breaks for smokers, and more intimate conversation. Over time, trust was built as the most vulnerable members realized that the researchers and the local organizations were serious about addressing the important community issues.

Although the overall purpose of the study was determined by us, the steering committee members worked together to create the principles that would guide the study. They also spent a lot of time developing the questions that would guide the study design.

Early in the research process, we made a commitment to utilize citizen researchers in the study. This approach increased trust and engaged a self-help organization to assist the steering committee in hiring three of their members as citizen researchers. Joanna Ochocka, one of the main researchers, had experience with citizen researchers and she played a strong role in training and supporting the citizen researchers in their work.

The design for the research was developed collaboratively. After much discussion, it was agreed that a three step process made sense. In the first phase, previous research related to the topic was reviewed and interviews were conducted with key informants to identify their insights on the key study questions. Phase II involved documents analysis of the three organizations and interviews with staff and users in those organizations. Phase III included an analysis of the information and development of themes and patterns that highlighted impacts for each of the local organizations and the entire community. The citizen researchers played a role in all three phases, working closely with the main researchers as well as the steering committee.

The themes from this study turned out to be powerful. The research showed that this one community was willing to embrace new approaches in the way vulnerable citizens were supported. There were several lessons and insights in the study on how communities could enhance support and participation. During the last few months of the study, we worked with the steering committee to create a variety of ways of disseminating the knowledge and themes from the research. Newsletters, community forums, conference presentations, journal articles, and a book were all ways that we communicated the lessons from this research (Nelson, Lord, & Ochocka, 2001).

Disseminating knowledge. In CBR, themes and findings are shared with all stakeholders, who in turn have the opportunity to reflect on their relevance and meaning. In many ways, effective communication of research results helps to mobilize knowledge for the wider community. The format for dissemination must speak to citizens and also be useful in contributing to social change. CBR researchers use traditional forms of dissemination, such as written reports and journal articles, as well as more innovative communication strategies, such as community forums, in-depth case reporting through narrative and storytelling, photo elicitation, theater presentations, and videos.

CONCLUSION: CBR-CD AND COMMUNITY CHANGE

In this chapter, we have explored why community-based research is important. We now know how CBR relates to community development and can enhance the process of community change. Accordingly, it is now possible to summarize this chapter with highlights from our understanding of what we see as the major parallels between community development and community-based research (see Table 10.4).

Leisure, sport, and tourism professionals have traditionally been concerned with programs and services. As some in the profession more fully embrace a community development approach, the role of community-based research will increase. New people entering the profession need to be equipped to understand and lead community development and community-based research endeavors. As we have noted, some of the skills required to play this role include knowledge of community change processes, commitment to asset-based approaches, ability to work from principles, and strong facilitation skills. As importantly, the attitude or mindset we bring to this work can enhance this new approach to professional practice. Professionals who are dedicated to building the capacity of community will have a mindset that honours citizen engagement, social change, good process, and research that starts with and fully involves the community. The widespread use of CBR would have a significant impact on the way community development is practiced. Using the principle-based mindset in Table 10.4, accompanied by the skill sets and practices we have outlined in this chapter, will help to ensure that significant impact becomes a reality.

Finally, we need to consider how public policy can be impacted by the powerful connection between community-based research and community development. Local governments and funding bodies can encourage the utilization of community-based research in ways that impact policy development. For example, municipal governments often have citizen engagement policies, which could be greatly strengthened using a CBR approach. Similarly, leisure, sport, and tourism professionals could make use of CBR in evaluating programs and services, such as those based in community centers. CBR also has usability in larger State or Provincial studies that are designed to provide information for leisure, sport, and tourism policymakers.

TABLE 10.4 TEN POWERFUL PARALLELS BETWEEN COMMUNITY DEVELOPMENT AND COMMUNITY-BASED RESEARCH

1. Dissatisfaction with traditional approaches
2. Driven by community concerns
3. Concern for marginalization of citizens
4. Collaboration with multiple stakeholders
5. Participatory (engaging citizens in design and implementation)
6. Asset-based/strength-based
7. Empowering process (individual and community)
8. Using innovative approaches to change
9. Ongoing co-learning (among researchers, community leaders, and citizens)
10. Building local capacity (citizens, organizations, or neighborhoods)

As community-based researchers, we hope that you see the value of CBR as an approach that is fundamental to community development, wherever research is required in order to move community development forward. We have emphasized knowledge, attitudes, and skills that can enhance the parallels between CD and CBR. Each of us entered this work because we were dedicated to building strong communities that included everyone (Lord & Hutchison, 2016). For us, community is the heart of community-based research. Bringing this commitment to the work always grounds us in the idea that CBR and CD, when done well, can significantly contribute to building inclusive communities.

REFERENCES

Action Research. Retrieved from http://arj.sagepub.com/

Arai, S., & Pedlar, A. (1997). Building communities through leisure: Citizen participation in a healthy communities initiative. *Journal of Leisure Research, 29*(2), 167–182.

Ateljevic, I., Prichard, A., & Morgan, N. (2007). *The critical turn in tourism studies: Innovative research methodologies.* Oxford: Elsevier.

Canadian Journal of Action Research. Retrieved September 1, 2014 from http://cjar.nipissingu.ca/index.php/cjar

Centre for Community-Based Research. (2014a). Definition of community-based research. Retrieved from http://www.communitybasedresearch.ca/Page/View/CBR_definition

Centre for Community-Based Research. (2014b). *Principles that guide our work.* Retrieved from http://www.communitybasedresearch.ca/Page/View/Principles

Chalip, L. (Ed.). (1997). Action research and social change in sport: An introduction to the special issue. *Journal of Sport Management, 11,* 1–7.

Cresswell, J. (2013). *Qualitative inquiry and research design: Choosing among five approaches* (3rd ed.). Thousand Oaks, CA: Sage Publications.

Dupuis, S. (1999). Naked truths: Toward a reflective methodology in leisure research. *Leisure Studies, 21,* 43–64.

Dupuis, S., Whyte, C., Carson J., Genoe, R., Meshino, L., & Sadlerd, L. (2012). Just dance with me: An authentic partnership approach to understanding leisure in the dementia context. *World Leisure Journal, 54*(3), 240–254.

Fortune, D. (2011). *Participatory approaches to re-imagining women's social inclusion as social justice: Experiences of community after federal incarceration in Canada* (Unpublished doctoral dissertation). University of Waterloo, Waterloo, ON.

Freire, P. (1970). *Pedagogy of the oppressed.* New York: Seabury.

Frisby, W. (2006). Rethinking researcher roles, responsibilities, and relationships in community development research. *Leisure/Loisir 30*(2), 437–446.

Frisby, W. (2002). The actualities of doing community development to promote the inclusion of low income populations in local sport and recreation. *European Sport Management Quarterly, 2*(3), 209–233.

Frisby, W., Reid, C., Millar, S., & Hoeber, L. (2005). Putting "participatory" into participatory forms of research. *Journal of Sport Management, 19*(4), 367–386.

Gamble, J. (2008). *A developmental evaluation primer.* Montreal: J. W. McConnell Foundation.

Gillies, J., & Dupuis, S. (2013). A framework for creating a culture of inclusion: A participatory action research approach. *Annals of Leisure Research, 16*(3), 193–211.

Henderson, K. (2006). *Dimensions of choice: Qualitative approaches to parks, recreation, tourism, sport, and leisure research.* State College, PA: Venture Publishing.

Hutchison, P., & Lord, J. (2012). Community-based research and leisure scholarship: A discernment process. *Leisure/Loisir, 36*(1), 65–83.

Jason, L., Keys, C., Suarez-Balcazar, Y., Taylor, R., & Davis, M. (Eds.). (2004). *Participatory community research: Theories and methods in action.* Washington, DC: American Psychological Association.

Kindon, S., Pain, R., & Kesby, M. (2007). *Participatory action research approaches and methods: Connecting people, participation and place.* New York: Routledge.

Kirby, S., Greaves, L., & Reid, C. (2006). *Experience research social change: Methods beyond the mainstream.* (2nd ed.). Peterborough, ON: Garamond Press.

Lewin, K. (1946). Action research and minority problems. *Journal of Social Issues, 2*(4), 34–46.

Lord, J., & Hutchison, P. (2016). *Pathways to inclusion: Building a new story with people and communities* (3rd ed.). Concord, ON: Captus Press.

Mertens, D. M. (2009). *Research and evaluation in education and psychology: Integrating diversity with quantitative, qualitative, and mixed methods.* Los Angeles: Sage Publishing.

Minkler, M., & Wallerstein, N. (Eds.). (2011). *Community-based participatory research for health: From process to outcome* (2nd ed.). Hoboken, NJ: John Wiley & Sons.

Nelson, G., Lord, J., & Ochocka, J. (2001). *Shifting the paradigm in community mental health: Towards empowerment and community.* Toronto, ON: University of Toronto Press.

Ochocka, J., & Lord, J. (1998). Support clusters: A social network approach for people with complex needs. *Journal of Leisurability, 25*(4), 14–22.

Olds, K. (1998). Urban mega-events, evictions and housing rights: The Canadian case. *Current Issues in Tourism, 1*(1), 2–46.

Patton, M. Q. (2011). *Developmental evaluation: Applying complexity concepts to enhance innovation and use.* New York: Guilford Publications.

Patton, M. Q. (2001). *Qualitative research & evaluation methods.* (3rd ed.).Thousand Oaks, CA: Sage Publication.

Pedlar, A. (1995). Relevance and action research in leisure. *Leisure Sciences, 17*(2), 133–140.

Reason, P., & Bradbury, H. (Ed.). (2008). *The Sage handbook of action research: Participative inquiry and practice.* Thousand Oaks, CA: Sage Publishers.

Reeve, P., Cornell, S., D'Costa, B., Janzen, R., & Ochocka, J. (2002). From our perspective: Consumer researchers speak about their experience in a community mental health research project. *Psychiatric Rehabilitation Journal, 25*(4), 403–408.

Reid, D. (2006). Community development, leisure research, and practice. *Leisure/Loisir, 30*(2), 315–332.

Stoecker, R. (2013). *Research methods for community change: A project-based approach.* (2nd ed.). Thousand Oaks, CA: Sage Publications.

Van de Ven, A. (2007). *Engaged scholarship: A guide for organizational and social research.* Oxford, UK: Oxford University Press.

Veal, A. (2011). *Research methods for leisure and tourism: A practical guide.* (4th ed.). Harlow: UK: Prentice-Hall/Financial Times.

11

COMMUNITY ORGANIZING

Rudy Dunlap and Heather Mair

COMMUNITY ORGANIZING: INTRODUCTION AND SCOPE

It might begin by chatting with a neighbor in your front yard or by reading a friend's social media post online. It might progress to a small group meeting at the local coffeehouse or pub, and it might culminate with a protest at city hall or an organized project in your neighborhood. The process of *community organizing* takes many forms, but it almost always entails what C. Wright Mills (1959/2000) described as the recognition that our everyday, private troubles are inextricably linked to larger social issues. Expressed another way, community organizing is the process of sharing our individual frustrations, indignations, or fears with others until they are transformed into shared issues that concern the welfare of an entire community (Staples, 2004). While such frustrations often exceed the scope of one neighborhood or city, many national or international movements originated in the troubles of everyday life as initially experienced by a handful of individuals.

As was set out in Chapter 1, the term community has evolved to encompass numerous 'communities of interest' (e.g., identity communities, online communities, brand communities). Grassroots organizing has typically emerged in 'communities of place' (e.g., neighborhoods, cities) as people share experiences that are embedded within a particular geographic locale. Indeed, the issues that provoke the organizing process emanate from shared experiences that encompass the breadth of community life, ranging from the need for clean water and air, to the fear of violence based on one's identity, to the need for a safe and convenient public spaces in which to recreate.

Our goal with this chapter is to briefly survey the nature and history of community organizing while also exploring its relevance for community development practice. Before moving on, however, it is worth noting that community organizing and community development may be thought of as distinctly different endeavors. For example, Matarrita-Cascante and Brennan (2012) sought to conceptualize the myriad ways community members can participate in development (see Chapters 1 and 3 for more on the forms of CD). Importantly for our purposes, the notion of grassroots organizing fits within the broader type of community development that is concerned with *self-help*. Matarrita-Cascante and Brennan further distinguish this from directed or *imposed* forms of CD):

> The major contribution of self-help forms of community development is that it provides residents with capacities necessary to take over the direction of change in their locality... particular emphasis is placed on the enhancement of the human resource of the community resulting in high levels of learning outcomes for local residents. (2012, p. 300)

Despite such intellectual conceptualizations (see Christenson & Robinson, 1989), the *practice* of community development has traditionally been associated with the development of infrastructure particular in partnership with not-for-profit organizations, such as community development corporations (CDCs), with government entities and citizen groups (Stoecker, 2003). Such arrangements often yield changes to a community's infrastructure that can have a marked effect on residents' quality of life. However, despite its potential to affect profound changes on individuals' health and well-being, community development practice has also been critiqued for how its reliance on established bureaucracies and institutions has tended to reinforce status quo political and economic relations (Stoecker) and ultimately failed to produce real changes in power dynamics.

By contrast, community organizing endeavors to fundamentally alter the balance of power within a given community by giving its members voice and agency. Since the time of the settlement movement in North

America in the late nineteenth century, grassroots organizing has addressed all manner of issues, both progressive and conservative, and has done so in any number of ways. *The process of community organizing entails individual members of a community coalescing around an issue of shared interest in order to affect change* (Ohmer & Brooks III, 2013; Rubin & Rubin, 2005). As such, it is distinctive from other forms of community development to the extent that individual members of a community work together to identify 'problems in common,' and more importantly, to create a shared vision of the future.

MODELS OF COMMUNITY ORGANIZING

The term *community organizing* often brings to mind images of confrontation; for instance, lines of protesters carrying signs and chanting slogans in response to misdeeds of a larger, more powerful entity. This form of organizing is exemplified in labor protests by the Back of Yards Campaign in 1930s Chicago (Fisher, 1984) or efforts in 1980s by the Dudley Street Neighborhood Initiative to halt illegal dumping in their neighborhood (described in the textbox below, see also Medoff, 1994). Such scenes are exemplary of a *conflict model* of community organizing in which citizens organize to wrest power from those individuals and entities perceived to wield it unjustly. While such actions are evocative, they overshadow the countless hours of discussion and relationship building that serve as the foundation of any organizing process. Indeed, community organizing is not inherently confrontational and may often take a more conciliatory approach as is done in the community building or *consensus model* of organizing.

> **Conflict Model of Community Organizing**
>
> *An approach that treats organizing as an adversarial activity involving two or more parties with opposing interests. This approach assumes that organizing activities result in winners and losers, and it often mobilizes residents around issues of social justice.*

The conflict model of community organizing, also referred to as the power or Alinsky model takes for granted that community organizing is a struggle undertaken by individuals who lack power (the 'have-nots') against those who have power (the 'haves'). As such, organizing is understood as being adversarial, class-based, and necessarily resulting in win-loss outcomes. The conflict approach has typically been used to address economic issues, such as predatory lending or mortgage redlining, and political issues, such as suppression of voter registration or racial profiling (Fisher, 2009). Not surprisingly, the conflict model has flourished in times and places where we have seen pronounced economic and social inequalities.

> **Consensus Model of Community Organizing**
>
> *An approach to organizing that aims to build social networks and trust among parties with differing interests. This approach assumes that organizing activities result in mutually beneficial, win-win outcomes. Consensus organizing typically mobilizes residents for the purpose of establishing relations prior to addressing issues.*

Often, an incident or an issue will spark the creation of a grassroots organization, community organizers using the conflict approach may build on the infrastructure of an existing organization (e.g., a church, a neighborhood association) in order to initiate the organizing process. Though often seemingly obvious, the first step in the organizing process is one of a facilitated, exploratory discussion in which community members work to identify their mutual concerns and visions for the future. These initial discussions may take a considerable amount of time, depending on organizers' facilitation style. Having identified or 'framed' issues of mutual concern, organizers and community members identify discrete actions and objectives and set out a plan for achieving them (see Chapter 7 for more on the planning process). Responsibilities are delegated accordingly and community members engage in a process of education during which the issue at hand is publicized within the community-at-large and additional members of the community are invited to participate. The initial organizing process culminates in some sort of prominent action or event (e.g., a protest march, a rally), undertaken by a large number of people in an effort to garner media attention and compel change. Below, we offer a simple dichotomy (conflict vs. consensus) as a way of sorting different approaches to community organizing, but it is also worthwhile to consider the concept and its characteristics generally.

THE CONFLICT MODEL AT WORK: THE OCCUPY MOVEMENT

In 2011, Adbusters magazine posted the following call to action:

"Alright you 90,000 redeemers, rebels and radicals out there, On September 17, we want to see 20,000 people flood into lower Manhattan, set up tents, kitchens, peaceful barricades and occupy Wall Street for a few months."

2000 American protesters moved into Zuccotti Park and built an encampment. The park was located in the heart of the financial district in New York City and activists said they were there to protest the "damaging influence of corporations on politics as well a social and economic inequality." Despite warnings of legal repercussions, and facing violence, hundreds of protesters stayed every night for two months. The Zuccotti protests inspired millions and long-lasting protests were undertaken in 500 cities around the world. Most of the encampments lasted for weeks, with some staying in place (taken down only by police force) until the end of November, 2011.

In keeping with the self-help tone of community organizing, the Occupy movement describes itself as leaderless:

"The #occupy movement has no official leaders. Anyone can be involved in the process and pick up the flag to address the problems they face in their community. We do not believe in placing the power of the movement in the hands of the few, but rather empowering everyone to be involved and share the responsibility together."

And the movement stands behind one demand, which is an outcome of events that have affected people personally (e.g., private troubles) but which are ultimately public issues:

"#occupy wants to end the relationship built on money and donations between our elected officials and corporate interests. We believe this relationship has led to rampant corruption and criminal activities that undermine our economic and political system. We simply want a system that operates in the interest of the people and to empower people to be a part of the process."

(http://www.occupytogether.org)

Since the protest in Zuccotti Park, a variety of occupy movements (e.g., occupy the farm) have sprung up around the US to organize around local, community-based issues. (http://whattheheckhasoccupydonesofar.com)

Community Organizer

The job of an organizer is to transform the interests of residents into coherent action. As opposed to espousing their own goals for action, organizers facilitate a democratic process in which residents forge their own goals and objectives for the future. Organizers focus on process by providing residents with strategy and tactics to achieve their vision of a better community.

In contrast to the conflict model, the consensus model of organizing, also referred to as the community building or social capital approach, rejects an adversarial approach. The consensus building model operates from the assumption that the fundamental challenge facing communities is the absence of robust social networks and civic institutions that facilitate public discourse about issues that affect communities. As the term community building suggests, the remedy is not confrontation, but rather the creation of partnerships and civic organizations that facilitate relationships that bridge social divisions (e.g., economic class, ethnicity) and the creation of social capital. As opposed to taking power from elites, the community building approaches endeavor to create a "newly functioning public sphere that attracts and engages more than a miniscule fraction of residents" (Traynor, 2012, p. 211). Given this emphasis, the consensus approach rests on two fundamental assumptions: first, that no groups or individuals should be excluded *a priori* from the organizing process; and two, that the organizing process can result in mutually beneficial outcomes for parties, even those with seemingly different agendas.

Which form of community organizing is appropriate for a given situation? As with most such hypotheticals, the answer is, 'it depends.' In situations characterized by glaring inequalities and exploitation, conflict may be the only viable approach. However, in situations where conflict is not imminent, a consensus approach might be the most efficient means for initiating a dialogue between parties. In reality, many organizing endeavors alternate between conflict and consensus approaches as the situation dictates (Ohmer & Brooks III, 2013) and conflict is often the pretext that brings different parties to the proverbial table.

Despite their differences, the conflict and consensus approaches to organizing both facilitate the involvement of residents in the affairs of their communities. As a result, involvement may yield an important sense of community attachment (Perkins & Long, 2002) or social integration (Speer, Jackson, & Peterson, 2001) that is important for both individuals' psychological well-being (Helliwell & Putnam, 2004) as well as the functioning of local government (Putnam, 1993). Additionally, both forms of grassroots organizing hold the potential to cultivate participants' 'civic skills,' which may in turn foster their involvement with other civic organizations and activities (Putnam, 1993). In other words, civic involvement may beget more civic involvement.

Application Question

Describe some contemporary organizing actions in your local community or society. Which forms of community organizing do they most resemble?

As will be made clear when we (briefly) discuss the history of community organizing, there is often a blend of both the conflict and consensus approaches. The next section presents the first part of a story, written by Rudy, which we feel exemplifies the relationship and the tension between these two approaches. As you read the story, pay attention to how the efforts of residents of the Crestview Neighborhood to secure a park juxtapose, intentionally or not, conflict and consensus as components in their campaign. As in Crestview's case, friendly conversations may ultimately give way to protest, which in turn sets the stage for future dialogue.

PARK PROMISES—PART I

Located in north-central Austin, Texas, the Crestview Neighborhood is often described as the perfect mix of 'old and new Austin' (Barnes, 2012). Primarily developed in the 1950s and 1960s, it showcases mid-twentieth century suburbia with a mix of single-family bungalows and ranches situated on quarter-acre lots. When first developed, Crestview was the 'nest' from which young post-war couples set out to build families and careers. Fifty years later, Crestview is once again being settled by young families who are drawn to its quiet streets, good schools, and proximity to amenities. Seemingly the perfect neighborhood for young, hip Austin families, Crestview lacks only one thing: a park.

Beginning in 2003, members of the Crestview Neighborhood Association entered into a dialogue with the owners of a privately-owned, five-acre lot to transform the land into a park. Mediated by an elected member of the City Council of Austin, these initial discussions resulted in a Neighborhood Development Plan that recommended the site be developed in to a park (Lanane, 2014). Despite the amicable nature of the process, negotiations regarding the terms of transfer dragged on and eventually the City Council member who had championed the issue moved on from office. As he departed, so did any momentum that had been built around the issue, and plans for the park receded from thought and expectation . . . until 2010.

Residents' hopes for a neighborhood park were renewed in 2010 with the formation of the Crestview Park Coalition (CPC). Whereas the negotiations in 2003 and 2004 had proceeded with the intent of building relationships and reaching a consensus decision, the CPC was borne of the view that the residents' efforts to gain a neighborhood park were more akin to a struggle for power than had previously been acknowledged. In an effort to raise awareness of the issue and focus residents' energy on the city government, the CPC and its members attended and spoke at city council meetings, gave interviews to local media outlets, created a web site, and printed signs for display in residents' front yards ("Crestview Park Now!"). In all of their activities, the CPC consistently reminded anyone who would listen that city government had promised a park for Crestview and had reneged on its promise (Crestview Park Coalition, 2013). The Coalition's effort reached a high point in June 2013 when it staged a 'Protest Picnic' outside of City Hall in downtown Austin, the purpose of which was to showcase the kind of activity that residents could not pursue in their own neighborhood.

A BRIEF HISTORY OF COMMUNITY ORGANIZING

As community organizing in contemporary society is characterized by conflict and consensus approaches, so too is its history. When the pendulum has swung between conflict and consensus, it has largely done so in response to prevailing economic conditions. In other words, as discussed below, grassroots organizing has taken on a consensus approach in periods of prosperity and then evolved towards conflict when a society's economic circumstances have made life near the bottom of the economic spectrum more desperate.

THE SETTLEMENT MOVEMENT

While the consensus, or community building, approach has been touted as a novel approach to community development (Traynor, 2012), in fact it aptly characterizes organizing's earliest incarnation in the settlement movement (Fisher, 1984), which can be seen as the genesis of numerous professional fields (e.g., community and public health, social work, community parks and recreation). Whereas previous efforts had been overtly charitable and paternalistic, the settlement movement, which began at Toynbee Hall in London, endeavored to work *with* the poor and immigrant populations of London to acculturate them to the refined values and morals of 'proper society.' Toynbee Hall served the dual role of providing much-needed social services (e.g., prenatal and infant care, employment services) as well as forms of cultural education (e.g., civics, table manner, personal hygiene) that helped its users better assimilate into the institutions of mainstream society.

The settlement idea was imported to the United States by Stanton Coit in 1886 and with it came a deliberate focus on the affairs of particular neighborhoods. Case in point, Coit's first iteration of the settlement house concept was located in the immigrant tenements of New York's Lower East Side and was called The Neighborhood Guild. Coit's work and that of his more famous successors, such as Jane Addams and Ellen Gates Starr, continued to focus on the affairs of individuals and families rooted in neighborhoods. For this reason alone, the settlement movement may be portrayed as the first widespread effort to foster community organizing in the United States.

Lauded for its successes in alleviating the crushing poverty and rampant discrimination that accompanied industrialization and urbanization in the United States, the settlement movement never sought to address the underlying political and economic conditions of its time (Fisher, 1984). With the exception of some of Jane Addams work, the settlement movement failed in its aspirations to work *with* the poor. In fact, settlement endeavors were characteristic of other progressive movements in the steadfast belief in the efficacy of expertise and professionalization. As opposed to being *of* the neighborhoods they served, settlement houses were created and administered largely by children of wealthy and established families in North America's major cities. As a result, the settlement movement and its leaders sought to address the ill effects of industrialization by promoting consensus with, rather than working against, their wealthy benefactors (Fisher).

ALINSKY AND CONFLICT

Settlement houses and similar efforts, such as the Cincinnati Social Unit Organization, continued to serve the poor and disadvantaged throughout the first half of the twentieth century. However, the stock market crash of 1929 and ensuing Great Depression dramatically altered the context of grassroots organizing. Whereas previous approaches had worked with elites in an effort to ameliorate the excesses of an inequitable system, the sustained poverty and unemployment wrought by the Depression brought into doubt the overall health and logic of the capitalist system. As the individual shock and shame of unemployment gave way to frustration and anger, efforts to organize for improved living conditions grew more militant and adversarial (Fisher, 1984).

No single name more aptly represents the history of conflict organizing than that of Saul Alinsky. Alinsky's signature accomplishments came during his organizing efforts with the Back of Yards Neighborhood Council (BYNC) on the south side of Chicago in the 1930s. During this period, south Chicago was a patchwork of different ethnic enclaves, e.g., Poles, Lithuanians, Czechs, who, when not engaged in outright 'turf wars,' remained socially segregated from one another. The area was also home to the city's infamous meat-packing industry, which employed the area's residents in dangerous work and at poverty wages. Alinsky, who was originally tasked with addressing juvenile delinquency, recognized immediately that the more pressing issue was the exploitation of workers by the large meat-packing companies, and this arrangement would endure so long as the workers remained separated by ethnicity and politics. Along with Joseph Meegan, a recreation coordinator for the City's Department Parks and Recreation, Alinsky worked with area churches and unions to bridge the existing ethnic divisions and unite residents in the context of the BYNC.

Notwithstanding Alinsky's and Meegan's leadership, the BYNC was designed to be radically democratic, a trait that would define Alinsky's work and his teachings to young activists (see Alinsky 1971). Through the BYNC, area residents identified issues that were important, principally their working conditions and its effects on their quality of life. Having set an agenda, Alinsky, Meegan, and other community leaders went about organizing a strategic campaign to force the meat-packing companies to address workers' demands. This campaign included tactics such as consumer boycotts, worker strikes, and a public relations blitz against the companies' labor practices, all of which resulted in concessions from the industry including a 40% wage increase (Fisher, 1984). In sum, the BYNC encapsulated the tactics that would define Alinsky's work for decades to come and the legacy of conflict-based organizing. These included the recruitment of existing community institutions into the organizing process, radically democratic participation on the part of members, the pragmatic use of varied tactics, and most importantly, a conceptualization of the process as a perpetual struggle of the people against the power monopoly of corporations and governments.

PARK PROMISES PART II: "A PROTEST PICNIC"

"Hold onto the ticket; I think she said that we can get our parking validated," Brad explained as we left the parking garage on the way to the Protest Picnic at City Hall. The comment struck me as odd and that perhaps this wasn't a 'real' protest if an attendee could get a parking validation. We pressed on in the direction of City Hall, wary of the noonday heat and hopeful that we could protest in the shade.

We rounded one corner of City Hall to find a collection of approximately fifty people staging what did indeed appear to be a picnic on the plaza in front of the building. Blankets were laid out over the sandstone pavers, children chased one another around obstacles, and people pulled food items from their coolers. We immediately sought out familiar faces and made introductions to new acquaintances. Lacking any picnic paraphernalia, much less any protest signs or placards, we found shady spots on the periphery of the gathering.

Presently two news crews arrived complete with professional-looking cameras and individuals whose appearance suggested they would be addressing the cameras at some point. The arrival of the cameras was quickly followed by the emergence of an officious looking man and a police officer from City Hall itself. These two conferenced with Andrea, the organizer of our gathering. Though Brad and I could not hear the exchange, the mutual nodding of heads suggested agreement, and the conversation ended with the two men from City Hall moving back towards the entrance to the building.

Andrea stepped up on a sandstone bench and yelled out to get our attention. Casual conversation ceased among the adults, while children continued to frolic through the proceedings. In an effort to overcome the passing traffic, Andrea practically shouted her address to us. She thanked us all for taking the time to attend and then re-hashed the narrative of Crestview's struggle to secure a park of its own in which residents could picnic and children could play. She concluded by explaining that our purpose today was to publicize the issue and to demonstrate to Austin's City Council that Crestview's residents would not cease to advocate for themselves. She concluded by explaining that we had approximately 45 minutes to stage our protest, a condition that once again seemed antithetical to the underlying idea of a protest.

Everyone took up large placards that read, "Crestview Park Now!" Brad and I looked amongst the crowd and finally found two signs of our own. People milled about and chatted, and I felt a momentary lack of direction. Quite all of a sudden, a high pitched voice yelled:

"WHAT DO WE WANT?!"

and it was quickly answered: "A PARK!"

"WHEN DO WE WANT IT?"

"NOW!"

"WHAT DO WE WANT?!"

This time in unison and much louder: "A PARK!"

"WHEN DO WE WANT IT?"

"NOW!"

The call and response continued and grew louder. Finally, the instigator of our chant, a woman named Deb, began marching in a circle around our group. Others quickly followed suit and presently we were parading around our own picnic as the cameras watched nearby. Our 'ring around the picnic' parade continued for several minutes until Deb decided to alter its course. She walked away from the circle followed by the remainder of the protesting picnickers and down the sidewalk and along the perimeter of City Hall. At a point several yards from our picnic, Deb stopped, pointed to a large window at street level, and explained that the City Council's chambers were on the opposite side of the window. "Let's make sure they hear us!" she explained. Our chants continued as we paraded back and forth in front of the window. It was impossible to tell due to the window's tinting whether anyone was actually meeting on the other side. Nonetheless our protest continued for a number of minutes.

Andrea re-appeared and directed us back to our picnic space. We complied, but made sure to walk directly in front of the two news cameras on the way back.

THE LEGACY OF CONSENSUS AND CONFLICT ORGANIZING

One of the most telling legacies of Alinsky's militant approach to organizing was the emergence of the civil rights and New Left protest movements of the 1960s. Exemplified by entities such as the Student Non-violent Coordinating Committee (SNCC) and the Students for a Democratic Society (SDS), the New Left placed a deliberate emphasis on radically democratic, community-level organizations that would in turn spark a national movement. This bottom-up approach to addressing segregation and discrimination in the American South was considerably more effective at gaining national attention than earlier top-down efforts on the part of organizations such as the NAACP (National Association for the Advancement of Colored People) (Fisher, 1984). The success of community-level civil rights efforts resulted in the continued use of conflict-oriented organizing throughout the 1960s and 1970s to address issues ranging from the redlining of neighborhoods of color to women's liberation to the environmental movement.

Whereas the legacy of conflict organizing is perhaps more prominent, consensus organizing is the more pervasive of the two related to contemporary organizing. Driven in part by the popularity of the social capital concept (see Putnam, 2000), many contemporary organizing efforts rest on the assumption that civil society is in disarray and that the organizing process should, first and foremost, strive to repair it by creating relationships among the community members and organizations.

The resurgence of consensus approaches has resulted from the failure of conventional development practices to revitalize economically depressed and blighted communities (Traynor, 2012). Whereas community development corporations (CDC) and private foundations have been adept at securing funds for the development of affordable housing in poor communities, they have traditionally been less able to mobilize community groups and residents in the service of broader revitalization activities (Traynor). Consensus efforts, also called community building, aim to build relationships between community members and other community entities (e.g., municipal government, banks, nonprofit organizations) in the hopes of cultivating residents' capacities to participate in the development process. The community building approach recognizes that efforts to develop community-based infrastructure stand a greater chance of success in the context of a vital and active civic life.

Application Questions

Think about Rudy's narrative of Crestview Park Promises. Which elements of conflict and consensus can you see at work in this story? What do you think the next step for this group should be? Develop two plans of action for the group—one using the conflict model and one using the consensus model. Which do you think is the most effective strategy at this point in the campaign for the park?

ORGANIZING FOR LEISURE, SPORT, AND TOURISM

The opportunity to experience leisure, recreation, and play have all been issues for which individuals and communities have organized themselves at one time or another. Consider Jane Addams's work to secure social services and provide recreational experiences in Chicago, the playground movement and its origins in Boston, Massachusetts to secure safe places for children to play, or workers' campaigns for shorter hours in towns and cities all across North America. Despite the recognition that leisure is a fundamental right (The Universal Declaration of Human Rights, Article 24), its absence from the lives of millions serves as a personal trouble that awaits provocation into a public issue (Mills, 2000).

Though often treated as an historical movement, the conditions that spawned the playground movement persist in many parts of North America. As noted in the park promises story, the Crestview Neighborhood and its Park Coalition are exemplary of the enduring lack of access to parks, green space, and community recreation centers. Not coincidentally, poorer neighborhoods of color are less likely to have ready access to safe recreational resources than their more affluent counterparts (Moore, Diez Roux, Evenson, McGinn, & Brines, 2008). The well-documented actions of the Dudley Street Neighborhood Initiative in the Dorchester-Roxbury Neighborhoods of Boston, Massachusetts also illustrate the continued need for public parks and green space in contemporary urban contexts. In a classic illustration of the blending of conflict and consensus organizing, the residents of Dorchester-Roxbury took control of a nascent development process within their neighborhood and charted a vision for their blighted neighborhood. Chief among their goals was the removal of industrial waste from their green spaces, the revitalization of local parks, and the establishment of a community recreation center (Medoff, 1994).

At a time of economic depression and heightened inequality, leisure, recreation, and play are often treated as frivolous and superfluous issues. Yet, the harm meted out by the disappearance of a living wage or the inaccessibility of health care is reflected not only by a rising tide of personal bankruptcies (Grusky, Western & Wimer, 2011), but also in the absence of free time to spend with friends and family. The disappearance and degradation of leisure due to longer working hours or, more insidiously, as a result of work's seepage into other domains of life has compromised societies' collective health and well-being (Kawachi & Kennedy, 2006). When understood as a casualty of economic and financial recession, the right to opportunities for leisure, recreation, and play may be seen looming in the background of the Occupy Wall Street encampments or at the protests of Wal-Mart workers for union representation. The struggle for economic security and fairness is *de facto* a struggle for the right to have leisure.

THE DUDLEY STREET NEIGHBORHOOD INITIATIVE (DSNI)

Formed in the Dorchester-Roxbury Neighborhoods of Boston, Massachusetts, DSNI offers a classic example of community organizing that addressed issues related to the need for public space and recreation. After the exodus of its original Italian and Irish immigrants in the 1960s, the neighborhood was settled by African American, Puerto Rican, and Cape Verdean families. This transition was accompanied by a policy of 'redlining' on the part of banks and mortgage lenders that made it impossible for residents to purchase property or build homes. The ensuing economic decline resulted in a neighborhood that was blighted by vacant lots and abandoned buildings that in turn facilitated numerous forms of criminal activity. Surrounded by illegal dumping and lacking safe green space for recreation, the different enclaves of Dorchester-Roxbury began to organize themselves in the hopes of fostering a transformation to their neighborhood.

When the City of Boston attempted to co-op their initial organizing efforts, residents re-asserted their control of the process, hired their own independent community organizer, and formed the Dudley Street Neighborhood Initiative (DSNI). Throughout the 1980s, DSNI recruited members from its neighborhood and engaged in a sustained campaign to draw attention to their plight. Activities included street corner protests of illegal dumping operations, press conferences to highlight government indifference, and neighborhood watches efforts to rid their public spaces of illegal drug and gang activity. Over the course of a decade, DSNI was able to secure the tool of eminent domain, the first instance of a neighborhood association doing so, for the purpose of buying and consolidating the neighborhood's patchwork of vacant lots. By the late 1980s, DSNI had secured the funding necessary to construct dozens of new housing units for its residents as well as the redesign of its public spaces. While the threats posed by economic instability remain, DSNI's accomplishments demonstrate community organizing's potential to address systematic discrimination and urban blight (Medoff, 1994).

> **Application Questions**
>
> *What barriers to access of public recreation resources exist in your community? What forms of community organizing might be used to best address such conditions?*

LEISURE AS A CONTEXT FOR COMMUNITY ORGANIZING

Within the field of community organizing, leisure is often overlooked as an issue about which community members organize themselves. If that is so, leisure's function as a way of organizing is even less well understood. The treatment of leisure as simply being a just reward for one's labors and a source of rejuvenation obscures the fact that it has also traditionally facilitated the social interactions whereby community organizing might arise.

Above and beyond mere sociability, leisure has been interpreted as being an activity through which individuals may realize their relations to the larger community and the body politic. Hemingway (1988) captures leisure's potential to influence the political life of communities is his treatment of leisure as the social context in which character and civic responsibility are cultivated. For those individuals who benefited from the economic privilege of their social status, Aristotle treated leisure as the activity in which citizens engaged with fellow members of the polis to pursue action related the political, social, economic, and religious affairs that determined the welfare of their community (Hemingway). By comparison, Aristotelian leisure is considerably more serious than its contemporary successor, to the point of even being described as the teleological end of human life (*Nichomachean Ethics,* 1177b4). The contrast of Aristotelian leisure with contemporary interpretations of leisure as being concerned with personal amusement and diversion could not be more striking, and it is these differences that set the stage for the notion of *civil leisure* (Mair, 2002).

CIVIL LEISURE

As opposed to simply reviving the classical conception of leisure as described by Hemingway (1988), civil leisure attempts to contrast dominant portrayals of leisure in contemporary society. Heather's work on her own and with colleagues (Mair, 2002; Mair, Sumner, & Rotteau, 2008), contrasts contemporary leisure, which is overwhelmingly individualistic and consumptive, with civil leisure which is deliberately social and critically reflexive. If contemporary leisure is focused predominantly on pleasure and enjoyment, civil leisure opens spaces for dialogue in the public sphere on topics that invite differing points of view (Mair, 2002). Though perhaps a small segment of societies' free time activities, civil leisure addresses precisely the sort of protest activities that arise from conflict-based community organizing. Further, as Heather has described, (Mair, 2002), civil leisure may often lead to activities, such as public protest, that subject participants to any number of physical, emotional, and/or legal harms. Nonetheless, civil leisure as manifested by organizing activities is undeniably expressive and creative, two characteristics that have frequently been associated with contemporary leisure (Kelly, 1982). Indeed, by casting individuals as participants in the civic processes that shape their communities, participation in community organizing is a form of collaborative expression that may transcend conventional lifestyle activities and individual preferences (Bellah et al., 1996).

Echoing the arguments underlying civil leisure, Glover and Stewart (2006) recast the phrase 'community recreation' to highlight its creative and progressive functions. Where community is typically understood as a setting in which recreation takes place and services are provided, Glover and Stewart have reappropriated recreation as a broader and more profound process that facilitates the relations between individuals that result in community. This conceptualization of community recreation does not take for granted that a collection of individuals within an arbitrary geographic boundary constitutes a community. Rather, their reinterpretation foregrounds the idea that groups of individuals are always recreating themselves as a collective that may provide some sort of group identity. Thus it is in such expressive and noninstrumental settings as public festivals and celebrations that individuals enact their connection and identity with others (Borgmann, 2013; Cook, 2003; Sharpe, 2008).

Recognizing the differences between community and communion (Yack, 1993), Glover and Stewart (2006) acknowledged the inherent clash of perspectives that the concept of community recreation implies. It is in the context of differing and potentially conflicting perspectives that community organizing stands to make its contribution to leisure. Community organizing, in its many forms, offers a powerful vehicle for the realization of civil leisure (Mair, 2002) and community recreation (Glover & Stewart). As opposed to the bureaucratic and corporatized nature of contemporary leisure services, the radically democratic ethos of conflict-based organizing provides a template for activity that allows individuals to realize their potential for collective action. Likewise, consensus-organizing models suggest ways in which citizens might realize their underlying connections to one another. In each case, place-based, citizen-driven action can chart a course for municipal leisure-service providers to take a more progressive approach to working with their communities.

> **Application Question**
>
> *In light of the concepts of civil leisure and community recreation, how might we, as advocates of leisure, engage our fellow community members in an effort to recreate our communities?*

CONCLUSION: LESSONS FOR THE CD PRACTITIONER

As we conclude this chapter, we would like encourage you to reflect on what this discussion might mean for the role *you* could play in your community (see Hutchison & McGill (1992) for more ideas). Here are some activities with which you may find yourself involved if you are assisting individuals or groups who face social injustice in your community:

- **Helping** to educate a group or individual engage with local authorities about an issue that is affecting them
- **Organizing** a meeting for a group or individuals to plan for a protest or a presentation to local authorities
- **Facilitating** a meeting between people who have a grievance and those who have the power to address that grievance
- **Advocating** for a group or individual who is facing social injustice (for example, writing a letter to the editor of the local paper or taking the lead in presenting issues to local leaders)
- **Coordinating** activities for individuals who may face barriers to participating in civil society
- **Connecting** individuals to one another so they may begin to share the issues that affect them and plan for a powerful, coordinated response for change.
- **Supporting** the empowerment of individuals or groups as they work to change their own lives.

Hutchison and McGill make it clear that recreationists who have a community development orientation (and vision) can and must make a difference—to help build alternatives—in these challenging times:

> The community vision pushes professionals and citizens alike to go beyond the current situation and begin building alternatives based on a deep caring and commitment to people who have been devalued. It requires recognition of the need for broader social change that will celebrate diversity and work at finding cooperative solutions to issues affecting all of us. (1994, p. 16)

As you finish this chapter, we'd like you to consider how you might envision a career that answers their call.

REFERENCES

Alinksy, S. (1971). *Rules for radicals: a practical primer for realistic radicals. Random House.*

Aristotle. (1984). Nicomachean ethics. In J. Barnes (Ed.), *The complete works of Aristotle* (Rev. ed.). Princeton, NJ: Princeton University Press.

Barnes, M. (2012, September 17). Mixing old Austin with new: Another generation of families, residents drawn to Crestview. *Austin American Statesman.* Retrieved from http://www.statesman.com/news/lifestyles/food-cooking/mixing-old-austin-new-another-generation-families-/nSC49/

Bellah, R. N., Madsen, R., Sullivan, W. M., Swidler, A., & Tipton, S. M. (1996). *Habits of the heart: Individualism and commitment in American life.* Berkeley, CA: University of California Press.

Borgmann, A. (2013). *Crossing the postmodern divide.* Chicago: University of Chicago Press.

Christensen, J. A., & Robinson, J. W. (1989). *Community development in America.* Ames, IA: Iowa State University Press.

Crestview Park Coalition (2013). Retrieved from http://park.crestviewna.org

Cook, D. T. (2003). Recreation. In K. Christensen & D. Levinson (Eds.), *Encyclopedia of community* (pp. 1146–1149). Thousand Oaks, CA: Sage.

Fisher, R. (1984). *Let the people decide: Neighborhood organizing in America.* Boston, MA: Twayne Publishers.

Fisher, R. (Ed.). (2009). *The people shall rule: ACORN, community organizing, and the struggle for economic justice.* Nashville, TN: Vanderbilt University Press.

Grusky, D. B., Western, B., & Wimer, C. (Eds.). (2011). *The great recession.* New York: The Russell Sage Foundation.

Helliwell, J. F., & Putnam, R. D. (2004). The social context of well-being. *Philosophical Transactions of the Royal Society, 359,*1435–1446

Hutchison, P., & McGill, J. (1992). *Leisure, integration and community.* Concord, Ontario: Leisurability Publications.

Hutchison, P., & McGill, J. (1994). New roles for recreationists. In G. L. Hitzhusen and L. Thomas (Eds.), *Global therapeutic recreation selected papers.* (pp. 9–16) University of Missouri.

Kawachi, I., & Kennedy, B. P. (2006). *The health of nations: Why inequality is harmful to your health.* New York: The New Press.

Kelly, J. R. (1982). *Leisure.* Englewood Cliffs, NJ: Prentice Hall.

Lanane, J. (2014, March 26). Crestview neighborhood pushes for a park. *Community Impact Newspaper,* Digital Edition. Retrieved from http://impactnews.com/austin-metro/central-austin/crestview-neighborhood-pushes-for-park/

Mair, H. (2002). Civil leisure? Exploring the relationship between leisure, activism, and social change. *Leisure/Loisir, 27*(3–4), 213–137.

Mair, H., Sumner, J., & Rotteau, L. (2008). The politics of eating: Food practices as critically reflexive leisure. *Leisure/Loisir, 32*(2), 379–405.

Medoff, P. (1994). *Streets of hope: The fall and rise of an urban neighborhood.* Boston, MA: South End Press.

Mills, C. W. (1959/2000). *The sociological imagination* (4th Ed.). New York: Oxford University Press.

Moore, L. V., Diez Roux, A. V., Evenson, K. R., McGinn, A. P., & Brines, S. J. (2008). Availability of recreational resources in minority and low socioeconomic status area. *American Journal of Preventative Medicine, 34*(1), 16–22.

Neulinger, J. (1981). *To leisure: An introduction.* Boston, MA: Allyn and Bacon.

Ohmer, M. L., & Brooks III, F. (2013). The practice of community organizing: Comparing and contrasting conflict and consensus approaches. In M. Weil, M. Reisch, and M. L. Ohmer (Eds.), *The handbook of community practice* (2nd Ed.) (pp. 233–248). Thousand Oaks, CA: Sage.

Perkins, D. D., & Long, D. A. (2002). Neighborhood sense of community and social capital: A multi-level analysis. In A. T. Fisher, C. C. Sonn, & B. J. Bishop (Eds.), *Psychological sense of community: Research, applications, and implications* (pp. 291–318). New York: Kluwer Academic-Plenum Publishers.

Putnam, R. D. (1993). *Making democracy work: Civic traditions in modern Italy.* Princeton, NJ: Princeton University Press.

Putnam, R. D. (2000). *Bowling alone: The collapse and revival of American community.* New York: Simon & Schuster.

Rubin, H. J., & Rubin, I. S. (2005). The practice of community organizing. In M. Weil (Ed.), *The handbook of community practice* (pp. 189–203). Thousand Oaks, CA: Sage.

Sharpe, E. K. (2008). Festivals and social change: Intersections of pleasure and politics at a community music festival. *Leisure Sciences, 30*(3), 217–234.

Speer, P. W., Jackson, C. B., & Peterson, N. A. (2001). The relationship between social cohesion and empowerment: Support and new implications for theory. *Health Education & Behavior, 28*(6), 716–732.

Staples, L. (Ed.) (2004). *Roots to power: A manual for grassroots organizing* (2nd Ed.). Westport, CT: Praeger Publishing.

Stoecker, R. (2003). Understanding the development-organizing dialectic. *Journal of Urban Affairs, 25*(4), 493–512.

Traynor, B. (2012). Community building: Limitations and promise. In J. DeFilippis and S. Saegert (Eds.), *The community development reader* (2nd Ed.) (pp. 209–219). New York: Routledge.

Yack, B. (1993). *The problems of a political animal. Community, justice, and conflict in Aristotelian political though.* Berkeley, CA: University of California Press.

12

COMPASSIONATE PEDAGOGY FOR REFLEXIVE COMMUNITY PRACTICES

Susan (Sue) M. Arai and Halyna Tepylo

KEYWORDS: Compassion, compassionate pedagogy, engaged embodiment, fear, joy, mindfulness, presence, serving, shame, suffering, vulnerability, witnessing.

> I began working for the neighborhood group. This was my dream job, making communities a better place and doing this part time while I finished courses in community advocacy. I wanted to help people. This position was in a neighborhood association, a not-for-profit organization at arm's reach to a local municipal government. I would play with kids, plan programs, foster wellness, create partnerships, help community grow, and finish my schooling. It was all planned out, my definitions were set. My first day of work, I walked into the community center with a big grin on my face . . .

Like Halyna describes in this opening vignette, we enter into community practice with hope, energy, and intention to use our minds, hearts, and passion for community. How soon we find ourselves, moment after moment, exposed to the joy, pain, and struggle of those around us and faced with complex decisions and negotiations wound around ethical concerns, justice, and democracy. To support us in this endeavor, this chapter is a call for compassionate pedagogy in community practices. By compassionate pedagogy we mean a mindfulness practice which engages embodiment and cultivates knowing and the presence of a community facilitator open to interconnectedness, who may move more deeply toward, and bear witness to, suffering rather than away from it. If we engage in community practices it is because we already have an intuitive awareness of suffering, oppression, or need for change in the world around us and have taken up a call to respond. We write this chapter from a place of knowing that it is our presence, our ability to engage in authentic relationships that sustains us, and others, as we move into the challenges and complexities of community practice. A capacity for deep reflection is needed for that kind of presence. This deep reflection is required to bring forth insight into experiences unaddressed or not spoken of, and in doing so we unveil forces that have been at work to immobilize agency and action in community practice. Compassionate pedagogy aims to deepen relationships at the foundation of community; it deepens implicit relational knowing at the foundation of trust. In so doing, compassionate pedagogy reopens us to joy in community practices. Compassionate pedagogy is not something to be achieved, or even something easily practiced. Consequently, this chapter is not to be read as a list of should dos, or have tos. This chapter is born from years of reflexivity on our own community practices, our willingness to explore with mindfulness and vulnerability our questions, feelings of failure, and painful moments in community practices which left us confused, lost, or sensing we had somehow missed our mark. We write this chapter to shed light on a path back to joy in community practices.

COMPASSIONATE PEDAGOGY IN THE CONTEXT OF TEACHING COMMUNITY PRACTICES

In this chapter we share experiences from our own classroom experience of compassionate pedagogy. This happened in a graduate course on community organizing and leisure facilitated by Sue and engaged in by Halyna. Engaging compassionate pedagogy requires fluid teaching spaces which blur lines between teacher and student, where learning spaces let go of structures and boundaries that separate and oppress us to give way to creating safe spaces and opportunities for meeting. Teaching from a place of compassionate pedagogy requires mindful openness and a willingness to co-create; to explore and share excitement, insight, passion, vulnerability, pain, and joy. It is born in dialogue. The focus was to write individual narratives from our experiences of community practices and reflect on them collectively each week, drawing connections to course readings chosen in response to the content of our narratives. In week one, we collectively discussed and shaped the assignment. From this dialogue, Susan wrote a description of the initial assignment to guide us as we wrote our narrative:

> Write a narrative of your experience in a community organization in which you played a role as a leader/teacher/volunteer/facilitator. In your narrative be sure to describe the community organization, people involved, and your role. As you write, think about the main story or stories about community you wish to reveal in your narrative (e.g., power, empowerment, bonds and connecting, leadership).
>
> As you write up your narrative: *place yourself in the role of the storyteller* and use "I" when needed; *write descriptively* providing as much detail as possible, including even what may seem like "inconsequential" or trivial details (i.e., it may be helpful to describe key images, sounds, tastes, smells, feelings or sensations, emotions); *describe events, actions, conversations, dialogue* without trying to interpret or explain what was happening (that will come later); and as you write, think about your *audience* and what you would like them to be able to know and feel as a result of reading your narrative.
>
> As a guideline, your narrative can be 2–4 pages in length (single-spaced) or longer or shorter if your narrative requires more or less space. Bring copies of your narrative to class next week so we can read them out loud and reflect collectively on each other's stories.

Excerpts in text boxes are from Halyna's narrative. Her experience reflects a moment many of us share, that first moment in community practice when we set out with hope and thoughts about possibilities, our best intentions, a foundation rooted in university education, and only a few community resources at our disposal.

> My first day of work, I walked into the community center with a big grin on my face. I was going to change the world, work hard, and be praised. This was the first time I had been given full decisive power. The community center I worked in represented municipal government. We had a small office tucked away in the corner. We were there out of convenience and cheap rent. I sat at my desk, crammed into a tiny office shared with my co-worker, and was told to start. With no idea what I was supposed to be doing, I spent the day looking at kids' games and attempted to make sense of my job by organizing the decade old information in folders appearing on my desk. Heaps of administrative paperwork barricaded the office from the outside world.
>
> When I started, I was met with dwindling participation numbers and budgets. I was told about horrible things my predecessor had done. I knew I needed to be better so I would not become the subject of this disdain. In my interview, I asked about community needs and how they were measured and understood. I was told to figure that out. This was something I was never able to do. Barriers, lack of time and interest from participants, and my inexperience in activating potential participants, became my excuses. University was designed to reward my regurgitation of buzzwords and lectures. The rigidity of my schooling resulted in only superficial knowledge about effective methods.
>
> I never heard of any community-driven needs assessments or true public participation. Everything we did was based on what we did historically and what the tight knit, three member planning committee thought. I felt constrained. Opinions and suggestions for kids' programming were gathered through surveys. I never received one back unless external motivation was offered. One person commented, "We love that we can win a $50 gift certificate." Congratulations? People didn't care enough to do this. Even the yearly mandatory public budget and strategy meeting was masked under a festival. I don't think anyone ever stopped to have a group conversation. I did not know what to do. Decisions were being made by a few key people—myself included.
>
> I felt I was a failure. I was also an outsider. I did not live in the community. How could I make improvements if I was not a part of the group? I did not understand what happens when our methods fail.

RISKING VULNERABILITY AND WITNESSING AS A PATH TO KNOWING

As Halyna's narrative unfolded she dug into painful moments in her experience of community practice. Carolyn Ellis (1999) aptly describes, "the vulnerability of revealing yourself, not being able to take back what you've written or having any control over how readers interpret it. It is hard not to feel your life is being critiqued as well as your work" (p. 672). As a reader, we ask you to hold Halyna's experience, her description, her emotion, her vulnerability, and her courage, and to do so with respect and without judgment. This is a true act of witnessing, hearing and holding Halyna's experience, letting her words land on your mind, body, and heart, to allow her words and experiences to impact and move you. To witness Halyna fully is to hold her experience without allowing our own assumptions, quick judgments, pity, or sympathy to close down the space for exploring the experience being described. Instead we enter into this exploration with curiosity, wondering, wanting to know more about what Halyna might have experienced. We must resist what Stacey Holman Jones (2005) refers to as the *rush to identification* involving a collapsing of me into you, and you into me. This acts to close down space for exploration, for understanding the experience of another from his or her position, it also shuts down engagement and responsibility. For example, in reflecting on the vignettes do you find yourself thinking "I know exactly what Halyna is talking about, I had that same experience when I . . ." or "I wouldn't have done it that way . . ." If you do, try to let go of these words to focus attention back on, and to enter more fully into, the experiences Halyna shares. In witnessing we hold space open for vulnerability, both the writer's and our own. In doing so, change within each of us becomes possible.

CULTIVATING COMPASSION—WITNESSING AND SERVING AS A FOUNDATION TO (INTER) CONNECTION

> I heard how successful our community group was in holding a community presence and fostering participation. I heard good things from actively involved staff, volunteers and participants. I was praised for what I did, partnerships I created, and how I interacted with people, but what I saw was clouded by my growing negativity. I saw a few people who wanted to stay busy. I saw people dropping kids off for free babysitting, not caring what they did. I saw youth voluntold to help, spending their time texting. I was overwhelmed.
>
> One man with a large family used our food cupboard every month, asking for toothbrushes and toothpaste. We were often in short supply and could not give out these items. Many negative comments were said about him, faulting him for being entitled. We did not know his situation. I didn't want to judge him, but his constant arguments and attempts to trick us into getting more frustrated me. Even more frustrating, was the power we had over something so small—we had toothbrushes and he could not have them. There were also complaints from volunteers and staff. Was I just as bad as them? I wondered about my values and desire to succeed in a community organization.
>
> I was caught in a cloud of negativity, both mine and others. I decided what was important because I ran the program and no one cared what I did as long as kids were safe and babysat. I became extremely anxious. I couldn't figure out what to do to be good at my job. My success was not from helping the community but by fitting in with those in charge. My coworker and I were in a space of negativity. " Exhausted, we did what we needed to do to get through the week. There was no passion. I ran through the motions. We complained, "I'm done for the week, I need a vacation" and "Not this person again. I can't deal with them right now." My mind was screaming. Volunteers told me they did not want to put in much effort since kids did not benefit from the programs anymore. With my desperate need to fit in and succeed, I imitated this behavior. I was overwhelmed. Cast aside was my naïve thinking that community groups can change the world. Dashed hopes of perfection caused my exhaustion and fueled my negativity. I decided I could no longer work there. Something needed to change and I decided it was me. I was questioning who I was, my roles, others' roles, and the ability for things to get better. I was scared that I did not know the answer. I left because I couldn't be the answer and that was a failure. Upon announcing my decision to leave, I was greeted with sadness and praise of my work. Pleasing to my ego, but

not worth the everyday struggles. I realized job success was not the point . . . I reflected on the positive aspects of the organization—the youth leadership program helped teenagers gain skills, eager university volunteers were willing to learn and help plan, children had support, and executive members were interested in community well-being—indicating people cared enough to be active. Still, the negatives churned in my mind. What happens to the community when the organization fails it?

As frustration, sadness, and struggle grow, our call for compassion deepens. Compassion is mistakenly thought of as a trait of a community developer. Compassion is not a static trait one is born with. In each moment, compassion is "born of our willingness to meet pain rather than to run from it" (Feldman, 2005, p. 2). Therefore, compassionate pedagogy is an ongoing action of cultivating compassion in moments when we are faced with pain of another, conflict, loss, betrayal, and disappointment. Compassion emerges when walls of judgment and defensiveness crumble, clouds of confusion dissipate, and waves of fear and anguish dissolve into the tender softening of acceptance, patience, and openheartedness. Compassion is the "expression of a liberated heart" (Feldman, 2005, p. 7) offering us refuge as we feel our hearts open to our own experience and touch the broken hearted experience of another. As Christina Feldman (2005) writes:

> Life cannot be controlled or predicted. In moments of pain, fear, anger, and the desire for self-protection are provoked to the surface. In those moments, you face a choice–your heart can close, your mind recoil, and your body contract, or you can dive deeply inward to find and nurture the balance, resilience, and courage that allow you to deepen and care (p. 3).

How then do we deepen and cultivate our capacity for compassion? Our ability to be compassionate with others begins first with our ability to deeply reflect on our own experience and be compassionate with ourselves. That is why this narrative reflection of Halyna's is so important. Compassionate pedagogy necessitates witnessing our own pain and suffering as a precursor to understanding and serving to witness the pain and suffering of others. In witnessing we do not attempt to fix—no solution, no advice, no prescriptions are offered. We do not attempt to help by doing for others. Instead we witness and "[t]he innate compassion of simply being received and listened to" provides person(s) we serve to "listen to the cries of her own heart with compassion" (Feldman, 2005, p. 26). At the heart of this is the belief that individuals possess an inherent energy, passion, and agency to be rekindled through practices of compassion.

> *Exercise.*
>
> *Recall a moment in community that left you feeling stuck in some way.*
>
> *Where do you hold tension in your body? Jaw? Shoulders? Stomach?*
>
> *Lightly bring awareness to that spot in your body.*
>
> *What emotion do you feel arising in that spot? Sadness? Fear? Anger? Rage? Hatred?*
>
> *What stories do you tell about the situation, people involved, yourself?*
>
> *Envision those stories as a train leaving the station. Watch them go. Let it all go.*
>
> *Stay with the feeling in your body.*
>
> *As you patiently watch, stay open to what emerges.*

The call in this moment was for each of us (Halyna, Sue, and you, the reader) to hold and witness Halyna's narrative with compassion. Gestures of compassion do not have to be grandiose. We enter into compassion without wanting to fix a problem or another person. In making this shift to compassionate pedagogy we must let go of our sense of ourselves, our identities, as helpers and fixers. Marilyn Friedman (1995) writes about "the legitimacy of communal norms and traditions that are supposed to define the moral starting points of community members" (p. 192). The moral starting point Halyna went into the position with was to help others, and not to be a judge of who deserved what, but her views of helping were challenged. Negative comments about people who used the food bank forced Halyna to reevaluate her identity as a helper, and the nature of providing for others. Jean Vanier (1998) describes the difficulties and dangers in forming relationships with human beings who touch our hearts recalling from his own experience, "I was frightened of being swallowed up by her pain and her need" (p. 70). It is in these moments when our hearts are touched that we are vulnerable. In 1997, Susan Arai wrote about resisting the temptation to do for others, noting from her own experience, "I was inclined to be a doer. However, my desire to act quickly to alleviate pain and suffering had to be controlled, for in the end, it would have hindered the [empowering nature of the] process" (p. 9). Halyna struggled between organizational pushes and pulls of individuals and felt swallowed up by pain and need surrounding her. Parents spent countless hours supporting children's pursuits and working to support their family, asking for help in the only ways they could. Halyna reflects how she and coworkers judged who they would *help*, and who they would force barriers upon, and how asking people to conform to rules created confusion and a hard distrust of both the system and individuals.

Instead of helping or fixing, we turn to compassion in the spirit of serving others. We engage compassion in each small moment rather than through a quest to achieve a grandiose goal (a fix) that leaves us feeling like a failure, like trying to end poverty, putting a stop to racism, or creating an ideal community in which people do not experience isolation. It is about turning to the pain of knowing that this act in and of itself will not end racism, poverty, homophobia, ableism, or disease; rather it is part of millions of act that collectively create the conditions for these ends to unfold. It is not an attempt to fix or help but a commitment to serve the conditions that contribute to those ends; to transform through compassion each moment of injustice, fear, pain, hatred beginning with those that appear in relation to the narrative. Compassion is born in each moment of practice, one pebble on the path that leads us to the ending of suffering. The practice is one of engaged embodiment—to pay attention to your internal experience—to notice those moments when we feel our walls go up, our breathing stop, our jaw clench, and then to breathe, and open to reflect on the messages contained within this experience.

Exercise.

Remember, this is not an attempt to fix you or to engage in some ongoing self-improvement project that has to be accomplished before you can engage with others in community. If you find yourself turning the sharp edge of judgment, fault-finding, and blame on yourself, this is not compassion. Let judgment, fault, and blame go, another train leaving the station.

As you reflect on that moment in which you felt fear, or anger, or hatred, how might you find compassion for yourself?

How might you soften this place that feels hard and rigid?

Gently focus awareness into this space and feel the edges of your experience. How hard or tight does that spot feel? Feel to the edges of the tightness, where does it end in your body?

Breathe into that spot of anger, fear, hatred, and send yourself a smile for your humanness. Give it space to unfold and move into a deeper knowing.

Finding compassion in these moments is foundational to our community practices; to our dialogues, connections, networks, and creation of communities. As Feldman (2005) describes, "[f]inding compassion for yourself in those moments is the forerunner of being able to extend compassion without conditions to others, whose rage, fear, withdrawal, disconnection, and confusion are no different than your own" (p. 11). Consequently, compassionate pedagogy requires an engaged presence and attending to your own experience to expand your capacity to be present for others. As you come to "understand the pain of those experiences in your own heart and are willing to be present and be intimate with that pain, you can find the steadfastness and courage to be present for another person entangled in some pain" (Feldman, 2005, p. 11).

EMBRACING SHAME AND SUFFERING, AWAKENING TO THE FULL CATASTROPHE OF COMMUNITY

> Arbitrary boundaries defining our community meant we served a wide variety of people with different mindsets and personal situations. To deliver flyers advertising programs, I had to cross a field, a business plaza, and a busy road. I could not walk this area to get to the locations of programs. I had to drive. Along the road, nestled at the outskirts of town, I saw beautiful brick houses, manicured lawns, and families at play. Money. "Keep driving," I told myself. Around the corner were cooperative housing units. I

entered the shared entranceway to reach the mailboxes. It was dirty. It reeked of smoke, urine, and poverty. The contrast in worlds was palpable and confusing, "was I not just in a different place?" Programs also were segregated and closed to specific groups because we could not individually meet the needs of everyone.

As the community center was at the edge of the community, we had outsiders using our programs. Programs in their community catered to the well off, ours the opposite. Many people with low incomes came from outside of our boundaries to participate in our free programs. This created smaller groups within our own community. We also had to strongly suggest outsiders use offerings in their own community. Subsidies were available but created embarrassment for many. It made me sad, sadness led to shame, and shame lead to fear.

It was easy to lose focus on the goals of the neighborhood group. I saw the same kids, volunteers, adults, and programs every day. Maybe we were helping these kids gain skills but we were not addressing the issue of community. How can we create a sense of community when no one wanted to participate? There was no strong sense of community, just static mini-communities. However, we were given status and congratulations for our "community" without anyone actually examining what our community really was, and without listening to active or passive members. "Buzzwords" of community allowed us to validate ourselves.

As Halyna continued to reflect on her narrative, the divided nature of this community became clearer. Members belonged to their own internal communities. Volunteers and staff also had their own community—one that created barriers for participants, and may have been at the root of people feeling fear and shame for using services. Perhaps this method of community development rooted in communities of place was better suited to a pre-modern world in which individuals' purposes were predetermined? Geographic boundaries of the neighborhood association set who was a "member," but with technology and media outlets, members had the freedom to participate in whichever community they wished. They were discouraged from promoting use of other group's services even if doing so served members of the community.

As we joined Halyna in exploring her narrative, we held space for holding and witnessing her disappointments and her tears. We gave space to explore the disillusion that Blackshaw (2010) states we tend to overlook in community studies. We opened space for questions: Were programs offered as a means to an end? Who and how did it serve? For parents, programs meant free babysitting where kids could play organized games with others. For some children programs provided friendships and meaningful activity, and for others, community participation meant having rules, activities, and discipline forced upon them. Blackshaw (2010) questions whether inclusion in community can be achieved when it is undesired, or if it even should be a goal of community development in a forced community.

As we notice tensions and ways people are harmed in community practices, and reflect on our role in these practices, our own feelings of embarrassment, guilt, or shame may arise. With this often comes an attempt to hide, get rid of, or to admonish self for feeling what is human. We try to banish our anger and feelings of pettiness, or feel ashamed for feeling greed or a grasping for control. As Feldman (2005) describes:

> [p]ride becomes the new focus of your endeavors to perfect yourself, and then you are horrified to find it replaced by greed. At some point, it may dawn upon you that the entire project is motivated by nonacceptance and idealized notions of perfection (p. 11).

Consequently, in practicing compassionate pedagogy we consider our humanness in all feelings and experiences—insecurity, control, fear, confusion, anger, guilt, shame—and hold it all; that is, as we engage in community practices we hold what Jon Kabat-Zinn (1990) refers to as the "full catastrophe."

Exercise.

Go inward and look at the things you say to yourself about feelings you have. How are you engaged in self-blame, self-judgment to clamp down on your fear, insecurity, shame etceras? How might you instead open to the full catastrophe and engage compassion for yourself and others?

When this happens, we often find ourselves as community practitioners falling into despair, depression, and overwhelm. Our practices of self-blame, self-judgment, fault-finding, defending are acts of violence against self. At other times, attempting to free ourselves from the shackles of shame we throw judgment and blame on people around us, perpetuating a violence against others and promoting the division of self from other. Both—our inward and outward projections of blame and judgment—perpetuates division, isolation, and feelings of deep loneliness which are the doorway to despair and exclusion. Instead of participating in these acts of violence toward self and others, what if we took up Christina Feldman's suggestion to hold the question of "how you would respond if you knew that anger, fear, resistance, and anxiety might be lifelong companions?" (p. 12). As she notes:

> You could continue to deny them, condemn them, or try to purge them from your heart. Or you could explore the possibility of a radical change of heart. Is it possible to embrace all that you are most prone to condemn or fear with receptive kindness? Can you accept the moments of anger and fear as guests, be willing to receive them with kindness without feeling obliged to serve them a five-course meal? No one likes being angry or afraid, but they are not your enemies. They are painful feelings that invite investigation, understanding, and tenderness. You can learn to accept these feelings with equanimity and allow them to arise and pass without blindly identifying with them or acting upon them. It is often the hardest moments of our lives that we find the deepest compassion. To postpone compassion is to postpone your capacity to engage with your life in the fullest and wisest way (Feldman, 2005, p. 12).

Once we become comfortable with looking into the doorway of our own pain and suffering, it becomes a doorway into insight and understanding of the experiences of others.

Exercise.

Reflect on the following question: How might the pain and suffering you are experiencing mirror the experiences of people in the community you serve?

Compassionate pedagogy is about realizing interconnectedness. It helps us see beyond right and wrong, us and them, and instead reminds us of the universal nature of human experience. As Feldman (2005) reminds, "there is no pain you can experience that has not been experienced before by another in a different time or place. Our emotional world is universal" (p. 14). Therefore, compassionate pedagogy is an ongoing practice. It is not something we will ever get perfect or right. It is not as if one day we will always be compassionate and never feel the grips of anger or hatred, the heartbreak of injustice, or fear in the face of violence. In our lifetimes we will not likely see the end of racism, poverty, ableism, misogyny and other forms of hatred, violence, and oppression. Again and again you will be asked to "open your heart and receive it. 'This also, this also' is the essence of compassion. Over and over you are asked to meet change, loss, injustice, and over and over you are asked to find strength to open when you are most inclined to shut down" (Feldman, 2005, p. 13).

What often obscures our ability to look more deeply and engage compassion in community practices is the label or symbol of community imposed on it; that is, we begin with the label of community rather than people and understanding the unique relationships, patterns, and knowledge contained within. Blackshaw (2010) notes symbols of community are often forced upon regions, in this case, the neighborhood. Furthermore, symbols of community are passed down through education systems and policies. Halyna was an outsider obligated to look on the group as a community. This label was given to make the group meaningful. Administrators knew community because they viewed it through this symbol. Instead of meaningfully examining more naturally imagined communities emerging from within, success was defined by how well one could speak to the label of community and provide symbols of community that state how well the community was achieving its goals. Halyna described it felt like she and the organization's structure were blind to community needs and possibilities. Instead their focus was on making procedures work and ensuring positive symbols of community—the great programs and supports being offered—were promoted. With supporting numbers and artifacts, thank-you cards received, Halyna described how it was easy to show participation rates and goal attainment to people who never looked beyond reports. Never did an outsider of the staff and main volunteer group get to hear about challenges within the group unless the input could be used to obtain more funding. The problem, Blackshaw (2010) states, is community becomes a "signature" word, "[i]t comes with the promise to consign the present to the future and with it limit the possibilities of choice concerning anything from geographical spaces to social identities, from cultural difference to political exigencies" (p. 129). While Halyna writes about believing this symbol of community initially, she started to question procedures and goals. In embracing shame and suffering within our community practices we are able to lift the illusion of community and witness the experiences that truly lie within. Čulík speaks of "kitsch" as "that beautiful lie, which hides all the negative aspects of life" (cited in Blackshaw, 2010, p. 43). Often when the symbol of community is invoked, community it is seen as inherently positive. Through compassionate pedagogy we embrace the full catastrophe of community to uncover new ways that collective community can be a force for change when change is needed.

TOWARD HEARTFUL AND EMOTIONAL RELATIONSHIPS OF POWER

Rather than relationships rooted in economic transactions and utilitarian benefits, compassionate pedagogy requires relationships rooted in emotional connection. Compassionate pedagogy requires that we patiently wade through actions tied to individual and collective fears, greed, or apathy and emerge into more heartful engagement of power relations. In the following excerpts, Halyna's reflections began to explore her experience through the lenses of academic literature that tells us how to engage in community practices. We further reflect on these ideas to elaborate on the practice of compassionate pedagogy.

Exercise.

Reflect on connections you have experienced in community. What is the root of those connections? What is the quality and strength of those connections?

> Michael Fabricant and Robert Fisher (2002) speak about engagement, participation, relationships of community within the program, and networks to the broader community. While our organization had the latter two, we scrambled with engagement and participation. We struggled to nurture emotional connections. Our outreach was mostly in the form of pamphlets delivered door-to-door, offering little motivation. Susan Stall and Randy Stoecker (2005) speak of "community as a liminal space" (p. 196), at the crossroads of public and private life. We had many connections to outside private and public resources that created links for participants, but the linkages were very distinct. We didn't allow the linkages to be an intersection, a space for joint growth, but rather they were a way to create a barrier and separate programs; a participant could either come to our food closet, or use food closets in another geographic area, not both. This only furthered the direction of our neighborhood association to exist solely to provide individual solutions to temporary needs.

Holding this reflection creates opportunity for us to reflect on how we might engage community practices to create emotional connections in community space, for new ways of engaging that do not simply reproduce the transactional nature of social and economic networks. Halyna describes how they resisted change in their community practices; how loosening their grip on history (i.e., this is how we have always done it), would require them to take risks, make themselves vulnerable, and move in ways that engaged people in different ways. This movement requires embracing our fears, the many and the multiple, that arise individually and collectively in community practices. As Jean Vanier (1998) observes, "Fear is at the root of all forms of exclusion, just as trust is at the root of all forms of inclusion" (p. 71). This was further reflected in Halyna's next reflection:

> I identify with Jean Vanier's (1998) own reflections, "I am beginning to discover how fear is a terrible motivating force in our lives" (p. 71), and "[f]ear demands the status quo" (p. 73). This fear of failure arises in my narrative. With my structured upbringing and past education, I needed to follow regulations and succeed in my job. I failed at making connections with members but I was able to make connections to other agencies and administrations. They were like me, and I was successful in dealing with similar people. I had not yet learned how to open myself up to difference. In the same light, this fear of failure led me to not question policies, or group norms, essentially maintaining the status quo. I had what Vanier describes as "an immature heart" and my ideas of community had to be questioned before I could realize how a difference could be made. As I learn from experience, I am able to gain a freedom from conformity. I began to understand Jean Vanier's (1998) statement about his own experience, "I tend to conform to what is expected of me and am fearful of going against the norm or of what my 'superiors' want of me. Is there a fear in me of being seen as guilty if I go against the norm?" (p. 93). More and more I

understand my tendency towards this, and now work to challenge myself to resist.

I struggled with the notion of job success. I had to work hard to be successful and wanted to continue this trend by fitting into the work environment. I belonged in the community of staff, not in the community experiencing and participating in programs. Boundaries between groups arising as a result of fear of unknown others restricted trust. I began to wonder: Did children who attended the games night feel they belonged? Did adults who found social networks with parents struggling with similar issues consider it community? If the neighborhood group were collectively empowered, what would programs be like?

A focus on needs and what was broken kept me fixated on what was wrong with the group, instead of what was right. I kept a smile on my face at work pretending all around me was positive, but soon drained of energy I was not able to keep this façade. John Kretzman and John McKnight (2005) emphasize, "nonprofit organizations are much more powerful community actors when they are not exclusively focused on needs, problems, and deficiencies but are effectively connected to the resources, or assets, of the local community" (p. 1). A focus on the assets would have allowed me as a leader to serve in connecting people with resources, and each other. A community can help each other grow, learn each others' abilities, and learn that each can play a meaningful role (Fabricant & Fisher, 2002). If we were able to open a space where community-minded volunteers could lead this, the organization would have been more successful. To do so, we needed to lean into our fear of giving up our power. Within the model the group worked, there were people in power who did not want to break down power they held. As Jean Vanier (1998) reminds us, "leaders consider themselves as generally in the right. It is part of the paradigm we have created: if you have succeeded in making your way to the top, then, by definition, by the law of natural selection, the values for which you stand have been authenticated" (p. 75). Instead, true leaders need to work to build relationships and trust with the community, to create space for people to express fears of participating, fear of stigmas, and fear of exclusion. I am also learning that leaning into fear requires much patience (Arai, 1997; Vanier, 1998).

Exercise.

How might fear be sitting within your community practices?

What fears arise within you? What do you notice about how you respond?

How does fear impede our ability to work together?

How might we begin a conversation about this fear?

Once we have walked into our fear it creates space for imagining a different way of being together, or creating imagined communities. When community is looked at as imagined, people create their own interpretations of community and determine the meaning it plays in their own lives (Blackshaw, 2010).

Some participants developed bonds with others attending programs, events, or sharing in their children's experiences but they may not have felt community. I smile as I remember a parent speaking to me about her six year old son's birthday party and how he had an invitation for someone he had met through the group. Though he did not know the other boy's name, they formed a bond with each other from day one. Another time, we wondered why no one had shown up for a busy cultural program designed to support people who are new immigrants to settle in the region. We later found out participants missed the program because they joined together to visit a group member who was in hospital undergoing cancer treatments.

Creating a community of place, the program structure allowed the subcultures Marilyn Friedman (1995) speaks of, to grow to form relationships and capacity in other ways. Jean Vanier (1998) speaks to humans wanting to be with others like themselves. Countless examples proved this to be true. However, this imposed neighborhood group did nothing to address diversity and fear of others who were different. Here, I reached another impasse as I reflected on how the organization strengthened community ties among some and yet, left large barriers for others. As Susan Stall and Randy Stoecker (2005) would have us reflect, we failed to provide a space of connection between haves and have-nots. Walls of resistance were allowed to be built within a diverse community. Perhaps the value of imposed neighborhood groups is the possibility for programs to offer a place for future bonds and future capacity to grow in diversity. Offering services some may be afraid or embarrassed to need, such as a food bank, may have led to fear of participating in other programs.

Segregation appearing in the community made sense. People wanted to be with like people who had similar needs. To be inclusive, we needed to embrace fear and open to trusting others, and look at our practices that brought shame to participants, "break[ing] down the prejudices and protective walls that gave rise to exclusion in the first place" (Vanier, 1998, p. 84). Marilyn Friedman (1995) challenges the view that we must belong in one community at a time; rather, through freedom of choice, individuals may belong to any number of communities. How might our practices of community development encourage the fluid movement of people within and across networks, recognizing interconnections we have to many communities that support our flourishing?

Building from the idea of choice, compassionate pedagogy requires an understanding of the vagaries of politics and a different understanding of power so that we might negotiate power and resist oppressions, compassionately. Our ability to engage empowerment (Arai, 2007) and resistance (Shaw, 2006) in our practices of community organizing requires we become aware of the inner workings of power. Consider Halyna's reflections in the following text box:

Neighborhood association volunteers and staff started out with heart on a path to help, but when a leader responsible for facilitating social capital has no power or knowledge to do so, programs and helpers become complacent and energy for community practices stagnate. In our neighborhood association there were a few volunteers who reflected what Susan Arai (2000) described as citizen volunteers who "identify strongly with their chosen pursuit" (p. 342). When the power of the municipality is coupled with a "lack of clear understanding of ways to achieve social change," individuals in the neighborhood association who invested heart into their work were pushed into labor volunteer roles destined to carry out the will of the municipality. Arai (2000) notes how great frustration arises when citizen volunteers are forced into roles associated with labor volunteers creating less "thick trust" and identification with the organization as they are asked to play a more passive role in the vision and direction of the organization. A shift occurred as citizen volunteers turned into frustrated labor volunteers, and this imposed helplessness contributed to a loss of energy and care put into efforts. Inner-conflict occurred within me; torn between change, wanting to help moved by feelings in my heart, and going through the labor of performing the motions of programs, I lost trust in my ability to make a difference in the organization with which I identified. It challenged my spirit. What is the point of being an involved citizen when all you are is labor?

Thich Nhat Hahn (2007) believes many individuals start on the right path along the road to power working towards good but get lost along the way with shifting goals of power and success interfering with happiness. Through my journey, power and success interfered in two ways. First, I had an inner desire to succeed. To fit in and avoid criticism I imitated others in the organization who had lost their passion. This interfered with my ability to serve. Second, I recognize that although I had a lot of power, I also lacked power to make changes. My initial approach full of hope and heart was abruptly halted when I realized my true position as labor. With compassion for myself, this required me to shift my understanding—my position did not have to be a powerless laborer. I could use my power to serve neighborhood citizens to realize their citizenship, to work to reduce power imposed by centralized organization structures, to serve to increase local ability to develop community, and to use the municipal-neighborhood group's assets and resources toward this end.

A FINAL REFLECTION FROM HALYNA

Beginning with such a positive entrance into community practice, it was troubling to leave this job 11 months later. I felt I failed. My journey started with me idolizing community development as a sacred and beautiful concept; I naively believed everyone could have a better life by participating in programs and services and that I could *help* this occur. My hopes of perfection shrank with my frustration and anxiety but through this experience I learned community practice is not easy and participating in a helping environment is not inherently good. Many times I gave up hope but I was not ready to stop believing in the possibility for community members to grow together as leaders, to open a space to build community.

Earlier in my reflections I asked, "what happens to a community when the organization fails it?" Perhaps a better question is: What happens when the community is built "with a focus on deficiencies and needs" (McKnight as cited in Fabricant & Fisher, 2002, p. 12)? I came to terms with power and decision making in a community organization. It appears that the definition of community an organization imposes may prevent community from forming in its truest sense—from within. I struggled to place a sense of community on the group but it was not my place to do so. Stories of friendships and support are reminders that individuals make strong connections, even in a system of heavy administration. My challenge was not in failing to create programs used by all, but to realize I could help facilitate inclusive programs for people who wanted to be included, and participation elsewhere could mean individuals had successfully found their own meaning. Upon reflection, I understand the community group needed to open a space to develop trust among members to grow together and create a better community, but also needed to support welcoming others to the group so that the group's capacity could expand (Arai & Pedlar, 2003).

I know I needed a different approach to learning, and to have patience with myself and processes along the way. We must stop to appreciate small things that bring support, joy, and community. Without this, one can get lost in the bureaucratic rigidness that creates an atmosphere of helplessness. In bureaucracy-designed groups, there is no "common history, a shared culture, and an apparent sense of purpose" (Blackshaw, 2010, p. 120); and this proved to be the case in our neighborhood association. However, it may be that the strength lay in developing the capacity of the neighborhood through programs leading to subcultures of imagined communities from within. Community is a place found through individuals' own meanings as people create their identities before community (Blackshaw, 2010).

Revealing these thoughts through narrative is a hard task in confronting what I thought were my failures and raw emotions in the experience. Once separated from the situation, I started a journey of compassionate pedagogy toward understanding how power, individuals, participation, and my own role and reflection, influence the growth and longevity of a community. Reflecting on my experience created a starting point to understand community organizations as a vehicle for social change, even when it does not fit into my predefined "perfect" community. I have come to challenge politics and power associated with top-down organizational roles in community practices, and wonder about a space where conflict among partners results in meaningful starting points. I have learned my quest to serve requires me to invest in more powerfully understanding what I believe in, rather than focusing on personal "success." Social change is not possible when leaders follow, or even when outside leaders lead without fostering reciprocal leadership relationships with community members. A shift needs to occur whereby space is created for fear to be expressed and explored in community relationships, creating opportunity for this conversation to emerge into trust and collective power in relationships. Most of all, I need to be better able to appreciate the small things that made the community beautiful and what the community did gain. Participating in the recreation programs and community gatherings offered a space for community to develop relationships and create their own subcultures. In seeing the positives, I can keep faith in the process that the community can continue to grow, despite existing barriers.

I leave these reflections feeling much more empowered to learn more than before. I am beginning to look back on my experiences with insight. I use Thich Nhat Hanh's (2007) words "we don't allow ourselves to be carried away by despair, anger, or negativity, because our insight tells us exactly what to do and what not to do to change the situation" (p. 26) as a reminder of mindfulness in my journey of learning and growing in this act of compassionate pedagogy.

This is now the space to turn inward and reflect on your own experience:

What came up for you as you read the chapter?

What do you notice about your willingness to sit with and feel into difficult emotion?

What is it like for you to witness someone else's vulnerability?

How does this touch into your own vulnerability?

What does that tell you about your own experience with community practices?

What would you change in your approach to community practices?

REFERENCES

Arai, S. M. (1997). Empowerment: From the theoretical to the personal. *Journal of Leisurability, 24*(4), 3–11

Arai, S. M. (2000). Typology of Volunteers for a changing sociopolitical context: The impact on social capital, citizenship and civil society. *Loisir et société/Society and Leisure, 23*(2), 327–352.

Arai, S., & Pedlar, A. (2003). Moving beyond individualism in leisure theory: a critical analysis of concepts of community and social engagement. *Leisure Studies, 22*(3), 185–202.

Blackshaw, T. (2010). *Key concepts in community studies.* Los Angeles: Sage Publications

Ellis, C. (1999). Heartful autoethnography. *Qualitative Health Research, 9*(5), 669–683.

Fabricant, M., & Fisher, R. (2002). Agency based community building in low income neighborhoods: A praxis framework. *Journal of Community Practice, 10*(2), 1–22.

Feldman, C. (2005). *Compassion: Listening to the cries of the world.* Berkeley, CA: Rodmell Press.

Friedman, M. (1995) Feminism and modern friendship: Dislocating the community. In P. A. Weiss & M. Friedman (Eds.), *Feminism and community* (pp. 187–207). Philadelphia: Temple University Press

Hahn, T. N. (2007). *The art of power.* New York, NY: HarperCollins Publishers.

Holman Jones, S. (2006). Autoethnography: Making the personal political. In N. K. Denzin & Y. S. Lincoln (Eds.), *Sage handbook of qualitative research (3rd ed.)* (pp. 763–791). Thousand Oaks, CA: Sage.

Kabat-Zinn, J. (1990). *Full catastrophe living: Using the wisdom of your body and mind to face stress, pain, and illness.* New York, NY: Bantam Dell.

Kretzman, J. P., McKnight, J. L., Dobrowolski, S., & Puntenney, D. (2005). *Discovering community power: A guide to mobilizing local assets and your organization's capacity.* Evanston, IL: Northwestern University, School of Education and Social Policy, Asset-Based Community Development Institute.

Shaw, S. M. (2006). Resistance. In C. Rojek, S. M. Shaw, & A. J. Veal (Eds.), *A handbook of leisure studies.* New York: Palgrave Macmillan.

Stall, S., & Stoecker, R. (2005). Toward a gender analysis of community organizing models: Liminality and the intersection of spheres. In M. Minkler (Eds.), *Community organizing and community building for health (2nd ed.).* (pp. 196–217). New Brunswick, New Jersey: Rutgers University Press.

Vanier, J. (1998). From exclusion to inclusion: A path of healing. In *Becoming Human* (pp. 69–103). Toronto, ON: Anansi.

PART C
CONTEMPORARY CONTEXT AND FUTURE DIRECTIONS

13

RECREATION, DEVELOPMENT, AND YOUTH

Brett D. Lashua

INTRODUCTION: READING RECREATION

The title of J. D. Salinger's well-known book *The Catcher in the Rye* (1951) was once puzzling to me: what is a "catcher in the rye"? Although required to read it years ago in high school, it was not until I started working in the field of youth recreation that I read the book again, more leisurely this time, that the title's meaning came into sharper focus. The protagonist, 17-year old Holden Caulfield, reveals the source of the title when describing a lucid dream:

> Anyway, I keep picturing all these little kids playing some game in this big field of rye and all. Thousands of little kids, and nobody's around—nobody big, I mean—except me. And I'm standing on the edge of some crazy cliff. What I have to do, I have to catch everybody if they start to go over the cliff—I mean if they're running and they don't look where they're going I have to come out from somewhere and catch them. That's all I do all day. I'd just be the catcher in the rye and all. I know it's crazy, but that's the only thing I'd really like to be. (p. 173)

For youth recreation practitioners working in the 'field,' this vision is allegorical, evoking visions of programs that 'save' young people from all sorts of dangers, as well as protecting an ideal vision of 'youth' itself. My rediscovery of this book coincided with working with young people labeled 'at-risk' which challenged my practical and academic knowledge of youth recreation and communities (see Lashua, 2010). In my first 'real job' in recreation, I helped deliver a program for adopted young people with disabilities who had spent years in group homes or were separated from siblings in different foster placements (Lashua, Widmer, & Munson, 2000). Many participants were struggling to adjust to the changing circumstances of their lives. In hindsight, I might say that they had already gone over the cliff that Holden was so worried about. Yet, they had survived, and the purpose of the recreation program where I worked with them was not to save anyone but to offer respite, a moment to pause their everyday lives, and reconnect (with siblings and others) who had lived through similar experiences. They were part of a community that I could never fully comprehend. This was highly educational for me, and the experience also allowed me to see Holden Caulfield in a new, more critical view: he is an unreliable narrator (see Edwards, 1977) and I was not buying into his desperate vision of youthful innocence anymore.

This chapter asks what students and practitioners might learn about youth, recreation and community from reading books such as *The Catcher in the Rye.* More broadly, it grounds youth recreation and community development concepts through young adult (YA) fiction—i.e., popular books geared for readers from ages 12–20—and I argue that many of these books are more than revelatory; they are also instructive.

Although I use a playful approach to studying recreation through reading, the chapter takes youth leisure and community development seriously, by taking young adult fiction seriously, and tracing lines of understanding that may be developed between the two. In what follows, I first set out some common themes, plot conflicts and resolutions I perceive in YA books. The chapter's second section provides a framework for thinking about the construction of 'youth' as a historical and social category, and considers the role that YA books play in such constructions. The next section offers a snapshot of youth recreation and community development themes in Michael Grant's (2008) *Gone,* read along with other YA books. *Gone* provides a fantastic example; the book's central plot device is that in the blink of an eye, every person 15 years old or over vanishes: they are 'gone.' The story that results offers a strangely compelling case study of youth and community development, not far from William Golding's (1954) *Lord of the Flies,* and also eerily echoing the adult-free vision of Holden Caulfield from *The Catcher in the Rye.* Finally, I consider common themes across these books in view of youth and community development models: in the absence of adults, how does community develop amongst young people left on their own? In the fantastic worlds and 'strange zones' (Shaw, 2013) of fiction that allow readers to consider different social realities, why do adult-free communities often fail so spectacularly? What are the lessons to be learned?

YOUNG ADULT FICTION

Although its roots may be traced back at least as far as the end of World War II, young adult fiction—from classics including J. D. Salinger's (1951) *The Catcher in the Rye,* William Golding's (1954) *Lord of the Flies,* J. R. R. Tolkien's (1954) *The Lord of the Rings* trilogy, and C. S. Lewis' (1950) *The Chronicles of Narnia* series, to more recent publications including Philip Pullman's (1995–2000) *His Dark Materials* trilogy, J. K. Rowling's (1997–2007) *Harry Potter* books, Stephanie Myers' (2005–2008) *Twilight* saga, Cassandra Clare's (2007–2014) *The Mortal Instruments* cycle, Malorie Blackman's (2001–2008) *Noughts & Crosses* five-book set, James Dashner's (2009–2011) *The Maze Runner* series, and Suzanne Collins' (2008–2010) *Hunger Games* trilogy to name just a few—is a relatively recent, often controversial and hugely popular genre. The numbers alone are staggering: Salinger's novel has sold around 65 million copies, Meyer's work achieved over 85 million books sold, and with Rowling's work surpassing an astonishing 450 million book sales worldwide. Beyond sheer quantities, the impact and influence of the ideas these books contain and stimulate is worth scholarly consideration.

While a few leisure scholars have commented on recreation and reading (e.g., Bairner, 2012; Pike, 2013; Stebbins, 2013), there is virtually nothing in the recreation and leisure studies scholarship about young adult literature. In other fields, researchers have explored social issues presented in YA fiction, such as teens' social and emotional development (Hebert & Kent, 2000), eating disorders in adolescent boys (Muise, Stein, & Arbess, 2003), LGBTQQ sexualities (Cart & Jenkins, 2006) and myriad other aspects of youth identity development (Bean & Koni, 2003). This scholarship shows that through YA books readers might learn something about the issues that shape young peoples' lives. This chapter is concerned with what YA fiction might mean to readers in terms of recreation, youth and community development.

Typically intended for youthful audiences and featuring teenage protagonists at critical moments of 'growing up,' the genre offers a means to facilitate the critical exploration of youth-adult relationships. *The Catcher in the Rye,* one of the most frequently banned books in American schools, is a scathing critique of contemporary American adult culture. Focused on the experiences of "a recently expelled 17-year-old prep school kid adrift in New York, calling damnation on a world of middle-aged phonies" (Walsh, 2013, p. 37), Caulfield's imagery of children running off a cliff (and his need to stop them from falling) is a stark metaphor for leaving childhood with an accompanying loss of innocence (and playfulness) in the absence of genuinely 'good' adults.

Furthermore, many YA books are fantastically otherworldly. By shifting reality—e.g., magic, vampires, werewolves, aliens, and other extraordinary creatures exist—many books are also fantastically sociological (i.e., questioning taken-for-granted constructs of everyday 'reality'). That is, they defamiliarize the familiar and open different windows into understanding otherwise easily overlooked personal, social, and developmental experiences of young lives in transition: changing family relations, emerging sexualities, shifting friendships, exclusion of difference, new leisure experiences, untapped freedoms, and new-found independence. That is, they alert us that the social world is 'made up,' and can be re-made in novel ways.

A CRITICAL THOUGHT EXPERIMENT—QUESTION REALITY?

It is difficult to suspend one's own perceptions, to make the familiar seem strange. The sociologist Howard Becker (1971, p. 10) wrote: "It takes a tremendous effort of will and imagination to stop seeing only the things that are conventionally 'there' to be seen." One of the key points that I hope to make across this chapter is that young adult fiction allows readers to 'shift the frame' of their own lives and see their everyday social relations in new ways, from a different angle. What if—as in *Harry Potter*—everything that you thought was true about yourself, your family, and the world was revealed to be untrue? "You're a wizard, Harry!" Hagrid lets slip, and the world is full of magic. This textbox 'critical thought experiment' asks you to try to shift the frame, to question reality, and to see what you have perhaps never seen, often hidden before your own eyes (which in itself is a very neat kind of magic).

Pretend you are an alien from another world, or you have met an alien and are giving your visitor a tour, watching the behaviors of the humans around you in order to puzzle out their lives. Consider which of the mundane, everyday things people normally do which would make very little sense to an alien. Think about how, without contextual knowledge, so many things people do actually make *almost no sense at all*—How would you describe aspects of your daily routine to someone who had no knowledge of 21st Century Earth culture? For example, from alarm clocks, to showering habits to breakfast meals, to commuting across cities (all while online with smartphones), the morning routines of millions are potentially incomprehensible. Why do we do what we do? Additionally, are the unwritten 'rules' of our social worlds utterly strange? Consider parental, familial, friends, or romantic relations—if asked, how would you explain these to an alien? What about power and privilege: Try explaining to your visitor why some people are treated better or given certain advantages over others. Why do some people have excessively luxurious lives, when so many have so little? With a sharper sense of defamiliarizing the familiar, consider recreation: How would you explain youth recreation, and why youth recreation programs are important, to an alien? What other examples can you think of and how might you see them anew, and more critically?

Following from this thought experiment, YA literature—especially when it involves a strange otherworldliness—allows us to imagine a shifted reality. This kind of shift can help us to see that social reality is already 'made up' and then also to appreciate that *it can be changed*. Other realities are possible, maybe not with supernatural beings, but perhaps one with more equitable relations? Malorie Blackman's (2001) *Noughts & Crosses* offers a great case in point. This 'alternative reality' book envisions a world where black people ("crosses") are the sociopolitical and economic elite, and white people ("noughts") are an oppressed underclass. This simple reversal of the existing racial hierarchy invites readers to recognize their role in its (taken for granted) reproduction or to challenge it in their actual lives. Such awareness or 'consciousness' is an important part of a critical education; it is the beginning of empowerment, which may lead to radical community development (Ledwith, 2005). This is a crucial first step, to see that things have been constructed in particular (often particularly awful and unjust) ways.

A BRIEF HISTORY OF THE SOCIAL CONSTRUCTION OF 'YOUTH'

The advent and growth of the young adult literature genre in the 20th Century reflects broader historical changes in the social construction and categorization of 'youth.' It mirrors wider social changes that have reconfigured the transitions between childhood and adulthood and the meanings attached to the liminality, or *in-between-ness* of 'teenagers' or 'youth' (Coles, 2000; Henderson, Holland, McGrellis, Sharpe, & Thomson, 2007; Morrow & Richards, 1996). What is 'youth,' 'young adulthood' or 'teenage'? What processes define and mark out this 'life stage'? After all, many such markers are not biological, but social, including achievements in education, employment, housing, and romantic/interpersonal relations (i.e., being an 'adult' is, perhaps, marked out by having a university degree, career, house, marriage, children, etc.; but what achieved social status marks out 'youth'?). In other words, the notion of 'youth' should been taken as much as an artificial social category as any other, such as 'race,' class, gender or ability, rather than existing as a predetermined 'natural' one. Because socially constructed, the boundaries and definitions of youth are fluid, shifting and political, always entangled in power with an adult 'other' (Bennett, Cieslik, and Miles, 2003) as young people transition from being children to becoming adults.

The sociology of youth transitions has attempted to map out the stages and characteristics of growing up from childhood into adulthood (Chamberlayne, Rustin, & Wengraf, 2001; Furlong & Cartmel, 1997; Hall, Coffey, & Lashua, 2009; Henderson, et al., 2007; Kehily, 2007; Wyn & White, 1996). Once seen as a linear progression along relatively stable steps and stages into adulthood, becoming an adult is now theorized as a much more complex and complicated process. Not only is employment no longer the primary register of achieved adulthood, "young people's transitions to adulthood are increasingly framed in relation to individuals tracking back and forth across a number of thresholds (for example, education, training, work, family and consumption)" (Hall, Coffey, & Lashua, 2009, p. 551). For example, how was adulthood (in North America) once linked to finishing high school and turning 18 years old? Is someone a 'youth' at age 17 in high school, then suddenly an 'adult' at age 18 in employment? How has this idea changed (or not)? Through questions such as these, researchers of childhood and youth have challenged "developmental narratives in which youth appears as a distinct life course stage separated out from adulthood" (Hall, Coffey, & Lashua, p. 555). Some have referred to "emerging adulthood"

(Tanner & Arnett, 2009), to characterize a long and winding road to adulthood that stretches from the late teens through one's late twenties. As the ideas of youth transitions become more blurred, so too have the categories (e.g., youth, teenager, young adult, emerging adult) that had described the stages of those transitions.

YA fiction illustrates these blurry transitions and identity categories. For example, in some books, youthful innocence and purity are extended, such as in the first books of Meyer's *Twilight* series, where the eternally 19-year-old vampire Edward shows reluctance to corrupt or change Bella Swan into a vampire (*read:* an 'adult') too. Holden Caulfield's vision of a 'catcher in the rye' operates in a similar sense, to arrest the onset of adulthood. In such analyses, young people are often romanticized; 'youth' are characterized as in need of shielding and protection. Alternately, in some tales young people are presented as little devils in need of guidance, restraint, or correction, such as in some of Charles Dickens' famous stories. In both views, youth are positioned as subordinate to adult control, or attempts at control, and this power dynamic forms the basis of what has been widely referred to as the 'problem of youth' (Holloway & Valentine, 2000).

The 'problem of youth,' as a line of sociological enquiry, can be understood as a means of maintaining adult control over young people as well as a matter of 'damage limitation' for youth during supposed transitions into adulthood. The field of youth recreation (and its services) is deeply caught up within these traditions (Lashua, 2010). Examples are numerous; e.g., Jang and Dworkin (2012, p. 27) note: "Since youth living in neighborhoods with high crime rates can be exposed to illegal activities or violence and spend time with deviant peers, formal OST [Out-of-School-Time] programs can *protect* youth from negative societal influences" [my emphasis]. Some theorizations have described these viewpoints as Apollonian and Dionysian (Jenks, 1996; Holloway and Valentine, 2000), after the Roman gods Apollo (the stern figure of righteous restraint) and Dionysus (the pleasure-seeking figure of playful abandon). Dionysian children are seen as impish pleasure seekers, or 'little devils,' in need of protection and moral guidance. Captured in phrases such as 'spare the rod and spoil the child,' Dionysian approaches to childhood reflect Puritan, and later, Victorian (Dickensian) views that discipline is needed to save children from themselves (Ansell, 2005). This is a view that might be seen in YA books such as *Lord of the Flies*. For Ansell (2005), Dionysian thinking dominated Western views of childhood until the early 20th Century, after which Apollonian views gained wider acceptance.

Apollonian views assert that children are essentially good—'errant angels'—and need protection from the corrupting forces of wider, adult influences. This view became increasingly widespread in the 20th Century and accompanied the rise of the YA genre. The innocence and purity of children has been extended and projected through 'youth' and 'teenage' years. For Rudd (2014, p. 138) this view is carried over from the Romantics of the 19th Century who:

> Rounded out and mythologised this new being, the child, as innocent, pure and, therefore, unsullied by adult society. By the end of the Victorian period, the 'cult of the child,' as it became known, was at its height, with the desirability of remaining a child, a Peter Pan, in the cultural ascendant.

The legacy of the Apollonian view is that childhood is an ideal time to be preserved and enjoyed as long as possible, and young people need adult protection from the dangers of the world (see Figure 13.1).

Young Adult literature highlights both perspectives, often ambiguously. Examples abound, including Harry Potter's coming to terms with his parents' violent death, or the absent fathers in the lives of Sam Temple (*Gone*) and Clary Frey (*The Mortal Instruments*), or Holden Caulfield's disillusionment with adult society; other books centralize sexuality (e.g., *Twilight*). Once taboo topics such as sex, death, war, genocide, abuse, racism, and drugs are increasingly seen as necessary topics for youth to know about and discuss with each other, parents, or other adults. In most instances, these books link with Apollonian views that young people need to know what is 'out there' in order to be better prepared for, and protected from, some of life's harsher realities. Viewed in the aggregate, both Apollonian and Dionysian models illustrate the 'problem of youth' or 'crisis of youth' (Holloway & Valentine, 2000) as a socio-historical construct: the problem or crisis has changed over time, and continues to change. However, both present a deficit model in which youth are seen as problems to be managed. The bones of this framework are evident in research in other fields, such as adolescent development, where the period of 'youth' has been described as a time of 'storm and stress' (*sturm und drang*) (Ayman-Nolley & Taira, 2000; Steinberg & Lerner, 2004) that has come to typify the unruly 'teenager' in the late 20th Century (Nichols & Good, 2004; Offer & Schonert-Reichl, 1992).

Young Adult fiction has played a significant role in reflecting, shaping, and in some books over-spilling this framework, particularly in terms of what it means to be

Dionysian	Apollonian
Children should be seen and not heard Children need protection from themselves Childhood is a time to learn discipline	Childhood is a time for play and not for work Children need protection from the world Children are innocent Children are passive Childhood should be happy

Both
Childhood is a time set apart from the adult world Children belong in families Children are closer to nature than adults Children are incomplete—less than adults

FIGURE 13.1 "WESTERN CONCEPTS OF CHILDHOOD: LEGACIES OF THE DIONYSIAN AND APOLLONIAN VIEWS" (ADAPTED FROM ANSELL, 2005, P. 11)

a young person, and what signifies 'coming of age' as an adult. That is, YA literature is very much a part of constructing and maintaining the boundaries of childhood, youth, and adulthood. The separated sections of a library or bookstore prove this point well enough, despite any number of YA books that expose and shatter these essentialized views. Caught between being romanticized or demonized, children and young people "can no longer be routinely mistreated, but neither can they be left to their own devices" (James, Jenks, & Prout, 1998, p. 14). It in this sense of being left to their own devices, with Apollonian and Dionysian constructions in mind, I turn to a brief synopsis of an exemplary book in the YA genre, Michael Grant's *Gone*.

GONE: YOUTH, RECREATION AND COMMUNITY DEVELOPMENT IN AN ADULT-FREE WORLD

Gone (2008) is the first in a six-book series by Michael Grant about young people in the fictional town of Perdido Beach, California, a place of mixed economic, political, and social fortunes. As such the town may be seen to represent a microcosm of American society (and more generically, globalized 'Western' societies), replete with class inequalities, ethnic divisions, sexism and homophobia, disability discrimination, and ideological clashes over religion, education, sport, and government. The book's protagonist, Sam Temple, is a 14-year-old high school student living with his mother on the poorer, disadvantaged side of town. Sam is a bit of a slacker, though an avid surfer, with his best friend and fellow outcast, Quinn. Other characters include Edilio, a gay young Latino; Caine, a wealthy and cruel student at a nearby boarding school; and Astrid, an intelligent young woman from an affluent neighborhood across town. Nicknamed "the genius," Astrid has a younger, autistic brother, Pete (aged 4), who many taunt cruelly.

As noted earlier, the book's central plot device is that in the blink of an eye, every person 15 years old or over vanishes: they are 'gone.' Additionally, an impenetrable dome envelops the town and isolates the characters in an adult-free zone. The story that results is not far from Golding's (1954) *Lord of the Flies*, mashed-up with aspects of the TV mystery-drama series *Lost* (2004–2010) and also *Heroes* (2006–2010). As they struggle to come to grips with their new existence, some characters quickly take on 'adult' roles, for example, by looking after the infants left suddenly without carers. Others run riot in their unexpectedly lawless and wholly unsupervised context of excess 'leisure.'

Furthermore, in another strange twist, the youthful residents of Perdido Beach develop an array of wonderful and horrific superpowers (a metaphor for rapidly changing teenage bodies). These superpowers cause most of the characters to consider and treat one another as "freaks," thus illustrating further social divisions over difference and privilege (all superpowers are not equal; some are far better than others). In addition to physical changes, these superpowers represent self-actualization or fulfilling one's (grown-up) potential: as the cliché goes, with great power comes great responsibility—although many characters are unwilling to bear this mantle of power. In a further nod to the tribulations of growing up, the youthful residents of Perdido Beach attribute their transformations to strange events at a nearby nuclear power station, and refer to their area as the Fallout Alley Youth Zone, or FAYZ for short; this 'phase' is a stark metaphor for their transitional 'youth' status too. (In *The Catcher in the Rye* Holden Caulfield also commented on the idea of a 'phase': "I'm just going through a phase right now. Everybody goes through phases and all, don't they?" (Salinger, 1951, p. 15)).

In the chaos of the FAYZ, the young residents of Perdido Beach struggle to re-establish a community without adults. In effect, Sam, Astrid, Edilio, and others who rally as leaders must act as kinds of 'catchers in the rye' to save the hundreds of young people and children stuck in the FAYZ. To do so, I argue that they embark on a series of (very radical) community development exercises. In the penultimate section of the chapter I link these actions to the community development literature, particularly the work of Margaret Ledwith (2005).

GOING BUT NOT GONE: YOUTH RECREATION MODELS AND YOUNG ADULT LITERATURE

Before getting to *Gone* and Ledwith's radical CD work, I want to steer through a number of other YA books. This detour allows juxtaposing these books with some youth recreation and development theories and models. While these models—including Positive Youth Development (Lerner, Almerigi, Theokas, & Lerner, 2005), Hart's (1992, 1997) ladder of children's participation, Sheir's (2001) pathways to participation, and Jones and Perkins' (2005) continuum of Youth-Adult Partnerships—are illustrative of youth recreation and community development, they are also limited in terms of making sense of participation at both a conceptual and practical level. That is, the models are sometimes difficult to see in action, on the ground, and at a conceptual level they often lack contextualization, such as the socio-historical construction of the 'problem of youth' noted above. Arguably, YA fiction is useful to illustrate these models and show some critiques of them.

The common ground in most YA literature is that, in the storm and stress of teenage years, young people are unjustly dominated by adults. Consequently, characters often wish for, or actively pursue adult-free contexts. A world without grown-ups is found not only in *Gone*'s FAYZ but also other YA fictional worlds, including the unnamed island in *Lord of the Flies,* most of the settings at Hogwarts, parts of Never-Never Land, and entire regions of Narnia. At its most simplistic, the basic premise of this plot device is that in a world where adults oppress young people, youth would be better off on their own. Put another way, it could be argued that 'youth communities' are unjustly oppressed by adults; young people are not empowered or listened to often enough. Much of the critical youth recreation literature argues this too, including some of my own work (Lashua, 2006; Lashua & Fox, 2006, Lashua, 2010). Indeed, the wider academic literature on youth development supports the idea that young people need to be listened to and their voices heard in community development processes (Jones & Perkins, 2005; Hamilton & Hamilton, 2004).

What is interesting, conversely, in YA fiction—keeping in mind it is usually written by adults—is that a community of youth on their own is a treacherous, if not catastrophic terrain. Far from ideal adult-free worlds, youth-only communities are almost always written as dystopian spaces. This doomed view is important because it cautions that neither adult-free nor adult-centered approaches to youth community development are workable. It invites collective action, while also caution: what often passes as collective action is perhaps not very 'collective' at all. Models of recreation, youth and development, not least those concerning community development, are many, including the ones that circulate through the chapters within this volume. Although they explain some aspects of youth development, they are ultimately lacking in critical aspects and often insufficient to the task.

For example, the 'deviant' wanderings of Holden Caulfield (e.g., he runs away from school, goes to nightclubs, gets drunk, visits prostitutes, etc.) may be viewed through (and offer a critique of) theories of Positive Youth Development (Shinn & Yoshikawa, 2008; Witt & Crompton, 1996). The fundamental premise of Positive Youth Development (PYD) is that, rather than trying to correct what is 'wrong' with youth, recreation leaders and programs should try work with young people by engaging, sympathizing, and supporting youth in 'productive' activities (Damon, 2004). In a YA context, rather than focus on what Holden lacks—e.g., he is in need of greater discipline or protection, or that he needs to be "cured" of his depression in order to achieve an absence of negative or undesirable behaviors—a PYD approach would seek to understand and encourage the gifts and talents that he has. Models of PYD view young people in regard to their potential, and collaborative efforts are sought to "offer young people the opportunities to learn and use the skills involved in participating actively in their communities and in making productive and positive contributions to themselves and their families and society" (Lerner, Alberts, Jelicic, & Smith, 2006, p. 21). However, the challenge raised by books such as *The Catcher in the Rye* allows readers to question the adult worlds that young people are invited to productively and positively contribute to. The adults in Holden's life—including the ones he did not see initially as "phonies"—treat him abysmally: they pretend to listen to him, he suspects one teacher wants to molest him, and his parents institutionalize him. Adults make Holden the 'problem' in need of a solution yet his view is exactly the reverse—the adult world is the problem and he does not want other children (especially his beloved younger sister Phoebe) to enter into it.

Through such examples, YA fiction helps to shift and broaden the frame from traditional 'storm and stress' constructions of teenage lives and 'the problem of youth.' In *The Catcher in the Rye,* Holden's storm and stress is not of his own making and he rejects the adult world. In a recreation context, *why should young people participate in programs that are part and parcel of power relations that oppressively (if silently) label youth as problems?* Positive youth development moves away from 'youth-as-problem' perspectives without, however, going far enough to question dominant social relations more broadly: why should Holden want to contribute productively and positively to his social world (e.g., school and family), all of which he sees as hopelessly corrupt? A similar world-weariness is evident in *Gone* when Sam comments: "This world is changing all the time. Animals. People. Who knows what's next? We didn't make this world, we're just the poor fools who are living in it" (Grant, 2008, p. 506).

Other development models can be seen threaded through analyses of YA literature. For example, Arnstein's (1969) "Ladder of Citizen Participation" (see Chapter 3, this volume)—reconfigured as Hart's (1992, 1997) "Ladder of Children's Participation" (see Figure 13.2)—may be used to consider youth-adult relations in numerous plotlines. Robert Muchamore's *CHERUB* book series about orphans (ages 10–17) recruited to become spies by the British Secret Service offers excellent examples of plot conflicts, during spy missions, at almost every stage of Hart's ladder.

In addition to Muchamore's *CHERUB* novels, Rowling's *Harry Potter* books also offer illustrative examples of Hart's ladder, particularly where the young protagonists struggle to succeed in the absence of shared decision making with adults. Similar models to Hart's can be viewed in Scheir's (2001) "Pathways to Participation" and Jones and Perkins' (2005) "Continuum of Youth-Adult Relations." Scheir's model simply does away with Hart's lowest three levels of nonparticipation. Where Hart refers to projects involving shared decisions between adults and youth as 'true participation' ("Rung 8"—see Figure 2) Jones and Perkins (2005) conceive a Youth-Adult Partnership (YAP), a point of stasis along a continuum between adult and youth control where an equal partnership is achieved. That is, youth and adult participants have equal chances in utilizing skills, decision making, mutual learning, and independently carrying out tasks to reach common goals.

However, larger conceptual questions about these models of youth participation remain unaddressed. Whether on a ladder, pathway, or a continuum, what is lacking in these models is an ability to critically assess the wider social, historical, and political context that subsumes these frameworks. For Collins and Ison (2006) the ladder does not go far enough to understand participation in terms of wider (e.g., dominant) social structures and neglects the context in which participation is conceptualized. For example, in Hart's model in Figure 13.2, the ladder is not simply 'floating' in the air; what are the foundations (ideas) that it is stands upon? Malone and Hartung (2010, p. 24) caution that "[w]ithout a theoretical framework, models or 'how-to' guides have flourished, and it is not always clear what has informed their construction." Program goals such as empowerment or encouraging young people to be "active citizens" often rest rather uneasily on uncritical or undertheorized assumptions about the benefits of participation. Malone and Hartung add that many programs are only seen as 'participatory' when adults initiate or recognize them as such; this ignores the 'organic' ways many young participants might have already been engaged in participatory processes without adults. If youth are not seen as 'problems' to be solved, the participatory practices shown on the ladder will be dissimilar to those represented on a ladder stood upon different constructs of youth. Rather than deviance, practices seen as 'nonparticipation' might be reconceived as resistance to, or rejection of, an oppressive social order (Nayak, 2009; Willis, 1977). Such critiques challenge us to understand the root issues of

(Re)Consider this?

Take a moment to reconsider youth recreation programs that you have been involved in before, either as staff or participant. Try to imagine what these experiences would have been like if they had been designed and delivered on a different 'rung' on Hart's ladder or different point on the continuum of Youth-Adult Relations. Can you envision any programs or activities that needed to be adult-led? Conversely, are there any instances when a youth-only approach would have been more appropriate or successful? Finally, can you rethink previous events that could have been much better if their planning and implementation had been shared, more equitably, between young people and adults? How so?

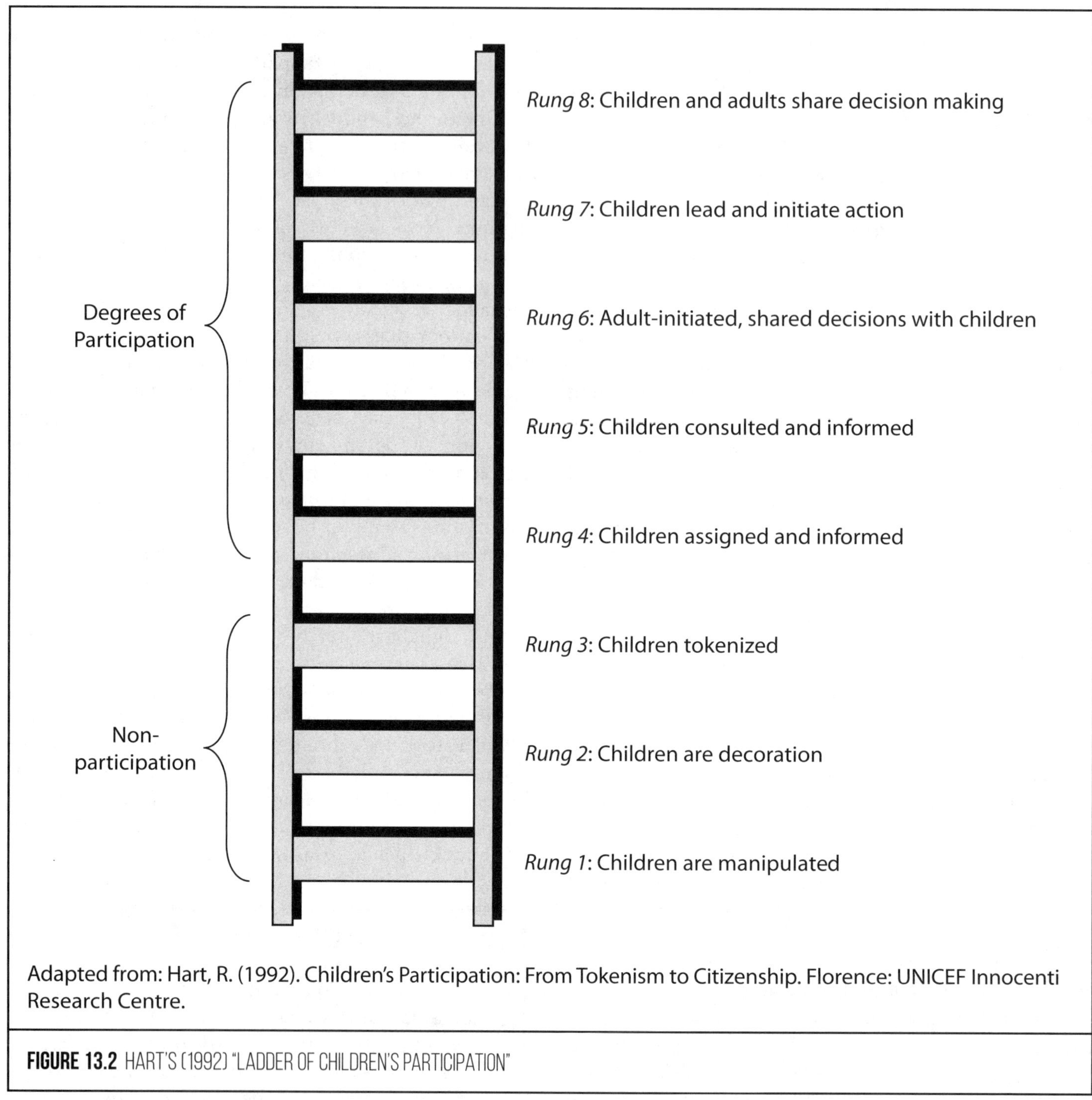

Adapted from: Hart, R. (1992). Children's Participation: From Tokenism to Citizenship. Florence: UNICEF Innocenti Research Centre.

FIGURE 13.2 HART'S (1992) "LADDER OF CHILDREN'S PARTICIPATION"

youth recreation provision, and invite more radical approaches to youth participation.

RADICAL YOUTH COMMUNITY DEVELOPMENT

In this final part of this section I bring together some of the ideas present in YA literature, the history and construction of 'youth' as a social category, and the example provided by *Gone,* through the radical Community Development approaches promoted by Margaret Ledwith (2005). Based in part on the work of Paolo Freire, for Ledwith (2005, p. 1) "Radical community development" involves:

- Commitment to collective action for social and environmental justice
- This begins a processes of empowerment through critical consciousness and grows through participation in local issues
- Calls for an analysis of power and discrimination in society
- The analysis needs to be understood in relation to dominant ideas and the wider political context
- Collective action, based on this analysis, focuses on the root causes of discrimination rather than the symptoms

The call to challenge and change social inequity requires collective action that begins with critical consciousness. Like the 'thought experiment' earlier in the chapter, Shor (1992, p. 122) offers that "Community development begins in the everyday reality of lives by 'extraordinarily re-experiencing the ordinary.'" In *Gone,* as in many YA books, it often takes a supernatural event to prompt this awareness. Thankfully, the simple act of (thoughtfully) reading YA literature also offers possibilities for raising critical consciousness, creating awareness of social and environmental inequalities, and understanding of how they circulate through the practices of everyday life. Participation in local issues is demanded, by default, in adult-free zones such as the FAYZ; examples such as this invite attention from readers to reconsider their current levels of involvement in local communities.

Books like *Gone* also illustrate the consequences of events precipitated by rapid escalation from complete noninvolvement to total involvement in community affairs, albeit without the mentoring, guidance, and collaboration of adult allies. Local participation requires collective action, and this collective action requires a range of youth and adult collaborators. In *Gone,* Sam, Astrid, Edilio, and Quinn suddenly find they must step in to act as decision makers to organize, feed, police, and protect the youth and children in the FAYZ. Although they struggle valiantly to meet the enormity of the task they are presented with (including a civil war between factions of teenage mutants with superpowers), they lack the experience and guidance of knowledgeable adults to help them through some of their most basic challenges, and social order quickly disintegrates. Here, questions of leisure loom large: in the absence of adults, schools, work, and other structures, what are they young people in the FAYZ to do with themselves? An extreme state of excess leisure, perhaps, is as dystopian as a state of no leisure at all. Although many YA books can be seen as Apollonian—Grant's construction of youth and community in *Gone* is largely Dionysian. Like *Lord of the Flies,* in the FAYZ youth need protection from themselves and discipline in order to survive. The absence of adult collaborators, while liberating at first, is ultimately catastrophic.

As noted earlier (see also Chapter 3), many youth and community development models inadequately address questions of power in society. In her analysis of the historical development of community development, Ledwith notes that CD rose against the (UK) welfare state's social control functions: "community work presented itself as a radical alternative to social work, which it caricatured as 'soft policing.' Similarly, youth work was dismissed as a means of simply keeping working class kids off the streets" (2005, p. 11). That is, adult power remains paramount, and youth empowerment is only possible within certain adult-defined limits. Similar characteristics can be traced through youth recreation (Lashua, 2010; Outley, Bocarro, & Boleman, 2011), and here we might also ask: what are the social control functions of youth recreation programs? Do models of participation offer more than 'soft policing' to simply keep troublesome 'kids' off the streets? How so (or not)?

CASE STUDY: PARTICIPATION AS SURVEILLANCE?

A new youth club had recently been opened in a former shop on a neighborhood estate in a small town. Following the closure of its main industries, the town had struggled with unemployment and hopelessness that had followed the breakdown of its 'traditional' community. As part of a large-scale regeneration plan to combat deprivation in the area, each neighborhood had a new youth club. Young people, it seemed, mattered to the future of the town! Working within a research team from Cardiff University, I attended evening sessions in several new youth clubs across a two-year period. In each club, young people were issued membership cards and required to sign in and out for each evening's session. While this made sense for health and safety reasons, it also meant that whenever there was a problem (e.g., a crime) in the area during youth club hours, local police would visit the youth club first. There they would check to see who was not present that evening, and immediately they would have their first suspect. Thus in one view the club was simply a place to keep young people together and out of trouble in the evenings; its membership cards and sign-in sheets were a way to keep tabs on *who was where*, and the youth club became just another form of youth surveillance. Rather than developing new opportunities, experiences and skills with young people, provision in the clubs seemed to be another way to temporarily 'contain' them—a form of soft policing that primarily served to keep them out of trouble. This, it seemed to me, was a missed opportunity to engage with young people to help reshape the town. What kinds of *community development* do you think would have been better suited to this kind of area and to these young people?

YA books also show how power circulates not only through youth-adult relations, but also through social differences such as class, education, sexuality, 'race,' and ability. In *Gone,* social hierarchies are shown through traditional markers of power (e.g., between 'rich kids' in private school versus 'poor' ones in public schools), and also through strange and wonderful *super*powers: between those characters with desirable superpowers (e.g., being able to run supernaturally fast) and undesirable ones (e.g., turning into a person made of gravel). As part of the storyline, these superpowers help to 'defamiliarize the familiar' and show how communities often fragment along lines of difference. In *Gone*'s vacuum of adult power, factions develop in the FAYZ that jockey for dominance by attracting and enlisting those with the most useful superpowers. As life in the FAYZ becomes increasingly difficult (e.g., a shortage of food), the youth-only community is divided, inequitably, along lines of power, privilege, and attempts to secure (or resist) dominance. These examples link readily into Ledwith's framework for considering the wider sociopolitical context in which community development occurs.

In order to untangle community power relations, Ledwith (2005) emphasizes the relationship of empowerment and stories as a means to link the "deeply personal and the profoundly political" (p. 61). This allows the use of stories to connect people to collective action in order to foster change. She offers:

> Life is a fiction. We tell and retell the stories of our lives differently according to our audience, our recollection and our insight; thus stories become shaped by time and space and understanding, and the *telling of stories can, in turn, be the vehicle of our understanding.* (Ledwith, 2005, p. 62, emphasis added).

Following Ledwith, YA books offer important stories useful for understanding the construction of relations between youth and adults, as well as recreation and community development. The trick, or task, here is in the connection of what Griffiths (2003) referred to as "little stories" (those of individual's everyday lives) to "grander concerns like education, social justice and power" (p. 81). In this regard, for Ledwith (2005), community development starts with shared stories based on critical reflection that prompt collective action.

As a vehicle for understanding community development (through raising critical consciousness), YA literature offers a potentially powerful and compelling way to connect 'little stories' to 'grander concerns' (or in the words of the American sociologist C. Wright Mills (1959), to see 'personal troubles' instead as 'public issues' (see Lashua, 2013)). *Gone* centralizes inequities related to class, education, ethnicity, and ability; *Noughts & Crosses* highlights racialized hierarchies of power and injustice; the *Harry Potter* series, although less centrally, highlights matters (among others) of social class hierarchies through its critiques of 'pure blood' families, 'mudbloods' and lesser factions such as 'squibs,' 'muggles,' and house elves; and *The Hunger Games* explores power and domination through youth leisure as a form of 'bread and circuses' (in Latin, *panem et circenses*). The fictional nation comprised of the 13 Districts in the *Hunger Games* novels is also called Panem. Bread and circuses are entertainments offered by the ruling classes to distract a population from more serious grievances and concerns (see Spracklen, 2009)). These examples offer useful points of entrée into critical awareness of the circulation of power, privilege, and reproduction of social inequalities: if readers can begin to see these processes in YA books, can they then also see them in their own everyday lives?

CONCLUSION

It is easy to dismiss YA literature and the ideas it illustrates as lightweight, unchallenging, or silly (Bloom, 2000). However, for better or for worse, more people will read YA fiction than will read the academic scholarship on youth recreation and community, and it is important for recreation scholar-practitioners to engage with the genre. Throughout this chapter I have argued that YA literature offers surprising points for critical evaluation of youth recreation and community development. That is, sometimes 'unreal' worlds of fiction provide a fantastic window through which to see and question the 'real world.' Certainly the 'reality' of the category of 'youth' should be questioned, and in this regard I offered a brief account of the socio-historical construction of youth. The sociological literature shows how 'youth' have been conceptualized as Dionysian and Apollonian—as little devils or little angels—in need of adult authority, control, and protection. This model, I argued, underlies much of the YA fiction and also models of youth participation. Regarding the latter, YA fiction can also be a useful way to understand recreation and community development theories and to illustrate where they are undertheorized.

As an alternative, I made links to the "radical community development" espoused by Ledwith (2005, p. 1) "founded on a process of empowerment and participation. Empowerment involves a form of critical education that encourages people to question their reality: this is the basis of collective action and is built on principles of participatory democracy." Arguably, the transfer of young adult fiction themes to recreation and youth development practices and understandings allows for a shift in focus, via case studies that expand upon concepts such as power, privilege, and oppression (see Chapter 9), in order to view youth and community development through a different, critical lens. Most of the YA books noted in this chapter are illustrative of these concepts. They are also often easy-to-read, yet engaging and informative; it is never too late to read them, at any age. To paraphrase a famous quip (originally about children's literature) from C. S. Lewis: a young adult story that can only be enjoyed by young adults is not a good story in the slightest.

REFERENCES

Ansell, N. (2005). *Children, youth and development.* Abingdon: Routledge.

Arnstein, S. R. (1969). A Ladder of Citizen Participation. *Journal of the American Planning Association, 35*(4), 216–224.

Ayman-Nolley, S. & Taira, L. L. (2000). Obsession with the dark side of adolescence: A decade of psychological studies. *Journal of Youth Studies, 3*(1), 35–48.

Bairner, A. (2012). Between flânerie and fiction: Ways of seeing exclusion and inclusion in the contemporary city. *Leisure Studies, 31*(1), 3–19.

Bean, T. W., & Koni, K. (2003). Developing students' critical literacy: Exploring identity construction in young adult fiction. *Journal of Adolescent and Adult Literacy, 46*(8), 638–648.

Becker, H. S. (1971). Footnote, added to the paper by M. Wax and R. Wax (1971), Great tradition, little tradition and formal education. In M. Wax, S. Diamond, and F. Gearing (Eds.), *Anthropological perspectives on education* (pp. 3-27). New York: Basic Books.

Bennett, A., Cieslik, M., & Miles, S. (2003) *Researching youth.* Basingstoke: Palgrave Macmillan.

Blackman, M. (2004). *Noughts and crosses.* London: Random House.

Bloom, H. (2000, July 11). Can 35 Million Book Buyers Be Wrong? Yes. *The New York Times,* p. A26.

Cart, M., & Jenkins, C. A. (2006). *The heart has its reasons: Young adult literature with Gay/Lesbian/Queer content, 1969–2004.* Oxford: Scarecrow Press.

Chamberlayne, P., Rustin, M., & Wengraf, T., (2001). *Biography and social exclusion in Europe: Experiences and life-journeys.* Bristol: Policy Press.

Chen, L. (2009) An analysis of the adolescent problems in *The Catcher and the Rye. Asian Social Science, 5*(5), 143–146.

Clare, C. (2007) *The Mortal Instruments: City of Bones.* London: Walker Books.

Coles, B. (2000). *Joined up youth research, policy and practice.* Leicester: Youth Work Press.

Collins, K., & Ison, R. (2006). Dare we jump off Arnstein's ladder? Social learning as a new policy paradigm. *Proceedings of PATH (Participatory Approaches in Science & Technology) Conference,* 4–7 June 2006, Edinburgh.

Collins, S. (2008). *The hunger games.* New York: Scholastic Press.

Damon, W. (2004). What is Positive Youth Development? *Annals of the American Academy of Political and Social Science, 591*(1), 13–24.

Dashner, J. (2009). *The maze runner.* New York: Delacorte.

Edwards, D. (1977). Holden Caulfield: "Don't Ever Tell Anybody Anything." *English Literary History, 44*(3), 556–557.

Furlong, A., & Cartmel, F., (1997). *Young people and social change.* Buckingham: Open University Press.

Golding, W. (1954). *Lord of the flies.* London: Faber and Faber.

Grant, M. (2008). *Gone.* New York: HarperCollins.

Grant, M. (n.d.) *Michael Grant: Gone.* Retrieved from http://www.michaelgrantbooks.co.uk/gone/

Griffith, M. (2003). *Action for social change in education: Fairly different.* Maidenhead: Open University Press.

Hall, T. A., Coffey, A., & Lashua, B. D. (2009) Steps and stages: Rethinking transitions in youth and place. *Journal of Youth Studies, 12*(5), 547–561.

Hamilton, S. F., & Hamilton, M. A. (Eds.). (2004). *The youth development handbook: Coming of age in American communities.* Thousand Oaks, CA: Sage.

Hart, R. A. (1997). *Children's participation: The theory and practice of involving young citizens in community development and environmental care.* New York: UNICEF.

Hart, R. A. (1992). *Children's participation: From tokenism to citizenship.* Florence, Italy: UNICEF/International Child Development Center.

Hebert, T. P., & Kent, R. (2000). Nurturing social and emotional development in gifted teenagers through young adult literature, *Roeper Review, 22*(3), 167–171.

Henderson, S., Holland, J., McGrellis, S., Sharpe, S., & Thomson, R. (2007). *Inventing adulthoods: A biographical approach to youth transitions.* London: Sage.

Holloway, S., & Valentine, G. (Eds.). (2000). *Children's geographies: Playing, living, learning.* London: Routledge.

James, A., Jenks, C., & Prout, A. (1998) *Theorising childhood.* New York: Teacher's College Press.

Jang, J., & Dworkin, J. (2012). Mothers' Satisfaction with Youth Out-of-School-Time Programs. *Journal of Youth Development, 7*(4), 25–36.

Jenks, C. (1996). *Childhood.* London: Routledge.

Jones, K. R., & Perkins, D. F. (2005). Determining the quality of Youth-Adult Relationships within Community-Based Youth Programs. *Journal of Extension, 43*(5). Retrieved from http://www.joe.org/joe/2005october/a5p.shtml

Kehily, M. J. (2007). *Understanding youth.* London: Sage.

Lashua, B. D. (2013). Community music and urban leisure: The Liverpool One Project. *International Journal of Community Music,* 6(2), 235–251.

Lashua, B. D. (2010). Are you listening? The practice of possibility. In K. Paisley and D. Dustin (Eds.), *Speaking up/speaking out: Addressing social and environmental injustice in the leisure services profession,* (pp. 73–82). Champaign, IL: Sagamore.

Lashua, B. D. (2006). 'Just another Native'? Soundscapes, Chorasters, and Borderlands in Edmonton, Alberta, Canada. *Cultural Studies—Critical Methodologies,* 6(3), 391–410.

Lashua, B. D., & Fox, K. M. (2006). Rec needs a new rhythm 'cause rap is where we're livin.' *Leisure Sciences, 28*(3), 267–283.

Lashua, B. D., Widmer, M. A., & Munson, W. W. (2000). Some well-deserved "R & R." *Parks & Recreation, 35*(5), 56–63.

Ledwith, M. (2005). *Community development: A critical approach.* Bristol: The Policy Press.

Lerner, R. M., Alberts, A. E., Jelicic, H., & Smith, L. M. (2006). Young people are resources to be developed: Promoting positive youth development through adult-youth relations and community assets. In E. G. Clary & J. E. Rhodes (Eds.), *Mobilizing adults for positive youth development: Strategies for closing the gap between beliefs and behaviors* (pp. 19–39). New York: Springer Science + Business Media, Inc.

Lerner, R. M., Almerigi, J. B., Theokas, C., & Lerner, J. V. (2005). Positive Youth Development: A View of the Issues. *Journal of Early Adolescence, 25*(1), 10–16.

Lewis, C. S. (1950). *The chronicles of Narnia.* New York: HarperCollins.

Malone, K., & Hartung, C. (2010). Challenges of participatory practice with children. In B. Percy-Smith and N. Thomas, (Eds.), *A handbook of children and young people's participation: Perspectives from theory and practice* (pp. 24–38). London: Routledge.

Marx, K. (1852). *The Eighteenth Brumaire of Louis Bonaparte.* Retrieved from https://www.marxists.org/archive/marx/works/1852/18th-brumaire/ch01.htm

Meyers, S. (2005). *Twilight.* New York: Little, Brown and Company.

Mills, C. W. (1959). *The sociological imagination.* Oxford: Oxford University Press.

Morrow, V., & Richards, M. (1996). *Transitions to adulthood: A family matter.* York, UK: Joseph Rowntree Foundation.

Muchamore, R. (2004). *CHERUB: The recruit.* London: Hodder and Stoughton.

Muise, A. M, Stein, D. G., & Arbess, G. (2003). Eating disorders in adolescent boys: A review of the adolescent and young adult literature. *Journal of Adolescent Health, 33*(6), 427–435.

Nayak, A. (2009). Beyond the pale: Chavs, youth and social class. In K. P. Sveinsson (Ed.), *Who cares about the White working class?* (pp. 28–35). London: Runnymede Trust.

Nichols, L. S., & Good, T. L. (2004). *America's teenagers-myths and realities: Media images, schooling, and the social costs of careless indifference.* New Jersey: Lawrence Erlbaum Associates, Publishers.

Offer, D., & Schonert-Reichl, K. A. (1992). Debunking the myths of adolescence: Findings from recent research. *Journal of the American Academy of Child and Adolescent Psychiatry, 31,* 1003–1014.

Outley, C., Bocarro, J. N., & Boleman, C. T. (2011). Recreation as a component of the community youth development system. *New Directions for Youth Development, 2011*(130), 59–72.

Pike, E. C. J. (2013). The role of fiction in (mis)representing later life leisure activities. *Leisure Studies, 32*(1), 69–87.

Rowling, J. K. (1997). *Harry Potter and the philosopher's stone.* London: Bloomsbury.

Rosenthal, G. (2004). Biographical research. In C. Seale, G. Gobo, J. F. Gubrium and D. Silverman (Eds.), *Qualitative research practice* (pp. 48–64). London: Sage.

Rudd, D. (2014). A coming or going of age? Children's literature at the turn of the twenty-first century. In S. Wagg and J. Pilcher (Eds.), *Thatcher's grandchildren? The politics of childhood in the twenty-first century* (pp. 118–138), Basingstoke: Palgrave Macmillan.

Salinger, J. D. (1951). *The catcher in the rye.* New York: Little, Brown and Company.

Scheir, H. (2001). Pathways to participation: Openings, opportunities, and obligations. *Children & Society, 15*(2), 107–117.

Shaw, D. B. (2013). Strange zones: Science fiction, fantasy and the posthuman city. *City: Analysis of Urban Trends, Culture, Theory, Policy, Action, 17*(6), 778–791.

Shinn, M., & Yoshikawa, H. (2008). *Toward positive youth development: Transforming schools and community programs.* Oxford: Oxford University Press.

Shor, I. (1992). Empowering Education: Critical Thinking for Social Change. Chicago: University of Chicago Press.

Spracklen, K. (2009). *The meaning and purpose of leisure.* Basingstoke: Palgrave Macmillan.

Stebbins, R. (2013). *The committed reader: Reading for utility, pleasure and fulfilment in the twenty-first century.* Toronto: Scarecrow Press.

Steinberg, L., & Lerner, R. M. (2004). The scientific study of adolescence: A brief history. *The Journal of Early Adolescence, 24,* 45–54.

Tanner, J. L., & Arnett, J. J. (2009). The emergence of "emerging adulthood': The new life stage between adolescence and young adulthood. In A. Furlong (Ed.), *Handbook of youth and young adulthood: New perspectives and agendas* (pp. 39–45). Routledge: New York.

Tolkien, J. R. R. (1954). *The lord of the rings.* London: George, Allen and Unwin, Ltd.

Walsh, J. (2013, September 8). Catch him if you can. *The Sunday Times, Culture Magazine,* pp. 37–38.

Willis, P. (1977). *Learning to labour: How working class kids get working class jobs.* Farnborough: Saxon House.

Witt, P. A., & Crompton, J. L. (1996). *Recreation programs that work for at-risk youth: The challenge of shaping the future.* State College, PA: Venture Publishing, Inc.

Wyn, J., & White, R. (1996). *Rethinking youth.* London: Sage.

14

SPORT IN THE COMMUNITY: AN OVERVIEW AND ASSESSMENT OF 'SPORT FOR DEVELOPMENT AND PEACE'

Simon C. Darnell

INTRODUCTION

On August 3rd, 2013 the United Nations (UN) General Assembly approved a motion to recognize April 6th—the date of the opening of the first modern Olympics in Athens in 1896—as the International Day of Sport for Development and Peace. This announcement marked the latest step in the recognition and institutionalization of the nascent 'Sport for Development and Peace' (SDP) sector, a term that refers to the range of stakeholders and organizations now working to mobilize sport in the service of international development and peace building (see International Platform—Sport for Development, 2014). Many of these programs and organizations look to sport as a way to increase local opportunities for education and health, promote social cohesion and the integration of marginalized groups, and/or support community building in post-conflict situations.

As a researcher trained in the sociology of sport, I came to be interested in the question of whether sport can indeed make a positive contribution to international development and peace in the ways suggested by the SDP sector. Sport sociologists had for years discussed and debated the extent to which sport yields positive and/or negative social impacts; the explicit organization of sport to make a positive contribution to development and peace offered me a chance to pursue these questions in a new context. The emergence of the SDP sector also presented an opportunity to think about how the context of international development might be changing the purpose and experience of sport, particularly at a community level. As a doctoral student, I sought to understand the experiences of young Canadians that served overseas in the International Development through Sport Program operated by Commonwealth Games Canada. Since then, I have interviewed various officials from SDP organizations, and looked at how countries like Cuba use sport as part of their foreign policy and international outreach to 'developing' countries.

In this chapter I offer an overview of various types of SDP initiatives, paying particular attention to community-focused programs that design and provide sport and physical activity opportunities or stage local sports events. I identify some important contributions of such initiatives. However, I discuss how these programs may serve to define, and therefore to *confine*, what constitutes 'development.' In this way, I present some of the ethical challenges and dilemmas in approaching, defining, and operationalizing community-based development through sport, and ask questions about how to approach SDP in an ethical and progressive manner.

WHAT IS 'SPORT FOR DEVELOPMENT AND PEACE'?

DEFINING THE FIELD

There is no single definition that encapsulates all of the activities, policies, and programs within the SDP sector. However, these organizations generally strive to mobilize the popularity and interest in sport, and draw on sport's pro-social and positive pedagogical dimensions, in ways that meet international development goals. In this way, the practice of *sport-for-development* "... aims to engage people from disadvantaged communities in physical activity projects that have an overarching aim of achieving various social, cultural, physical, economic, or health-related outcomes" (Schulenkorf and Adair, 2014, p.3).The outcomes that are often pursued are those that are compatible with the United Nations' Millennium Development Goals (MDGs) (Figure 14.1), which are the social development targets for 2015 set by the international community, and include such goals as the eradication of extreme poverty and the achievement of universal education (UNDP, 2014). For the purposes of this chapter, then, the term Sport for Development and Peace (SDP) is a moniker for the sector of stakeholders that promote, advocate, organize, implement, and evaluate sport activities designed to meet goals like the MDGs (see Giulianotti and Armstrong, 2014).

While the SDP sector may not be able to achieve all eight of these goals, recent analyses have identified four main categories of initiatives within the SDP sector based on the development goals they pursue: social inclusion, health and education, poverty reduction, and peace and reconciliation (Giulianotti and Armstrong, 2014). Social inclusion programs in SDP seek gender empowerment, opportunities for persons with a disability, and improved self-esteem and self-efficacy of individuals or communities on the social margins (see Coalter, 2013). In a related fashion, health and education programs in SDP strive to improve education and health outcomes by using sport as a hook that attracts participants and students. Poverty reduction programs in SDP attempt to mobilize sport in ways that connect people to employment prospects or even create new opportunities for economic development or growth. Finally, peace and reconciliation efforts in SDP organize sport as an opportunity to rebuild communities in ethnically divided or post-conflict societies, by bringing together former, or even current combatants and supporting the rehabilitation or reintegration of child soldiers.

There are many SDP organizations doing work in these four areas. One example of a social inclusion-oriented SDP program is SCORE, which operates sport programs across southern Africa and is designed to teach young people skills necessary for personal success and social contribution (score.org.za, 2014). A good example of a health and education SDP program is EMIMA, an organization based in Dar Es Salaam, Tanzania that uses sport to increase awareness and knowledge of HIV/AIDS and sexual health within communities (sportanddev.org, 2014).

Alive & Kicking is a social enterprise operating at the community level in Kenya, Zambia, and Ghana and works toward poverty reduction by manufacturing sports equipment with local labor and materials to support employment (aliveandkicking.org, 2014). And, a good example of an organization aiming to promote peace and reduce conflict is Peace Players International, which organizes sport programs to bring together youth from communities divided by conflict. Initiatives in this category in particular tend to stage sports events as festivals in order to inspire community pride and interaction (see Schulenkorf, 2012). With these different categories in mind, it is possible to identify some similarities across the sector.

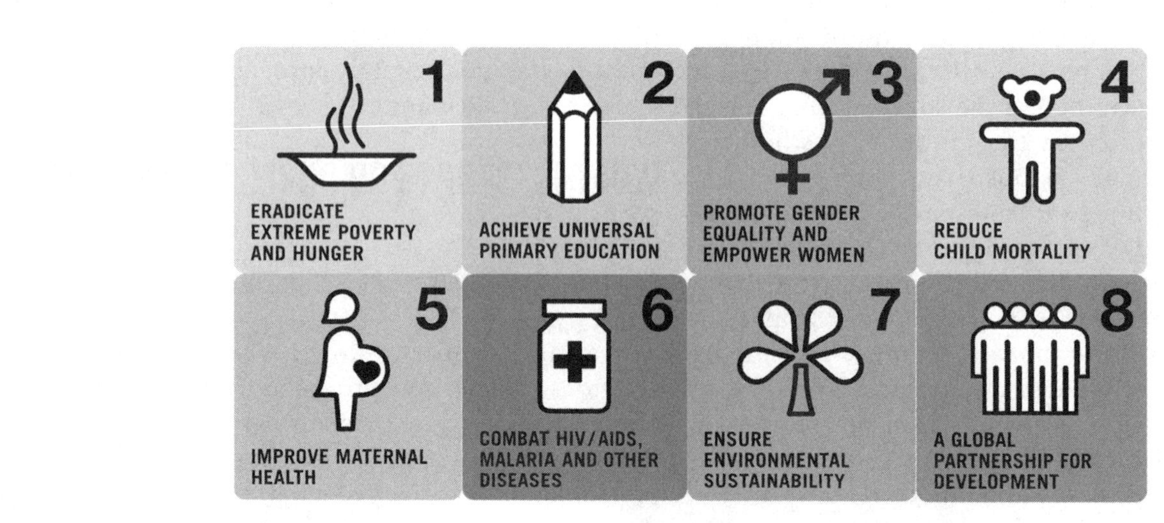

FIGURE 14.1 UN MILLENNIUM DEVELOPMENT GOALS (HTTP://WWW.UN.ORG/MILLENNIUMGOALS)

PROFILE OF A SDP ORGANIZATION: PEACE PLAYERS INTERNATIONAL

Peace Players International (PPI) was founded in 2001 on the premise that "children who play together can learn to live together." The organization operates programs in four regions with a long history of violent conflict: Northern Ireland, Cyprus, South Africa, and Israel/Gaza. PPI's mission is "to unite, educate, and inspire young people in divided communities through basketball." (www.peaceplayersintl.org/about, para 2)

Integral to its programming are its core elements of frequent, long-term integration, local leadership development, and the incorporation of a peace and leadership curriculum. On its website, Peace Project International describes its methodology:

> *Children first start working with PPI in a "single-identity" context, building trust with teammates and coaches and familiarizing themselves with PPI's curriculum. They then come together with their peers from the "other side" for the first time in a special event known as a "twinning," where PPI's trained coaches use basketball, the curriculum, and their facilitation skills to help players build the respect and understanding that leads to lasting friendship. Over time, "twinnings" accelerate in frequency, as participants and families become more comfortable with the process. Ultimately, PPI aims to work with young people not only throughout an entire year, but year-over-year as well, laying the foundation for life-long change.* (http://www.peaceplayersintl.org/why-it-works/methodology, para 2)

Throughout the program, children engage in formal peace and leadership education that aims to help them make connections between the experiences they are having with their teammates and coaches and the conflicts that exist beyond the courts. The curriculum involves both guided discussions about theories of peace and conflict and on-court activities to help teach specific ideas. One on-court activity is described on the PPI website:

> *For example, in one drill, coaches will instruct players not to pass to one of their teammates, who is not informed of the coaches' direction until after the drill is over. When the excluded player finally does get the ball, almost invariably he or she will act selfishly as well, not passing to teammates and hurting the team in the process. After explaining what they asked the team to do, PPI's trained coaches use this experience to facilitate a discussion about anti-social behavior and how we often reciprocate the very actions we resent in others. By giving young people a language to describe personal and communal conflict, this curriculum helps them extend the lessons they learn within PPI to their lives far beyond the court.* (http://www.peaceplayersintl.org/why-it-works/methodology, para 7)

After the children graduate out of the program at age 14, they are invited to take on leadership roles in the program, where they serve as assistant coaches and mentors.

TRENDS IN SDP

The variety of organizations and initiatives under the title of SDP, and the different development goals pursued by such programs, can make it difficult to establish commonalities. However, there are several themes that tend to hold across SDP in its current formation.

First, SDP organizations and stakeholders tend to share, and even promote, an understanding of, or belief in, the universal popularity and nearly essential positive aspects of sport, often suggesting that sport can bring together diverse groups of people in an inclusive and socially productive manner. For example, when commenting on the announcement of April 6th as the International Day of Sport for Development and Peace, United Nations General Assembly President Vuk Jeremic stated:

> *"Sport can be a powerful handmaiden for peace and reconciliation. It can bring us closer through shared celebration of achievements of universal appeal and attraction"* (UN, 2013).

Similarly, Jacques Rogge, then the president of the International Olympic Committee (IOC), proclaimed:

> *"In effortlessly throwing asunder all human barriers, sport is indeed the world's universal language"* (UN, 2013).

On the one hand, this notion of sport as a *universal language* has benefits to the SDP sector; it sets a tone of inclusive practice, and attempts to avoid complicity in the engrained political and social divides that have led to, and helped to maintain, development inequality and/or conflict. Making reference to the universality of sport is therefore useful for promoting its utility and applicability for development, part of what Coalter (2013) refers to as the 'conceptual entrepreneurship' of sport-for-development policy and practice. At the same time, the notion that sport's popularity or global recognition transcends local diversity of culture, or hierarchies of gender, race, or class, is contested within the academic discipline of sport sociology. Indeed, sociologists of sport have often concluded that the social and political organization of sport—particularly traditional, competitive sport—serves to secure male dominance, exacerbate violence, and reinforce hierarchies of race and class as much as, or even more than, it challenges such structures (see Coakley, 2011). Similarly, the selective human rights records of some global sports organizations (including the IOC) make it difficult to simply accept claims of sport's inherent or universal social positivity (see Hoberman, 2011). In addition, and discussed further below, the notion of sport as universal does not necessarily diminish the practical difficulties or ethical dilemmas of the actual work of sport-for-development.

> **Application Questions**
>
> *Do you think the notion of "sport as a universal language" is applicable and/or appropriate to the pursuit of community development through sport? In what ways?*
>
> *In what ways do you think structuring community development programs on the notion that sport is universal might be inappropriate or even detrimental?*

The second theme that tends to hold across the SDP sector is that its leadership rests with civil society actors, like non-governmental organizations (NGOs), as opposed to national governments. Whereas international development was traditionally led by nation-states, particularly through policies of foreign aid, the highest profile and most active organizations of the SDP sector tend o be non-governmental and pursue development goals beyond national interests. According to Coalter (2013, p. 153), this leadership of civil society actors in SDP was facilitated by a 1990s shift in the international development paradigm itself, one that moved away from foreign aid and towards "the potential of social capital, community, and social relations to contribute to various types of social development and economic growth." This shift sparked a general trend toards non-governmental policy and programming in response to development inequality, what some critical scholars have referred to as 'NGOization' (see Choudry and Kapoor, 2013). In other words, SDP is often conceptualized as part of a global civil society that seeks to contribute to the social good and "fill development and welfare gaps, especially where local civil societies are small or underdeveloped" (Giulianotti, 2011a, p. 211).

Related to the centrality of global civil society actors within the organization and implementation of SDP is a third theme, namely that SDP at a local level often connects to, and is influenced by, global events and transnational forces of politics and economics. These include sports mega-events like the Olympic Games or FIFA World Cup, international financing in the form of sponsorship from transnational corporations, or the charitable proceeds from international celebrities (see Darnell, 2012). Such global influences do not necessarily prevent independent, community-based initiatives in SDP, but they have been found to influence what occurs at the local level of sport-for-development. For example, in my research into SDP (Darnell, 2012), program officials and policymakers working in the sector described how sports mega-events help to draw public attention to the social significance, importance and benefits of local sport-for-development efforts. This is particularly the case when such events are hosted in 'developing' countries, like the 2010 FIFA World Cup in South Africa, or cities like the 2016 Summer Olympics to be held in Rio de Janeiro, Brazil. Similarly, celebrity athletes can bring legitimacy to SDP by lending their name and image to such initiatives, or by financing programs themselves through their charitable foundations (see the Roger Federer Foundation, 2014).

In this way, SDP is not separate from, but in fact embedded in, the world of international sport. SDP is similarly connected to the structures of international development funding or aid, a system that still tends to see relatively rich countries and organizations support activities in poor communities. These funding systems can have real effects on sport-for-development on the ground. For example, Hayhurst (2013) conducted research into an SDP partnership between a European-based transnational corporation, an international NGO also based in Europe, and a local NGO in Uganda. Her results illustrated a *corporatization* of sport-for-development, in which the funding from these European organizations was accompanied by encouragement—and even an expectation—that Ugandan girls and women become independent and responsible social entrepreneurs. Notably, the local NGO in Hayhurst's (2013, p. 299) research worked to similar ends, but did so largely ". . . in order to gain autonomy and sever their dependency on donors." This type of research highlights some critical questions about local SDP initiatives. For example, how politically and economically autonomous are they? Is the practice of SDP *challenging* or *confirming* the traditional flow of development aid from relatively rich countries and communities to the relatively poor or underserved countries? Questions also remain as to the effects and impacts of SDP programs and policies on the ground, and this is the focus of the next section.

THREE IDEAL TYPES OF SDP INITIATIVES

According to Giulianotti (2011a), SDP research to date has tended to be contextual and case-based as opposed to thematic, analytical or generalizable. In attempting to fill this gap, and based on research with different kinds of SDP organizations, Giulianotti proposes three models of SDP organizations that seek peace and/or reconciliation through sport. These are offered not as specific examples, but rather as ideal types, ". . . encapsulating particular characteristics of SDP projects within idealized, homologous forms" (Giulianotti, 2011a, p. 213). The differences between the three types of SDP organizations are based on their institutional features, properties, social relations of engagement, and methods of monitoring and evaluating their work.

While actual SDP organizations may not fit neatly into any single one of these categories, the similarities and differences between the ideal types help to illustrate the various approaches available for peacebuilding and conflict resolution through sport.

Three ideal types of SDP organizations focused on peace and reconciliation:

1. Technical organizations—These tend to bring external, scientific and impartial perspectives to problems of conflict; seek direct and quantifiably measureable outcomes through interventions; and deploy well-established, competitive sports that are structured and externally monitored.

"The 'technical' SDP model is underpinned by a 'realist,' positivistic, instrumental philosophy, which assumes that specific societies encounter 'real,' objectively-identifiable social problems" (Giulianotti, 2011a, p. 215).

Peace Players International (discussed above) demonstrates elements of a technical organization: it brings an external and neutral perspective to areas of conflict, it includes peace and leadership curriculum across all of its programs, and it tends to use well-established sports like basketball as the basis of its activities.

2. Dialogical organizations—These tend to bring education and mediation support to specified community and social groups; pursue practices that confront and challenge the foundations of inter-communal conflict; deploy a 'train the trainers' approach to ensure program sustainability; modify existing sports in pursuit of integration and cooperation; and favor participatory techniques for monitoring and evaluation.

"Dialogical approaches seek to facilitate the positive re-foundation of social relations between communities. SDP agencies offer guiding mediation to build new meanings between the divided parties, practicing a dialogical pedagogy that engages and teaches user groups" (Giulianotti, 2011a, p. 218).

Peace Players International also demonstrates elements of a dialogical organization: it offers leadership training to graduates to support the sustainability of the program, it modifies sports like basketball so as to integrate opportunities for players to learn about conflict resolution, and it tailors its programs according to the local context in which they operate.

3. Critical organizations—These tend to seek facilitating roles that pursue long-term transformation of relationships within divided communities; maintain fluid roles and horizontal (versus top-down) power relationships amongst diverse

community groups; connect sport to other cultural activities and even create new games that may be free of the history of conflict; and tend to eschew structured monitoring and evaluation altogether.

"The (critical) model pursues transformations in relationships between divided communities and in how SDP work is conducted. The underlying philosophy is that effective peace-making emerges from long-term learning experiences among self-directed learners" (Giulianotti, 2011a, p. 220).

While Peace Players International may not show obvious signs of a critical organization, it does aim to engage youth in long-term learning, and to discuss critical issues in ways that encourage young people to grapple with the complexities of growing up in a post-conflict society. (http://www.peaceplayersintl.org/why-it-works/methodology, para 8)

Application Questions

Imagine you have been commissioned by an international development funding agency to propose a sport program based on one of the ideal types developed by Giulianotti. This program that you are developing should be designed to make a positive contribution to social inclusion and conflict resolution in a community that has experienced recent violence from ethnic-based conflict (revisit Chapter 3 for information on social inclusion).

What strengths and weaknesses can you identify within each of the three ideal types?

Based on these strengths and weaknesses, which of the three ideal types do you think provides the best model for pursuing locally relevant and sustainable community development and peacebuilding? Why?

Describe what a process of community development and peacebuilding might look like if your chosen program was successful in meeting its goals.

RESEARCH IN SDP: DO SDP PROGRAMS MAKE A DIFFERENCE?

There has been a host of recent research into the field of sport-for-development and the SDP sector. Taken together, the results of these studies are best described as equivocal. Therefore, this section provides an overview of research showing SDP programs serving development in generally successful and progressive ways, but also findings that suggest such initiatives may serve to constrain development, in both theory and practice.

SDP SERVING DEVELOPMENT

The plethora of recent research into SDP has documented a range of positive results from such initiatives, suggesting that if properly designed and implemented, sport programs can and do contribute towards the achievement of development goals like the MDGs. For example, research into the EMIMA program (cited above) found that young people in Tanzania who participated in sport-based extracurricular education programs were better prepared, and therefore more likely, to engage in safe and healthy sexual behaviors (Roberts et al., 2012). According to the authors of the study, the results show that "the sport-based approach is an effective means of communicating desirable information about safe sex behaviors to a population of at-risk adolescents" (Roberts et al., 2012, p. 156). In a similar manner, researchers like Kay (2009) have concluded that sport-based programs offer girls and young women an opportunity to assert their agency and independence amidst relations of gender dominance and structures of patriarchy. Kay (2009) found that girls who participated in the GOAL project in Delhi, India acquired important information about reproductive health and demonstrated improved confidence and assertiveness in the face of gender oppression.

Sport programs, events and participation have also been found to make a positive contribution towards social inclusion and post-conflict resolution. Gasser and Levinsen's (2004) study of the Open Fun Football Schools in the former Yugoslavia, and Sugden's (2010) assessments of the Football 4 Peace project in Israel, have cautiously concluded that sport can bring people together within ethnically divided communities in ways that may contribute towards reconciliation. Similar research in Cambodia, a country marked by a history of genocide and high levels of contemporary poverty, has suggested that sport programs—like the Siem Reap Hotel Football League—offer a communal space and a relatively safe platform in and through which to discuss and confront social divisions and inequalities (Okada and Young, 2011).

There is even evidence that sport can make a positive contribution to economic development and can help individuals and groups to achieve upward social mobility. In addition to Hayhurst's work, showing the potential for sport-based social entrepreneurship in poor communities, researchers like Spaaij (2011) have found that participation in sport can develop social capital, which individuals are able to use to help find employment and achieve some economic security.

OPEN FUN FOOTBALL SCHOOLS (OFFS)

In 1998, the Cross Cultures Project Association, a Danish organization, started a program called Open Fun Football Schools (OFFS) in Bosnia and Herzegovina, following the violent breakup of Yugoslavia. Recognizing that communities in Bosnia and Herzegovina were living with the effects of the war, and that ethnic divisions had been exacerbated and entrenched through violence, OFSS was designed to bring children together from different communities, particularly those that had been on opposite sides of the conflict. Five-day football programmes were designed and delivered during school vacations, with a focus on fun and inclusion more than competition and winning. Eventually, the program was rolled out in all of the countries of the former Yugoslavia, as well as some in the Middle East.

In their assessment of OFSS, Gasser and Levinsen (2004) drew attention to the fact that the program had been successful because of input and cooperation from a range of stakeholders and participants, including the children who played the games, but also the school's trainers and coaches, local clubs and municipalities, and even parents and the public. This last group was key, as seeing their kids play football resulted in "parents' mutual concerns for their children outweigh(ing) the mutual hostility bred by the war" (Gasser and Levinsen, 2004, p. 465). Overall, Gasser and Levinsen concluded that the success of the program was not just that it encouraged children from different ethnic communities to participate together in sport, but also that children's families as well as football clubs and community leaders had come to support the program. Thus, football was positioned as part of a long and broad process of post-war reconciliation. In Gasser and Levinsen's (2004, p. 471) words: "OFFS long-term success hinges on the successes of the local officials, international organizations, international and national sporting bodies and others who work to develop Bosnia and Herzegovina as a multiethnic nation."

These are all important research findings that demonstrate positive development outcomes achieved at the local or community level through sport initiatives and programs. In addition, though, there are limitations to such initiatives and thus the need for caution regarding the potential for SDP programs to constrain development.

SDP CONSTRAINING DEVELOPMENT

First and foremost, the positive impacts of SDP cited above are complicated by research findings that demonstrate not all participants derive the same benefits from sport-for-development, at the same time or in the same ways (Coalter, 2013), making it difficult to generalize results across the sector or connect such results directly to sport. More broadly, though, is the question of how development is approached and defined in the field of SDP. David Black (2010) has argued that the term *development* is often ambiguous in both its theoretical deployment and its practical application, suggesting that it has no inherent definition within the field of sport-for-development. In a similar fashion, Coalter (2013) has contended that deploying the term development leads to blind spots in SDP practice because important aspects of process, policy and critical inquiry can be overlooked or obscured. In his words:

> ". . . the term development conceals much more than it reveals and contains mostly unanswered questions about the nature and extent of relations between the micro level (e.g., the possible impact on the individual of participating in a sport-for-development programme), the meso level of organizations, institutions and communities and the macro level of economy, government and a globalized world" (Coalter, 2013, p. 20).

These kinds of critical insights draw attention to the fact that a definition of development is never pre-given in the field of SDP, but is in fact beholden to processes that takes place through policy, and at the level of program implementation. Such processes of defining development and implementing programs, if conducted in an informed and ethical manner, pay critical attention to 'top-down' versus 'bottom-up' strategies, the political ideology to which programs subscribe, and the various ways in which development can be interpreted and defined (Black, 2010).

POLICYMAKING IN SDP

Contributing to the institutionalization of the Sport for Development and Peace (SDP) sector of recent years has been the publication of several significant policy documents identifying the problems to which SDP initiatives should attend and the ways in which SDP programs should best set about addressing these problems. These documents reveal how the process of sport-for-development is imagined, particularly by those in positions of authority or those who are best able to guide local-level practices. Lyndsay Hayhurst (2009) has offered an important examination of these policies, based on a discourse analysis of six SDP policy documents published between 2003 and 2008, three by the United Nations and three by the Sport for Development and Peace International Working Group (SDP IWG).

Hayhurst uses a theoretical perspective known as 'governmentality' to understand policies not for the ways they restrict people's behavior but rather for the ways they structure relations of power that serve to encourage people to act in particular ways. In her analysis, policies are not simply means to ends, but ways in which knowledge and practices become recognizable, reasonable or normal.

After analyzing these documents, Hayhurst then offers three theses for understanding policy and understanding practice in the field of SDP. Her first thesis is that the wide range of issues, problems, priorities, and actors in SDP makes for policies that often lack clarity and may even be "convoluted, congested and embedded in a system of increasingly political relationships and rationales that continue to perpetuate its discourse in an eternally circuitous manner" (Hayhurst, 2009, p. 213). This thesis draws attention to the ways in which development institutions often have to define and justify their own positions and importance within a crowded field of actors—as much as or even more than they work to design policies and programs that meet the needs of their partners or recipients.

Second, Hayhurst argues that within these policies, the people who live in the Global South or what Hayhurst refers to as the 'Two-Thirds World'—meaning the relatively poor people who are the targets and presumed beneficiaries of SDP programs—are often positioned as 'passive recipients' of policies derived by the "political agendas and interests of donors, UN agencies and NGOs" (Hayhurst, 2009, p. 215). The implication is that there is a tendency for the goals of development to be identified, defined, and justified by development organizations rather than through the actions of local people.

Third, according to Hayhurst's analysis, SDP policies are often compatible with, and may even be 'wedded to,' neoliberal understandings of international development that advocate for entrepreneurial, competitive and un-regulated responses to the problems of development inequality such as poverty, lack of education and poor health. To this end, SDP policies seek to facilitate partnerships between NGOs and the private sector in ways that will encourage people in the Two Thirds World to become more efficient, and self-sufficient, within an increasingly global marketplace. Yet by pursuing development in these ways, these policies tend *not* to support government oversight or regulation, nor do they call for welfare state assistance in the tradition of social democracy.

The significance of Hayhurst's analysis is not that these goals of development are objectively wrong, or that people in the Two Thirds World do not want to be equal partners within the framework of international capitalism. Rather, the point is that the establishment of development priorities or goals—as often takes place through the process of policymaking—never occurs in a social or political vacuum, and is always influenced by the relations of power and authority in which they are constructed. In this way, pursuing and/or analyzing community development through sport is not simply a technical exercise or a question of what works and does not work; critical reflection is called for regarding how SDP policies confirm and/or challenge social hierarchies and inequality on a global scale.

These concerns are not just theoretical in nature, but connect to the practical challenge of SDP work as identified within the research literature. For example, in my own research with Canadian volunteer interns serving abroad in sport-for-development, I found a tendency among volunteers to interpret development in relation to individual achievement, terms that made sense to them based on their own class position and positive experiences with sport in Canada (Darnell, 2010). Interns' desires to reproduce such experiences for less privileged others through sport-for-development were laudable but also served to reduce development to a process of social reproduction. In this case, social reproduction meant that the possible definitions of development were constrained to a process of preparing marginalized people and communities to conform to, or even survive amidst, the structures of poverty and inequality (see Hartmann and Kwauk, 2011). In the specific field of SDP, this process can be further enforced if and when understandings of sport's contributions to development are not specific, empirical or critical, but rather "based on idealistic and popular ideas" (Coalter, 2010, p. 296). The descriptions of sport by Jeremic and Rogge, cited above, are examples of such popular and largely idealistic accounts.

Still, research does suggest that program officials and practitioners are working towards SDP practice that tries not to impose, reduce, or constrain the definition of development at the local or community level. Indeed, some SDP officials have demonstrated the willingness and ability to reflect critically on the power relations, and have shown a commitment to providing opportunities through DP rather than implement predetermined projects and goals (see Giulianotti, 2011b). What this means, though, is that the practical challenge of developing and implementing sport-for-development programs lies less with measuring outcomes and achieving targets and more with "establishing locally relevant models for programme implementation processes that harmonise all stakeholder objectives" (Richards and Foster, 2014, p. 169).

LOCAL INTERPRETATIONS OF SDP

Some analyses of sport remind students and scholars of the significance of local interpretation and agency in the relationship between sport and social development. Andrew Guest (2009) conducted an important study int SDP that helps to illustrates how such programs may be conceptualized by stakeholders and also how they may be interpreted at the local or community level in ways other than intended.

First, Guest shows that the Olympic Movement of the 1950s and '60s, under the leadership of International Olympic Committee President Avery Brundage, tended to view sport as a means of 'civilizing' and 'developing' Africa through colonial notions of universal humanism. Against this historical backdrop, Guest offers an ethnographic account of programs delivered by *Olympic Aid,* an international NGO and the precursor to *Right to Play.* In the early 2000s, *Olympic Aid* developed and delivered sport programs in Angola that were designed to facilitate life skills of self-esteem and teamwork for the local community. Guest's research, though, shows that these goals of community development were at cultural odds with local priorities of employment and the building of tangible, economic competencies. He argues that such results illustrate local agency, and perhaps even resistance, to the implementation of development programs that lack relevance and meaning, and also serve to remind researchers and practitioners that sport and/or community development are likely to hold various meanings for different people in different cultural and sociopolitical contexts. The results further illustrate a dogged philosophy of *modernization* within SDP, where sport is often viewed as 'universal' and therefore presumed to overcome the challenges of culture and inequality that make development work so difficult.

The implications of Guest's study are potentially profound. He demonstrates that the social meanings and values attached to, or promoted through, sport and SDP are not essential or universal. In fact, there is always a possibility, and perhaps even a probability, that the meanings of sport and development promoted by practitioners of SDP programs will not align with local people. As Guest (2009, p. 1348) writes:

> *". . . the general lesson from the history and practice of the Olympic Movement's grassroots outreach to Africa is that sport has diverse local meanings that go beyond type and form. Thus, while global sports programmes often make some effort to*

include local types of sport and games, cultural meanings for sport are deeper and more complex than the form of activities. It is not enough, for example, to simply include local sports and games within programming—an idea that Coubertin himself envisioned as part of his proposed African games during the 1920s. Indeed, although people in Pena had some indigenous sports and games, they were most enamoured with the familiar Olympic sports of soccer and basketball. They were not, however, enamoured with the idea of using sports to develop 'life skills' such as self-esteem and teamwork (nor did they necessarily feel that particular versions of self-esteem and teamwork were essential for healthy development). Thus, rather than simply altering the form of sporting activities, cultural diffusion alters meanings."

CONCLUSION

This chapter has drawn out some common themes and practices within and across the burgeoning Sport for Development and Peace sector and used these themes to address possibilities and limitations in the mobilization of sport to meet international development goals. This literature illustrates that there is significant institutional and practical diversity across the sector. Similarly, the research in the field suggests strong possibilities for supporting development through sport, as well as the need for critical caution about the impact and ethics of SDP program and policy development. In conclusion, two points are worth considering, particularly for the ways in which they may inform progressive SDP practice and research in future.

First, any positive achievements or developments documented by SDP practitioners or experienced by participants need to be understood as more than simply evidence of sport's development contribution. In addition, such results need to be conceptualized theoretically, and/or in terms of process, particularly if they are to be attributed to sport or deemed replicable in other social and geographic circumstances (see Coalter, 2013). A chore of SDP practice and research then, is not just adjudicating whether sport-for-development works (or does not) but understanding *how* and *why* it works (or does not).

Second, despite the fact that this chapter has tended to focus on the international SDP sector, particularly given its increasing profile and reach, it would be a mistake to conclude that social development through sport can only occur in poor or marginalized communities when implemented by external organizations. As Fokwang (2009, p. 198) has argued, the community-level significance of soccer in countries like Cameroon demonstrates that there are "institutions or organizations in 'poor' countries that have evolved local grassroots mechanisms for self-help, often by-passing the state or local government." Recognizing, and making sense of, such sport-for-development programs that are community formed and focused is part of the ongoing struggle to balance local agency and autonomy against global forces and international power structures that form the field of SDP (see Lindsey and Grattan, 2012). In turn, understanding the interplay of these various influences can help to produce research and practice that is contextually relevant, ethical and effective.

Application Questions

Imagine you have just accepted a placement as a volunteer for an SDP organization in a rural community in southern Africa, the Caribbean or South East Asia. You will be there for 8 months working with local people with a goal to organize sport towards improving education opportunities and achievements, promoting good practices of health care and healthy behavior among the residents, and supporting the place of girls and women within the community.

What would you do to prepare for such an experience? What would you want to know before you left?

Can you identify 3–5 issues for self-reflection that you would consider before you left? Why these issues? How do these issues connect to the ideas and research discussed in this chapter?

What do you think would be the most rewarding part of this work? What would be the hardest or most challenging?

REFERENCES

Alive and Kicking. (2014). Retrieved from http://www.aliveandkicking.org

Black, D. R. (2010). The ambiguities of development: Implications for 'development through sport.' *Sport in Society, 13*(1), 121–129.

Choudry, A., & Kapoor, D. (Eds.). (2013). *NGOization: Complicity, contradictions and prospects.* London & New York: Zeb Books.

Coakley, J. (2011). Youth Sports What Counts as "Positive Development?." *Journal of Sport & Social Issues, 35*(3), 306–324.

Coalter, F. (2010). The politics of sport-for-development: limited focus programmes and broad gauge problems? *International Review for the Sociology of Sport, 45*(3), 295–314.

Coalter, F. (2013). *Sport-for-development: What game are we playing?* London: Routledge.

Darnell, S. C. (2010). Power, Politics and" Sport for Development and Peace": Investigating the Utility of Sport for International Development. *Sociology of sport journal, 27*(1).

Darnell, S. C. (2012). *Sport for development and peace: A critical sociology*. London: Bloomsbury Academic Press.

Fokwang, J. (2009). Southern perspective on sport-in-development: a case study of football in Bamenda, Cameroon. In R. Levermore & A. Beacom (Eds.), *Sport and international development.* (pp. 198–218). Basingstoke: Palgrave Macmillan.

Gasser, P. K., & Levinsen, A. (2004). Breaking post-war ice: Open fun football schools in Bosnia and Herzegovina. *Sport in Society, 7*(3), 457–472.

Giulianotti, R. (2011a). The sport, development and peace sector: A model of four social policy domains. *Journal of Social Policy, 40*(4), 757–776.

Giulianotti, R. (2011b). Sport, Transnational Peacemaking, and Global Civil Society: Exploring the Reflective Discourses of "Sport, Development, and Peace" Project Officials. *Journal of Sport & Social Issues, 35*(1), 50–71.

Giulianotti, R., & Armstrong, G. (2014). The Sport for Development and Peace Sector: A Critical Sociological Analysis. In N. Schulenkorf & D. Adair (Eds.), *Global sport for development: Critical perspectives* (pp. 15–32). Basingstoke: Palgrave MacMillan.

Guest, A. M. (2009). The diffusion of development-through-sport: Analysing the history and practice of the Olympic Movement's grassroots outreach to Africa. *Sport in Society, 12*(10), 1336–1352.

Hartmann, D., & Kwauk, C. (2011). Sport and development: An overview, critique and reconstruction. *Journal of Sport and Social Issues, 35*(3), 284–305.

Hayhurst, L. M. (2009). The power to shape policy: Charting sport for development and peace policy discourses. *International journal of sport policy, 1*(2), 203–227.

Hayhurst, L. M. (2013). The 'Girl Effect'and martial arts: social entrepreneurship and sport, gender and development in Uganda. *Gender, Place & Culture*(ahead-of-print), 1–19.

Hoberman, J. (2011). The myth of sport as a peace-promoting political force. *SAIS Review, 31*(1), 17–29.

International Platform—Sport for Development. (2014). Retrieved from http://www.sportanddev.org

Kay, T. (2009). Developing through sport: Evidencing sport impacts on young people. *Sport in Society, 12*(9), 1177–1191.

Lindsey, I., & Grattan, A. (2012). An 'international movement'? Decentring sport-for-development within Zambian communities. *International Journal of Sport Policy and Politics, 4*(1), 91–110.

Okada, C., & Young, K. (2012). Sport and social development: Promise and caution from an incipient Cambodian football league. *International Review for the Sociology of Sport, 47*(1), 5–26.

Peace Players International. (2014). Retrieved from http://www.peaceplayersintl.org

Richards, J., & Foster, C. (2014). Sport for Development Programme Objectives and Delivery: A mismatch in Gulu, Northern Uganda. In N. Schulenkorf & D. Adair (Eds.), *Global sport for development: Critical perspectives* (pp. 155–172). Basingstoke: Palgrave MacMillan.

Roberts, G. C., Maro, C., & Sorensen, M. (2012). Using Sport to Promote HIV/AIDS Education among At-risk Youths in Sub-Saharan Africa. In R. J. Schinke & S. J. Hanrahan (Eds.), *Sport for development, Peace and social justice* (pp. 149–162). Morgantown, WV: Fitness Information Technology.

Roger Federer Foundation. (2014). Retrieved from http://www.rogerfederer foundation.org

Schulenkorf, N. (2012). Sustainable community development through sport and events: A conceptual framework for Sport-for-Development projects. *Sport management review, 15*(1), 1–12.

Schulenkorf, N., & Adair, D. (2014). Sport for Development: The emergence and growth of a new genre. In N. Schulenkorf & D. Adair (Eds.), *Global sport for development: Critical perspectives* (pp. 3–14). Basingstoke: Palgrave MacMillan.

SCORE. (2014). Retrieved from http://www.score.org.za

Spaaij, R. (2011). *Sport and social mobility: Crossing boundaries* London: Taylor & Francis.

Sportanddev.org. (2014). EMIMA. Retrieved from http://www.sportanddev.org/connect/organisation.cfm?org=161

Sugden, J. (2010). Critical left-realism and sport interventions in divided societies. *International Review for the Sociology of Sport, 45*(3), 258–272.

UNDP (2014) The Millennium Development Goals: Eight Goals for 2015. Retrieved from http://www.undp.org/content/undp/en/home/mdgoverview/

UN. (2013). UN Assembly Proclaims 6 April International Day of Sport for Development, Peace. Retrieved from http://www.un.org/apps/news/story.asp?NewsID=45689#.U1fK_cdwapo

15

COMMUNITY DEVELOPMENT AND ECONOMIC DEVELOPMENT: WHAT IS THE RELATIONSHIP?

Rhonda Phillips

INTRODUCTION

It can be a bit risky to tell a Southerner to "share your personal perspectives" as the editors did with the instructions on writing this chapter. So it is with a bit of risk I will first tell you a story before we delve into the intricacies of community and economic development. It is definitely a personal story and if told properly, it will circle back to our topic, eventually.

Growing up in the rural Southeastern US, I was struck even as a young child by the lack and wanting of many of our neighbors struggling to keep apace of rapidly changing economic conditions. As the US began "deindustrialization" in the 1960s and 1970s, it hit my region hard. Dependent upon relatives holding jobs far away—in places such as Detroit, or on off-shore drilling rigs in the Gulf of Mexico—residents of rural regions of the Deep South were severely impacted by deindustrialization because the money did not flow home like it did in the past. Worse, the textile mills and other US industries dependent upon low-cost labor scattered throughout the South began to shut down as I entered my teens and by the time I was a freshman in college, the region and the rest of the US were in the recessionary times of the early 1980s. The jobs that I grew up hearing my relatives and neighbors talk about were essentially gone—a thing of the past, without any hope of return. Options for many others left town as the last parts assembly plant headed to Mexico with its 600 jobs.

My piney hills region was one of mostly small farmers (at least for those who stayed behind) and in tandem with deindustrialization came the compression of the agriculture industry in the US. This hit at the heart of rural Americans' lifestyle, literally driving out the small farmer as they struggled to sell their crops or buy winter feed given the dizzying fluctuation of prices and demand. Coupled with rapid changes starting in the 1960s and accelerating in the 70s and 80s in agriculture and trade policy (think federal subsidies for certain crops, price fixing on agricultural products, etc. and you've got the picture), it was no longer feasible to keep land in production. The impact on small farmers was huge, with no recourse for many but to let land lay fallow, and many gave up farming altogether. From 1950 to 1975, the number of farms in the US decreased by half (along with people leaving these areas too) while the size of farms that remained doubled in acreage (Barber 2014). Without the scale of large farms as in the Midwest and other regions of the US, it was impossible to compete with crops grown for commercial markets, such as soybeans, where scale and quantity are essential. Cotton had disappeared as a viable option long ago in the 1960s when the transition to mechanized harvesting made it too expensive for small-scale farmers to grow. Predominately through policy, along with other changes in agricultural technology, we grew ourselves out of the small farm culture and its small town economies.

I watched this transition and was one of the last of the small Southern farm kids in my region to experience the richness of a rural community with a reasonably viable economy. There were verdant farms everywhere and to see a fallow field was a rarity in the 1960s and into the 1970s. By the mid-1980s, there were almost no farms left. The last dairy closed shortly after, and in town the gin and the feed mill were but rusty reminders of more prosperous times. I may sound positively ancient with this next bit but growing up, there were massive wood pickle vats owned by a small local company that made dills (you could smell it for miles around when they were at the end stages of processing). It was right on the train track, which still ran at the time to collect the various crops to take to larger cities. Better yet, a kid could pick up some summer money picking cucumbers and hauling in the large bags, along with all the other pickers for the day on the back of a pickup truck and riding to town to sell them to the pickle company (I know, it is been outlawed since to ride in the back of open trucks, especially sitting on top of huge burlap "croker" sacks of cucumbers). Nothing quite like a check made out in your own name resulting from the veritable fruit of your own labor when you are 12 years old. It could be that I am just waxing nostalgic but if there are no part-time summer jobs, what do youth turn to instead?

My memories of these type activities were shared by other rural residents too. Experiences such as buying meat and others things you did not want to or could not grow yourself from your neighbors or local businesses. We were "buying local" and were "locavores" before it became popular. I knew every family's name for miles radiating out from our farm. The community gatherings were things of lore, with potluck dinners and sorghum syrup making in the fall and on and on. It was here that I first learned about cooperation, as well as the idea of community working towards a goal when my father helped establish an agricultural cooperative organization—a collective of small farmers—to sell fresh vegetables to large markets several hours away.

Fast forward a few decades: over half the farms are gone in my home county, down to 337 farms from 744 in 1974, reflecting the national trend mentioned earlier. Many of these farms are not the same as the diverse crops of my youth, they are instead holiday tree farms, or other types of tree farming, with some commercial chicken or cattle farms interspersed. The landscape is dramatically different, and the majority of the former pastureland is now covered in pine trees for selling as pulpwood and lumber. Population decreased about 13% from the time I was born until 2012, and many people drive the 70-mile roundtrip to the closest city for work, or, as I did, many just leave. Now, my home county is among the poorest in the nation, with median household income, and housing values well below state averages. Unemployment rates are still in the double digits. More disturbing is that the county made national headlines in the early 2000s in a story that chronicled the move of the illegal drug trade from urban to rural areas. I have no data to back this up—only anecdotal observations—but I can say that while visiting, one hears small aircraft flying over late at night and there are very expensive cars parked outside ramshackle homes, and these both could perhaps be considered indicators of illegal drug trade. Locals say that shipments are dropped in remote locations and runners collect them in cars that speed through the county at night without headlights.

I do not return home as often as I should.

> **Application Question**
>
> *Draw on your personal experience, the experiences of family and friends, or conduct some research on a rural area near you. How has it been impacted by changing economic conditions?*

WHAT DOES ECONOMICS HAVE TO DO WITH THIS?

Economic doctrine would indicate that the rational decision is to let market supply and demand dictate, and if some communities fall by the wayside, so be it. In other words, if there is no longer any "demand" for small farms and towns, then let it fade away—never mind how policy may have spurred their demise! I was struck by the severity of this via observations in my own home region and later when discussions about letting the Great Plains return to the wild came about in the 80s, after agricultural decline was hitting unprecedented levels (if you are interested in learning more, just search for the Buffalo Commons, or explore the history of how the Great Plains' rich resources were plowed under, literally, culminating in the Dust Bowl of the 1930s). It is a difficult thing to let places go—their history matters to some of us. It is more rational to think in terms of demand yet we are still talking about people, no matter how few are left in the rural areas. Throughout the rural and urban US landscape, you can see remnants of former communities where the economy of the area or region did not or could not adjust to changes. In some branches of economics, such as Keynesian or public choice in which the government can help by supporting demand for goods and services, interventionist government policies could help communities adjust to the vagaries of free market economics (for more details on Keynesian economics, look into the history of the Great Depression and the recovery mechanisms). Numerous attempts to do so have been made over the years throughout the US and in most countries, some successful and others not as much. Options are to intervene or to let the chips fall where they may and economists and policymakers have different stances on what constitutes the best approach. All of this is to say that without a healthy economy, most towns and cities cannot sustain themselves over the long-term, no matter the size.

So what is a community to do to remain viable and enjoy well-being given some of these difficulties we have just discussed? There are many elements that make a community strong yet economics can "make or break" the ability to survive. For example, having connections between all sectors, whether private, nonprofit, or public, makes a difference in helping communities build capacity and resilience to economic challenges. Dedicated partners, residents, leaders, and other civic and social entrepreneurs (those who combine the spirit of enterprise with the spirit of community) are needed to help build durable and resilient economies (Phillips et al., 2013).

WHAT'S ECONOMIC DEVELOPMENT?

It was 1980 when I first heard this term. My father shared a newspaper article with me that the region's university had just initiated one of the nation's first graduate programs in economic development, with the mission of helping a poverty stricken region regain strength. Although I was a first semester freshman, I was hooked. Can we really influence outcomes and make things better? Could it help, and where do we start? It was the natural choice for me to pursue. I found that as a policy approach, practice and profession, economic development is somewhere in the middle between well-meaning intervention and hands-off market capitalism that the practice of economic development falls in the US and Canada. Mostly it is an uneasy territory of being "business friendly" with low taxes and plenty of subsidies for private corporations in the attempt to lure them to one of many competing areas, whether a city, a county, a state or province, or even competition among countries for businesses to locate in their jurisdiction. At the same time, economic developers see the need for stable jobs and improvements in quality of life for the residents they represent. Economic development is often referred to by economists and policymakers as "local-level" economic development, or community (level) economic development as it is typically place-focused.

The evolution of the definition of economic development through time shows a transition to incorporating more qualitative aspects (e.g., quality of life, climate considerations, walkability, presence of biking paths, access and enjoyment by residents to arts, culture, and nature), rather than just a single-minded focus on quantitative indicators such as numbers of jobs. The following shows this evolution, beginning with the American Economic Development Council's 1984 definition (this group is now the International Economic Development Council):

> (Economic development is) the process of creating wealth through the mobilization of human, financial, capital, physical and natural resources to generate marketable goods and services. The economic developer's role is to influence the process for the benefit of the community through expanding job opportunities and the tax base (AEDC 1984, p. 8).

Hmm . . . this sounds a bit limiting but then it was 30 years ago, and we would hope to have expanded our thinking by now. Long ago it was pointed out that if the focus is predominately on job and wealth creation, it will be easier to lose sight of broader issues affecting community quality of life in other domains (Beauregard 1993). Economic well-being that includes both quantitative and qualitative indicators is more often mentioned now. According to Forman and Mooney (1999), there has long been emphasis in both practice and process for economic development to embed various levels of approaches: organizational (developing leaders), product development (investments to maintain or improve infrastructure), market development (enhance the economy), business development (nurture start-ups and existing businesses), and workforce development (improve local talent and skills).

Economic development as a practice and profession grew out of the desire to attract businesses and residents to areas open to growth. In the 20th century, it focused on attracting manufacturing to the southern tier of the US, and later was adopted by all regions as a way to market their areas as places to locate and expand businesses. During the 1980s, we shifted to more of a focus on "growing our own," with small business entrepreneurship and creative ways to finance and promote new ideas. It was during this time that I set my sights on becoming an economic development professional and threw myself into learning all about helping entrepreneurs incubate new ideas. Over the next few decades, the emphasis shifted to a broader perspective of incorporating sustainability concepts, as well as improving quality of life.

Application Questions

Take a look at your local newspaper. How prominent is economic development in the local conversation? To what extent is economic development seen as a solution to local problems?

As thinking about economic development has evolved and shifted to being more inclusive of impacts on where we live (our places), definitions began to reflect a broader role of community:

> We maintain that community economic development occurs when people in a community analyze the economic conditions of that community, determine its economic needs and unfilled opportunities, decide what can be done to improve economic conditions in that community, and then move to achieve agreed upon economic goals and objectives (Shaffer, Deller, & Marcouiller, 2006: 61).

Without explicitly stating it, this definition implies that social capital is instrumental to success, or what the authors refer to as decision-making capacity in a community. It is what Mattessich and Monsey (1997) referred to as the extent to which members of a community can work together effectively which we can consider a resource just like any other form of capital providing value to communities.

When we started including dimensions other than economics, things began to change; definitions, policies, and actions reflected more sustainable development aspects, and incorporated environmental issues alongside social equity considerations. Anglin's definition (2011) includes both social equity and sustainable development:

> Community economic development, and its values and practices, are indeed important strategies to help forge a stronger base for addressing key challenges going forward such as (1) development that protects the environment while opening opportunities for the poor to build wealth and opportunity, and (2) assisting in the larger project of strengthening the economic competiveness of cities and regions.

Should economic development be more oriented towards an overriding end result: the improvement of human well-being? The obvious answer is yes. However, the reality is that economic development practice and outcomes is often driven by a focus on the generation of wealth. Perhaps it cannot be helped, yet I would like to think that we can move as societies towards what E. F. Schumacher (1973: 191) stated in his elegant classic, *Small is Beautiful, Economics as if People Mattered:*

> Economic development is something much wider and deeper than economics, let alone econometrics. Its roots lie outside the economic sphere, in education, organisation, discipline, and, beyond that, in political independence and a national consciousness of self-reliance.

I found Schumacher's work much later on in my quest of learning about economic development. His work resonates with me deeply, because it focuses on people and promoting development of, and for, people—something that is sometimes overlooked in economics. How I interpret what he is saying in this quote is that economic development is more than the mathematics of equations, and it can have a synergy greater than economics. He also admonished that if wealth or materialism is the central focus of our economies, then the unlimited expansion this implies cannot fit within the limitations of nature (for example, no system whether human made or natural can sustain unlimited growth). We have found this to be true with the advent of environmental crises and recognition of the need for sustainable development. The question we are asking now is: can there be a more "gentle and elegant" orientation for economics, as Schumacher called for 40 years ago? In other words, can economics, and economic development, be focused on people and their needs more fully? The human element—things like trust, relationships, respect, and needs—must be addressed within the economic framework, and while not always an easy thing to do, it is required if communities are to build capacity and resiliency for fostering durable, local economies (Phillips, Seifer & Antczak, 2013).

COMMUNITY DEVELOPMENT, AS IF PEOPLE MATTERED . . .

Later in my learning journey, I became more and more interested in community development, with its principles, ideas, and engaged practice. These approaches are so broad and inclusive of many elements, and having more residents thoroughly embroiled in its processes is inherently appealing. Community development is a rich and varied area of practice and study, evolving from social action of earlier times around tenement housing and infrastructure improvement with the Progressive Movement in the late 1800s. Later, the women's and civil rights movement, and the need to address poverty spawned tens of thousands of community development corporations (CDCs) or initiatives. Several years ago, I had the pleasure of visiting the very first CDC in the US to receive federal funding–Bedford Stuyvesant Restoration in New York City—and was in awe of what they have accomplished since their founding in 1967. Here was the idea in action that people can identify their challenges, design approaches, build connections and resources, and tackle the issues as a team.

I quickly learned that people have always been front and center in community development, no question. For example, the Community Development Society, founded in 1970, states its practice principles as the following:

- Promote active and representative participation toward enabling all community members to meaningfully influence the decisions that affect their lives.
- Engage community members in learning about and understanding community issues, and the economic, social, environmental, political, psychological, and other impacts associated with alternative courses of action.
- Incorporate the diverse interests and cultures of the community in the community development process; and disengage from support of any effort that is likely to adversely affect the disadvantaged members of a community.
- Work actively to enhance the leadership capacity of community members, leaders, and groups within the community.
- Be open to using the full range of action strategies to work toward the long-term sustainability and well-being of the community (CDS, 2014).

It felt to me that expanding the development net with community development was essential and my forays into community development later led me to serve as editor of the primary journal of this discipline in the US. In the Deep South, this would call for the old adage of "throwing a rabbit in a brier patch" (rabbits love briers) and I felt at home in this discipline.

It is often considered that community development deals with the "soft" side of development—social dimensions, issues of equity, environmental protection, advocacy for those who may not have voice in their community, etc. The practice of community development often yields processes and outcomes that significantly impact overall quality of life and well-being in communities, and there's nothing "soft" about that so the descriptor in this context really means the *intangible aspects of development.* This could include negotiating, building relationships, and fostering sense of belonging and place. I will draw the comparisons more fully later, but suffice it to say that all of these soft dimensions contrast to some of the more "hard" aspects of economic development.

I consider community development as both a process and an outcome, with the following definition:

> *A process: developing and enhancing the ability to act collectively, and an outcome: (1) taking collective action and (2) the result of that action for improvement in a community in any or all realms: physical, environmental, cultural, social, political, economic, etc. (Phillips & Pittman, 2014, p. 8).*

In other words, it is a way to get things done that need doing in a community, as decided upon by the collective wit, wisdom, and desires of its members. Community development focuses more on the overall place and a broad range of dimensions encompassing collective well-being.

BRIDGING COMMUNITY AND ECONOMIC DEVELOPMENT

The relevance of the question of the relationship between community development and economic development matters insomuch as to the degree it impacts a community's ability to thrive. If the focus of economic development is predominately on the creation of jobs, then likely other important aspects will be neglected. Based on our own experiences as residents of communities, we inherently know that job growth alone will not be enough to make a community a desirable place to live, work, play, and prosper. On the other hand, if economic development approaches incorporate a wider perspective and consider domains beyond the economic, then it may address broader desires of a community. Conversely, if community development does not include economic considerations as part of a broader framework, then it may not be sustainable over the long-term (and most would not want the outcome for their town that I witnessed in my own).

> *Community economic development is "a merging of aspects of the fields of community development and economic development, implying practice aimed at community betterment and economic*

improvement at the local level, preferably encompassing sustainable development approaches" (Phillips & Besser, 2012, p. 6).

A way to connect the two areas is to think of community development as *producing* the assets to improve quality of life while economic development can help *mobilize* these assets to the benefit of the community with improved investment and quality of life outcomes, especially those related to economic dimensions. In an ideal situation, there would be a merging of aspects of both fields. In other words, can we find a more expansive and inclusive approach to improving our communities across a spectrum of outcomes—better access to services including education, cleaner energy and efficient transportation modes, representation and equity for all, and opportunity for livelihoods that can foster decent quality of life?

The following figure (15.1) probably best illustrates this idea of combining the two. Note that the capacity building process inherent in community development leads to social capital (the first component on the left side of the figure), which in due course results in community development outcomes (hopefully desirable ones decided upon by members of the community). Those communities with the ability to act—social capital—can in turn generate more desirable economic development programs, processes and outcomes should they want to pursue these goals. This is the mobilization of resources discussed earlier. Notice the box at the top of the figure, community development outcomes—when communities take action, they create and maintain effective economic development programs mobilizing resources. Improvements in the physical, social, and environmental domains of community can result in more desirable economic outcomes as well. This chain depicts an iterative cycle that can result in improved quality of life via community economic development. While community developers might not think they are practicing economic development and vice versa, this figure shows that we all practice *community economic development.*

Application Questions

Could you see how the "chain" could be used to think through a situation in a community where action was needed? For example, if a place wanted to promote green businesses, where would you start?

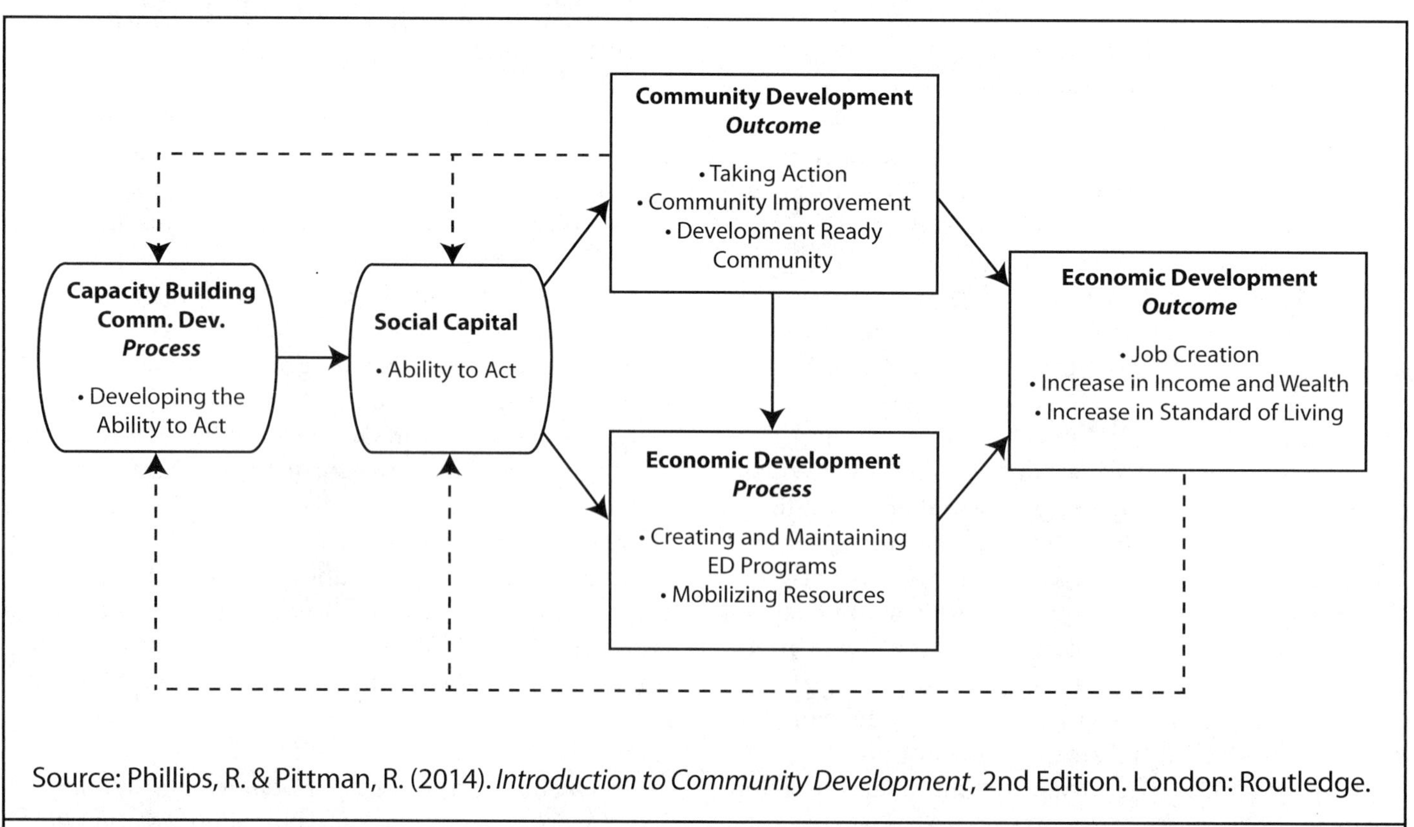

Source: Phillips, R. & Pittman, R. (2014). *Introduction to Community Development*, 2nd Edition. London: Routledge.

FIGURE 15.1 COMMUNITY AND ECONOMIC DEVELOPMENT CHAIN

SO WHAT ABOUT CED (COMMUNITY ECONOMIC DEVELOPMENT)?

I was 17 when the mayor of my home town (technically I lived well outside the town but it was the only place around so I claim it), a progressive thinker of the 70s wanted to reinvigorate it by reclaiming historical attributes. There was a railroad depot of considerable significance, and at the time, brick streets handmade and hand-laid generations earlier. Not to mention that a nearby small town's claim to fame was their bank having been reputedly held up in the early 1930s by Bonnie and gang, of Bonnie and Clyde fame, so one could see potential in this area. The small Main Street had some admirable facades from an earlier era, and there were still ornate iron hitching posts up and down the streets for when wagons and horses were the mode of transportation. The idea was that it could be an antiquing destination and perhaps some of the Victorian era homes could become bed and breakfast inns for short visits by tourists drawn to the improved ambience of the place. The old cotton and grain mill just a little further down Main Street could be reclaimed into some sort of museum or gallery. There was even an ice factory just off Main Street that was quite interesting, and all the buildings were solidly made red brick from the clay of the area. We could perhaps be like a bit larger town a few hours north of us, a place where tourists flocked. A movie had even been filmed there. People were abuzz with possibilities and ideas flowed openly, even the young people like me were included and I had a conversation with the mayor that I am sure later helped me select my career path.

The potential transformation of my hometown did not happen. Instead, the town retreated with the next election and sealed its fate as a dying place by paving over the brick streets, plastering aluminum siding over every brick façade as was done in towns throughout the US in the 1970s, and pulling up the hitching posts—all in the name of progress. The mill and gin and ice house have crumbled and there is no sign of anything of historical interest other than the courthouse, which mercifully was spared the aluminum treatment. Apathy, in many ways, plays a more major role than other factors in the demise of many communities. It is considered a fatal flaw in both community and economic development parlance. It, along with the lack of hope, seals the fate quicker than just about anything else. On the brighter side, hope can indeed spring eternal and be recovered, as many places have shown. Tiny Roslyn, Washington (population 875) became the film site for a popular television series in the 1990s; even smaller Helen, Georgia (population 526) recreated itself as an Alpine Village, attracting several thousand residents to the surrounding area and a slew of artists and crafts businesses. Hope is our ally in community and economic development.

As noted, viable development has happened in many other places. Numerous examples abound of how economies have turned around and generated benefits. The first book I wrote was about some of these places that dared to go ahead and try it, small places throughout the US that took a chance on redevelopment strategies based on arts and culture, historic preservation, or even creating "surreal" environments to attract new residents, visitors, and businesses. There was something different about these places that somehow defied the odds and were able to not only survive, but in some cases thrive. These are the communities that are exceptional and the American writer Gertrude Stein, had she visited them, could not have said, "there isn't any there there" as she did when she visited other cities, implying that there are communities with no distinguishing characteristics and lacking vibrancy or a definitive sense of place. These communities I explored in this book used innovative approaches to encourage development in ways that built on unique aspects of that place, and serve to garner investment, historic preservation milestones, tourism, and other revenue-generating activities. Underutilized resources have been capitalized upon to generate desirable outcomes for these areas; sometimes these resources were inherent to the community, other times they literally had to be created (Phillips 2002).

I want to point out that tourism-based strategies are often pursued by communities as a way to encourage community economic development outcomes. Tourism does not always result in success stories; yet when it is coupled with community-based development approaches and strategic economic development investments, it can (Chapter 16 offers a case study of tourism as community economic development). Tourism is certainly an economic activity, with demand and supply and consumer-driven impacts—just as any other major economic sector—with potential valued-added implications, as Reece explains (2010). These value-added implications may be better incomes, more choices of businesses for residents, improved infrastructure and amenities and so on. At that same time, there are significant economic costs associated with tourism, ranging from incidental to opportunity costs to inflation, and overdependence (Wall and Mathieson 2006). There are numerous sociopolitical and cultural impacts of tourism and must be considered in planning and design of tourism-based development approaches (Baud-Bovey and Lawson 2000). These impacts place it squarely in the domain of community development. Thus, tourism can be viewed as part of both economic development and community development approaches, assets, and outcomes.

TASTING AS GOOD AS IT LOOKS: BURLINGTON, VERMONT'S FOOD-BASED COMMUNITY ECONOMIC DEVELOPMENT APPROACH

The good winds of fortune blew me into Burlington, a small city (40,000) just south of the Canadian border, on the shores of Lake Champlain. I lived there for over a year, and relished the community development in action witnessed firsthand. For a former farmer, it was paradise—here was a city integrated with its local food system, par excellence! Let me give you a bit of a summary, and then encourage you to visit so you can see (and taste) for yourself.

• The Intervale Center is a 350-acre urban farm, with wetlands, fields, trails, and wildlife corridors home to over a dozen independent farm businesses. Hundreds of residents use the area for recreation and to buy food produced on the farms. And buy they do—approximately 10% of Burlington's food is produced at the Intervale Center, including for the local hospital, schools, and community supported agriculture members (CSAs). Farm viability programs help support the regions' food system and promote viability. Events and fairs are held regularly at the Intervale, organized as a nonprofit enterprise. This is impressive as the Intervale was a former dumping ground, literally. Future plans include utilizing waste steam generated by the power plant on the site for heating greenhouses to grow even more food. The Intervale is also home to Gardener's Supply, a 100% employee-owned company.

• The City government commissioned the Urban Agriculture Task Force for residents to find ways to make the local food system even stronger by designing a comprehensive Urban Agriculture Food Policy. The recommendations were adopted by City Council in 2012. (This is community development in action, to be certain—residents identifying issues, challenges and opportunities and making the recommendations to local government).

• Development of a Fresh Food Corridor to promote education and consumption of healthy foods.

• Economic development plans include approaches around value-added food sector planning, to seek out opportunities for producing food products in the city.

• ONE World Markets, where refugees who've relocated to Burlington showcase their products and develop business ideas—many of these focus on cultural and ethnic food products. The City of Burlington has organized this event.

For more information, see *Sustainable Communities, Creating a Durable Local Economy* (London: Earthscan, 2013), a book I wrote with my colleagues Bruce Seifer and Ed Antczak about Burlington's community economic development adventures.

Application Questions

Consider Burlington's food-based community economic development approach. What aspects of the approach do you think are most important for residents? For businesses? For policymakers or elected officials?

Now, back to my story—why did I tell you this? Not necessarily to illustrate best practices (although I want you to be inspired to seek those out) but rather to invoke the counterfactual; what if the residents had decided to pursue a different path, one of engaged community economic development? Could innovative and creative development approaches have been a way to help stem the loss of people, investment, and sense of place? By rebuilding the local food shed, would the community have been positioned to partake of the new "local" movement sweeping across many areas? Would community development processes have helped build community capacity/social capital to empower us to chart our future, rather than be blown by the winds of economic forces far beyond our control? Inspiring others to create a collective vision or even the glimmer of potential for an alternative healthier future is the value of this story. There are many examples where good community economic development process and approaches have yielded viable outcomes and I have managed to live in a few of them. Burlington, Vermont is one of them (see text box). The potential of bringing together community and economic development approaches is significant and in places where this is done well, the result can be improved quality of life and a more sustainable community.

Application Questions

Think of a community in which you would like to live in the future. What are the main features of the place that attract you? Of these, can you explain which are most influenced by community development? How about those most influenced by economic development?

REFERENCES

Anglin, R. (2011). *Promoting sustainable local and community economic development.* London: CRC Press.

Barber, D. (2014). *The third plate: Field notes on the future of food.* New York: The Penguin Press.

Beauregard, R. (1003). Constituting economic development: A theoretical perspective. In R. Bingham and R. Mier (Eds.), *Theories of local economic development: Perspectives from across the disciplines.* Newbury Park, CA: Sage.

Baud-Bovey, M., & Lawson, F. (1998). *Tourism and recreation handbook of planning and design.* Oxford: Architectural Press.

Community Development Society (CDS). (2014). Principles of good practice. Retrieved from www.comm-dev.org

Forman, M., & Mooney, J. (1999). *Learning to lead: A primer on economic development strategies.* Seattle, WA: Washington State Community, Trade and Economic Development.

Graham, C. (2011). *The pursuit of happiness: An economy of well-being.* Washington, DC: Brookings Institution Press.

Hannon, K., & Knox, D. (2010). *Understanding tourism.* Thousand Oaks, CA: Sage.

Mattessich, P., & Monsey, B. (1997). *Community building: What makes it work: A review of factors influencing successful community building.* St. Paul, MN: Wilder Foundation.

Phillips, R. (2002). *Concept marketing for communities: Capitalizing on underutilized resources to generate growth and development.* Westport, CT: Praeger.

Phillips, R., & Pittman, R. (2009). *An introduction to community development.* London: Routledge.

Phillips, R., & Besser, T. (2013). *Community economic development.* London: Routledge.

Phillips, R., Seifer, B. F., & Antczak, E. (2013). *Sustainable communities: Creating a durable local economy.* Abingdon, England: Routledge.

Reece, W. S. (2010). *The economics of tourism.* Upper Saddle River, NJ: Prentice Hall.

Schumacher, E. F. (1973). *Small is beautiful: Economics as if people mattered.* London: Harper & Row.

Shaffer, R., Deller, S., & Marcouiller, D. (2006). Rethinking community economic development. *Economic Development Quarterly, 20*(1), 59–74.

Wall, G. & Mathieson, A. (2006). *Tourism: Change, impacts and opportunities.* New York: Pearson/Prentice Hall.

16

TOURISM AND COMMUNITY EMPOWERMENT: THE CASE OF A TANZANIAN MAASAI COMMUNITY

Christine Buzinde and Heather Mair

INTRODUCTION

A large part of the world's population is made up of a diverse group of indigenous populations such as the Maasai of Tanzania, the Maya of Mexico, the Maori of New Zealand, and the First Nations People of Canada, to name a few. A look at the history associated with many indigenous populations often indicates that they have endured numerous hardships and atrocities brought about by colonialism and other forms of control over their people and lands. The effects of years of control over indigenous communities are still evident today in many parts of the world. For instance, indigenous populations often have higher poverty rates, in comparison to nonindigenous groups, because they tend to be geographically, economically, and politically marginalized.

Governments, international organizations (*e.g.*, the World Bank) and/or tourism industry representatives often encourage marginalized indigenous communities located within lesser economically developed (LED) nations to invest in tourism development so as to improve their economies. They often dictate the type of tourism development communities should engage in as well as the rules of engagement. Such a development model, which can be referred to as a *top-down approach,* has been criticized principally because it tends to exclude local community members from the tourism planning process. As a result, it offers few to no mechanisms through which community members can determine whether they want to engage in tourism nor how to develop tourism in a way that suits community needs and wants.

As authors of this chapter, we are sharing our view that understanding how tourism development can contribute to community well-being and social change is an important area of scholarship. Further, we are committed to the notion that when tourism development tends to solely focus on economic parameters, it risks ignoring issues such as community well-being and power. As you will see below with our discussion of Christine's work in Tanzania, we are deeply interested in interested in understanding how community members negotiate tourism development and how tourism impacts community life.

Research increasingly shows that it is through community involvement that tourism development can become successful in enhancing the social, cultural, economic, and environmental aspects of a given community (Mair & Reid, 2007; Sofield, 2003; Taylor, 1995). However, we should not idealize the concept of community empowerment because even when community members are involved in decision-making processes, tourism development can still occur in a haphazard manner, for instance due to locals' lack of knowledge, and this can be detrimental for the collective (Mair & Reid, 2007). Nevertheless, it should be noted that being involved can empower community members to take control and ownership of any development processes. A development model that accounts for community involvement is commonly referred to as a *bottom-up approach.*

DEFINITION OF EMPOWERMENT

At the individual level, empowerment can be defined as "agency or the expansion of individuals' choices and actions primarily in relation to others" (Kilby, 2010, p.33). At the community level, empowerment can be defined as "a group's... capacity to make effective choices, that is, to make choices and then to transform those choices into desired actions and outcomes" (Alsop, Bertelsen, & Holland, 2006, p. 10). In the context of tourism, community empowerment allows for "a relatively equitable distribution of local benefits in terms of revenues and employment" and it results in "a relatively high degree of control by local residents for administering tourism services" (Mitchell & Reid, 2001, p.115).

The goal of this chapter is to introduce the concept of community empowerment as it relates to tourism development. Within tourism development processes, government officials and tourism industry representatives play a variety of different roles that can foster, or hinder, a sense of empowerment amongst local members of any community. When a bottom-up approach to development is adopted, the roles that members of the two-abovementioned groups enact can empower communities by involving community members in decision making, planning, policymaking, as well as overall management of tourism. By contrast, when a top-down approach to development is adopted, government officials and tourism industry representatives are more likely to impose planning strategies that exclude community members from key decision-making meetings, and by so doing disempower the community. We prefer the bottom-up approach because it is inclusive in nature and it assumes that community members are equal stakeholders in the tourism development planning process. Additionally, the bottom-up approach allows for community 'buy-in' so it has the potential to neutralize the emergence of tensions between government officials, tourism industry representatives and members of a given community [see Chapter 7 for more on planning and community development). This chapter draws on the case study of the Maasai of Esilalei Village in Tanzania. In discussing the concept of empowerment, this chapter highlights positive outcomes but it also alerts the reader to the ongoing challenges faced by the Esilalei community.

THE MAASAI OF ESILALEI VILLAGE

We use the Esilalei Village as a case study in this chapter to provide an example of the various ways in which empowerment related to tourism development can take place. The village of Esilalei is located in Tanzania (East Africa) approximately 107kms west of the metropolitan town of Arusha. Esilalei is located close to a major highway that transports international tourists from Arusha to world-renowned national parks like Ngorongoro Conservation Area (NCA) and Serengeti National Park. Manyara Ranch borders the eastern boundaries of the village. The land on which Manyara Ranch is situated originally belonged to the Maasai (they abandoned it in the early 1900s due to a tsetse fly infestation) before it was taken over by private investors and later by the Tanzanian government under the National Ranching Corporation (NARCO) (Goldman, 2011; Hodgson, 2001). In the late 1990s when Tanzania undertook efforts to liberalize its economy, the African Wildlife Foundation (AWF) established the Tanzania Land Conservation Trust (TLCT) which currently has a 99 year lease on the land that commenced in 2001 (Sachedina, 2008). Approximately 2,370 Maasai pastoralists reside in Esilalei.

COMMUNITY EMPOWERMENT

A look at the historical evolution of the concept of empowerment reveals that the genesis of the term is closely linked with the civil rights movement and feminist theorizations in the 1960s. At that time, this concept was used to highlight social and political circumstances that prevented certain members of society (e.g., women or people of color) from realizing their full potential (Friedmann, 1992). Since the 1960s, the term empowerment has evolved to reflect various disciplinary approaches including political science, nursing, development and tourism studies, to name a few (Sofield, 2003). According to Rappaport (1987), empowerment is "a mechanism by which people, organizations, and communities gain mastery over their affairs (p. 122). Gilchrist (2009) defines it as the process of improving "people's capacity to influence the decisions that affect their lives" (p. 66).

The term empowerment implies that individuals have power over a given situation and power to enhance their circumstances by removing constraints and roadblocks that prevent them from acquiring resources that contribute to quality of life or any desirable life situation. Empowerment at the community level can serve to dismantle the challenges that prevent a community from enhancing its circumstances (i.e., social, cultural, economic, environmental). It is "a central principle of community development" (Gilchrist, 2009, p. 66), which according to Sofield (2003) can be regarded as "a process or an outcome" (p. 83). According to Scheyvens (2003) empowerment can reflect various aspects of a community; consequently, one can speak of various *forms of empowerment,* such as cultural empowerment, social empowerment, economic empowerment, and psychological empowerment, among others. Examples of the aforementioned four types of empowerment are described in the subsequent section utilizing the Esilalei Village as a case study.

Application Question

Have you ever traveled to a country that is considered to be a developing or less developed country?

A. If you have, reflect on your experiences there as a tourist. What kinds of activities did you engage in? Who did you meet? Where did you stay? As you read through the case study and learn about this case of community empowerment through tourism, look back at your reflections and compare your experiences with this case. Do you think that the kind of tourism you engaged in enhance the power of members of the communities you visited? Why or why not?

B. if you have not experienced this kind of travel, try to imagine what your experiences might have been like. What kinds of activities might you engage in? Who do you think you would meet? Where would you stay? As you read through the chapter and learn about this case of community empowerment through tourism, look back at your reflections and compare your experiences with this case. Do you think that the kind of tourism you engaged in enhance the power of members of the communities you visited? Why or why not?

2. Draw on your personal experience, the experiences of family and friends, or conduct some research on a country that is considered to be a developing or less developed country. What do you know about the kinds of tourism developments (if any) there? As you read through the case study, consider whether this kind of approach to community empowerment and tourism exists in the country you chose to focus on.

CASE STUDY

CULTURAL EMPOWERMENT: IMPLEMENTING CULTURAL BOMAS

The Maasai are traditionally a nomadic people; however, during the British colonial era, the government forced them to stop their nomadic lifestyle and to settle down in a designated area (Goldman, 2011; Hodgson, 2011). The British colonial era, which followed German occupation of Tanzania throughout World War I, took place during 1918 to 1961. Tanzania was declared an independent state (from British rule) in 1963 but unfortunately land policies endorsed by local government continued to disfavor Maasai land tenure needs (Hodgson, 2001). For example, the natural landscapes they customarily journeyed through, as nomads, became prime properties for high-end gaming and nature-based tourism for expatriates and Western tourists. The Tanzanian government sold and resold various plots of land, located in or close to areas where Maasai previously resided, to foreign investors. As a result, Maasai communities were constantly relocated to remote areas. This form of targeted displacement, which aims to evict and/or relocate a particular group of people from their place of residence is referred to as gentrification.

In Tanzania, the Maasai are generally regarded as a proud ethnic group that has retained ties to its traditional customs against all odds. Some non-Maasai Tanzanians as well as certain foreigners regard Maasai adherence to tradition as 'unmodern' and backward. Such views are in part, due to recurring media accounts that erroneously limit Maasai to portrayals of a primitive or prehistoric group of people despite the fact that such stereotypes have little to do with the contemporary Maasai people (Hodgson, 2001). Interestingly, the uniqueness of Maasai cultural traditions is a key motivating factor that lures many international tourists to Maasailand, by so doing enhancing Maasai's sense of pride in their culture and generating much-needed income to the community. The Maasai have used their popularity with international tourists to leverage land tenure with the local government. This strategy has been relatively successful in that the community has been able to fend off (at least for now) government plans to once again evict the Maasai. However, due to the recent economic downturn, land scarcity and continued disregard for indigenous ways of life, the Tanzanian government is once again proposing to evict Maasai from their current location so as to expand game reserves for nature tourists.

The Maasai are a people whose culture has been on display for international tourists for decades. Years of exposure to tourism have benefited the Maasai people in many ways but it has not been without costs. One of the biggest challenges they faced in the late 1970s early 1980s was invasion of privacy as tourists tended to wander into Maasai homesteads uninvited. Such tourist practices interrupted the sequence of day-to-day activities undertaken in Maasai homesteads. The increase in tourist numbers exacerbated the problem. The Maasai decided to remedy the problem by creating pseudo Maasai villages (referred to as cultural *bomas*) that could orient tourists to Maasai culture while concurrently shielding the community from invasion of privacy. Cultural *bomas* are visible in Kenya and Tanzania (two nations in which Maasai reside) and they are exemplars of the ways in which indigenous communities are effectively minimizing negative impacts induced by tourism while maximizing positive outcomes.

The creation of cultural *boma*s is also an attempt by the community to claim ownership of the land or what Sofield (2003) refers to as traditional or legitimate empowerment. This form of empowerment is derived from indigenous customs that inform cultural knowledge and mores. For instance, a quintessential example of traditional empowerment within the Maasai community is the fact that as a collective, the Maasai have taken control of (empowerment) the development of cultural tourism on their communal lands. They are empowered to take matters into their own hands because they regard themselves as the (traditional and) rightful owners of Maasai lands and culture and accordingly, they regard themselves as the only legitimate group with the power to sell Maasai land and/or culture. It is important to note that it is crucial to transform traditional empowerment into legal empowerment (Sofield, 2003) because such a measure would ensure that community members have legal backing, particularly in this case of land tenure. The community has actively worked on selecting aspects of Maasai culture that can be sold for tourism. The cultural tourism products presented by the Maasai to tourists include: cultural festivals, dances, and local tours to sacred places, to name a few. Hence, the Maasai are a clear example of a community empowered to bring about desirable outcomes for the collective through cultural tourism development, but also one constrained by injustices imposed by the local government.

FIGURE 16.1 IMAGE OF TRADITIONAL HUTS THAT COMPRISE THE CULTURAL BOMAS

SOCIAL EMPOWERMENT: PROVISION OF SOCIAL SERVICES

There is power in numbers and location and in the case of the Maasai, their minority status and residence in the hinterlands of the nation means that access to social services is rare and often nonexistent. Furthermore, funds for social services fluctuate as ruling political parties and political agendas change. Cognizant of the oscillating trends in government funded social service programs, the Maasai act as stewards of community well-being within their villages. For instance, funds accrued from the cultural *bomas* are used to improve building structures that house clinics and schools as well as repair roads. Donations from philanthropists, who arrive to the community as tourists, are also often geared towards social services that benefit the collective. The process of allocating accrued tourism revenue to social services (e.g., building roads, schools) is a direct outcome of a form of empowerment that can be referred to as social empowerment (Scheyvens, 1999).

By developing cultural bomas, the Maasai have implemented what Sofield (2003, p. 335) refers to as "the path for [an] adaptive response" to cultural/ethnic tourism development, which when applied to "indigenous ownership and control is absolutely fundamental to empowerment" (p. 276). In fact, high levels of control and ownership, which are characteristic of bottom-up approaches to tourism, can "counter some of the disempowering tendencies of economic globalization and tourism development" (Mair, Reid, & George, 2005, p. 166) and foster a sense of community empowerment (Mitchell & Reid, 2001).

ECONOMIC EMPOWERMENT: IMPLEMENTING MECHANISMS FOR INCLUSIVE WEALTH

Prior to the development of the *bomas* there was no mechanism for the Maasai to benefit economically from tourism because there was no established tourism product in the community. The cultural *bomas* are inhabited based on need. That is, elders are informed of families in dire need of financial assistance, perhaps for a medical procedure or for nourishment. The elders then choose the individuals who temporarily inhabit the cultural *bomas* on a rotational basis. Part of the funds accrued during individuals' one to two months stay in the *bomas* are equally distributed to those residing in the *boma* and the remaining funds are used to replenish funds for social services.

This inclusive approach to wealth redistribution is laudable particularly when one considers that communities dependent on tourism often exhibit large wealth gaps between the 'haves' and 'have-nots' (Britton, 1982). For instance, this gap is evident in nations like Mexico, particularly in the city of Cancún, where international hotel corporations exhibit magnificent waterfalls on their colossal properties while neighboring communities, inhabited by indigenous hotel workers (of Mayan descent), have no infrastructure for running water (Aguilar & De Fuentes, 2007). Esilalei is certainly an example of a community working towards inclusive wealth but it should be noted that even such laudable efforts are often plagued with corruption and/or mismanagement. Furthermore, existing structures of power and/or lack of spaces for community dialogue may lead to disproportionate distribution of revenue accrued from tourism. Communities do not always consist of a "homogenous, egalitarian group with shared goals" (Scheyvens, 1999, p. 248), thus internal issues of power can possibly thwart efforts aimed for the collective good. There are also *opportunity costs* (i.e., making a choice between one thing and another where one must consider risks and opportunities) associated with tourism development, which from an economic perspective means that when resources are invested in tourism the opportunity to invest in other important industries (e.g., the transportation industry) is lost. Allocating all investment opportunities towards the tourism industry can be problematic because it forces communities to further depend on a volatile industry and it does not provide an economic 'safety net,' in the form of other economically viable industries.

PSYCHOLOGICAL EMPOWERMENT: EMPOWERING WOMEN

Within some LED nations, women are respected but perplexingly also relegated subordinate roles. For instance, traditionally in the Maasai community, a woman only becomes recognized as a key member of society when she becomes a mother of healthy offspring and/or once she becomes a senior citizen and gains elderly status. By contrast, within contemporary Maasailand, economic empowerment through tourism has elevated Maasai women's status. Women tend to populate cultural *bomas* on behalf of their family (polygamous in nature) and they occupy their time there with craft and/or souvenir making in hope of selling these products to tourists. Unlike the entry fee which is split between community projects (i.e., roads, schools) and the families in need, the funds accrued from individual selling of crafts are remitted directly to the respective artists. Craft making thus becomes an activity that grants women economic power and economic independence. Many Maasai women use the personal funds to purchase cows for their family, an act that also contributes to elevation in status. The act of being able to purchase a cow is regarded very highly within the Maasai community because the cow is regarded as sacred and viewed as a giver of life.

Additionally, as a result of tourism in Maasailand, many Maasai girls and women are often recipients of philanthropic endeavors championed by tourists. For instance, some tourists donate funds to respective Maasai communities or to local non-governmental organizations (NGOs) that focus on primary and secondary education for Maasai girls or businesses enterprises for Maasai women. While these are rough estimates based

FIGURE 16.2 IMAGE OF ELDERLY MAASAI WOMEN (PHOTOGRAPH BY CHRISTINE BUZINDE)

on conversations with local leaders, these funds could range from $100 (USD) to $1000 (USD) per year, depending on the number of donors and the magnitude of each donation. Thus, the space in which the touristic encounter takes place is concurrently the locale in which concerted efforts to enhance Maasai women's status through education and enterprise take place.

Primary education for Maasai girls translates into knowledge of health issues and economic management in the household and it also provides a vital prerequisite for those who choose to pursue postgraduate studies. In this case, the development of a cultural tourism program designed and implemented by the Maasai empowers a traditionally disempowered sub-group, Maasai women. Selling souvenirs in the bomas enhances Maasai women's capacity to augment their income and this results in personal or psychological empowerment.

Women, much like their male counterparts, play an in important role in any community. In fact, one can go as far as to say that within LED nations, women play a vital role in the managing and enhancing their family's quality of life. Research on development and micro-enterprises in LED nations indicates that for instance, women in Africa are often very successful business innovators whose contributions help boost the economies of their home nations (Mayoux, 2001; Kimbu, 2014). Additionally, research on micro-loans in LED nations indicates that not only are women the highest ranking recipients of such funds they are also more likely, in comparison to their male counterparts, to yield profits and repay the loans; however, one can not lose sight of the fact that their male counterparts may retain control (Kilby, 2010). Indeed, women's entry into capitalist enterprises may lead to heavier workloads at work and home and may bolster gender inequity (Kilby, 2010).

CONCLUSION

Community empowerment is an important concept within the context of tourism development because an empowered community can utilize tourism as a vehicle through which to enhance community services and well-being. For instance, in the case of the Maasai, the community had the power to mobilize resources and utilize tourism as a tool through which to redistribute wealth in the community. Similarly, Maasai women were empowered to make crafts of their choice to sell to tourists. The accrued income from craft making contributed to the elevation of women's status within the community, perhaps further empowering and motivating them to find novel and meaningful ways to sustain themselves and their families economically.

The Maasai case study is a form of what Sofield (2003) refers to as resident responsive tourism and within this context residents are empowered in a variety of ways to take control of their circumstances (i.e., cultural, social, economic, and psychological empowerment). The community may possess a certain level of power but there are often tourism development decisions made *outside* the community (Reid & Sindiga, 1999), such as whether tour operators choose to take tourists to Maasai villages and if so, which cultural *bomas* in a given village they select to direct tourists to. It can be argued that the Maasai, in this case study have what Sofield (2003) broadly refers to as traditional empowerment, which enables them to develop cultural tourism and allows them to claim 'traditional' ownership of the land on which they reside based on cultural lineage. However, they are reliant on support from for example tour operators to ensure that tourists are indeed taken to the cultural *bomas*. Additionally, they are dependent upon government policies that legally grant land tenure. Accordingly, it is important for community members to complement traditional empowerment with legal empowerment because the latter is vital as communities work towards long-term enhancements to overall community well-being. In conclusion, the dynamic nature that characterizes societies worldwide means that the Maasai story shared in this chapter is not static but rather that it is part of a continually unfolding history of the Maasai people of Esilalei, Tanzania.

REFLECTION QUESTIONS

1. What first steps would you take to ensure that your community is empowered to invest in a form of tourism development that is beneficial to your community? What challenges other than the ones mentioned in the chapter do you foresee?
2. Do you think that all types of tourists appreciate the approach to tourism adopted by the Maasai? Please explain.
3. Imagine that you are an independent consultant who has been sent to a town hall meeting to discuss the pros and cons of displacing a community from an area that they have inhabited for decades. The town hall meeting has been set up to provide vital information to members of a community that is about to be displaced from their place of residence. In your town hall speech, reflect on the pros and cons related to the process of displacing a community and also be sure to discuss the relevance, if at all, of the concept of community empowerment.

REFERENCES

Aguilar, M. D., & De Fuentes, A. G. (2007). Barriers to achieving the water and sanitation-related Millennium Development Goals in Cancún, Mexico at the beginning of the twenty-first century. *Environment and Urbanization, 19*(1), 243–260.

Alsop, R., Bertelsen, M. F., & Holland, J. (2006). *Empowerment in practice: From analysis to implementation.* Washington, DC: The World Bank.

Britton, S. G. (1982). The political economy of tourism in the third world. *Annals of Tourism Research, 9,* 331–358.

Gilchrist, A. (2009). *The well-connected community: A networking approach to community development.* Bristol: The Policy Press.

Friedmann, J. (1992). *Empowerment: The politics of alternative development.* Cambridge: Blackwell.

Goldman, M. (2011). Strangers in their own land; Maasai and wildlife conservation in Northern Tanzania. *Conservation and Society, 9*(1), 65–79.

Hodgson, D. L. (2001). *Once intrepid warriors: Gender, ethnicity, and the cultural politics of Maasai development.* Indianapolis: Indiana University Press.

Kabeer, N. (2001). Conflicts over credit: re-evaluating the empowerment potential of loans to women in rural Bangladesh. *World Development, 29*(1), 63–84.

Kilby, P. (2010). *NGOs in India: The challenges of women's empowerment and accountability.* New York: Routledge.

Kimbu, A. N. (2014). Women, social entrepreneurship and tourism development in sub-Saharan Africa. Brugge, Belgium: 2014 Annual TTRA International Conference: Tourism and the New Global Economy.

Mair, H., & Reid, D.G. (2007). Tourism and community development vs. tourism for community development: Conceptualizing planning as power, knowledge and control. *Leisure/Loisir, 31*(2), 403–425.

Mair, H., Reid, D. G., & George, W. (2005). Globalization, rural tourism and community power. In D. R. Hall, I. Kirkpatrick, and M. Mitchell (Eds.), *Rural tourism and sustainable business* (pp. 165–179). Clevedon, UK: Channel View Press.

Mayoux, L. (1999). Questioning virtuous spirals: micro-finance and women's empowerment in Africa. *Journal of International Development, 11,* 957–984.

Mitchell, R. E., & Reid, D. G. (2001). Community integration: Island tourism in Peru. *Annals of Tourism Research, 28*(1), 113–139.

Rappaport, J. (1987). Terms of empowerment/exemplars of prevention: Toward a theory for community psychology. *American Journal of Community Psychology, 15*(2), 121–148.

Sachedina, H. T. (2008). *Wildlife is our oil: Conservation, livelihoods and NGOs in the Tarangire Ecosystem.* School of Geography and the Environment, University of Oxford: Tanzania. Unpublished dissertation from St. Anthony's College.

Scheyvens, R. (1999). Ecotourism and the empowerment of local communities. *Tourism management, 20,* 245–249.

Sofield, T. H. B. (2003). *Empowerment for sustainable tourism development.* Oxford: Elsevier.

Taylor, G. (1995). The community approach: Does it really work? *Tourism Management, 16*(7), 487–489.

17

AN EMERGENT CASE STUDY OF INTERactive: PROMOTING INTERCULTURAL UNDERSTANDING USING PHYSICAL ACTIVITY AS THE TOOL

Paula Carr and Wendy Frisby

INTRODUCTION

"We never stop becoming who we are"

(Nasib, INTERactive Member)

Nasib, who is in her 70's, felt very isolated when she moved from Fiji to Canada. Her illustrated and narrated story, which you can view and listen to on the website provided at the end of the chapter, provides a glimpse of her experiences as a newcomer who initially felt very disconnected and alone in her new surroundings. Eventually, Nasib took a risk and ventured out to the Collingwood Neighbourhood House (CNH) in the Renfrew-Collingwood neighbourhood in Vancouver where she met Kat, the CNH senior's coordinator who was also an alumnus from the School of Kinesiology at the University of British Columbia (UBC). Kat invited Nasib to come to a meeting about a community/university partnership that was forming to promote intercultural understanding in the diverse neighbourhood using physical activity as the tool. There Nasib met Jessica, a UBC student, who she now calls her "little sister" and the two women have forged a very close bond. Nasib went on to become an intercultural connector in Renfrew-Collingwood INTERactive (shortened to INTERactive in this chapter), the project that grew out of the partnership, and fondly calls all the people she meets her "new family."

Megan, another UBC student, helped to create the intercultural connector's card (see Figure 17.1) that Nasib takes to the sky train station and elsewhere to invite others to walk with her. As you can see, Nasib's card is multilingual and provides visual images to get her message across to others, who like her, do not speak or write English as their first language, an important consideration in our increasingly diverse world. The images on the card convey that one can meet to walk

FIGURE 17.1 INTERCULTURAL CONNECTOR'S CARD

INTERactive's Approach to Community Development

- Intentionally develop relational and collaborative approaches that connect diverse citizens and community organizations because more can be achieved working together than alone.
- Draw attention to the meanings, practices, and benefits of increased intercultural understanding.
- Increase opportunities to participate in traditional and non-traditional forms of physical activity to promote both intercultural understanding and health.
- Recruit and support intercultural connectors in the community who can reach out to those who are the most isolated and inactive.
- Create an environment of co-learning and experimentation to further develop skills and practices that encourage intercultural relationship building through shared activities.
- Utilize a diversity of methods to allow organic and structured community development processes to unfold.
- Develop a non-hierarachical approach to community organizing where everyone's assets are discovered and valued to encourage co-creation and co-leadership.
- Creatively utilize existing resources to strive for sustainability, rather than developing new programs.
- Share learning with others so that the impact ripples out.

with Nasib at 1:00 on Tuesdays at Collingwood Neighbourhood House on Joyce Street.

This case study is about Nasib and others involved in INTERactive that began two years ago. We are just two of those people—Paula is an intercultural neighbourhood developer and former executive director of CNH and Wendy is a recently retired professor in the School of Kinesiology at UBC. We acknowledge that other members of INTERactive would tell this story differently based on their own social locations and experiences with the project, but we would like to share our story with you in the hope that it will connect to your own pathways into and through community development—either now, or in the past, or in the future. Our story will help illuminate how community development approaches emerged through INTERactive and what the impact has been.

Our goals in sharing this case study are to: document the history of the community development process that is evolving in INTERactive; provide an example of how a community/university partnership can benefit the parties involved even when challenges are encountered; and share the story of INTERactive with others who may be interested in launching similar initiatives. To accomplish this we will discuss INTERactive's foundations and emergent community development processes, as well as its co-created activities, and share our stories of change and future directions.

INTERactive's Foundations and Emergent Community Development Processes

INTERactive is a neighbourhood-based initiative that is designed to promote intercultural understanding and relationship building using physical activity as the tool. Created by eight community partners, local citizens, and a university, it is a co-learning and co-creation approach to improving intercultural relations, health, and safety in the Renfrew-Collingwood neighbourhood. It is important to understand the history of the neighbourhood and its current culture, as this provided fertile ground for INTERactive to be launched and thrive.

The Neighbourhood Context

The Renfrew-Collingwood neighbourhood is a diverse and growing community situated in the east side of the City of Vancouver. It has a long history of expansion and decline with different approaches to community development, depending on the era. Originally, it was a hunting and food gathering area for indigenous peoples, then it hosted farmlands for the early pioneers, and eventually it became a transportation and business hub linking New Westminster, the first capital of British Columbia, to Vancouver. Its vibrancy began to decline due to industrial land development until the early 1980s, but this changed when Vancouver hosted Expo 86 and invited the world to visit, which happened at the same time that Canada was welcoming more new immigrants from different countries. The neighbourhood grew in population from 31,595 in 1986 to over 50,000 people today. In 1986, 30% of the population learned English as a second language, today that has risen to over 74%. It is estimated that a third of Renfrew-Collingwood's total population live in conditions of poverty. This neighbourhood is considered to be one of the most multicultural neighbourhoods in Canada and is a microcosm of other diverse cities (Carr, 2012).

During this period of growth, housing and transportation developments were a catalyst in bringing people in the neighbourhood together, which resulted in the formation of citizen-run organizations like CNH and the Collingwood Community Policing Centre. The founding members of the citizen-led organizations were actively involved in planning their new community. As people came out to public meetings and held dialogues to discuss the impacts of community growth, they started to get to know their neighbors (Cavers, Carr & Sandercock, 2005; Sandercock & Attili, 2005; Sandercock, Attili, Cavers & Carr, 2009). There were multiple streams of thinking about who should be moving into the neighbourhood. Some felt it was important to help those most in need, while others felt people with financial resources should be attracted to stimulate the business environment because high-need residents required social programs that drained limited community resources. Not surprisingly, these were emotionally charged discussions. In the initial years, most of the participation came from already organized groups and the earlier settlers living in the area, and they were not very successful in reaching out to culturally diverse and more marginalized residents.

Over time, CNH played a significant role in filling this void by including new immigrants and populations who were not well represented in community life, partly through their settlement and family support programs and services. Through advocacy and modeling respectful and collaborative approaches, staff and volunteers developed and implemented outreach and inclusion approaches that began to be practiced in other local institutions. This occurred because as CNH linked with isolated people, they connected them to other groups and organizations in the area and this process was reciprocated. In this way, CNH worked with other service providers to create a neighbourhood infrastructure and network that supported community service provider collaboration, while also developing meaningful working relationships with resident leaders. The stated values of CNH, which are infused into its community development practices, are:

- Cooperation and mutual respect among people
- Self-reliance of individuals and the empowerment of people and the Collingwood community as a whole
- Social justice and equitable treatment for all individuals
- Accountable to the community and responsive to its changing needs
- Full participation of all peoples in the social, cultural and economic life of the Collingwood community
- Valuing and recognizing the work and accomplishments of staff and volunteers and providing staff and volunteers with ongoing support, feedback, and continuous learning opportunities
- Resident involvement in problem solving and decision making
- Integration, collaboration and cooperation among service providers and within the organization and the Collingwood community
- Diversity and multicultural nature of the Collingwood community

There were and still are different roles that people take on to make the neighbourhood thrive—some strive to develop stronger and vibrant business districts, while others are involved in social services. There are people who take on roles to improve local schools and early learning centers. There are residents engaged in leading sporting and recreation activities. There are historians and people who advocate for saving historical landmarks, people committed to safety and community policing, health promotion, literacy, and so on. People usually initially get involved in single areas and later in multiple areas as they begin to see the connections in their work. Many people describe Renfrew-Collingwood as "a good place to grow" because efforts have been made to pay attention to working together and capacity building. When residents are asked "how they learn," their primary responses are from "each other" and "by doing." They experience community life together, experiment together, reflect together, address challenges together, and give each other feedback to improve access to community life for all residents. It was this foundation and the culture of the neighbourhood that laid the groundwork for INTERactive to be initiated with such a sense of community ownership and enthusiasm to experiment and co-create the project together.

Collingwood Neighborhood House's Mission

To promote the well-being of the Collingwood community by providing leadership and working collaboratively with individuals, families, agencies and other groups to develop and support inclusive, innovative, sustainable initiatives and services that respond to the community's social, educational, economic, health, cultural and recreational needs (http://www.cnh.bc.ca).

It is important to note that INTERactive is not a fixed program—rather it has been an emergent community process that has developed in a number of different directions as discussed in the next section. The first year's focus was on reaching people who were identified as not participating in community life through health promoting forms of physical activity, and taking actions to improve their access, removing barriers, and tapping into community creativity by working together.

As demonstrated in the INTERactive storytelling project that paired community members with UBC students to create eight illustrated stories of the impact of the project, the seeds were planted when Andrea, a doctoral student in Kinesiology at UBC introduced her aunt Paula to Wendy. Andrea was keen to make this bridge because she saw synergies when she heard Paula talking about the intercultural work she did in the community and Wendy talking about her research and a course she was developing on interculturalism, health, and physical activity at UBC. A meeting was soon organized at CNH that community members, community partners, and UBC students attended and enthusiastic interest was expressed in working collaboratively together to create a project that would strive to achieve two main goals:

1. to promote intercultural understanding using physical activity as the tool
2. to build capacity for interculturalism both in the community and at the university

WHAT IS INTERCULTURALISM?

Initially there was confusion about what interculturalism is and this remains an ongoing challenge that we are tackling through various forms of communication. While there are many different definitions of interculturalism in the literature, members of INTERactive decided to hold a workshop to develop their own definition of it, which is: "embracing diversity, fostering awareness, connecting people, and creating something new together in our neighbourhood." Creating something new could include, for example, building new relationships, trying new activities, breaking down assumptions about others, and using existing resources in creative new ways. The short form definition that some INTERactive members use to describe interculturalism is "doing something new with someone who is not like you."

Interculturalism differs from multiculturalism, which is a policy that Canada and many countries around the world have adopted and is designed to protect the freedom of newcomers to practice their own cultural traditions within a new host country (Banting & Kymlicka, 2012). Multiculturalism focuses primarily on ethnicity because the policy arose as a response to rising immigration rates, but this is only one aspect of one's identity. While many are proud of living in countries that are responding to ethnic diversity, multiculturalism policy has also been criticized for encouraging people to stay within their own ethno-cultural groupings (Frisby, Thibault & Cureton, 2014).

Interculturalism is thought to be the next wave in policy approaches because it considers ethnicity in addition to a number of other intersecting dimensions of one's identity including gender, age, place of birth, socioeconomic status, disability, health, religion, sexuality, and so on. An intercultural approach, whether it is legislated as official policy or not, acknowledges that while people share many similarities such as the desire for health, safety, and a sense of belonging in one's community, we are also different from each other in a variety of ways. It is by learning about our similarities and differences through social connections that we can break down stigmas, silos, stereotypes, and conflicts to help build vibrant, enriched, more tolerant, and welcoming communities.

WHY USE COMMUNITY PHYSICAL ACTIVITY TO PROMOTE INTERCULTURALISM?

The Renfrew-Collingwood neighbourhood has a long history of promoting interculturalism, including the utilization of leisure activities. One example is the beautification project in Slocan Park that brought community members together with local artists to create pathways, improve lighting, paint murals, carve totem poles, redesign children's playgrounds, and create community gardens. Covered areas and field house improvements were also built for community meetings, arts production, and exercise. While physical activity is already offered by a number of community partners and other groups in the neighbourhood, it had yet to be an explicit focus for encouraging intercultural understanding in ways that also promote physical, mental, and community health. It is well known that physical activity is important in the prevention of chronic diseases and there is growing evidence that it can also play a role in promoting mental health, as long as meaningful social interactions are fostered (Lee, Frisby, & Ponic, 2014). Unfortunately, positive social interactions are not always adequately encouraged on the playing fields and in other recreation spaces, and they may even become harmful if bullying, racism, sexism, ageism, ableism, and homophobic behaviors are allowed to occur (Tirone, 2010). Knowing the potential trouble spots with physical activity programs, some of the ways that INTERactive has intentionally fostered social interaction to promote intercultural understanding include:

- providing opportunities for people to introduce themselves and tell their stories in ways that are comfortable for them
- setting ground rules for respectful interactions
- creating buddy systems
- finding translators for community members who do not speak the dominant language
- developing a collaborative approach to decision making
- encouraging intergenerational and cross-cultural discussions
- inviting community members to teach non-traditional activities

Many of the physical activities that we can learn from each other, whether it is Aboriginal games or dances originating from another country, are low-cost, fun, can be learned quickly, and can also be adapted for different age groups and persons with disabilities.

Application Questions

Think of a community development initiative. Do you see any additional benefits to taking an intercultural approach in that initiative? How could it be incorporated?

Just some of the intercultural physical activities we have tried in the community and at the university include: Zumba, bocce, blind running, capoeira, shorinji kempo, tinikling, sepak takraw, and stick pull. These activities can teach us much about the world around us as they all have interesting histories that are sometimes tied to religion, celebrations, popular culture, struggles between social classes and political groups, as well as different cultural understandings of health. The focus on sharing and co-learning fit with our ideas about community development because community knowledge about different physical cultures from around the world are valued and residents are encouraged to become teachers so that more diversified options are available to a wider range of people (Donnelly & Nakamura, 2006). Community members who have become leaders and teachers in INTERactive have told us that being able to contribute in this way has also deepened their sense of belonging in the neighbourhood.

Application Questions

Are there non-traditional leisure activities that you or family members know that you could teach to others? How would you incorporate positive social interaction to promote intercultural understanding and relationship building into the teaching of this activity?

HOW IS INTERactive ORGANIZED?

The following diagram (Figure 17.2) illustrates INTERactive's non-hierarchical organizational structure that strives to honour the assets, skills and knowledge brought by all who participate in it. The four circles convey that there is no one leader because everyone is a co-leader of the project. In this way, we are all teachers and learners (Freire, 1970). Members of each circle meet on a regular basis and the entire group comes together several times throughout the year to co-create new ideas and activities, hear about and celebrate successes, devise strategies for overcoming challenges, discuss and coordinate plans, and develop ways to enhance communications and outreach. Nancy has played a crucial community development role by supporting and coordinating all four circles through their respective and collective work by helping them build their capacity and confidence to try new things.

Another main challenge has been providing the time and space to allow people to generate different ideas and feel comfortable with an organic and constantly evolving process. In top-down approaches to organization, there is a tendency to direct actions without consultation or input. In contrast, INTERactive aims to move away from an expert syndrome that is controlled by a few people and towards a process in which everyone feels valued and is seen as an expert. In this transition,

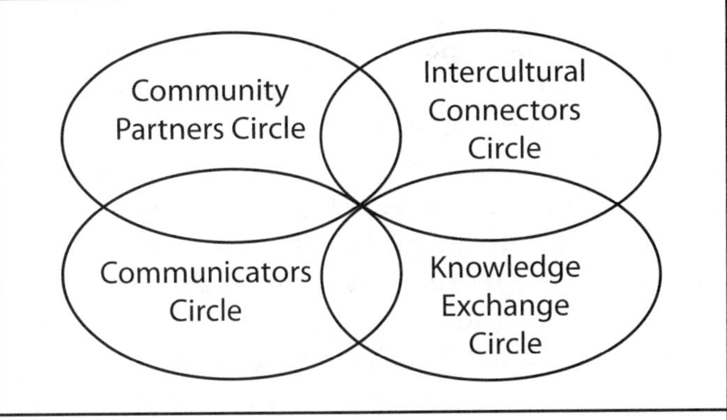

FIGURE 17.2 INTERactive's NON-HIERARCHICAL ORGANIZATIONAL STRUCTURE

it can feel uncomfortable and very confusing at first and we have certainly heard this throughout the evolution of INTERactive. Over time, however, most members have become more comfortable with the non-hierarchical structure and collaborative process that has taken us in a variety of directions. While our intercultural community development approach has been time-consuming, it has also created a sense of ownership when everyone's input is valued as much as possible, even though not all of that input can always be put into action because of the rich number of ideas generated. As Reid, Tom, and Frisby (2006) discussed in their analysis of the complexities of community action, some ideas may be good ones but may not feasible for various reasons, while other ideas may not be possible initially but may be implemented at a later date.

In INTERactive, the *Community Partners Circle* is comprised of Collingwood Neighbourhood House, Collingwood Community Policing Centre, Spectrum Society for Community Living, Renfrew Park Community Centre, Windermere Family of Schools, Better at Home for Seniors, Collingwood Business Improvement Association, Evergreen Health Centre (VCH), and the School of Kinesiology at UBC.

Early in the project, the community partners assisted with identifying people they knew who were not being reached and recruiting members of the following groups to join the *Intercultural Connectors Circle*: new immigrants, single parents, middle year children, Aboriginal residents, people with mental health challenges, isolated seniors, and people living in poverty. Intercultural Connectors is the circle that Nasib belongs to. We have found that having community members connect with other community members has been the best way to grow INTERactive. One of the unique features of the intercultural connectors is that they are not limited to connecting with just their peer group (which is often the approach), rather they are supported and encouraged to reach out beyond their peers to model intercultural relationship building. The connectors were found through a call out to community partners and citizens and were supported by mentors Kat and Emanuela, who encouraged the intercultural connectors to share and utilize their assets and gifts for reaching new people. The mentors also helped to orient the intercultural connectors to opportunities for both participating in and contributing to physical activities that helped to bridge new relations. To fulfill their outreach roles, many of the intercultural connectors sampled existing physical activities in the neighbourhood, discovered new ones and continued to share this with people, who they often met with in non-traditional settings like stores, their housing units, and other public spaces like parks or while waiting for transit.

The Communicators Circle, which is comprised of several community members and UBC students, has also been instrumental in spreading the word through social media, articles in the community newspaper, and face-to-face communications. For more information and to see communication examples, several links are provided at the end of this chapter.

Application Questions

What do you think INTERactive's logo conveys about the project? Think of different community development project. If you were to draw a picture of that project to explain it to a neighbor who may not hear or understand your language, what would your picture look like?

The *Knowledge Exchange Circle* is made up of university students and faculty and community members who are interested in disseminating research, best practices, and other information related to the project. Several UBC students have been involved in INTERactive through community-based experiential learning projects that are tied their university course on interculturalism, health and physical activity, and many have continued to volunteer long after they completed the course.

How is INTERactive Resourced?

We have heard and read about several community development projects involving leisure in the past, but it was not always clear how they were funded and resourced. Knowledge about fundraising and maximizing the use of existing resources is an important skill for anyone working in this field. While a key aim of INTERactive is to combine existing resources and develop new approaches to current work rather than starting costly new programs and services, it was still necessary to do some fundraising to provide honoraria and pay for meeting expenses and event-related costs. Some funding has been made available by community organizations like the Vancouver Foundation, an organization that is committed to strengthening

To successfully apply for funding to support community development projects, applications must usually demonstrate:

How the project contributes to the goals of the funder

The contributions and roles of partners

The expected outcomes and impact

How information about the project will be communicated

connections and engagement in communities, and governments interested in building welcoming and inclusive communities. In the first year, financial support came from CNH, the Vancouver Foundation, the Renfrew Park Community Association, and the Province of BC in partnership with the City of Vancouver. Additional support for the second year was received from the Healthy Living Program (Vancouver Coastal Health region) and the Vancouver Film Studio (a local business supporting intercultural community building). Some one-time funding was also received from UBC including the President's Office, the Centre for Community Engaged Learning, the Faculty of Education, and the School of Kinesiology because student learning, community engagement, and intercultural understanding are key strategic goals of the university.

The diversity of funding sources has its advantages. One advantage is that it broadens the reach and ownership for new and innovative projects like INTERactive. It also allows for greater sustainability as no one funder can put an initiative in jeopardy if they decide to cease their funding. However, other major challenges are that most funding is for 'one-time only' and it requires expertise and dedicated time to write proposals to various funders and seek out additional sources of support. This process also requires a great deal of administration and accountability as funders often have different evaluation and reporting requirements. We continue to meet with various stakeholders and funders to better build capacity and support to ensure the long-term sustainability of INTERactive, but this remains an ongoing challenge.

Application Questions

What types of challenges do you think could be encountered when adopting an intercultural approach to community development? What are your suggestions for overcoming them?

INTERactive's Co-Created Activities

In its first year, INTERactive could point to a number of successes. For example, the partners supported the intercultural connectors and together they reached over 450 people from various backgrounds. All of them reported trying new physical activities and forming new relationships. The community partners also adjusted physical activities to be more culturally diverse, supported the participation of parents and children, and developed walking clubs and spontaneous activities in outdoor public spaces that got people moving one step at a time. Examples of leveraging existing resources included partners adjusting schedules and fees, increased and coordinated promotion, learning from each other, and working together to reach deeper into the neighbourhood to encourage more active living. The core group of 60 people reached out to their different networks and connections to share the approaches and to encourage more co-creation and co-learning. The following provides examples of the INTERactive's co-created activities that have emerged since the projects inception.

Zumba in the Park

Over 250 people attended a movie night at Slocan Park sponsored by the Collingwood Community Policing Centre (CPC) and Collingwood Business Improvement Association (CBIA). The movie night had been designed to bring leisure activities into local parks as a way of promoting safety, but watching a movie is a sedentary activity. As a result, some of the movie night organizers, who were also partners in INTERactive, wondered if and how physical activity could be incorporated into the event in ways that would promote intercultural understanding and relationship building. They decided to try Zumba, an African and Latin based exercise program that is fun and easy to learn before the movie started. CNH found an instructor that the Collingwood Community Policing Centre paid for, Patrick (from INTERactive's Communication Circle) videoed the activity (see the website for it at the end of the chapter), and now several individuals and groups use the video to encourage movement at public gatherings. The video has been a very effective in communicating what INTERactive is about because it shows over 200 diverse people exercising, smiling, and interacting with one another. This summer, the CPC and the CBIA held physical activities before each movie in their international film series, illustrating how the success of the initial event has radiated out. Wendy has also shown the video to various audiences at UBC and to leisure researchers at an Australia and New Zealand Association of Leisure Research Conference (ANZALS) and encouraged them to dance to it with her. Most had never tried Zumba before but found it easy to do and it generated lively discussion afterwards, along with relationship building and mutual learning, while taking a healthy exercise break in a largely sedentary day (Frisby, 2014).

PARENTS, CHILDREN, AND TEACHERS

The intercultural connectors had met many parents and children who desired to be more physically active but had encountered language, a lack of culturally relevant activities, time, fees and schedules as barriers. Local partners began to examine ways to reduce fees, offer incentives to participate, and move schedules so children and parents could share a time to exercise at their own levels. They also began to give tours of community offerings in first languages. Parents and children formed a group and started their own activities in local parks and neighbourhood streets, which was often facilitated by Axel, a 10-year-old intercultural connector who was supported by Jules, a UBC student. This had led to a new initiative for next year where parents, teachers, and students in local schools will be learning and co-creating activities that bridge intercultural relations.

REACHING OUT THROUGH EVERYDAY ACTIVITIES

Another example of an emergent intercultural activity occurred when David (from INTERactive's Communication Circle) was inspired by a dance walking video he saw from New York. He sent a challenge out to people to meet at a public place and dance walk together. It was then suggested that we dance walk around the Collingwood-Joyce sky train station as people came home from work. Subsequently, a group of 20 formed. They danced around a local park, picking up five to ten more people along the way. As a larger group, they then went over to the train station and dance walked people down the street, encouraging another five to ten people to join in. In only 30 minutes, 40 people took a routine everyday activity and added more physical activity into it while also having fun with their neighbors, most of whom they had never met before.

COURSE DEVELOPMENT AT UBC

As stated earlier, one of the goals of INTERactive was to build capacity for intercultural understanding both in the community and at the university. An example of the latter is the new course on *Interculturalism, Health, and Physical Activity* in the School of Kinesiology at UBC. Students have worked collaboratively with the instructor to create assignments and learning opportunities that better prepare them for intercultural community development work in an increasingly diverse world. At the beginning of each class, two students present a short current event that they see connecting to the course content, along with their analysis of whether and how it helps to promote intercultural understanding. Students also complete a learning journal, present an analysis of an intercultural physical activity that they tried but were previously unfamiliar with, and work on an on-campus or off-campus community-based experiential learning (CBEL) project that involves presenting their recommendations to various groups and organizations. Some of these CBEL projects in the course are connected to INTERactive and INTERactive members, including Nasib, have come to class to tell their stories to promote two-way learning between the community and the university. Kat was uniquely positioned to perform a crucial bridging role between the university and community because she was a former graduate student who also worked in Renfrew-Collingwood. Understanding both contexts well, she was able to strengthen relations and cross-pollinate information and opportunities for co-learning and the co-creation of activities amongst community members and students.

STORIES OF CHANGE AND FUTURE DIRECTIONS

Almost every day INTERactive members hear a story about a new physical activity that is being tried or a new relationship that is being formed. This gives us an indication that the project is helping to create a new culture in the neighbourhood and at the university. Examples include mothers sharing yoga time with their children, community groups building physical activities into their regular programming, staff teams holding walking meetings in the workplace and around the neighbourhood, people identifying places where neighbors are physically active, and using public spaces for spontaneous walking, biking, wheelchair movements, running, and so on. At the university, INTERactive was profiled in the working draft of UBC's Intercultural Understanding Strategic Plan. Meetings have also been held with key university leaders to discuss the long-term sustainability of community engagement projects like INTERactive. Students are also talking about INTERactive across campus, such as at a workshop organized by the student-led UBC Mental Health Network.

This year, we plan to build on the co-created activities from INTERactive's first two years as follows.

- Sharing the stories of active living in an intercultural environment to stimulate more interest and motivation to "try something new with someone not like you."
- Community and student teams are working on animating neighbourhood streets and the university. This is an alternative to the reliance on organized programming and moving toward encouraging people to just take a few minutes to be active (like in the dance walking example provided earlier). They will be creating signage (with images instead of words to account for language differences) allowing people to see the benefits of taking the stairs rather than elevators and seeing the health benefits of developing and deepening social relationships. Walking, wheelchair, and biking clubs will be encouraged and supported. Games like community treasure hunts are being explored because they are a great way to bring different generations together to discover the neighbourhood's intercultural treasures.
- The INTERactive connectors along with many others in the neighbourhood who are connecting with people (workers, students, business owners, and neighbors) will be continually oriented to the neighbourhood opportunities and offerings around physical activity and leisure. They will also come together to share and learn about ways to increase intercultural connections, communication, and engagement through an INTERactive learning series.
- Donna, a UBC graduate student, and Vive, a UBC alumni who works at CNH (who are both members of INTERactive's Knowledge Exchange Circle), worked together to create an *Intercultural Physical Activity Instructional Guide* for teachers, parents, student leaders, and others to teach non-traditional activities. Training the trainers will be the next wave of getting this initiative embedded in community practice and culture change.
- Wendy, Donna, and Shawn are writing a workbook titled *Interculturalism, Health and Community Physical Activity* that is designed to share learning about INTERactive and other community-based research projects with other communities.
- Another goal is to strengthen the UBC and Renfrew-Collingwood relationship by involving students beyond one class, one semester, and one department.
- Plans are percolating to involve more people and build stronger connections with the Renfrew-Collingwood Food Security Institute, local artists, and by influencing built environment plans for greater health outcomes.

FOR MORE INFORMATION, CHECK OUT:

Where Strangers Become Neighbours is a documentary on the evolution of the Renfrew-Collingwood neighborhood. http://www.cnh.bc.ca/neighbourhood-stuff-to-do/film-where-strangers-become-neighbours

The Interculturalism 101 document that INTERactive members developed to communicate what interculturalism is and why it is important. http://www.cnh.bc.ca/neighbourhood-stuff-to-do/about-interactive

INTERactive's illustrated stories. http://www.cnh.bc.ca/neighbourhoodstuff-to-do/about-interactive

The INTERactive blog that provides information and updates. http://www.cnh.bc.ca/rcinteractive

The video of community members doing Zumba in the park. http://www.cnh.bc.ca/zumba-in-the-park

The Intercultural Physical Activity Instructional Guide by Lee and Wong (2016) is available at http://www.cnh.bc.ca/neighbourhood-stuff-to-do/interactive or http://www.jwsporta.ca

The City of Vancouver's Healthy City for All Strategy. http://www.vancouver.ca/people-programs/healthy-city-strategy.aspx

- INTERactive aims to inform and being informed by the City of Vancouver's *Healthy City for All Strategy* as it integrates many of the components within the strategy and offers an applied example for development in other neighbourhoods.

CONCLUSION

In closing, this case study of INTERactive illuminates the community development processes and structures involved in this unique community-university partnership, along with the some of the challenges encountered and the impacts it is having. The long history of community development in the Renfrew-Collingwood neighbourhood set the stage for INTERactive's birth and is largely responsible for its flourishing and growth. While interculturalism is a new term for many, the way members of INTERactive collectively define it—as "doing something new with people not like you"—builds upon and overcomes some of the limitations of multiculturalism policy. We invite you to consider how projects like INTERactive could be improved and how you might integrate an intercultural approach into your own community development work. In this way, you may be able to find ways to add to and build upon the stories told in this chapter. We believe an intercultural approach will be essential when working, living and playing in an increasingly diverse world and that physical activity and other forms of leisure have an important role to play in promoting intercultural understanding.

REFERENCES

Banting, K. & Kymlicka, W. (2012). Is there really a backlash against multiculturalism policies? New evidence from the Multiculturalism Policy Index. GRITIM Working Paper Series, No. 14, GRITIM: Queen's University.

Carr, P. (2012). Growing an Intercultural Neighbourhood, Growing a Civil Society. Retrieved from http://www.cnh.bc.ca/wp-content/uploads/2012/10/Intercultural-Book-LPIV-lores-Sept2012.pdf

Cavers, V., Carr, P., & Sandercock, L. (2005). *How strangers become neighbours: Constructing citizenship through neighbourhood community development*. Social Sciences and Humanities Research Council and the National Metropolis Project.

Donnelly, P., & Nakamura, Y. (2006). Sport and multiculturalism: A dialogue. Report for Canadian Heritage. Toronto, ON: University of Toronto Centre for Sport and Policy Studies.

Freire, P. (1970). *Pedagogy of the oppressed*. New York: Herder and Herder.

Frisby, W. (2014). Critical commentary: Moving from multiculturalism to interculturalism through leisure, *Annals of Leisure Research*. *17*(4), 1–5.

Frisby, W. Thibault, L. & Cureton, K. (2014). Multiculturalism and federal sport policy in Canada. In Ian Henry and Ling Mei Ko (Eds.), *International handbook for sport policy* (pp. 106–116). London: Rutledge.

Lee, D., Frisby, W., & Ponic, P. (2014). Promoting the mental health of immigrant women by transforming community physical activity. In L. Greaves, A. Pederson, & N. Poole (Eds.), *Gender transformative health promotion for women* (pp. 111–128), Toronto, ON: Canadian Scholars Press.

Lee, D., & Wong, V. (2016). *Activities for everyone, everywhere: An intercultural physical activity guide*. Vancouver: RC INTERactive and JW.

Reid, C., Tom, A., & Frisby, W. (2006). Finding the 'action' in feminist participatory action research. *Action Research*. *4*(3), 313–330.

Sandercock, L., and Attili, G. (2005). *Where strangers become neighbours: The story of Collingwood Neighbourhood House*. Retrieved from http://www.cnh.bc.ca/neighbourhood-stuff-to-do/film-where-strangers-become-neighbours/

Sandercock, L., Attili, G., Cavers, V., & Carr, P. (2009). *Where Strangers Become Neighbours: Integrating Immigrants in Vancouver, Canada*. New York: Springer Publishing Company.

Tirone, S. (2010). Multiculturalism and leisure policy: Enhancing the delivery of leisure services and supports for immigrants and minority Canadians. In H. Mair, S. M. Arai, & D. G. Reid (Eds.), *Decentering work: Critical perspectives on leisure, social policy, and human development* (pp. 149–174), Calgary, AB: University of Calgary Press.

18

MARGINALIZATION, INCLUSION, AND COMMUNITY DEVELOPMENT: WHAT THIS MEANS FOR WOMEN WHO HAVE SPENT TIME IN PRISON

Darla Fortune

> *In its purest sense, the term 'community development' refers to the collective means by which the ideal conditions of freedom and security—human kindness, mutual respect and recognition, tolerance, care, solidarity and social justice—might be achieved* (Blackshaw, 2010, p. 186).

The purpose of this chapter is to explore ways community development can contribute to the inclusion of one of our most marginalized groups of citizens in Canada—women who have spent time in a federal prison. Inclusion for women returning to community from prison became a topic of interest for me a number of years ago when I was both a volunteer and a student research assistant at Grand Valley Institution for Women (GVI), a women's federal prison in Kitchener, Ontario.

My first introduction to GVI was through Stride Night, a weekly recreational program offered by Community Justice Initiatives (CJI). Stride Night was developed by CJI to offer a space for women at GVI to come together with community volunteers and connect over shared leisure interests. Through these interactions, relationships form and reciprocal understanding develops between women and volunteers. Such relationships and understandings are intended to contribute to more knowledgeable communities that can better support women's reintegration.

During my time at Stride Night I heard many women express an interest to have Stride happen in community so they can continue to connect with volunteers after they leave prison and maintain the supportive relationships they developed. I suspect such sentiments were indicative of the fear and insecurity women have about entering a less-than-supportive community where they risk being isolated and excluded on the basis of stigma and difference. I became more attuned to the fear women have as they enter community when I was a member of a Stride Circle supporting a woman who entered community after a lengthy period of incarceration.

A Stride Circle is comprised of a group of volunteers, often recruited through Stride Night, who establish supportive relationships with a woman in GVI and maintain these relationships in community. As part of a Stride Circle I developed a deeper appreciation for the complexity associated with entering community after release from prison and the many needs women have for emotional support and practical assistance. My involvement in a Stride Circle made it difficult for me to imagine how women can even begin to negotiate the systemic barriers that preclude inclusion (e.g., barriers to accessing affordable housing, finding employment, and participating in community leisure programs) without having a social support system in place. I also realized, however, that the support provided by Circle volunteers is merely a drop in the bucket in terms of what must be done to create a more inclusive and socially just environment for women being released from prison. This realization led me to embark on a participatory action research (PAR) study with women who were living in the community after release from GVI. The study aimed to critically examine normative aspects of inclusion and explore how issues of difference, power, and marginalization shape inclusion efforts. Findings suggested that deep societal change is needed for women to truly experience inclusion upon their release from prison and highlighted a role for community in supporting personal change and growth.

My experiences as both a volunteer and a student researcher shed light on the chronic exclusion that women experience before, during, and after their incarceration. I have hope, however, that change is possible in terms of women's prospects for inclusion and I see a clear role for community development principles to be used to guide strategies for inclusion. With this in mind, I have three main goals for this chapter:

1. To expand readers' understanding of the marginalization and exclusion experienced by women who spend time in federal prison
2. To outline ways community development can advance inclusion efforts
3. To share learnings and offer suggestions that can help foster inclusion for people who experience chronic marginalization

I set the stage for the discussion that follows by describing the process and impact of marginalization.

THE PROCESS AND IMPACT OF MARGINALIZATION

The term marginalization describes the process of being relegated to a position of reduced social importance by dominant members of society (Hines, 2012). Hines explained that marginalization occurs because the dominant society benefits from having certain groups of people depicted as undesirable. The impact of marginalization is that whole groups of people are "expelled from useful participation in social life and thus potentially subjected to severe material deprivation and even extermination" (Young, 1990, p. 53). Marginalization also results in "the deprivation of cultural, practical, and institutionalized conditions for exercising capacities in a context of recognition and interaction" (Young, p. 55).

Given that marginalization often coincides with insufficient income for an acceptable standard of living, little opportunity to participate in social and economic activities, and a diminution in health-related quality of life (Layton & Wilson, 2014), individuals experiencing marginalization are often recipients of social services (Pedersen et al., 2012). Marginalization can also result in individuals having social networks that consist mostly of professionals and therefore are not reciprocal (Pedersen et al.). A lack of opportunity for reciprocity makes it difficult for individuals to move beyond being recipients of support and achieve equity in their social relations. For further discussion on marginalization and oppression, see Chapter 9.

While marginalization and exclusion are often used interchangeably, exclusion can also be considered the main consequence of being marginalized. Perpetuated by differences in race, class, gender, age, religion, disability, and sexual orientation, exclusion exists when people lack opportunity for full participation in the social and economic benefits of society (Ratcliffe, 2000; Wilkinson & Marmot, 2003). With systemic oppression related to race, class and gender contributing greatly to exclusion, it is not surprising to find that women, people who are non-white, and people living in poverty and/or with a disability top the list of those most in need of strategies to help facilitate inclusion (Labonte, 2004). Individuals who have spent time in institutions such as prisons are also particularly vulnerable to enduring exclusion (Wilkinson & Marmot, 2003).

Women in prison are more likely than not to have lived in poverty prior to their incarceration (Pedlar, Arai, Yuen & Fortune, 2008; Richie, 2001). There is also racial disparity in women's prisons that has not gone unnoticed. In Canada's prisons, for example, black and Aboriginal women are disproportionately over-represented (The Canadian Human Rights Commission, 2003). Consequently, there are compounding and intersecting factors influencing women's exclusion. In the next section I will describe how the exclusion and marginalization already present in women's lives is subsequently deepened by incarceration.

DEEPENING EXPERIENCES OF MARGINALIZATION AND EXCLUSION THROUGH INCARCERATION

Persistent unemployment and related poverty is a shared reality for many incarcerated women (Richie, 2001), making it difficult for them to be included in the social and economic activities within their communities. Prospects for inclusion are further diminished when women who spend time in prison are depicted by others in community as evil, aggressive, and pathological outcasts (Pedlar, Arai, & Yuen, 2007). This depiction can result in public opposition to opportunities and experiences designed to enhance women's well-being and connection to society. For example, Pedlar et al. reported on the public backlash over a workshop offered in GVI that was intended to provide women with the chance to socialize and learn strategies to improve their health and wellness.

Researchers have often emphasized the importance of supportive family relationships for women leaving prison and trying to make a fresh start in the community. For example, Nelson, Deess, and Allen (1999) found that family encouragement and emotional support were related to female offenders' reintegration success in terms of obtaining employment and abstaining from using illegal substances. Alongside work and family, Uggen, Manza, and Behrens (2004) identified civic reintegration as another important aspect of reintegration. Civic reintegration, referred to being productive and giving something back to society (e.g., participating in paid employment and paying taxes, volunteering one's time) is considered to be critical to discontinuing criminal activity and helping formerly incarcerated individuals transform their identities from "deviant" to "law-abiding citizens" (Uggen et al.).

As the paragraph above suggests, women entering community from prison are likely to continue to experience exclusion if they do not reintegrate in the areas of civic duty, work, and family. However, the idea that work and family are inherently positive aspects of women's lives has been highly contested. For many women, security when it comes to either employment and/or family relationships has never been a reality (Pedlar et al., 2008; Richie, 2001). The high incidence of women in federal prisons who report being abused by a family member (Richie, 2001) suggests family is often not a source of comfort or support. Moreover, theories on women's criminality have identified gender-related oppression in the family as being at the root of women's illegal activity (Morash & Robinson, 2002). Therefore, to expect them to fit back into work and family domains based on constructions of economic independence and responsibility (Uggen, Manza, & Behrens, 2004) can be unrealistic.

The effects of exclusion include material deprivation, marginalization from social activities, reduced access to public resources, alienation from decision making and civic participation, and isolation from community (Galabuzi, 2004). When people are chronically excluded and come to believe they are devalued members of society, their health is often compromised (Ponic & Frisby, 2010). Given that inclusion strategies are considered to be well suited for addressing health inequities (Belle-Isle, Benoit & Pauly, 2014), I see a strong link between such strategies and approaches to community development. Community development workers and community-based health promoters often work to address health concerns by facilitating inclusion (Ponic & Frisby, 2010). In the section that follows I discuss how I see principles of community development guiding inclusion strategies for women entering community after incarceration.

HOW CAN COMMUNITY DEVELOPMENT GUIDE INCLUSION?

Critical of the power imbalances that create exclusion, Salojee (2005) argued that inclusion strategies must incorporate new ways of thinking about the problems of injustice and inequality. For Salojee, inclusion encourages respect for differences and the removal of barriers for participating in the social life of our communities. I have argued elsewhere (Fortune & Arai, 2014) that fostering inclusion necessitates paying attention to social justice and creating an inclusive democracy that provides space for discussion about oppression and discrimination. Ideally, inclusion supports the conditions necessary for all individuals to exercise capacities, express experiences, and participate in determining actions—what I see as the essence of community development (Seebohm, Gilchrist & Morris, 2012).

Rose and Thompson (2012) described their experience as community development workers in an Australian community experiencing high unemployment and concentrations of people living on government benefits. Their community development approach was guided by four principles: power-sharing; operating from a strengths-based perspective; engaging in reflective practice; and prioritizing access and equity. I consider these to be powerful principles that can enhance the inclusion of marginalized individuals in decision-making structures that affect their lives. Next, I provide tangible examples of initiatives that are putting these principles into practice to support the inclusion of women entering community after incarceration.

POWER-SHARING

In community development practice, power-sharing generally refers to supporting community identification of priorities; respecting decision making and working to ensure community members have opportunities to take action. Rose and Thompson (2012) made efforts to share power by ensuring the groups and individuals they worked with had the information and opportunities necessary to make decisions and act on these decisions. An example of power-sharing with women who are incarcerated can be found in the Inside-Out Prison Exchange Program (www.insideoutcenter.org) that brings college and university students ("outside students") together with incarcerated men and women ("inside students") to study as peers in a class taught within prison walls. This program originated in the United States and was first introduced to the Grand Valley Institution in Kitchener, in 2011. People who have taught Inside-Outside courses describe the transformative potential that exists when students are brought together to study collaboratively across a range of boundaries (Hyatt, 2009). An inside student who completed a course described the power that comes when people, who may not believe they have talents and capabilities, are given the chance to discover what they are capable of and learn how they are connected to their community as well as to the rest of the world (Werts, 2013). Inside-Out serves as a power-sharing model because it encourages inside students and outside students to encounter each other as equal dialogue partners who together explore specific issues and ideas relating to the assigned readings and their own experiences (Butin, 2007). A passage from an essay written by Tiina, a former inside student at GVI, further highlights the transformative potential of Inside-Out:

> Inside-Out gave me a chance to interact in a meaningful way with the outside community, at the exact moment that I most needed it. I felt myself growing and changing and gaining confidence each and every time I spoke in class. I felt accepted and appreciated by my classmates and I learned to listen to and appreciate them as well (taken from The Inside-Out Centre Newsletter, volume 5, number 2, fall 2013).

OPERATING FROM A STRENGTHS-BASED PERSPECTIVE

Operating from a strengths-based perspective involves recognizing that all members of a community have significant strengths that can be mobilized to create change. Rose and Thompson (2012) used a strengths-based approach by co-identifying strengths with marginalized residents and encouraging the sharing of these strengths through structured groups and activities. Stride Night is an example of a program that operates from a strengths-based perspective. As mentioned, Stride Night creates a space for women at GVI to come together with community volunteers and connect over shared leisure interests. A range of recreation activities are available, such as art and crafts, physical activities and sports, and coffeehouse nights involving music and poetry readings. I have seen firsthand how these activities enable women at GVI and volunteers to demonstrate skills and interests not readily apparent in a prison context. It is not uncommon during coffeehouse nights, for example, to see women and volunteers playing various musical instruments and singing together. The musical talent that surfaces during coffeehouse nights can be astounding and I am not the only one who has joked about sneaking in a recording device to reveal the next music sensation.

Sharing skills and interests at Stride Night sets the stage for reciprocal relationships that are based on recognition of humanity (Yuen, Thompson, and Pedlar, 2006). CJI takes the strengths-based perspective one step further with a program called Fresh Start Creations. Women involved in Fresh Start Creations use their skills to create works of art, such as custom jewelry and picture frames, to be sold in the community with proceeds donated to local charitable organizations. A participant of Fresh Start Creations spoke of the joy she derives from being able to use her creative skills as a way to give back to community:

> I'm really pumped about this project because it creates the space for us to explore our creativity. But it's also a genuine partnering arrangement based on one common thread—giving back to the community in order to move forward (taken from CJI newsletter, June 2009).

ENGAGING IN REFLECTIVE PRACTICE

As discussed in Chapter 9, engaging in reflective practice entails reflecting on and critically questioning our personal values and actions in a process of continuous learning. Rose and Thompson (2012) engaged in reflective practice by critically examining how they were helping to meet the needs of the community and reflecting the community's strengths. Reflective practice also pushed them to question whether their actions may have been getting in the way of community or individual empowerment.

Engaging in reflective practice necessitates critically examining the ways some of our practices and policies may perpetuate, rather than ameliorate exclusion. I consider this process to be an imperative for individuals and organizations working with any marginalized group to bring about social change resulting in inclusion.

For community development strategies to effectively promote inclusion, practitioners must critically reflect on how they may not always be inclusive in their attitudes and actions. Botes and van Rensburg (2000), for example, identified the paternalistic attitude of professionals as a key impediment to participatory community development. They explained that professionals, whether consciously or unconsciously, can dominate decision-making processes, particularly when working with less vocal and marginalized groups. This impediment underscores the importance of reflective practice and offers a reminder that we move closer to inclusion when we draw from the wisdom of people who experience marginalization and create opportunities for people to speak for themselves. Without critical reflection, individuals and organizations intending to bring about social change in terms of inclusion may actually be contributing to paternalistic policies by not addressing and challenging power imbalances present in our society (Shakir, 2005).

PRIORITIZING ACCESS AND EQUITY

When we prioritize access and equity we work to ensure that needs of the most marginalized groups in a community are being addressed. For Rose and Thompson (2012), prioritizing access and equity meant identifying additional resources that can be designated for the benefit of citizens who experience marginalization. An example of an initiative that aims to identify how community resources can be best used to benefit women being released from prison is an annual community engagement forum that is organized in a partnership between GVI and the local community. The most recent community forum focused on the role of recreation and leisure in women's reintegration process. Past forums have looked at the ways women can be better supported regarding employment, housing, and mental health. Each forum has provided a venue for women, both formerly and currently incarcerated, to speak directly to the issue based on their personal experiences and needs. Time was also devoted to engaging various community organizations and members of the community in discussions aimed at trying to address the issue at hand from different perspectives. A discussion question from the recreation and leisure forum, for example, asked people to identify how the leisure needs of women entering community can be better supported. Tangible outcomes from these forums included a local fitness center offering to provide women at GVI with fitness and nutrition programs and an entrepreneurial course initiated by business leaders who are donating their time and expertise to teach women at GVI business skills they may use upon release.

There are several ideas derived from the community development principles and examples shared in this section that I consider to be key learnings. I believe these learnings can be applied not only to women entering community after incarceration, but also when working to foster inclusion for people who experience chronic marginalization. The learnings are outlined in the section that follows.

KEY LEARNINGS I HAVE GLEANED FROM COMMUNITY DEVELOPMENT PRINCIPLES

When I combine community development principles with my personal experience and review of relevant literature, I conclude that there are three critical components that need to be in place in the community for people who are marginalized to be truly included: recognition of humanity, sense of solidarity, and social justice.

RECOGNITION OF HUMANITY

When talking about the nature of interactions between inside students and outside students involved in the Inside-Out Prison Exchange Program, Hyatt (2009) observed that the more opportunity non-incarcerated people and people who are incarcerated have to encounter each other as peers, the more they see each other's humanity and the more they question the fairness and integrity of the criminal justice system. Research has also shown that when community volunteers and women in prison come together in leisure, there is a recognition of humanity, respect, and growth that occurs for both women and volunteers (Pedlar, Yuen, & Fortune, 2008). Resulting relationships that develop are constructive not only for incarcerated women, but also for volunteers (Yuen et al., 2006). Volunteers take their experiences with women they meet and the criminal justice system back to the community, often challenging community perceptions and myths about women who are incarcerated. Recognizing the humanity of people who are marginalized is a necessary first step to valuing their unique skills and abilities, which I believe is a precursor to real inclusion.

McKnight (1995) recommended that policies and practices guiding inclusion should reduce dependence and increase interdependence by focusing on the gifts and capacities of people who have been excluded from community life. Block (2009) also reminded us that we take steps toward inclusion when we view our differences as sources of community vitality. For this to happen, as can be seen with both the Inside-Outside Prison Exchange Program and Stride Night, I believe there need to be opportunities to connect across our differences.

> Can a show like *Orange is the New Black* push us to re-examine what we think about women in prison and the issues they are faced with?
>
> It is quite likely that you are familiar with the hit series, *Orange is the New Black (OITNB)*. It is also quite likely that before this series aired in the summer of 2013, you had not given much

thought to women in prison. Perhaps now you are beginning to question the fairness of the criminal justice system and are wondering about who is behind our prison walls and what pathways led them there. At least I hope this is what *OITNB* might accomplish and its unexpected popularity gives me reason to be optimistic. An article written for Huffington Post by Rachel Simon (see "Has 'Orange is the New Black' made post-convict life easier for prisoners?" posted July 9, 2014) suggests that as a result of *OITNB*, people are beginning to see that women who go to prison are not the "scary, unsympathetic characters" they are often made out to be. Simon also acknowledges that while the stigma women face when they leave prison still exists, "for the first time, people are wondering why."

OITNB is based on a bestselling memoir of the same name by Piper Kerman. During a radio interview Kerman explained that she wrote the book so people will have a different and multi-faceted sense of who is locked up in prison today and why there are there. Her experience in a women's prison led her to conclude that there needs to be a lot more prevention in communities around issues such as drug addiction and violence (aired on Q, CBC radio, August 15, 2013).

Whether *OITNB* can spark any real change in terms of how society deals with issues related to addiction and violence remains to be seen. While I am aware of justifiable critiques based on feminist and anti-racist analysis, I also applaud the book and the series for opening up a world from which too many of us are hidden and for humanizing women who are seldom thought about in such a way.

SENSE OF SOLIDARITY

I use the term *solidarity* to describe the unity that exists between people who share common interests and are committed to working together to advance these interests. Describing a participatory action research project undertaken with women released from a prison in San Diego alongside community members who were part of a faith-based community, Parsons and Warner-Robbins (2002) explained how participants came together across differences to engage in research and develop mutually agreed upon goals. Together they identified programs, transportation, housing, and community awareness as being key ingredients for helping women enter community after incarceration and worked collaboratively for positive changes in these particular areas.

As the study by Parsons and Warner-Robbins (2002) demonstrates, when women are engaged as partners and their needs are placed at the heart of community development initiatives (Ritchie, 2001) we see solidarity in action. Working in solidarity can happen when we move away from expert-driven policymaking models and facilitate the active participation of people in decisions that affect their lives (Belle-Isle, Benoit & Pault, 2014). I believe that working in solidarity encapsulates community development at its most participatory since it can ensure the most marginalized citizens are being listened to and included (Botes & van Resburg, 2000).

Think back to the community engagement forums I described earlier. These forums bring together various people in community who are interested in working together for a common purpose. The most compelling aspect of each forum is the words and stories shared by women who are speaking directly from their own experiences. The women's stories form the focal point for the discussions that follow. However, without community members present to listen to and learn from the women's experiences, little would change in terms of improving women's transition from prison to community. Solidarity emerges when women share their wisdom with members of the community who may be unaware of the challenges associated with entering community after a period of incarceration and together they identify and tackle the changes needed to enhance the transition process.

AN EXAMPLE OF SOLIDARITY THROUGH THE ARTS

In March 2014, University of Waterloo Drama students presented a play called *From Solitary to Solidarity: Unravelling the Ligatures of Ashley Smith*, which explored issues of mental health in the context of the story of Ashley Smith, a teenager who died at GVI in 2007. When the story behind Ashley's death went public, it ignited controversy and sparked a national debate about the treatment of people with mental illness within Canada's prison system. The play was a collaborative performance aimed at trying to understand the life and death of Ashley Smith. During the performance, students investigated the social and political consequences of broken correctional and mental health institutions (UW Drama and Speech Communication, March 19, 2014).

Another play based on the story of Ashley Smith is called *Watching Glory Die*. Playwright Judith Thompson uses this play to convey a political message about our shared responsibility for injustice. *Watching Glory Die* was also inspired by a sense of solidarity, most evident when Thompson explained her reason for writing the play: "I owe it to Ashley. I want to give her what I can" (The Canadian Press, April 21, 2014).

It is worth noting that in response to public outcry and a damning coroner's report on the circumstances surrounding Ashley's death, the Canadian government announced a pilot project that will send women with severe mental illness who break the law to provincial treatment centers rather than correctional institutions (CBC News, April 30, 2014). It is also worth noting that that in December 2014, the government rejected the major recommendation put forth in the coroner's report: to restrict the use of solitary confinement in Canadian prisons. Retired Supreme Court justice Louise Arbour, who spearheaded an inquiry into conditions in women's Canadian prisons nearly 20 years earlier, argued the reason little has changed with respect to Canada's use of solitary confinement over the decades is that "inertia easily settles. There's no big lobby, there's no pressure on the government. Prisoners are a well-identified unpopular minority" (CBC News, December 11, 2014). Arbour's comments capture the need for solidarity to move people to act in order for social change to occur. Her comments also highlight the difficulty in achieving social change pertaining to issues affecting individuals who are marginalized.

Application Questions

Please think about a social issue with which you are familiar but not directly affected. What might provide you with a sense of solidarity with people who are directly affected by this issue? What steps do you think could be taken to promote shared responsibility for addressing this particular issue?

While facilitating the PAR study focused on inclusion with women living in community after a period of incarceration, I learned that solidarity matters as much in research with marginalized individuals as it does in practice. For inclusion to be a reality for women entering community after incarceration, it cannot be something they work toward on their own. Accounts of research that have reported positive results involved women working alongside others who share their goals and are committed to working across difference (e.g., Parsons and Warner-Robbins, 2002). Ultimately, such research speaks to our capacity for seeing the humanity in people marginalized by oppressive structures, valuing the skills and abilities of all people in community, and recognizing a personal responsibility to share in the quest for social justice.

SOCIAL JUSTICE

Bell (1997) explained that social justice holds to a vision in which individuals are both self-determining and interdependent while there is a sense of social responsibility aimed at addressing social inequities. The PAR study I conducted with women who had spent time in GVI led me to conclude that if principles of social justice guided inclusion efforts, there would be dialogue and negotiation aimed at reimagining inclusion and creating a space that is hopeful and inclusive for *all* citizens (Fortune & Arai, 2014). Social justice necessitates a collective obligation to make right the injustices that exist in our communities. This can start with prioritizing access and equity in terms of time and resources (Rose & Thompson, 2012). However, social justice also moves us toward acknowledging our shared responsibility. Shared responsibility is a much discussed but seldom acted on concept when it comes to women leaving prison and entering community. Yet, since women's quest for personal change and growth is dependent on the extent to which there is support and shared responsibility for addressing issues of inequality, inclusion must be viewed as an aspect of social justice.

A primary goal for Stride Night is that women who are incarcerated and volunteers from the community spend time together and build relationships that will continue after a woman leaves prison (Yuen et al., 2006). Continued relationships between women and volunteers are supported through Stride Circles. Grounded in principles of restorative and social justice, the support network provided by Stride Circle is intended to offer practical assistance and hope for women reintegrating into society. Restorative justice is a theory of justice that is grounded in the belief that crime involves disruptions in relationships. This theory emphasizes the involvement of those directly involved and affected by criminal behavior in a cooperative process aimed at repairing harm and rebuilding broken relationships (Zehr, 2002). Volunteers are not only instrumental in helping women find housing, employment, and social opportunities—they offer much-needed emotional support as well (Fortune, Thompson, Pedlar & Yuen, 2010). This is one example of community members sharing responsibility for creating a more socially just community.

We also move closer to promoting social justice when we begin to question and disrupt unexamined and taken-for-granted practices that contribute to inequality and injustice (e.g., the treatment of people with mental illness within Canada's prison system brought to light by Ashely Smith's story). Butin (2007) identified the Inside-Out Prison Exchange Program as an exemplary model of justice-oriented education because it pushes students to re-examine their knowledge and it introduces tensions and dilemmas relating to crime and justice that need to be reflected upon before they can be addressed.

Application Questions

Can you think of examples of situations when people have had opportunities to dialogue across differences? How did this opportunity help people re-examine their preconceived ideas about social issues (such as poverty or mental health)? How might you create similar opportunities in your future work or research?

As seen in examples of programs such as Inside-Out, Stride, and the community engagement forums held at GVI, community organizations are well positioned to promote inclusion when they have a social justice orientation and adopt participatory processes (Belle-Isle, Benoit & Pault, 2014) aimed at greater empowerment for people experiencing marginalization. Organizations operating from a social justice mandate are also increasingly recognizing the inclusionary potential of leisure for people who are marginalized (Trussell & Mair, 2010).

RECOGNIZING LEISURE AS A VEHICLE FOR INCLUSION

Pedlar (1996) argued that we need to better understand how recreation and leisure can support community development. She observed a widening gap between those who are advantaged and those who are disadvantaged in society and called on practitioners and researchers to recognize the vital role recreation and leisure can play in enhancing the quality of community life.

Unfortunately, quality of life benefits that can be derived from leisure are not easily obtainable for people who experience chronic marginalization. For example, women entering community after incarceration may experience a heightened sense of exclusion when trying to access leisure opportunities, particularly when the associated cost is unaffordable and fee reduction programs perpetuate stigma by requiring disclosure of a criminal record (Yuen, Arai, & Fortune, 2012). Inequality in terms of leisure provision is most disconcerting when we consider that a lack of healthy leisure activities was reported to be among eight factors most associated with women's re-arrest (Andrews, Bonta, & Wormith, 2006). Moreover, barriers to accessing leisure often intensify feelings of exclusion (Reid, Frisby, & Ponic, 2002). Challenges associated with leisure provision notwithstanding, it has been argued that when leisure is at its best, it becomes a vehicle for helping people link in to social life, which aids the goal of inclusion (Trussell & Mair, 2010). For example, as Fortune and Yuen (2015) found, participation in a community arts program enabled women who were formerly incarcerated to experience inclusion because the program provided them with an opportunity to explore new identities as artists, engage in acts of citizenship, and find a personal sense of belonging.

We bring others into a community as citizens when we include them in relationships where their capacities can be expressed and where they are no longer defined by their deficiencies (McKnight, 1995). For women currently in prison, this happens through programs such as Stride Night. Interactions between women and community members during Stride Night provide opportunities for connections that are built on shared interests, talents, and capacities (Pedlar, Yuen, & Fortune, 2008). Findings from a study by Yuen et al. (2012) suggest that if leisure providers in the community find ways to emphasize the contributions, interests, and talents of women who have spent time in prison, while paying attention to relationship development between women and others in community, they will be taking steps to reduce marginalization and build more inclusive communities.

In their book *The Abundant Community,* McKnight and Block (2012) discussed the importance of making people's gifts and capacities visible. Many of the suggestions they offered for doing this included leisure. Suggestions included holding gatherings where youth learn about music, poetry, storytelling, and dance from artistic neighbors, having neighborhood hikes, monthly potluck dinners, and creating community gardens. By making gifts and capacities visible and connecting community members across perceived boundaries, leisure has an important role to play when it comes to supporting the inclusion of individuals who are marginalized.

Application Questions

Please think about a time when a leisure experience connected you with someone across a range of differences. Did you discover this person had skills and abilities that were surprising? How do you think leisure can best create opportunities for all members of our communities to learn about and share their skills and abilities? How does leisure in this sense lead to a broader recognition of humanity?

CONCLUDING REMARKS

It is commonly acknowledged that for women who enter community after a period of incarceration to experience inclusion, their community conditions must change (Pedlar et al., 2008; Pollack, 2009; Ritchie, 2001). However, when the right supports are provided, women can also be instrumental in bringing about change within their communities. I am confident that as women work in solidarity with others in community who share in the responsibility for social justice, they will begin to unleash their gifts and capacities, subsequently contributing to inclusion and helping to build stronger communities. Since women often come from and return to disenfranchised communities (Richie, 2001), their gifts and capacities are sure to be much welcomed and needed resources.

Addressing inclusion is not only good for the well-being of marginalized individuals and groups, but also for the wider community (Crisp, Taket, Graham, & Hanna, 2014). John McKnight (1995) argued that the capacity of the community is diminished whenever certain segments of the population are marginalized due to unequal access to resources and power imbalances and this marginalization goes unnoticed or unchallenged by the rest of the community. Community is strengthened when people work together to combat inequalities and "improve their collective conditions of existence" (Blackshaw, 2010, p. 164). My hope for this chapter is that the ideas and examples presented provide the impetus to challenge marginalization and exclusion through community development practice and research, which values and incorporates the knowledge and capacities of individuals who are marginalized.

Application Questions

Identify people in your community who are most susceptible to experiencing marginalization. Reflect on the nature of their marginalization and then draw from the four principles outlined by Rose and Thompson (2012) to consider how a community development approach could enhance inclusion for the people you have identified.

REFERENCES

Andrews, D. A., Bonta, J., & Wormith, J. S. (2006). The recent past and near future of risk and/or need assessment. *Crime & Delinquency, 52,* 7–27.

Bell, L. A. (1997). Theoretical foundations for social justice education. In M. Adams, L.A. Bell, & P. Griffin (Eds.), *Teaching for diversity and social justice* (pp. 3–15). New York, NY: Routledge.

Belle-Isle, L., Benoit, C., & Pauly, B. (2014). Addressing health inequities through social inclusion: The role of community organizations. *Action Research, 12,* 177–193.

Blackshaw, T. (2010). *Key concepts in community studies.* London: Sage Publications.

Block, P. (2009). Community: *The Structure of Belonging.* San Francisco, CA: Berrett-Koehler Publishers, Inc.

Botes. L., & van Rensburg, D. (2000). Community participation in development: Nine plagues and twelve commandments. *Community Development Journal, 35*(1), 41–58.

Butin, D. W. (2007). Justice-learning: Service-learning as justice-oriented education. *Equity and Excellence in Education, 40,* 177–183.

Canadian Human Rights Commission. (2003). *Protecting their rights: A systemic review of human rights in correctional services for federally sentenced women.* Ottawa, ON: Author.

Crisp, B. R., Taket, A., Graham, M., & Hanna, L. (2014). Implementing the social inclusion agenda. In A. Taket, B. R. Crisp, M. Graham, L. Hanna, S. Goldingay, & L. Wilson (Eds.), *Practicing social inclusion* (pp. 249–256). New York, NY: Routledge.

Fortune, D., & Arai, S. M. (2014). Rethinking community within the context of social inclusion as social justice: Implications for women after federal incarceration. *Studies in Social Justice, 8*(1), 79–107.

Fortune, D., Thompson, J., Pedlar, A., & Yuen, F. (2010). Social justice and women leaving prison: Beyond punishment and exclusion. *Contemporary Justice Review, 13*(1), 19–33.

Fortune, D., & Yuen, F. (2015). Transitions in identity, belonging, and citizenship and the possibilities of inclusion for women leaving prison: Implications for therapeutic recreation. *Leisure/Loisir, 39*(2), 253–276.

Galabuzi, G. E. (2004). Social exclusion. In D. Raphael (Ed.), *Social determinants of health: Canadian perspectives* (pp. 233–251). Toronto, ON: Canadian Scholars Press.

Hines, J. M. (2012). Using an anti-oppressive framework in social work practice with lesbians. *Journal of Gay & Lesbian Social Services, 24,* 23–39.

Hyatt, S. B. (2009). Creating social change by teaching behind bars. *Anthropology News,* January 2009, 24–28.

Labonte, R. (2004). Social inclusion/exclusion: Dancing the dialectic. *Health Promotion International, 19*(1), 115–121.

Layton, N., & Wilson, E. (2014). Practicing inclusion in policy design for people with disabilities. In A. Taket, B. R. Crisp, M. Graham, L. Hanna, S. Goldingay, & L. Wilson (Eds.), *Practicing social inclusion* (pp. 54–64). New York, NY: Routledge.

McKnight, J. (1995). *The careless society: Community and its counterfeits.* New York: Basic Books.

McKnight, J., & Block, P. (2012). *The abundant community: Awakening the power of families and neighborhoods.* San Francisco, CA: Berrett-Koehler Publishers.

Morash, M., & Robinson, A. L. (2002). Correctional administrators' perspectives on gender arrangements and family-related programming for women offenders. *Marriage & Family Review, 32*(3), 83–109.

Nelson, M., Deess, P., & Allen, C. (1999). *The first month out: Post-incarceration in New York City.* New York, NY: Vera Institute of Justice.

Parsons, M., & Warner-Robbins, C. (2002). Formerly incarcerated women create healthy lives through participatory action research. *Holistic Nursing Practice, 16*(2), 40–49.

Pedersen, P. V., Andersen, P. T., & Curtis, T. (2012). Social relations and experiences of social isolation among socially marginalized people. *Journal of Personal and Social Relationships, 29*(6), 839–858.

Pedlar, A. (1996). Community development: What does it mean for recreation and leisure? *Journal of Applied Recreation Research, 21*(1), 5–23.

Pedlar, A., Arai, S., & Yuen, F. (2007). Media representations of federally sentenced women and leisure opportunities: Ramifications for social inclusion. *Leisure/Loisir, 3*(1), 255–276.

Pedlar, A., Arai, S., Yuen, F., & Fortune, D. (2008). *Uncertain futures: Women leaving prison and re-entering community.* Retrieved from http://www.ahs.uwaterloo.ca/uncertainfutures/

Pedlar, A., Yuen, F. C., & Fortune, D. (2008). Incarcerated women and leisure: Making good girls out of bad? *Therapeutic Recreation Journal, 42*(1), 24–36.

Pollack, S. (2009). "Circuits of exclusion": Criminalized women's negotiation of community. *Canadian Journal of Mental Health, 28*(1), 83–95.

Ponic, P., & Frisby, W. (2010). Unpacking assumptions about inclusion in community-based health promotion: Perspectives of women living in poverty. *Qualitative Health Research, 20*(11), 1519–1531.

Ratcliffe, P. (2000). Is the assertion of minority identity compatible with the idea of a socially inclusive society? In P. Askonas & A. Stewart (Eds.), *Social inclusion: Possibilities and tensions* (pp. 169–185). New York, NY: St. Martin's Press.

Reid, C., Frisby, W., & Ponic, P. (2002). Confronting two-tiered community recreation and poor women's exclusion: Promoting inclusion, health, and social justice. *Canadian Women's Studies, 21*(3), 88–94.

Richie, B. E. (2001). Challenges incarcerated women face as they return to their communities: Findings from life history interviews. *Crime and Delinquency, 47*(3), 368–389.

Rose, V. K. & Thompson, L. M. (2012). Space, place and people: A community development approach to mental health promotion in a disadvantaged community. *Community Development Journal, 47*(4), 604–611.

Saloojee, A. (2005). Social inclusion, anti-racism and democratic citizenship. In T. Richmond & A. Saloojee (Eds.), *Social inclusion: Canadian perspectives* (pp. 180–202). Halifax, NS: Fernwood Publishing.

Seebohm, P., Gilchrist A., & Morris, D. (2012). Bold but balanced: How community development contributes to mental health and inclusion. *Community Development, 47*(4), 473–490.

Shakir, U. (2005). Dangers of a new dogma: Social inclusion or else...! In T. Richmond & A. Saloojee (Eds.), *Social inclusion: Canadian perspectives* (pp. 203–214). Halifax, NS: Fernwood Publishing.

Trussell, D. E., & Mair, H (2010). Seeking judgment free spaces: Poverty, leisure, and social inclusion. *Journal of Leisure Research, 42*(4), 513–533.

Uggen, C., Manza, J., & Behrens, A. (2004). 'Less than the average citizen': Stigma, role transition and the civic reintegration of convicted felons. In S. Maruna & R. Immarigeon, (Eds.), *After crime and punishment: Pathways to offender reintegration* (pp. 258–290). Cullompton, Devon, UK: Willan.

Werts, T. (2013). Tyrone Werts: Reflections on the Inside-Out prison Exchange Program. *The Prison Journal, 93*(2), 135–138.

Wilkinson, R., & Marmot, M. (Eds.). (2003). *Social determinants of health: The solid facts* (2nd ed.). New York, NY: World Health Organization.

Young, I. M. (1990). *Justice and the politics of difference.* Princeton, NJ: Princeton University Press.

Yuen, F., Arai, S.M., & Fortune, D. (2012). Community (dis)connection through leisure for women in prison. *Leisure Sciences, 34*(4), 281–297.

Yuen, F. C., Thompson, J. E., & Pedlar, A. (2006). Volunteering and engagement in leisure: A restorative justice approach to working with incarcerated women. *Restorative Directions Journal, 2*(1), 23–35.

Zehr, H. (2002). *The little book of restorative justice.* Intercourse, PA: Good Books.

19

THE PAST AND FUTURE OF COMMUNITY DEVELOPMENT THROUGH LEISURE

Alison Pedlar

There are many ways of describing what community development is. Like others you have encountered in this book, I believe community development works toward bringing about change and improvement in people's lives. Community development seeks to enhance people's life conditions, in order that they may enjoy the benefits of citizenship. In large part, these benefits are simply human rights, including access to education, shelter, nutrition, recreation and sufficient resources to ensure self-determination, health, and well-being.

In bringing my thoughts together to write this chapter, I looked back at my work over two decades. It is evident that much of my current thinking mirrors what I considered to be central to community development and recreation and leisure in the 1990s. In 1996, I raised concerns about the challenges facing our field. Now, almost 20 years later, it is disquieting to realize how these same concerns persist.

> During the current period of restructuring and public sector concern for deficit reduction, there is a particular need to consider whether the field cannot in fact contribute more broadly to the quality of community life. This suggests that as an alternative to the product/income generating orientation to leisure and recreation, we ought to rethink the ideas behind community development. The widening gap between those who are advantaged and those who are disadvantaged in society makes it increasingly urgent to more fully understand the ways in which recreation and leisure can foster community development and the role of the citizen and practitioner in that process (Pedlar, 1996, p. 7)

Rather than concluding that community development is something of a lost cause, since little has changed in 20 years of practice, I will suggest that social, environmental, economic, and political structures shift in such a way that it is important for us as community development students, teachers, and practitioners to reflect and refresh our praxis. My purpose here is to look at the evolution of my understanding of community development and how community development can function as a vehicle for enhancing people's life circumstances. It is my hope that these reflections will provide some illumination of the processes, challenges, and enormous rewards that community development can bring, from a personal, collective, and professional perspective.

The seeds of community development in general begin to take root through education, which leads to an emerging awareness and possibly a questioning of the status quo. Such questioning is seen as a precursor to individual and collective consciousness raising. Indeed, community development and its corollary community organizing have been catalysts for social and political movements that draw together people who may be questioning and/or experiencing discontent with the status quo. It is such discontent that generally leads to people seeking change in their individual and collective lives.

AN EMERGENT CONSCIOUSNESS-RAISING

In the early 1960s, I returned to Britain from Kenya, immediately prior to its gaining independence from British rule. As a 20-year old white woman of considerable privilege, I found the British class system so rigid that I was unsure of how to fit in, of how I wanted to fit in. I witnessed struggles, particularly by and on behalf of people of color, as they suffered systemic discrimination. The contrasts and tensions were striking in terms of people's ability to participate as equal members of society in such a politically rigid and socially divisive class structure.

I also questioned why women mostly remained on the fringes of mainstream social, political and economic life. The working poor, the unemployed, and people with disabilities were virtually invisible, often living in wretched conditions with little hope of a better future, without the rights or responsibilities and privileges which one would expect all citizens to enjoy.

Disadvantage and discontent around denial of rights bubbled up in some groups who came together to organize for change as part of social movements seeking change across a wide spectrum of communities of interest. In the UK and other parts of the world, activists were fighting for change. There was the peace movement, the labor movement, the feminist movement, the environmental movement, and the faint beginnings of agitation for gay rights.

I decided to leave England in 1971 and applied to immigrate to Canada, to what I was anticipating would be a more equitable, cohesive, and just society. This was the era of Pierre Trudeau who was twice Prime Minister of Canada from 1968–1979 and again from 1980–1984. It was a time when it seemed to me social cohesion could and indeed would exist alongside multiculturalism, and collective and individual opportunity in my adoptive country.

Shortly after arriving in Canada, I entered university, partly in order to learn more about the country I had chosen to make my home. As well, I simply had a thirst for education. I decided to study city planning. In the 1970s, urban renewal and gentrification of low-income neighborhoods were seen as the way to combat the inner-city decay that occurred across North American cities after the flight to the suburbs of younger families, pursuing the dream of a single-family dwelling. While in planning school, I studied regulatory instruments such as planning acts and planning by-laws that are all part of what one might call "the planner's toolbox." These instruments governed the so-called revitalization movement. Concurrently, I began to see that there were powerless populations whose communities were forever altered, but whose needs and preferences were essentially ignored by planning practice. The planner's toolbox seemed to me to be especially well equipped to handle the physical face of the city, but lacked instruments for improving the social or human dimensions of urban life. City planning and development as managed out of city hall struck me as being designed strictly as a haves vs. have-nots venture.

My hunch about the inadequacies of the planner's toolbox was reinforced when I took up my first appointment as a city planner. I became a housing planner with a large urban municipality. I was now to see those zoning by-laws in action and was to conduct research on housing needs in that municipality. I was really not good at this work. I had preconceived ideas of what was needed, and so did the council and development industry that tended to be grounded in interests that were critical to the municipality for the economic health of the area. Turns out, our views on these matters were seriously divergent.

Can you identify any "tools" used in recreation, leisure or sport that might function in unhelpful ways for the community, individual, and practitioner?

What do these look like?

What are the pitfalls of such tools?

How do we show ourselves to be viable professionals without them?

I began to ferret out hopeful signs of resistance to development pressures in Canada's major urban centers. I found a few, notably in Toronto and Montreal. Community organizers were working to counter the pressures of city hall, gentrification, and the urban renewal industry. They called for participatory planning processes to try to ensure citizens in vulnerable neighborhoods had some say over their lives. For instance, the community organizing work in low-income neighborhoods, such as Trefann Court in Toronto, fought to end the displacement of urban poor populations and signaled the beginnings of the reform movement. Community organizer, John Sewell, and others, were successful in halting the mass removal of communities from neighborhoods that were slated for replacement by monolithic low-income apartment towers, such as in Toronto's Regent Park and St. James Town.

In Montreal, residents of Milton Parc faced incredible odds when their neighborhood was threatened by plans for a huge modern commercial development. Houses were knocked down. There were no facilities for people who lived in what ended up feeling like a war zone. Young people with nothing to do in the ravaged neighborhood organized themselves around spaces where people's homes had once stood, and started to use the empty spaces to play recreational basketball and the like. The people of the neighborhood determined they were not going to let the demolition continue. Working together they built one of Canada's most successful examples of citizen-led collaborations involving community and government.

The result was a housing cooperative that enabled the community to survive and flourish, preserving architecturally significant buildings, accommodating a socially, ethnically, and economically diverse population. This happened in large part because of the grassroots organizing that lead to social animation, rarely seen in planning around neighborhoods inhabited by the poor and powerless.

Here are principles of sound grassroots organizing and change that are drawn from my observations of the community development experiences of Montreal's Milton Parc and Treffan Court in Toronto.

PRINCIPLES OF GRASSROOTS ORGANIZING AND CHANGE

People self-determine their own direction

If outside organizers come in, they should leave decisions to the community

Enable creativity of community to guide

Assist in formal negotiations with official power brokers, such as municipality

Facilitate rather than dictate

Support strengths identification within the community

Organize meetings in spaces and places that suit people, not the authorities

Africville in Nova Scotia fared less well in terms of the efforts of the citizens to save their community. There, many Black Nova Scotians had carved out a life, but faced isolation and extreme poverty. The decision to relocate the people of Africville was based on urban renewal and business interests. Powerless, the people whose homes were systematically leveled were placed in scattered social housing developments around Halifax and beyond.

Other examples of failure in terms of human devastation that results from bad professional practices involved relocation of Aboriginal communities. The Davis Inlet Innu community is just one example. Relocated, with no regard for, or engagement of, these communities, the challenges of crisis identity and hopelessness continue for the displaced individuals—displaced by distant "authorities" who have little sensitivity for the damage done to the affected populations.

In the 1970s and into the early 1980s, institutions that housed huge numbers of people with mental health and intellectual disabilities were closing. The deinstitutionalization movement is something that I subsequently became immersed in, but for now, in the course of my job as a professional planner in the early 1980s, I became aware of the challenges in trying to locate sites for group homes. These were relatively small congregate settings, generally with 3 to 5 bedrooms, to house people released from institutions into the community. Some people returned to their family homes, but generally people were placed in group homes, or boarding houses. Some ended up in shelters. Others ultimately found themselves living on the street. This was the beginning of what is today almost taken for granted—every city will have homeless people in its midst, referred to as *hard to house* by the authorities. With respect to group homes and congregate living situations, exclusionary zoning by-laws stipulated where these could and could not locate. Often these decisions were driven by an exclusionary mentality backed up by a toolbox of instruments that prohibited organizations from developing housing in decent neighborhoods for people who were deinstitutionalized.

These were among my early introductions to urban and regional planning in which the power of city hall and other levels of government seemed to be removed from the citizens whose interests they were purportedly representing. It seemed that planning practice was insensitive to social justice considerations. After a couple of years in planning practice, I returned to graduate school to pursue a doctorate, in the course of which I was able to look more closely at the opposing narratives around community well-being and exclusion of some of society's most vulnerable citizens that I had witnessed in practice.

GAINING PERSPECTIVE

Back in graduate school, I searched for an understanding of ways to counter such dominant ideologies as individualism and corporatism. In the paragraphs below, I highlight some of the writings that were most helpful to me.

My explorations lead me to communitarianism as a possible antidote to the forces of individualism, big government, and corporate interests that appeared to be blind to the interests of local communities, whose residents were displaced from their homes and local places of employment as a result of the drive of the development industry.

> *The "communitarian" community is more than a mere association; it is a unity in which the individuals are members. This membership is neither artificial nor instrumental, but rather has its own intrinsic value. This is in contrast to the individualist conception of community, which communitarians hold to be superficial, even obnoxious.* (Avineri & De-Shalit, 1992, p. 4)

The communitarian thought of Robert Bellah and his colleagues in *Habits of the Heart* (1986; 1996) captured for me the essence of fragmented communities and societies. Their research included extensive interviews with hundreds of Americans on a range of issues including social justice, work, and civic affairs. Their findings supported the contention that fragmentation was endemic to urban life and had deeply divisive influences on what had once been regarded as public goods. Access to healthy and safe recreation, public libraries, festivals, and other common spaces where communities could thrive, became secondary or nonexistent in people's everyday lives.

> In 1986, Robert Bellah said:
>
> *There are deep structural problems in our society: economic, political, social institutional. What we are suggesting is there is also a problem of language—of having lost touch with, or finding it increasingly difficult to express, those impulses, those commitments that really do tie us to one another, that identify us through those ties and commitments, not against them.* (www.robertbellah.com/lectures_4.htm)

Among other works that deepened my understanding of communitarianism and guided my thinking around community and community development were those of Etzioni, founder of The Responsive Communitarian Platform in the early 1990s. Writing on the *Spirit of Community* (1993), Etzioni brings into sharp focus the distinctive character of community, in contrast to formal institutionalized services, which score high on fragmentation, but low on responsiveness and social cohesion.

> *True, there is, quite properly, in any relationships or community some vague sense of appropriate reciprocity, of the need to contribute to a climate of mutuality. But basically people help one another and sustain the spirit of community because they sense it is the right thing to do* (Etzioni, 1993, p.145).

As well, Charles Taylor in *Sources of the Self: The Making of Modern Identity* (1989), deepened my understanding of the self in community, in contrast to instrumentalism and fragmentation.

> *To take an instrumental stance to nature is to cut us off from the sources of meaning in it. An instrumental stance to our own feelings divides us within, splits reason from sense. And the atomistic focus on our individual goals dissolves community and divides us from each other* (Taylor, 1989, p. 500).

Social relationships and connections between people as they impact both individual and collective well-being were more recently further elaborated in Richard Putnam's *Bowling Alone: The Collapse and Revival of American Community* (2000).

> *Whereas physical capital refers to physical objects and human capital refers to properties of individuals, social capital refers to connections among individuals—social networks and the norms of reciprocity and trustworthiness that arise from them. In that sense, social capital is closely related to what some have called "civic virtue." The difference is that "social capital" calls attention to the fact that civic virtue is most powerful when embedded in a dense network of reciprocal social relations. A society of many virtuous but isolated individuals is not necessarily rich in social capital.* (Putnam, 2000, p. 19)

For me, the ideas behind social capital and human interdependence began to take hold. This academic thought is relevant to community development, providing tangible conceptual working tools which are helpful in understanding community building in the context of leisure and recreation and well beyond.

Other writing that I found especially helpful included the philosophy of the city (*The Good City*) promulgated by Haworth, my mentor and life partner. The thoughtful and practical lessons contained in his 1963 book focused attention on the centrality to a good city of two conditions, opportunity and community. His thesis was that the latter, community, is often lost as specialization and industrialization diminish prospects for the common life, and common concerns are lost to individual interests at the expense of community; again fragmentation. Haworth's work was very influential in the emergence of my perspective on individual well-being and community welfare.

Additionally, in her seminal book, *The Death and Life of Great American Cities* (1961), the urbanist, Jane Jacobs, stressed the urgency of not allowing inner cities to decay and the importance of maintaining the link between people, place, and collective well-being. She focused our attention on the inner city and working to ensure its survival. Her writing alerted us to the dangers of acquiescing to the pressures of, for instance, commerce and transportation routes that would annihilate the heart and soul of the inner city.

My appetite for what scholars as well as community activists had to say about reinvigorating and energizing the common interest lead me to explore further theoretical thought, including the essays in the 1987 collection of papers edited by John Forester in *Critical Theory and Public Life*. It was in this collection that I was first introduced to the ideas around critical theory as it relates to the exercise of power by the professional and institutional forces that subjugate public participation and citizen engagement in planning. Add into this mix my graduate school reading of Freire *Pedagogy of the Oppressed* (1970), which gave me insight into the relevance of education, civil action, community organizing, and the confluence of theory and practice, as Freire names it, praxis. Freire talked about the importance of freedom being attained or acquired by the oppressed, as opposed to being given to people.

> *The point of departure of the movement lies in the people themselves. But since people do not exist apart from the world, apart from reality, the movement must begin with the human-world relationship. Accordingly, the point of departure must always be with men and women in the "here and now", which constitutes the situation within which they are submerged, from which they emerge, and in which they intervene.* (Freire, 2002, p. 85)

Although this deeply influenced my thinking I didn't realize it till later when I began to further understand empowerment: empowerment not being something you give to people like a ticket to a hockey game, but something that people claim for themselves (Pedlar, Haworth, Hutchison, Taylor & Dunn, 1999). This is key to the community development venture.

Not infrequently, urban renewal has displaced poorer neighborhoods in favor of more tax lucrative business and commercial interests. Some communities started to pay heed to the warnings of people like Jacobs who saw this trend as crushing the life from cities. Those who were able began to organize to resist powerful redevelopment activities. Saul Alinsky is recognized as the first modern day community organizer to raise deep concerns about the injustices and oppression in poor inner-city neighborhoods. His work in the 1930s with Back of the Yards in Chicago and other depressed neighborhoods was to pave the way for many future organizing efforts, giving hope that it was possible to fight big business and city hall. Alinsky's *Rules for Radicals* (1971) remains essential reading for organizers and vulnerable communities.

Similarly, very practical guidance came from the works of people like John McKnight and John Kretzman, *Building Communities from the Inside Out: A Path Toward Finding and Mobilizing a Community's Assets* (1993). Their work was grounded in helping disenfranchised populations take control of their lives and provided communities with an arsenal of easily understood and practical approaches to community development. These helpful and workable approaches target communities' assets and strengths rather than their deficits. They encourage and enable people to pool resources, their social and human capital to undertake community development.

> *Thinking about your experiences with community, can you identify an especially empowering practice either in collective or individual terms or both?*
>
> *Was there any outside intervention or did all the action emanate from inside the community?*
>
> *Did change happen?*
>
> *Did it seem to be sustainable?*

Ultimately, my doctoral studies had much more to do with human services planning and community than with traditional urban planning. My doctoral committee was willing to let me pursue an understanding of the potential of planning practice and community development, by going beyond the physical and addressing the social elements of community and people's lives. Much of my doctoral work was done in Sweden, an enlightened society where social justice is at the fore of policy and praxis as evidenced in a commitment to the idea that the well-being of the individual is intricately tied to the welfare of the whole. I witnessed what would have been considered extraordinary measures in North America in welcoming people back to community from institutions. For instance, the question of integration was turned on its head by transforming former institutions into integrated living in open communities for all, people with disabilities, and people without, people with higher and lower incomes, all within the site of former gated "asylums."

During this time, I became aware of the grassroots movement that had formed around deinstitutionalization and people with disabilities. The recognition of those who had been disenfranchised and institutionalized came in large part through the social action of groups like People First and Mencap. They fought for the right to inclusion in all aspects of everyday community life, and it was here that I gained a deep understanding of the way that recreation and leisure are public goods and play a role in inclusion. Through persistent civil action and education, the disability movement ultimately raised the importance of self-determination in people's lives, demanding that those who had so long held power over every aspect of their lives do "nothing about us, without us." This principle is one which all community developers, policymakers, service planners, service providers, advocates, and friends of those communities they seek to enhance, would do well to remember.

INTERSECTION OF SOCIAL JUSTICE, RECREATION, AND COMMUNITY DEVELOPMENT

Modern day recreation is based in large part on social justice and a commitment to providing people in all income brackets and social classes with access to recreation, playgrounds, parks, and other communal spaces where people gather in play and at leisure. Accordingly, it is concerned with the public good, civil society and equity. For instance, recreation played an active role in the settlement house movement of the 1920s (Hillman, 1960), where people new to North America could live, work and play, fostering community spirit and collective well-being. Access to recreation provided restoration and educational opportunities for personal and social development. Indeed, recreation and leisure as a public good is rooted in inclusion, creativity, and collaboration, bringing people together to identify solutions to problems. Given the tenets on which recreation is based, it might well be considered an ideal space in which community development and citizen participation can happen.

Significant barriers to participation persist, however powerlessness that flows from lack of resources inhibits and often precludes participation and engagement in healthy free time leisure pursuits, particularly when poverty dominates as an overarching condition of everyday life. For instance, organizers in the Davis Inlet relocation efforts presumed that recreation could assist in working with the young people of the community. However, local people were not centrally involved at a grassroots level, and sadly, the effort flown in from the outside was probably too little too late and too detached from the people themselves. Not infrequently, disenfranchised communities are reluctant to participate and efforts to be more collaborative fail.

POSSIBLE PRECURSORS TO NONPARTICIPATION

Patronized and treated as subservient to service provider

Involvement essentially amounts to tokenism

Opinions ignored so community learns to "leave it to the expert"

Apathy after years of disappointment around broken promises

Practitioners reinforce stigma in "client" vs. partner status

Community disempowerment and its corollary, disenfranchised citizens, accepted as the norm

Municipal recreation departments have often been leaders in actually seeking to practice community development and bring citizens into partnership with recreation policy and program development. But there has been a tendency among some community development practitioners, especially in powerfully centralized city or municipal settings, to imagine that by using the word "community" in front of whatever service or program or committee they are concerned with, they are "doing community development." Clearly, it is a more complex and difficult undertaking than these practitioners imagine. It takes a certain openness and deep commitment to engage in collaborative action that does not present barriers to participation.

Some may say you cannot teach community development. But there are principles that are fundamental to community development that can be brought to the classroom. These include genuinely participatory decision making, grassroots problem identification and problem solving, and strengths and assets identification. Another important factor from a teaching/learning perspective is relationship building between teacher, student, and community member based in mutuality and reciprocal learning. This mutuality functions in much the same way as Paolo Freire's (1970) conscientization or critical consciousness raising among co-learners. The co-learner relationship is characterized by respect and equality. For the community development teacher, this means ongoing nurturing of the relationship. This takes time beyond the classroom and beyond the teaching schedule, time that not every teacher is willing or able to offer. As well, the relationship is dependent on openness on the part of the community and willingness on the part of the learner to enter the community and act in tandem with co-learners in the development endeavor. Clearly, this is not feasible if the learning is confined to the traditional classroom. Recreation has a clear advantage in this respect—it is rooted in participatory practice, reciprocity that seeks to resist the distancing and specialization that can come with professionalization.

Much has been written on the subject of the culture of professionalism and the detrimental impact of professional dominance, where the practitioner overwhelms or dominates the community and community development activity (Illich, 1971; McKnight, 1995). Although my observations may suggest that I see real disadvantages in professional activity in community development, this is not the case. Professional engagement in community development is absolutely critical in my view, but it is how professionalism is understood and implemented that is important here. The professional community developer or organizer who is reflective and comes to their work with an openness and deep commitment to participation is a vital cog in the community development wheel. A reflective practitioner of the sort Schön (1983) envisaged, one who engages in a cyclical process of melding theory and practice, is key to genuine community development. This requires that the professional and the community engage in a process of examining, reflecting, and learning through experience, and consciously applying that learning back to practice. This is what makes the difference between genuine participatory community development and community management.

REFLECTING ON THE PAST AND A HOPEFUL FUTURE IN COMMUNITY DEVELOPMENT

Over a ten-year period, a group of colleagues and I carried out research with women in prison (Pedlar, Arai, Yuen, & Fortune, 2008). Our research examined the pathways that lead these women to prison. The majority of the women who we came to know through our in-depth qualitative research had come from disadvantaged communities. One of the most successful examples of community development that I have observed happened with this group of women in a place that is largely devoid of social animation and openness—a penitentiary. At the prison for federally sentenced women in Kitchener, Ontario, recreation is a community builder; it brings women together for a few hours a week in something called Stride Night to work in ways that have enhanced their lives both within the prison and on release into the community. The women who attend Stride Night soon realize that the success or failure of the night is entirely of their own making. Stride Night is not a required correctional program. While a gifted community-based facilitator is involved with them at Stride Night, the women choose whether to go to Stride Night, and they determine their engagement in the scheduled activity and the outcome of their participation. In this setting they experience freedom to be what they wish to be, and do what they can do to get there. Paradoxically, it is in prison that these women experience freedom to grow and flourish, experiencing the self in a way that is otherwise not possible, most especially in the tightly controlled environment of a penitentiary. This would not happen, however, without openness of staff within the prison, and the co-learner facilitator, engaging in reflective practice. Equally, the volunteers who come into the prison from the community-at-large and the incarcerated women experience an environment where they are able to build trust and authenticity in their relationships, both essential characteristics of community.

Perhaps my final observation of critical factors in sustainable community development has to do with economic realism. I have observed elsewhere that third way politics, with its emphasis on community action rather than government or state intervention, and where there is ostensibly a partnership between community and state, is not helpful if it becomes an avenue for government and the private sector to simply abdicate responsibility and "leave it to the community" (Pedlar, 2006).

Indeed, writing with Haworth in 2006, we spoke further to the relevance of state action and collective responsibility to community and individual well-being.

> *The larger thrust of communitarianism is to stress the importance of community for personal development and fulfillment. The point is not that we should ignore the values of individual rights and human flourishing, but that we should reject the naïve supposition that these can be protected outside community and in the absence of state action to promote public goods.* (Pedlar & Haworth, 2006, p. 524)

Some may claim that community development that requires financial support, especially from outside the community, is not community development. I would argue, however, that most often sustainable community development will not get off the ground without an infusion of financial resources. Some recent innovative financial collaborations exist such as social impact bonds where public and private investors support social and economic initiatives, providing funds, whether that be in the form of social bonds (Finance for Good, http://financeforgood.ca/social-impact-bonds-and-their-role-in-canada/) or start-up grants from community foundations and community micro-loans (http://community microlending.ca). Examples of economic community development illustrate how it is possible to build community where citizens participate in collective self-determining activities and receive an infusion of external resources. With the support of micro-loans providing small low-interest start-up loans for entrepreneurial efforts, participants are able to take control of their futures, as opposed to remaining objects of pity and social assistance. This perspective, based in real life experience, was captured recently by Ken Lyotier, the founder of *United We Can* in Vancouver. Mr. Lyotier was a dumpster-diver who worked with other street people to build a very successful and sustainable recycling operation in downtown eastside Vancouver, by going through dumpsters (CBC radio archives, Ideas, November 8, 2013). *United We Can* has social and human capital in vast quantities, but, as Mr. Lyotier says, "money is a great organizing tool" and their grassroots organization needed that initial financial capital investment of a micro-loan in order to build a viable and sustainable community-based operation.

> *Thinking about the claim that community development can only happen when leadership and resources come from within the community:*
>
> *What is the cost/benefit of an injection of outside financial resources to the community development effort?*
>
> *What is the cost/benefit of the involvement of an outside professional expertise to the community development effort?*

Community development will remain central to what we do in recreation, sport, and tourism as long as we care about democracy and civility. Indeed, democracy and civility are essential building blocks for inclusive societies. They ensure that we pursue collaboration, whether between teacher and learner, as *co-learners,* or between practitioner and citizen, as *community.* Similarly, authentic partnerships between public and private sectors, and between community and professionals, are the way forward. Unfortunately, in many North American jurisdictions the neoliberal ideology has taken hold, leading to an emphasis on reducing public spending, and a concomitant diminution of public goods. Result: communities face not only greater social imbalances and inequities, but greater challenges to community development efforts.

I suggested at the start of this chapter that many of the concerns around community development and changing life circumstances that existed some 20 years ago, persist today. I suspect though that those concerns look a bit different today, perhaps even more challenging for those wanting to improve the quality of life in our communities. Indeed, because of the social and fiscal conservatism that exists in the neoliberal political climate of the early 21st Century, community development in recreation, sport, and tourism requires new and more creative approaches to practice than may have been the case in the last century. These approaches include greater openness and mutuality between community members and professionals. Mutuality entails being open to social action that is born in community, enabling community competence. Community development in recreation, sport and tourism will function most effectively if the practitioner complements rather than dilutes communal coherence; in other words, embraces reciprocal learning and community empowerment. In my view, this is necessary if we are to bring about the positive community change that leisure, sport, and tourism are capable of providing.

REFERENCES

Alinsky, S. (1971). *Rules for radicals: A pragmatic primer for realistic radicals.* New York: Random House.

Avineri, S., & De-Shalit, A. (1992). Introduction. In S. Avineri & A. De-Shalit (Eds.), *Communitarianism and individualism* (pp. 1–11). New York: Oxford University Press.

Bellah, R. N. (1986). Individualism and Commitment in American Life. Lecture at University of California, Santa Barbara. Retrieved from www.robertbellah.com/lectures_4.htm

Bellah, R. N., Madsen, R., Sullivan, W. M., Swidler, A., & Tipton, S.M. (1986; 1996 updated edition). *Habits of the heart.* Los Angeles: University of California Press.

CBC radio archives, Ideas, November 8, 2013. *United We Can.*

Etzioni, A. (1993). *The spirit of community: Rights, responsibilities, and the Communitarian Agenda.* New York: Crown Publishers, Inc.

Forester, J. F. (Ed.). (1987). *Critical theory and public life.* Cambridge: MIT Press.

Freire, P. (1970; 2002 30th anniversary edition). *Pedagogy of the oppressed.* New York: Continuum.

Haworth, L. (1963). *The good city.* Bloomington: Indiana University Press.

Hillman, A. (1960) *Neighborhood centers today: Action programs for a rapidly changing world.* New York: National Federal of Settlements and Neighborhood Centers.

Illich, I. (1971; 1999). *Deschooling society.* New York: Marion Boyars Publisher.

Jacobs, J. (1961). *The death and life of great American cities.* New York: Random House.

McKnight, J. (1995). *The careless society: Community and its counterfeits.* New York: Basic Books.

McKnight, J., & Kretzman, J. (1993). *Building communities from the inside out: A path toward finding and mobilizing a community's assets.* Evanston, IL: Institute for Policy Research.

Pedlar, A. (2006). Practicing community development and third way politics: Still faking it? *Leisure/Loisir, 30*(2), 427–436.

Pedlar, A. (1996). Community development: What does it mean for recreation and leisure? *Journal of Applied Recreation Research, 21*(1), 5–23.

Pedlar, A., Arai, S., Yuen, F., & Fortune, D. (2008). *Uncertain futures: Women leaving prison and re-entering community.* Retrieved from http://www.ahs.uwaterloo.ca/uncertainfutures/

Pedlar, A., & Haworth, L. (2006). Community. In C. Rojek, S. Shaw, & T. Veal (Eds.), *Handbook of leisure studies* (pp. 518–532). Hampshire, UK: Palgrave Macmillan.

Pedlar, A., Haworth, L., Hutchison, P., Taylor, A., & Dunn, P. (1999). *A textured life: Empowerment and adults with development disabilities.* Waterloo, ON: Wilfrid Laurier University Press.

Putnam, R. D. (2000). *Bowling Alone: The collapse and revival of American community.* New York: Simon & Schuster.

Schön, E. (1983). *The reflective practitioner: How professionals think in action.* New York: Basic Books.

Taylor, C. (1989). *Sources of the self: The making of the modern identity.* Cambridge, MA: Harvard University Press.

AUTHOR BIOS

Susan (Sue) M. Arai is an Associate Professor in the Department of Recreation and Leisure Studies at the University of Waterloo, a registered psychotherapist with the College of Registered Psychotherapists of Ontario, and mindfulness practitioner. Sue's training and education has been achieved through a Ph.D. from the University of Guelph (Rural Studies), a diploma from the Toronto Institute for Relational Psychotherapy, and training in Mindfulness-Based Stress Reduction. Sue's research-teaching-practice emphasizes transformation and social justice through anti-oppressive, liberatory, and intersectional negotiations of difference in relationships and communities. Her research interests focus on mindfulness; trauma, mental health, and healing through leisure; therapeutic relationships; therapeutic recreation practices; and community inclusion and health promotion. Sue has worked with practitioners in hospitals, healthy communities initiatives, social planning councils, disability and mental health organizations, and community health centers in Ontario.

Christine Buzinde is an Associate Professor in the School of Community Resources and Development at Arizona State University, USA. Her research focuses on two areas: community development through tourism and the politics of tourism representations. Christine's research on community development adopts a grassroots approach and it aims to understand the relationship, or lack thereof, between community well-being and tourism development within marginalized and/or indigenous communities. She conducts research in Tanzania, Mexico, India, and the US.

Paula Carr has worked in the community sector and with municipal and provincial departments, supporting intercultural leadership for over 40 years in Canada. For 23 years, Paula was the Executive Director of Collingwood Neighbourhood House, which was the subject of the award winning film "Where Strangers become Neighbours" and recipient of the International BMW Intercultural Learning Award, Province of BC's Nesika Award and the City of Vancouver's Cultural Harmony Award.

John Colton teaches in the Department of Community Development and Environmental and Sustainability Studies at Acadia University in Wolfville, Nova Scotia, Canada. His research interests include community-based renewable energy and stakeholder engagement, aboriginal ecotourism and community development, and sustainable community development.

Simon C. Darnell is an Assistant Professor in the Faculty of Kinesiology and Physical Education at the University of Toronto. He studies the social, political, and historical relationships between sport, international development, and peace building. He is the author of *Sport for Development and Peace: A Critical Sociology* (Bloomsbury Academic, 2012).

Rudy Dunlap received his Ph.D. in Leisure Studies from the University of Georgia in 2008. He is currently an associate professor in the Leisure, Sport, and Tourism Program in the Department of Health and Human Performance at Middle Tennessee State University. In addition to coordinating the Graduate Program in Leisure and Sport Management at MTSU, Dr. Dunlap teaches undergraduate and graduate courses in community development, outdoor recreation, and qualitative inquiry. His scholarship explores leisure as a socio-cultural context in which community development and social change take place. During his own leisure, Dr. Dunlap gardens, cooks, mountain bikes, and chases his twins.

Michael Edwards is an Associate Professor in the Department of Parks, Recreation and Tourism Management at North Carolina State University. His research interests center on social inequality in access to sport and recreation as well as the role of leisure and sport in promoting rural community health development.

Wendy Frisby is a Professor Emeritus with the School of Kinesiology at the University of British Columbia. She has engaged with numerous community groups and has written extensively on participatory and community-based approaches to research. Her work has been acknowledged by a Shaw/Mannell Leisure Research Award, the Canadian Association for the Advancement of Women in Sport and Physical Activity (CAAWS) Influential Women Award, a National Academy of Kinesiology International Fellow, and the Earle Zeigler Lecture Award.

Darla Fortune is an Assistant Professor at Concordia University, Montreal, QC in the Department of Applied Human Sciences. She received her Ph.D. from the Department of Recreation and Leisure Studies at the University of Waterloo, ON. Her research is embedded in a concern for social justice and aims to create positive change in the lives of individuals who are most at-risk of experiencing exclusion from community. Her leisure includes attending community festivals and events, and taking part in her daughter's many adventures.

Karen Fox is a full professor with the Faculty of Physical Education and Recreation at the University of Alberta. Dr. Fox's research interests focus on how alternative leisure discourses and practices context dominant practices, takes seriously music-dance making, and attends to Indigenous life worlds. Her research methodology is grounded in participatory and reciprocal processes while inviting critique.

Karen Gallant is an Assistant Professor in the School of Health and Human Performance, Dalhousie University. Her research interests focus on citizen engagement and inclusion of marginalized populations in communities. Her research has explored the role of volunteering in furthering community vitality, and issues of inclusion, social support, and power for marginalized individuals, including older adults, people living with mental health issues, immigrants, and drug-addicted populations.

Troy D. Glover is Professor in the Department of Recreation and Leisure Studies at the University of Waterloo, the same institution from which he received his Ph.D. Focused primarily within an urban context, his research explores the role(s) of leisure in developing social capital and advancing transformative placemaking. His approach often favours a social ethic whereby community members are knowers of their own lived experiences with capabilities and entitlements to forward their own visions of a healthy community. Thus, Troy's research also aims to engage community members directly in dialogue to envision their aspirations for the future of their community. When not at work, Troy enjoys spending time with his children, even though they rarely let him sleep in.

Peggy Hutchison is Professor Emeritus from Brock University in Ontario who has researched, lectured, and advocated nationally and internationally in the area of community and inclusion for over thirty years. She is coauthor of many books such as *Pathways to Inclusion; Community, Integration, and Leisure;* and *Friends & Inclusion* and numerous articles and presentations which focus on belonging and relationship's importance to building an inclusive life for anyone who is marginalized in our society.

Amanda Johnson is a Professor in the Department of Recreation and Tourism Management at Vancouver Island University. Amanda's research focuses on community-based meanings of urban places and the landscapes of everyday life. Her work in community development includes research related to urban revitalization, brownfield redevelopment, leisure experiences in public spaces, and the social impact of displacement from community spaces.

John Lord is a community researcher and facilitator and is currently a partner in the Facilitation Leadership Group. He is cofounder, along with Peggy Hutchison, of the Centre for Community Based Research in Kitchener, Ontario, where he was the first director for many years. He has researched and published widely on innovative community supports and is the author or coauthor of several books, including *Pathways to Inclusion; Friends & Inclusion;* and *Facilitating an Everyday Life.*

Theron Kramer has extensive community development and evaluation/research experience as a manager, consultant, and volunteer with not-for-profit sector and government organizations. He was a Board member of the Centre for Community Based Research for many years. He is currently Co-Chair of the Community Research Ethics Office in Waterloo Region and member of the Research Ethics Board at Wilfrid Laurier University. Theron recently received the Queen Elizabeth II Diamond Jubilee Medal for outstanding community service.

Brett Lashua is a Senior Lecturer in the Carnegie Faculty at Leeds Beckett University. After studies at Kent State University, Brett completed his Ph.D. at the University of Alberta in 2005. His scholarship is concerned with the ways that young people make sense of their lives through arts, leisure and cultural practices, and how young people are "made sense of" through particular representational and narrative strategies. He coedited (with Karl Spracklen and Stephen Wagg) *Sounds and the City: Popular Music, Place and Globalization* (Palgrave, 2014). His leisure interests include hanging out with his two favourite people in the world, making (bad) pop music, and playing baseball.

Stephen Lewis is currently a Lecturer of Recreational Therapy at Clemson University. Stephen completed his Ph.D. in Leisure Behavior in Indiana University, and his Master's and Bachelor's degrees were both from Florida State University. Stephen's scholarship often focuses on issues of intersectionality, with special focus on LGBT issues, obesity-stigma, and disability studies.

Heather Mair earned a Ph.D. in Rural Planning and Development at the University of Guelph in Ontario, Canada. She is an Associate Professor in the Department of Recreation and Leisure Studies at the University of Waterloo. Her research interests include critical approaches to the study of leisure, sport, and tourism research. Heather is also interested in investigations of the roles leisure, sport, and tourism can play in community development, empowerment, and well-being. Her leisure includes watching curling and playing with her daughter, dog, and two cats.

David Matarrita-Cascante is an Associate Professor in the Department of Recreation, Park, and Tourism Sciences at Texas A&M University. His research uses community development and natural and environmental sociology frameworks. His work sits at the intersection of the above interests and various literatures including international development, amenity migration, tourism, protected areas, natural events, and community health.

Rasul Mowatt is an Associate Professor in Recreation, Park, and Tourism Studies at Indiana University. His main research and teaching areas are: leisure behavior, social justice, cultural studies, and critical pedagogy. While his sub-research and teaching areas are: racial identity, social inequity and leadership & management best practices, violence and deviancy, governmentality and policy analysis, participatory research, critical historical analysis, media and narrative analysis, visual methodology, and active learning.

Alison Pedlar received her Ph.D. in Urban and Regional Planning from the University of Waterloo. Her teaching and research activity focused on social policy, planning, and development of human services. Much of her work was conducted within a participatory and collaborative research framework, and included community development work with older adults, individuals with disabilities, incarcerated women, and other marginalized populations. Her primary research program was concerned with community, citizenship, social justice, and rights. She retired from the Department of Recreation and Leisure Studies at the University of Waterloo in 2007. Her leisure interests include discovering film, and city and nature walks.

Rhonda Phillips, Ph.D., FAICP, is Dean of Purdue University Honors College and a Professor in the Agricultural Economics Department. Previously, at Arizona State University, she served as a Professor in the School of Community Resources and Development as well as a Senior Sustainability Scientist in the Global Institute of Sustainability. She is author or editor of 20 books on the topics of community and economic development, community well-being, and quality of life and is President of the international Society for Quality-of-Life Studies. In 2016, she was elected to the College of Fellows of the American Institute of Certified Planners (FAICP), and held the Certified Economic and Community Developer (CEcD) designation for 17 years.

Don Reid is a Professor Emeritus in the School of Environmental Design and Rural Development at the University of Guelph, Canada. Dr. Reid's research focuses on community development and social planning, as well as tourism and leisure planning. Don's work is centered in Canada and Africa. Don has also been very active in community leisure planning both from a practical as well as an academic perspective. Additionally, Don has sole-authored three books (one in press), coauthored one book, jointly edited two books, and contributed numerous book chapters and journal articles, as well as a number of professional reports on these subjects. Don is an avid reader and world traveler.

Erin Sharpe is an Associate Professor in the Department of Recreation and Leisure Studies at Brock University. Her teaching and research interests center on examining relationships between leisure, community, and development. A leisure sociologist, her work is influenced by socio-spatial, post-structural, and post-colonial perspectives. Most recently, Dr. Sharpe was awarded a Social Sciences and Humanities Research Council of Canada grant to examine intersections between identity and neighborhood in the sporting lives of young people. Her leisure interests include family canoe trips, rowing, and walking the dog.

Halyna Tepylo received a BA in Honours Recreation and Leisure Studies from the University of Waterloo in 2010. She is currently working on a MA at the University of Waterloo studying leisure meanings and communication within settlement services. Her research interests include leisure and immigration; community inclusion, belonging, and participation; and sport development. In her leisure time, Halyna can be found curling, coaching, traveling, and enjoying the performance arts.

Alan Warner teaches in the Department of Community Development at Acadia University in Wolfville, Nova Scotia, Canada. His particular areas of expertise and research are community youth leadership, environmental education and community development and sustainable food systems.

Colleen Whyte is a faculty member in the Department of Recreation and Leisure Studies at Brock University. Her research program is focused on understanding the experiences of older adults within Canadian society, and the contributions of recreation and leisure to personal quality of living for older adults. She is a director with the Canadian Association for Leisure Studies, a member of the Canadian Association on Gerontology, and Therapeutic Recreation Ontario.

Felice Yuen is an Associate Professor at Concordia University, Montreal, QC in the Department of Applied Human Sciences. She received her Ph.D. from the Department of Recreation and Leisure Studies at the University of Waterloo, ON. Her research interests include using arts-based methods to understand how leisure can be used as context for community development, healing, advocacy, and empowerment. She enjoys playing guitar, eating, and going on adventures with her children and husband.

INDEX

OTHER BOOKS BY VENTURE PUBLISHING

21st Century Leisure: Current Issues, Second Edition
by Valeria J. Freysinger and John R. Kelly
Active Living in Older Adulthood: Principles and Practices of Activity Programs
by Barbara A. Hawkins
Adventure Programming
edited by John C. Miles and Simon Priest
Adventure Programming and Travel for the 21st Century
edited by Rosemary Black and Kelly S. Bricker
Boredom Busters: Themed Special Events to Dazzle and Delight Your Group
by Annette C. Moore
Brain Fitness
by Suzanne Fitzsimmons
Client Assessment in Therapeutic Recreation Services
by Norma J. Stumbo
Client Outcomes in Therapeutic Recreation Services
edited by Norma J. Stumbo
Conceptual Foundations for Therapeutic Recreation
edited by David R. Austin, John Dattilo, and Bryan P. McCormick
Dementia Care Programming: An Identity-Focused Approach
by Rosemary Dunne
Dimensions of Choice: Qualitative Approaches to Parks, Recreation, Tourism, Sport, and Leisure Research, Second Edition
by Karla A. Henderson
Diversity and the Recreation Profession: Organizational Perspectives, Revised Edition
edited by Maria T. Allison and Ingrid E. Schneider
Effective Management in Therapeutic Recreation Service, Third Edition
by Marcia Jean Carter, Christen G. Smith, and Gerald S. O'Morrow
Evaluating Leisure Services: Making Enlightened Decisions, Third Edition
by Karla A. Henderson and M. Deborah Bialeschki
Facilitation of Therapeutic Recreation Services: An Evidence-Based and Best Practice Approach to Techniques and Processes
edited by Norma J. Stumbo and Brad Wardlaw
Facilitation Techniques in Therapeutic Recreation, Third Edition
by John Dattilo and Alexis McKenney
File o' Fun: A Recreation Planner for Games & Activities, Third Edition
by Jane Harris Ericson and Diane Ruth Albright
Finding Leisure in China
by Geoffrey Godbey and Song Rui
The Game Finder: A Leader's Guide to Great Activities
by Annette C. Moore
Health Promotion for Mind, Body, and Spirit
by Suzanne Fitzsimmons and Linda L. Buettner
Human Resource Management in Recreation, Sport, and Leisure Services
by Margaret Arnold, Regina Glover, and Cheryl Beeler

Inclusion: Including People With Disabilities in Parks and Recreation Opportunities
by Lynn Anderson and Carla Brown Kress
Inclusive Leisure Services, Third Edition
by John Dattilo
Internships in Recreation and Leisure Services: A Practical Guide for Students, Fifth Edition
by Edward E. Seagle, Jr., Tammy B. Smith, and Ralph W. Smith
Internships in Sport Management
by Robin Ammon, Jr., Matthew Walker, Edward E. Seagle, and Ralph W. Smith
Interpretation of Cultural and Natural Resources, Second Edition
by Douglas M. Knudson, Ted T. Cable, and Larry Beck
Intervention Activities for At-Risk Youth
by Norma J. Stumbo
Introduction to Outdoor Recreation: Providing and Managing Resource Based Opportunities
by Roger L. Moore and B. L. Driver
Introduction to Recreation and Leisure Services, Eighth Edition
by Karla A. Henderson, M. Deborah Bialeschki, John L. Hemingway, Jan S. Hodges, Beth D. Kivel, and H. Douglas Sessoms
Introduction to Recreation Services: Sustainability for a Changing World
by Karla A. Henderson
Introduction to Therapeutic Recreation: U.S. and Canadian Perspectives
by Kenneth Mobily and Lisa Ostiguy
An Introduction to Tourism
by Robert W. Wyllie
Introduction to Writing Goals and Objectives: A Manual for Recreation Therapy Students and Entry-Level Professionals
by Suzanne Melcher
The Leader's Handbook: Learning Leadership Skills by Facilitating Fun, Games, Play, and Positive Interaction, Second Edition
by Bill Michaelis and John M. O'Connell
Leadership and Administration of Outdoor Pursuits, Third Edition
by James Blanchard, Michael Strong, and Phyllis Ford
Leadership in Leisure Services: Making a Difference, Third Edition
by Debra J. Jordan
Leisure and Leisure Services in the 21st Century: Toward Mid Century
by Geoffrey Godbey
Leisure Education I: A Manual of Activities and Resources, Second Edition
by Norma J. Stumbo
Leisure Education II: More Activities and Resources, Second Edition
by Norma J. Stumbo
Leisure Education III: More Goal-Oriented Activities
by Norma J. Stumbo
Leisure Education IV: Activities for Individuals with Substance Addictions
by Norma J. Stumbo
Leisure Education Program Planning: A Systematic Approach, Third Edition
by John Dattilo
Leisure for Canadians, Second Edition
edited by Ron McCarville and Kelly MacKay
Leisure, Health, and Wellness: Making the Connections
edited by Laura Payne, Barbara Ainsworth, and Geoffrey Godbey
Leisure in Your Life: New Perspectives
by Geoffrey Godbey
Leisure Matters: The State and Future of Leisure Studies
edited by Gordon J. Walker, David Scott, and Monika Stodolska

Leisure Studies: Prospects for the Twenty-First Century
edited by Edgar L. Jackson and Thomas L. Burton
Leisure, Women, and Gender
edited by Valeria J. Freysinger, Susan M. Shaw, Karla A. Henderson, and M. Deborah Bialeschki
Making a Difference in Academic Life: A Handbook for Park, Recreation, and Tourism Educators and Graduate Students
edited by Dan Dustin and Tom Goodale
Managing to Optimize the Beneficial Outcomes of Leisure
edited by B. L. Driver
Marketing in Leisure and Tourism: Reaching New Heights
by Patricia Click Janes
More Than a Game: A New Focus on Senior Activity Services
by Brenda Corbett
N.E.S.T. Approach: Dementia Practice Guidelines for Disturbing Behaviors
by Linda L. Buettner and Suzanne Fitzsimmons
Parks for Life: Moving the Goal Posts, Changing the Rules, and Expanding the Field
by Will LaPage
Planning and Organizing Group Activities in Social Recreation
by John V. Valentine
Planning for Recreation and Parks Facilities: Predesign Process, Principles, and Strategies
by Jack Harper
Programming for Parks, Recreation, and Leisure Services: A Servant Leadership Approach, Third Edition
by Donald G. DeGraaf, Debra J. Jordan, and Kathy H. DeGraaf
Recreation and Youth Development
by Peter A. Witt and Linda L. Caldwell
Recreation for Older Adults: Individual and Group Activities
by Judith A. Elliott and Jerold E. Elliott
Recreation Program Planning Manual for Older Adults
by Karen Kindrachuk
Reference Manual for Writing Rehabilitation Therapy Treatment Plans
by Penny Hogberg and Mary Johnson
Service Living: Building Community through Public Parks and Recreation
by Doug Wellman, Dan Dustin, Karla Henderson, and Roger Moore
A Social Psychology of Leisure, Second Edition
by Douglas A. Kleiber, Gordon J. Walker, and Roger C. Mannell
Special Events and Festivals: How to Organize, Plan, and Implement
by Angie Prosser and Ashli Rutledge
The Sportsman's Voice: Hunting and Fishing in America
by Mark Damian Duda, Martin F. Jones, and Andrea Criscione
Survey Research and Analysis: Applications in Parks, Recreation, and Human Dimensions
by Jerry Vaske
Taking the Initiative: Activities to Enhance Effectiveness and Promote Fun
by J. P. Witman
Therapeutic Recreation and the Nature of Disabilities
by Kenneth E. Mobily and Richard D. MacNeil
Therapeutic Recreation: Cases and Exercises, Second Edition
by Barbara C. Wilhite and M. Jean Keller
Therapeutic Recreation in Health Promotion and Rehabilitation
by John Shank and Catherine Coyle
Therapeutic Recreation Practice: A Strengths Approach
by Lynn Anderson and Linda Heyne